About the Author

The Word for Every Day is a treasury of readings Alvin N. Rogness has gathered in his career as a Christian pastor, author, speaker, and church leader.

He served congregations in Duluth, Minnesota, Ames and Mason City, Iowa, and Sioux Falls, South Dakota. For 20 years he served as president of Luther Theological Seminary, St. Paul, Minnesota.

His Christian service has taken him to Europe and Japan to conduct retreats and missions for U. S. armed forces. He has served on numerous national and international boards and commissions.

His articles and books include: the award-winning *Book of Comfort, Today and Tomorrow, Remember the Promise, The Jesus Life, The Land of Jesus, Bridges to Hope, The Touch of His Love, The Wonder of Being Loved, Living in the Kingdom, Forgiveness and Confession,* and *Captured by Mystery.*

The Word For Every Day

365 Devotional Readings

Alvin N. Rogness

AUGSBURG Publishing House • Minneapolis

THE WORD FOR EVERY DAY

Copyright © 1981 Augsburg Publishing House

Library of Congress Catalog Card No. 81-65650

International Standard Book No. 0-8066-1886-8

Scripture quotations unless otherwise noted are from the Revised Standard Version of the Bible, copyright 1946, 1952, and 1971 by the Division of Christian Education of the National Council of Churches.

MANUFACTURED IN THE UNITED STATES OF AMERICA

About this Book

When editors of Augsburg Publishing House suggested that I put together a book of 365 devotional readings, they gave me free rein in seeking sources. It has been an interesting assignment. I began thinking back to writers whose ideas had inspired me. I had many books on my shelves filled with my liberal marginal notes. To these I have reverted often. This book, besides containing my own offerings is therefore sprinkled liberally with quotations from authors who have stirred me. To them I express your thanks and mine.

The sequence of pages may follow roughly the church year, though not with any labored attempt at fidelity. At the close of the book are readings for Palm Sunday, Maundy Thursday, Good Friday, and Easter.

The aim of the book has not been chiefly to instruct but to edify. It is my hope that whether you select one page for each day's reading and Scripture and add your own meditation and prayer, or whether you dip in it now and then, it will bring comfort, hope, and courage into your life.

Newspapers and magazines trap us into today's fears and anxieties. These readings, I hope, will help us to recover our bearings as citizens of an eternal empire. This is not to diminish our responsibility for today's world, but to give us a solid place to stand as the storms swirl around us. After all, we are children of a heavenly Father who is the Lord of history. To him we go for grace; from him we receive guidance; in him we have life and hope.

Alvin N. Rogness

The book of Ecclesiastes must have been written in a time of catastrophe and despair. It is probably one of the most eloquently pessimistic pieces in all the world's literature. The first verse strikes the dark note: "The words of the Preacher, the son of David, king in Jerusalem. Vanity of vanities, says the Preacher, vanity of vanities! All is vanity. What does man gain by all the toil at which he toils under the sun?" Then follow the fourteen contrasts that embrace the whole of human existence, among them these:

> a time to be born, and a time to die;
> a time to plant, and a time to pluck up what is planted;
> a time to kill, and a time to heal;
> a time to weep, and a time to laugh;
> a time to mourn, and a time to dance;
> a time to keep silence, and a time to speak;
> a time to love, and a time to hate;
> a time for war, and a time for peace (3:2-8).

We cannot deny that we are caught in the flow of time. It is true that things and actions have *their* time. Nothing new comes out of this circle in which all life moves. However clever and industrious we may be, and however much we seem to accomplish, we must know that the whole structure may topple and our works wash away in the flood of the years. God's timing is hidden to us, and on our own our toiling and timing are of no permanent value.

But something has broken into this repetitious circle of time. Jesus said, "The time is fulfilled and the kingdom of God is at hand." God's timing breaks into this doleful tempo of our years. Something new has appeared. And this something new—his kingdom—can break into every minute, every hour, and every year of our lives.

Before Ecclesiastes ends, there appears a note, at once wistful and strident, "The end of the matter; all has been heard. Fear God, and keep his commandments, for this is the whole duty of man."

Set your minds on things that are above, not on things that are on earth. For you have died, and your life is hid with Christ in God (Col. 3:2-3).

The new year is a time for inventories. What assets do we have? It may be a bit embarrassing to list them because most of us have far more than we need. As the list grows, Thoreau's statement, "We are as rich as our ability to do without things," will haunt us.

There are assets which, understood as gifts, need not shame us. Health, the love of family and friends, work to do, opportunities for service—these are rich dividends.

In the wake of Christmas we should have no trouble placing at the top of any list the greatest gift of all—the Lord himself. "God so loved the world that he gave his only Son. . . ." In a profound sense, all the other good gifts of life are included in him. He brings them all.

Moreover, by his life, death, and resurrection, he has claimed us as sons and daughters, joint heirs with him to an imperishable kingdom. This is the gift to dwarf all others. We sing, "Jesus, priceless treasure."

A priceless gift has its awesome aspects. It is disconcerting to have the gift in your hands if you have no inclination to want it. If you do not want to be a child of God, it is a nuisance to have God knocking at your door with adoption papers in his hands. If you do not want a kingdom and palaces, it can be irksome to have someone hovering around trying to put a crown on your head. Of course God will not force the issue. But ever since Bethlehem, this old world has stirred uneasily, having the gift of Christ and a beckoning kingdom to deal with. We have gotten attached to the hovels, and the palace looks austere. We have settled down to being bellhops to our passions and to public opinion, and we do not like to be disturbed by Christ's announcement that we are created for rulership.

Only two options are open to us. We may accept the gift—and learn that in Christ we have privileges and responsibilities that make life enormously rich. Or we may, like Esau, exchange the right of our high station for matters of the moment. Whichever we choose, we are nobility—nobility in rebellion or indifference, but nobility still. We are created and redeemed to be nothing else.

The first option is as sublime as the other is base. God gives us the power to receive his priceless gift. Surmounting all the dazzling inventories of time is God himself, and nothing can separate us from his love in Christ Jesus.

Bless the Lord, O my soul, and forget not all his benefits (Psalm 103:2).

Our faces must be to the future. We dare not simply revel in the past, nor be engulfed by the present. We have responsibilities for the tomorrows. But in our day it is especially difficult to have bracing hope for the future. Problems of immense dimensions loom before us. We lose both heart and courage.

It is the church's ministry to put us on the path of the morrows with confidence and calm. This it can do only as it turns us around to view the faithfulness of God in the past. It says, "Remember the mercies and loving-kindness of your Lord. He who has not failed you in the past, will he fail you in the future?"

Remember how he led the children of Israel out of Egypt. Remember how again and again he brought them out of exile. Remember, above all else, how he sent his only Son to die and rise again for the sins of the world. Remember how he caused a small frightened band of followers to become apostles and missionaries the world over—until hundreds of millions of people embraced the faith and changed the course of history.

Perhaps within the boundaries of your own lives you can remember how the Lord has spared you. You were terrified by the possibility of harm. Your heart was filled with fear and anxiety. You lost sleep. Your courage and hope were all but gone. But most of your fears were unfounded. You were given strength. His mercy and his kindness saw you through in strange and wonderful ways. You never quite knew how, but blessings that you never expected came your way.

But the morrows will still hang heavy. Reason as we will, fears well up to rob us of mirth in the day and sleep at night. I pray the words of an ancient litany, "From the crafts and assaults of the devil, from sudden and evil death, from pestilence and famine, from war and bloodshed, from sedition and rebellion, from lightning and tempest, from all calamity by fire and water: Good Lord, deliver us." I substitute my own litany: "From exhaustion of energy, from pollution of air and water, from world hunger, from nuclear war: Good Lord, deliver us." But even my prayers tend to be a reminder of the uncertain tomorrows.

As I look back and begin counting my blessings, and rest back in those arms that have cradled and carried me through the years, I have the courage to look forward with calm and confidence.

Return, O my soul, to your rest; for the Lord has dealt bountifully with you (Psalm 116:7).

When I first heard Thomas Gray's poem, *"Elegy Written in a Country Churchyard,"* I found myself resisting the conclusion he drew as he contemplated the dead:

> Full many a gem of purest ray serene
> The dark unfathomed caves of ocean bear:
> Full many a flower is born to blush unseen,
> And waste its sweetness on the desert air.

With other lines I found it easier to agree:

> Perhaps in this neglected spot is laid
> Some heart once pregnant with celestial fire;
> Hands, that the rod of empire might have swayed,
> Or wak'd to ecstasy the living lyre.

To be sure, the accidents of time and place have prevented many people from having the opportunity for learning, from developing latent gifts, from finding the paths of power or riches. But does that mean that it is a life that has wasted its sweetness on the desert air?

With few exceptions, every life has fulfilled some purpose. However limited the opportunities or short the years, if it has not wantonly thrown itself away, it has become a component in God's great plan.

In my cousin's family, Jimmy, a child born with Down's syndrome, in his 13 years had become a blessing not only to his parents and sister and brothers, but in his affection for all people in the community he had endeared himself to hundreds. When his brave heart gave up one night, he was mourned like a hero or saint.

I have known parents whose child died a few moments after birth. For nine months they had sensed the wonder of budding life, had lavished affection upon him, had entertained dreams for him. As quickly as he had come, he was gone. Can one say that the wonder, the affection, and the dreams of nine months were of no account, or the lessons of grief that followed? Was the sweetness of those months wasted on the desert air?

Every child is dear to our heavenly Father. A person's worth has nothing to do with the length of his years, nor with his achievements. In some plan beyond our understanding, every life has eternal meaning.

For thou didst form my inward parts, thou didst knit me together in my mother's womb (Psalm 139:13).

One of the fine novels coming from Sweden in the midcentury was Hemmer's *Fool of Faith*. The setting is Finland during the Communist uprising of 1917. While the revolution succeeded in Russia, in Finland it was repressed, and the prisons were filled with the embittered men who had tried to overthrow the government and the church. The principal character in the story is Pastor Bro, the prison chaplain. The prisoners met him only with hatred and vindictiveness. Failing to reach them, one night in his quarters he prayed for guidance. His prayer took the shape of a question, "What would Jesus do if he were the chaplain of this prison?" The answer came, "Jesus would disguise himself as a prisoner, go beyond these gray walls, and minister from the inside."

The next day there were seven prisoners in a cell where there had been six before. Week upon week, Bro lived with the men in the vermin-infested prison. One day a man shared his hatred. He told how an official had seduced his wife. In fury he had taken his axe, climbed the hill to the great white house, intent on splitting the man's head. Not finding him, he had broken furniture until the police caught him. Bro heard him out, then said, "My friend, you used the wrong axe. You used the axe of revenge which never cut the chain that binds you; for revenge breeds hatred and hatred revenge, and you add link upon link to the chain that imprisons you. The axe you should have used is the axe the Lord Jesus used, and left for us to use—the axe of forgiveness. Forgiveness will cut the chain, and you will be free."

They were interrupted by a guard who came to report that the next morning one man from this cell was scheduled for execution. They could decide among themselves who it should be. They cast lots, and the lot fell to Bro. The next morning the firing squad noted something different in one of the men to die. He stood erect, shoulders back, chin up, a slight smile, a gleam in his eye—as if he were about to be decorated.

Jesus made friends of us all, and died for us all. His death has not softened the hearts of all or driven hatred from all. Nor has he assured us that we who follow him will always succeed in changing the hearts of people. Bro died never knowing whether his life in the cell had achieved anything except—and this is a great *except*—that he had had the honor of following in the footsteps of his Lord.

Greater love has no man than this, that a man lay down his life for his friends (John 15:12).

Lewis Browne in his well-known book, *This Believing World,* begins with these lines, "In the beginning there was fear; and fear was in the heart of man; and fear controlled man. . . . At every turn it whelmed over him. . . . All the days of man were gray with fear, because all his universe seemed charged with danger." A dismal picture.

Contrast this with the epic sweep of Chapter 1 in the Bible: "In the beginning God created the heavens and the earth. . . . God said, 'Let there be light'; and there was light. . . . And God said, 'Let us make man in our image, after our likeness; and let them have dominion over . . . all the earth. . . .' And God blessed them . . . and God said, 'Be fruitful and multiply, and fill the earth and subdue it. . . .' And God saw everything that he had made, and behold, it was very good."

Both these paragraphs describe our remote beginnings on the earth. In one, we are thrust unwillingly into a hostile world full of enemies; in the other, we are formed to have sovereignty over a world created for our dominion. In one, we are cringing creatures of fear; in the other, we are princes and princesses, enthroned to rule. Nor are these alternatives confined to our beginnings. Twentieth-century people may cower in fear as much as our prehistoric ancestors. Modern ingenuity is matched by modern insecurity.

Franz Werfel has described our present plight in the parable of the camel-driver who is being pursued by his enraged camel. To escape, he jumps into a well, and as he falls, his clothes catch on a root growing out of the wall of the well. There he hangs, suspended. He looks up and sees the maddened eyes of the camel looking down upon him. He looks down into the bottom of the well and sees the fieiry eyes of a dragon. As his eyes become accustomed to the light, he sees two mice, one white and one black, taking alternate bites at the base of the root.

Werfel says that man had thought to be the driver of a machine, but the machine, gone mad, has turned on him and threatens to destroy him. Man faces, on the one hand, the fury of the ungovernable machine, and, on the other hand, the prospect of catastrophic death. Meanwhile, time is running out—day and night, the white mouse and the black mouse.

A grim prospect indeed! It will take faith in a God who has given us the machine to use, and who can help us keep or regain control and avert falling into the flames of the dragon. Without this faith, we freeze in fear; we dishonor God and we renounce our high station.

Thy kingdom is an everlasting kingdom, and thy dominion endures throughout all generations (Psalm 145:13).

When all the sentimental "Home, Sweet Homes" have been sung, it still remains a hard and glorious fact that, whatever glories or pleasures the world may chance to provide, it is within the love of family that people find life's greater joys. In his autobiography, Malcolm Muggeridge, then a British reporter in Russia, tells of seeing his wife Kitty and their two little boys stepping down from the train after a long absence.

Such moments of happiness, looked back upon, shine like beacons, lighting up past time, and making it glow with a great glory. Recollecting them, I want to jump up and shout aloud in gratitude at having been allowed to live in this world, sharing with all its creatures the blessed gift of life. Alienation is to be isolated and imprisoned in the tiny dark dungeon of the ego; happiness to find the world a home and mankind a family, to see our earth as a nest snugly perched in the universe, and all its creatures as fellow-participants in the warmth and security it offers. Its very components, the very twigs and mud of which it is made, likewise participating. Then, indeed, all the world is a grain of sand, eternity in an hour, infinity grasped in one's hand. So, such moments of happiness comprehend a larger ecstacy, and our human loves reach out into the furthermost limits of time and space, and beyond, expressing the lovingness that is at the heart of all creation. Curiously enough, of all people, it was Karl Marx I thought of as we rode joyously up to Rossiniere; recalling how in one of his letters he describes to his wife the longing he has to return to Paris, where the family were then living, after one of his interminable quarrelsome conferences, and how the only lasting and satisfying joy he knows is to be with them and see around him their dear familiar faces. The memory of this letter stayed with me, I suppose, because of the contrast it offers with the efforts made in his name to promote the happiness of all mankind; in the result, so desolating, so bloody and so futile. Poor old Jewish enrage, whose furious indignation was to rumble and echo through the world for years to come—he, too, gratefully flying back to his nest.

How lovely is thy dwelling place, O Lord of hosts! My soul longs, yea, faints for the courts of the Lord: my heart and flesh sing for joy to the living God. Even the sparrow finds a home, and the swallow a nest for herself, where she may lay her young, at thy altars, O Lord of hosts. . . . Blessed are those who dwell in thy house (Psalm 84:1-4).

He said, "The first thing we do in moving to a new city is join a church." We were seated together on an airliner. His office had transferred him several times, uprooting his family, the last move to Denver. Their background was Presbyterian, and that's the church they joined wherever they went. "Not because denominations mean that much," he added, "but it's important to have some continuity in belonging."

I thought of families I knew that didn't bother to sink roots outside of the family itself, and how in this mobile age they were denying themselves another buttress against loneliness. To be sure, there are people who seem to need identity with a group less than others, but we are all social creatures and need to belong to others, both for what they may do for us and we for them.

As Christians we belong to the big family, the one, holy, Christian and apostolic church. Even more broadly than that, we belong to the one human family. But within both these families we need to find our own clusters, our own immediate family, our congregation, our community, our nation.

It has been interesting, and encouraging, to note how young people especially have been searching for their roots. The world is too terrifying and lonely to go it alone. Nor is this a sign of weakness. The rugged individualism so prized and needed in a pioneer society was probably never intended by God to be a model for his children.

God uses small clusters as laboratories to equip us to be servants in larger spheres. Within the family, and the more limited group of a congregation, for instance, we become servants of one another and become groomed to reach out beyond. No one can love or care for humanity as a whole without first learning to love and care for those who are near.

Only God, who is infinite, can hold all the people of the earth in his embrace. We, his children, must begin in the smaller classroom. And the classroom will become a fortress from which we can sally forth into the world to cheer the discouraged, to give warmth to the lonely, and to infuse the word with hope.

Now the company of those who believed were of one heart and soul, and no one said that any of the things which he possessed was his own, but they had everything in common (Acts 4:32).

I hadn't seen him in two years. During the years I had lived in this Midwestern city I had often eaten in his cafe. We became close friends. Coming as a young immigrant from Greece, he had worked long and hard until his eating place was the finest in town. Now, at 70, he was beginning to turn things over to his son. Seated with me at the table, he reflected on how well things had gone for him. He paused, tears formed in his eyes, and he said, "But, Al, I haven't taken time for my soul."

He was a successful man. He was reasonably rich. The community esteemed him. What else did he need?

Jesus once put it bluntly, "What is a man profited if he shall gain the whole world, and lose his own soul?"

It is as if each of us has a bag to fill. We use our years to fill them with good things, family, friends, money and property, honor, perhaps power. Then comes death, and we must leave the bags behind. If we have accumulated our cargo at the expense of our souls, then what? Everything is gone.

The soul itself has needs, quite apart from food, shelter—even honor. The soul has a life with God. It feeds on the Word and the sacraments. It grows through prayer and praise. It becomes strong as it reaches out to help others.

It is good for each of us to take stock. What if we were to die today? What would we leave behind? Memories that are cherished by our families and friends, we hope. Maybe some property or trust funds for our children. Perhaps the fruits of our labors, whether in business, in the home, in our professions. But we do leave it all behind!

Stripped of it all, we go on to live forever with our Lord. And it is his hope that we may have used the swift years on earth to prepare for the full life on the other side. If we have let that which is eternal about us wither and die from oversight, neglect, or even repudiation, the loss is enormous.

This is what my friend meant in his sad remark, "But I haven't taken time for my soul."

I remind you to rekindle the gift of God that is within you (2 Tim. 1:6).

In 1883, Krakatoa, a volcanic island between Java and Sumatra, exploded with the most terrific force known in natural history, resulting in tidal waves reaching as far as Madagascar. All vegetation and all life on the island were destroyed. A few years later, grasses and flowers began to appear, seeds carried across the sea by the winds and the birds until the island became a jungle again.

Jesus talked about the Word of God and the kingdom of God in terms of seed. Seeds may not be impressive; they may even go unnoticed. But who can calculate their power? God works in quiet and mysterious ways.

Read a newspaper, and you will be impressed by the struggles for power between nations, between industries, between people. In these struggles are ideas and events which quietly and unrelentingly are shaping the future. Only in retrospect will some astute historian be able to tell what were the significant forces at work, and these forces may not have had one line in the newspapers.

In my library I have a second-hand book, long out-of-print, *Gesta Christi,* by Loring Brace, in which the author traces the influence of the Christian faith in shaping the values and life of society across the centuries. The rights of women and children, the alleviating and eliminating of slavery, the care of prisoners in war, the duty of rulers— these and many other areas, he shows, have come under the quiet and sure power of the "seed." It has been said that in England the child-labor laws were changed through the sermons of John Wesley and the novels of Charles Dickens.

Years ago a young carpenter from Nazareth was executed in Jerusalem for disturbing the peace. By all the standards of power, the event should have been forgotten in a day. But he was "the Word made flesh." In a few years, his story and his kingdom had spread throughout the Mediterranean world, and in the 2000 years since, the event has been the most revolutionary force the world has known. It remains so still, all the armaments of the world notwithstanding.

His kingdom is still like a seed. It goes unnoticed. As they shape foreign policies, world statesmen rarely speak of it. But the kingdom is there in ways beyond calculation. For lo, said Jesus, the kingdom is within you.

It is like a grain of mustard seed, which, when sown upon the ground, is the smallest of all the seeds on earth . . . and becomes the greatest of all shrubs (Mark 4:31-32).

A literary critic has observed that modern novels rarely, if ever, have a redemptive character or motif. It is almost as if the writers do not like human beings. Dostoevski's novels, while describing life with all its sordidness, invariably have both motif and characters which are redemptive. Moreover, he reflects the Christian assessment of man, the "Old Adam" and the "New Man" struggling for ascendency. In his *Crime and Punishment* Raskolnikov has murdered Lizaveta, whom he thinks a worthless hag. Later he meets Sonia, a sensitive girl who, to provide food for her starving family, has become a prostitute. In their common misery they read together the story of the raising of Lazarus. Later still, we find this exchange:

"Well, what am I to do now?" he asked, suddenly raising his head and looking at her with a face hideously distorted by despair.

"What are you to do?" she cried, jumping up, and her eyes that had been full of tears suddenly began to shine . . . "Go at once, this very minute, stand by the cross-roads, bow down, first kiss the earth which you have defiled and then bow down to all the world and say to all men aloud, 'I am the murderer!' Then God will send you life again. . . . Suffer and expiate your sin by it, that's what you must do."

"No! I am not going to them, Sonia."

"But how will you go on living? What will you live for?" cried Sonia, "how is it possible now?"

They sat side by side, both mournful and dejected, as though they had been cast up by the tempest alone on some deserted shore.

"Have you a cross on you?" she asked, as though suddenly thinking of it. "No, of course not. Here, take this one, of cypress wood. I have another, a copper, one that belonged to Lizaveta. . . . I will wear Lizaveta's now and give you this. Take it . . . it's mine! It's mine, you know!" She begged him. "We will go to suffer together and we will bear our cross!"

"Give it to me," said Raskolnikov.

Jesus, deeply moved . . . cried with a loud voice. "Lazarus, come out." . . . The dead man came out (John 11:39-44).

God made you. More than that, he made you to be like him, in his image. He gave you the gift of freedom, the right to choose. He took the risk of having you vote against him and leave him. He wanted you with him, but only if in freedom you chose to be his.

God redeemed you. As God the Son, he came to the earth to recover those who in disobedience had elected to leave him. He went to a cross in death to do it.

God reshapes you. God the Holy Spirit is at work through the means of grace, Word and sacrament, to bring the whole weight of heaven to bear on you. He does not leave you alone. He calls you, pursues you, and catches up with you. If you will let him, he remakes you into the being he had wanted you to be from the beginning.

And when death closes the door on his further work with you on earth, he flings wide the door of the eternal Kingdom, makes perfect what he began here, and puts you to work again, to serve him and to enjoy him forever! What more can you ask?

Is it any wonder that the world, even we who are his, can't quite believe that people are that important in the universe? Dwarfed by the billions of bodies in billions of light-years of space, what are we but infinitesimal blobs of protoplasm that come and go like wind across the waste? But, says our Lord, we are heirs of an eternal kingdom, incredibly precious to the king. And nothing, said St. Paul, nothing, "neither death, nor life, nor angels, nor principalities, nor things present, nor things to come, nor powers, nor height, nor depth, nor anything else in all creation will be able to separate us from the love of God in Christ Jesus our Lord" (Rom. 8:38-39).

To be sure, evil is deeply entrenched in the earth, the evil resists the gentle pressure of God. God would like to eliminate wars and crime. He wants you to escape tragedy and pain and death. But the presence of selfishness, indifference, and hatred among us often makes it impossible for him to break through with his will and blessings. Eventually, when he winds up the present order and ushers in the new heaven and the new earth, then the hurdles of evil will be done away.

Meanwhile he has made it possible for us to live with him now, forgiven and reconciled, at work night and day at his great enterprise of mercy and justice for all men. Isn't this enough?

Be strong and let your heart take courage, all you who wait for the Lord! (Psalm 31:24).

I come to God, the Great Judge. I rest my case with him. It's a strange place to rest. I have never seen him nor touched him. There is no incontestable evidence that he exists at all. Nonetheless, I find comfort in resting myself, and my case, with him.

Perhaps it is not so strange after all. I am created precisely to come to rest in him, and therefore it's the most natural thing in the world. In fact, there is no other place for me to rest.

To come to terms with God, however, is not so easy. He is God. He sets the standards; he calls the shots. He judges the world, and he judges me. To come into his presence is not as casual a thing as dropping in on a friend for an evening. Each of us appears before him to be judged, to receive a verdict, to be accepted or rejected. Fortunately for us, he has promised not to evict anyone who comes. But this does not mean that he does not judge. In coming to him, we come to terms with our sins and wretchedness.

The apostle Paul says, "But with me it is a very small thing that I should be judged by you or by any human court. I do not even judge myself. . . . It is the Lord who judges me." No doubt Paul would not have dared to arraign himself before the high court of God if he had not already known the limitless mercy of that court. He recognized, however, that the human verdict was often in error, and that his own self-appraisal could be distorted. Only God has a right to give final sentence. Only God knows the hidden springs of the heart. But God knows. And this is both terrifying and comforting.

Terrifying as it is to appear before God stripped of any pretense, I must appear. I need to be judged. I must have a verdict. To be passed over, to be dismissed as if I am not important enough to be judged at all—this is more frightening than being convicted. To be adrift in the universe, unnoticed and unjudged, as if no one cares what I do or what I am—this is intolerable. "Set me free or send me to jail, but do not pass me by as if I am nothing." We need a God who judges us!

A boy of seven was adopted after having been shuttled from one foster home to another. Two months later someone visited the home and the boy announced proudly, "My father spanked me." Someone loved him enough to judge him. No longer was he passed by. He was accepted for judgment and for love. This is the cry of the human heart—the cry for a God who cares enough to judge!

Prove me, O Lord, and try me; test my heart and my mind. For thy steadfast love is before my eyes, and I walk in faithfulness to thee (Psalm 26:2-3).

LAW AND OBEDIENCE

If there is a God at all, he is the ruler of the universe. He has laws, laws for planets and laws for people. Planets obey him; people may disobey. They were given the gift of freedom, the right of choice. In this they resemble God. Let us ask some questions about God's plan for us and his law.

Why have laws at all?

We can well understand why they are necessary in nature, so that planets and galaxies stay within their orbits, so that chemical elements cannot willy-nilly change their structures. Without natural law there would be utter chaos. It is not quite as apparent with moral laws, the laws of God governing human behavior. We may get the notion that we can design these for ourselves, relying on ourselves to know what is best for our lives. To the extent that we ignore some basic, unchanging order of values (the moral law or the will of God), we tend toward anarchy, and we destroy ourselves. God gives us rules and laws to know right from wrong, good from evil, righteousness from unrighteousness.

But is his law too much for us?

Yes. How can anyone love the Lord with all his heart and his neighbor as himself? How can he be perfect as his heavenly Father is perfect? And yet that is what God asks.

What good is the law then?

By showing us that we cannot possibly fulfill the law, God turns us around to find another way to avoid despair and to please him. He turns us to Christ, God's Son, who became one of us, took our place, and obeyed perfectly all of God's law—for us! We throw ourselves on him for mercy and forgiveness. We rest our case with him. The futility of trying to obey the law is the very thing that drives us to Christ. This may seem to be a cop-out, freeing us from the law's judgment, and for a new anarchy.

Are we then through with the law and with obedience?

No, indeed. The law no longer threatens us. Our disobedience cannot separate us from God. We are forgiven and restored. Now we can turn to the law as something friendly, not threatening and condemning. The law becomes a guide, a road map which we cherish and use to find our way into the life God wants for us, the life which will release his blessings for us. Now we can love the law.

Open my eyes, that I may behold wondrous things out of thy law. I am a sojourner on earth; hide not thy commandments from me! (Psalm 119:18-19).

To join the ranks of God is more like enlisting in the army than joining a club. You may join Rotary or the Farm Bureau without altering the course of your life very much. But join the army, especially during wartime, and every area of your life, every habit, every plan may be radically changed. At the recruiting office you are asked for more than your good will and signature. Your very body comes under a new command.

It is significant that St. Paul tells his Roman congregation to present their *bodies* as a living sacrifice. It has always been easier to offer God something vague and indefinite, like praise or adoration, than to give something concrete. Most people are all in favor of God and mercy and righteousness. They are pleased to have their children interested in church and Sunday school, and are rather proud that one of their cousins became a minister or priest. But to have the church of God step in and demand their bodies, the time of their day, the labor of their hands—well, that's going a bit too far. If only Paul had said, "Present your good wishes, your sympathies, your occasional prayers, as a living sacrifice." But Paul made it rather rough when he said *your bodies*. That involves our eating and drinking, our working and resting, our speaking, our mating. And eventually it means that we are to place this world's economics and politics, its agriculture and industry, its arts and science, on the altar of God as our reasonable service.

This means, said Paul, that we be no longer conformed to this world. We are not to be regulated by, nor adjusted to, this world. We are to be *transformed*, to come under the policies of a higher world. A young soldier, awakened at six, cannot dismiss his sergeant by saying that while he is all in favor of this hour of rising for the army, his habit has been to rise at eight and he'd like two more hours of sleep. Having enlisted, he must conform; he must be transformed from his old habits into the routine of the army.

It is not enough for us Christians to be nice gentle people who get along well with our neighbors. If your neighbor, in drunken frenzy, beats up the newsboy, you'll have to collide with your neighbor. If as a new man on the police force, you find your fellow officers accepting bribes, you can't be nice about it. As Christians we have a prior obligation to a Kingdom, and to this Kingdom and its King we have pledged *our bodies*, our lives!

I appeal to you . . . by the mercies of God, to present your bodies as a living sacrifice (Psalm 12:1).

Most of us really do not want to be different from other people. Oh, we may enjoy some little differences, as in clothes or cars. But, for the most part, we find it most comfortable (and defensible) to do what others do. We are conformists.

The world has moved on to better things largely because there are people brave enough not to conform. Perhaps Jesus was the prince of nonconformists. Had he been willing to embrace the values of his culture and not offend the powers of his day, he need not have reached a cross. He conformed to something higher, to his Father and the Kingdom, and this got him into trouble. It earned him misunderstanding, disdain, rejection, hatred, finally death.

Not all nonconformists suffer such grim treatment. The world may be mildly amused and puzzled by them, and end up giving them grudging praise. Albert Schweitzer may be such an instance. To the bewilderment and disappointment of his generation, he turned his back on a brilliant European career as an organist and philosopher; he studied medicine and plunged into Africa to give his life in service to a primitive people of a different race. *How sad*, people in Europe thought; how sad that he would throw away his extraordinary talents and be forgotten. Before Schweitzer died, however, God had made his name the great world symbol of selfless Christian service.

In a less dramatic way, every community has nonconformists who win our praise. In one of my congregations there are two sisters who together have given over 70 years as Sunday school teachers. They did not conform to the general practice of "giving their fair share" of service. The couple who tithed 30% of their income—they were nonconformists. The family that adopted a black child who otherwise would be shuttled from one foster home to another—they were nonconformists.

Those of us conformists who think such service is carrying things a bit too far had better remember that if we claim Jesus at all, we ought to be caught in a style of life that will often carry us far beyond its established standards. It is the life of excitement and glory.

Do not be conformed to this world but be transformed by the renewal of your mind, that you may prove what is the will of God, what is good and acceptable and perfect (Rom. 12:2).

Nihil is the Latin word meaning *nothing*. The belief that life adds up to nothing is *nihilism*. The temptation to accept this belief is widespread. It lurks in each of us. The horizon of the future rolls with dark clouds, and no sunlight breaks through. Death, death for each of us and death for the planet, seems the only certain thing. This mood is not utterly new, but it is clearly with us now. Theodore Heimarck describes our plight.

> Despite the fact that human responses to this given limitation of life may be somewhat similar over the years, it would be very difficult to find any other era than our own when the number who have turned inward upon themselves and the number of badly frightened persons have been so great. Even those who could be classified as placid and phlegmatic find their strange peace shattered by the noise of the disconsolate, the frustrated, and the fear-frenzied. There is, without doubt, a new element in the present situation which had deepened the gloom and intensified the sufferings of restricted humanity.
>
> Raging or silent, straining or placid, mankind, sorely needing rescue, has managed to agree tacitly that the Owner tarries and dallies, and some have been persuaded that he is dead. Whether he is dead or merely silent, thousands of people have declared their intention of honestly facing this discomforting situation in the hope that they can, from within, muster sufficient courage to make possible a meeting with nothingness in calm dignity. It is precisely man's resignation to the tidings of the absent God that characterizes our culture today.

The writer of Ecclesiastes who thousands of years ago said "there is nothing new under the sun," probably would not agree that this dark mood belongs only to us moderns. Full into its teeth in every age we fling our faith in God. From Genesis to Revelation the Bible calls us to this God in whom there is comfort and hope. We who claim him as our heavenly Father have no right to collapse into despair nor yield to a life of meaninglessness. God is our refuge and strength.

I have seen everything that is done under the sun; and behold, all is vanity and a striving after wind. What is crooked cannot be made straight, and what is lacking cannot be numbered (Eccles. 1:14-15).

After John W. Coffey Jr. retired as a lieutenant colonel in the U.S. Air Force, he became a pastor. Later, when his son was in Vietnam, finding a dearth of Christian literature for the armed services, he wrote a book of meditations, *God Is My Pilot*. Here is a selection from the book:

Turning to the Lord is a complex maneuver. To turn *from* the concerns and desires of our hearts and to turn *to* the Lord is a radical change for the human heart. Nothing short of a miracle can accomplish this redirection of the soul.

It's like an Immelmann turn. This is an aerial maneuver in which an airplane reverses its direction while gaining as much altitude as possible. It's a half-loop with a half-roll at the top. The whole maneuver requires power in the airplane and coordination and timing on the part of the pilot.

This turning to the Lord is like that. It takes power, and it requires a close coordination with God.

And the power that brings us to God is not in us. It is of God, given to us in a Savior, a Lord. For this turning to the Lord is far more than turning over a new leaf, far more than a major overhaul of the soul. It's a *new creation*, a new birth, a new source of power. And the energy for this complex maneuver lies squarely in the One Son, Jesus Christ. He is the source of our new creation, our second birth. And His cross and resurrection transmit the power of God that uplifts and transforms us. Christ did not die to impress us, or to scare the "hell" out of us—but to create us anew. The Risen Christ is the living, present, and continuing creative Hand of God. Jesus Christ is just as creative now as He was at Calvary, as He was "in the beginning." As faith encounters Him, the power of God pulls us up and over; we are created anew. . . .

But it takes timing and coordination on the part of the pilot—time with God, and a response to the gentle pressures of the Holy Spirit. To gain altitude in this maneuver, to come close to God, we dwell on godly things, and we come to where we know he is—in His Word (you'll find Him in your Bible), in His sacraments, in His church. . . . Some call this life-giving maneuver conversion; others call it regeneration; others a second birth; still others, a renewal of your Baptism.

All the ends of the earth shall remember and turn to the Lord (Psalm 22:7).

One of the great preachers and educators of the Midwest was T. F. Gullixson, prairie pastor and seminary president. Addressing himself to our practice of ascribing rules to God when they had little or nothing to do with the will of God, he went back to his prairie years. If a man had a bull, he said, the farmer would be foolish to have bits of fencing built here and there within the large enclosure, giving the bull a chance to develop the habit of crashing through fences, including finally the real one.

Jesus disturbed people by seeming to ignore useless rules. The ancient Jews, for instance, had all sorts of rules about the Sabbath. When Jesus ignored some of them, people were offended and even enraged. Jesus reminded them that the Sabbath was made for man, and not man for the Sabbath. Or to put it another way, rules are made for man, and not man for rules.

We need to remember this basic principle of our Lord. We live in an age of rapid change, and some of us fear that elemental values are being lost. Most of these values have been expressed in the form of rules, and sometimes we fear that if the rules are broken or changed the values themselves will be lost.

When a few years ago men began growing beards and letting their hair grow long, the older generation feared that they had given up on the cherished values of society. Established rules of grooming were being defied, and anarchy was on the way! In the mail I received a letter from an old lady who wrote, "Last Sunday a young pastor preached in our church. He had a beard and long hair. He looked just like Judas." For her a shift in rules of hairstyles was betrayal.

Whenever we examine rules which people, not God, have made, we need to ask if they are necessarily the carriers of great value. Or can the rules go, and the values still remain? Can a man with a beard be as hard working, charitable, honest, and moral as a clean-shaven man? Of course he can.

A whole set of rules or practices have become guardians of values that God holds dear. The institution of marriage, for instance, which is enforced by rules of both church and state, is of great concern to God. To defy these rules is not only to fly in the face of custom but of God himself.

Open my eyes, that I may behold wondrous things out of thy law (Psalm 119:18).

In the book of Revelation we have the Lord's words to the seven churches, among them the church of Ephesus. After praising them for their patience and faithfulness, he says, "But I have this against you, that you have abandoned the love you had at first."

Jacob Tanner, who retired at 70 as professor of theology, and for almost another quarter-century taught religion at Waldorf College interprets this puzzling charge:

> The church at Ephesus is a typical example of legalistic sanctification. The church had toiled in patience. It could not bear evil men that called themselves apostles. It had suffered for Christ's sake and had not grown weary. This is a wonderful picture of congregational life. It would seem that there could be no flaw in its spiritual life. . . .
>
> Nevertheless Christ puts His finger on a most serious situation. The congregation had lost its first love. Their seemingly flawless congregational life had become Christian business, not a spiritual fruit. It was not an outflow of the intimate relation with the Lord characteristic of the first love. No longer was their conscience sensitively aware of the small everyday sins and failures. No longer was there a need of confessing their sins and failures. No longer was there an unquenchable thirst for the forgiveness of sins. No longer was there any irresistible longing for renewal and victory. Congregational life, as well as the life of the individual, had become a spiritual business proposition, a task of the highest importance indeed, but which had become spiritual routine. The motive back of it all was duty to God and the church, not love. It was the dignity of the congregation that must be maintained, the integrity of their confession, that is, the good name of the church and of themselves as church members.
>
> The life of the congregation had lost its evangelical motive and warmth and the flavor that comes out of a heart filled with humble gratitude. The change threatened the very existence of the church.

Remember then from what you have fallen, repent and do the works you did at first. If not, I will come to you, and remove your lampstand from its place (Rev. 2:5).

Perhaps we ought rather to ask: *what* or *whom* do we worship? Worship is not like jogging or calisthenics. It isn't something we do to make our souls feel better. Nor is it an exercise in aesthetics. In fact it is not primarily an exercise at all.

We come to meet God when we worship. Whenever we turn to find him, to thank him, to adore him, we worship. It may happen when we are jogging, or lying down, or in the midst of a busy office. More likely, we worship best in the singing of hymns and in the praying of prayers, with others who are also singing and praying. Always, however, the object is not simply to worship, but to face God.

The Wise Men from the East who came to Bethlehem were not on a 16-day excursion to see the sights of Palestine. They came to find and to give gifts to one they were convinced would be a great king.

The church is often preoccupied with styles of worship. And there are many. The quiet unadorned hour of silence and meditation appeals to the Quakers. The high altar and elaborate symbolism appeal to the Eastern church. Who is to say which style is better? All styles are good if the object is to meet God, to hear him, to thank him, to praise him, and to serve him.

We grasp some of the majesty and power of God as we peer through a telescope. We can be fascinated by God's diversity, and the infinitesimal, as we look into a microscope. We may sense the music of the spheres by hearing the song of birds and the wind in the trees. All this may give us an impulse to adore, but only if first we have met him at the foot of the cross, where the love of God breaks through in unrivaled radiance.

Even the most primitive people have had an intuitive sense of someone or something that ought to be worshiped, usually from fear and not from love. They sacrifice to the gods, or perhaps to their ancestors, in order to keep them from visiting disaster upon them. Christian worship is different.

We see God in the face of Jesus Christ, a face of great tenderness. In him the God of power has become the God of love. Overwhelmed by the mighty dimensions of that love, we fall on our knees to thank him, and we rise up to follow him. This is worship.

I will praise the Lord as long as I live; I will sing praises to my God while I have being (Psalm 146:2).

Few men in our generation have led as many to penetrating insights into our relation to God and to one another as Thomas Merton, the Trappist monk. In his book, *No Man Is an Island,* he speaks of friendship:

> Charity must teach us that friendship is a holy thing, and that it is neither charitable nor holy to base our friendship on falsehood. We can be, in some sense, friends to all men because there is no man on earth with whom we do not have something in common. But it would be false to treat too many men as intimate friends. It is not possible to be intimate with more than very few, because there are only very few in the world with whom we have practically everything in common.
>
> Love, then, must be true to the ones we love and to ourselves, and also to its own laws. I cannot be true to myself if I pretend to have more in common than I actually have with someone whom I like for a selfish and unworthy reason.
>
> There is, however, one universal basis for friendship with all men: we are all loved of God, and I should desire them all to love Him with all their powers. But the fact remains that I cannot, on this earth, enter deeply into the mystery of their love for Him and of His love for them.
>
> Great priests, saints like the Cure d' Ars, who have seen into the hidden depths of thousands of souls, have, nevertheless, remained men with few intimate friends. No one is more lonely than a priest who has a vast ministry. He is isolated in a terrible desert by the secrets of his fellowmen.
>
> When all this has been said, the truth remains that our destiny is to love one another as Christ has loved us. Jesus had very few close friends when He was on earth, and yet He loved and loves all men and is, to every soul born into the world, that soul's most intimate friend. The lives of all the people we meet and know are woven into our own destiny, together with the lives of many we shall never know on earth. But certain ones, very few, are our close friends . . . they are inseparable from our own destiny, and therefore, our love for them is especially holy: it is a manifestation of God in our lives.

No longer do I call you servants, for the servant does not know what his master is doing; but I have called you friends, for all that I have heard from my Father I have made known unto you. You did not choose me, but I chose you and appointed you that you should go and bear fruit and that your fruit should abide (John 15:15-16).

INTEGRITY

These words by Ralph Waldo Emerson, framed, have hung on the wall in our home for many years:

It is sublime to feel and say of another: I need never meet, or speak, or write to him: we need not reinforce ourselves, or send tokens of remembrance; I rely on him as on myself; if he did not thus or thus, I know it was right.

To be trusted never to lie or cheat, never to break a promise, never to deceive—to be accepted as such a person is probably the highest tribute the world can give. There are other desirable virtues too, of course, like patience, charity, cheerfulness. But basic to all is integrity. In a profound sense, the whole economic, political, and social order depends on people like that. They are the cement that holds everything together. If a bank teller, for instance, embezzled $100 (a trifling sum in the volume of the bank's business), he would lose his job for lack of integrity. The life of the bank itself depends on people who can be trusted with sums, large or small.

A mother may be disturbed by her child's quick temper, but far more worried if he lies and steals, even if they are little lies and trifling thefts. She knows that if he cannot be trusted in small things, he probably will not be trustworthy in big things. He may grow up to be a person without integrity, which means that he is corrupt at the center of his character.

You buy something in the store, and the cashier makes a mistake and gives you back a five-dollar bill instead of a one. You call this to her attention, and she is perceptibly grateful. Her confidence in the whole human race, too often shaken, is restored. You have not only saved her embarrassment; you have given her hope.

Years ago an immigrant farmer bought a cow for $100, on the assurance that she would yield a specified amount of milk. He discovered that she actually gave a fourth more—so he went back and gave the former owner an additional $25. Most of us would probably say that this was carrying integrity too far. But, had she given a fourth less, would we have been surprised to have him demand a refund of $25? He was a man of integrity.

A truthful witness saves lives, but one who utters lies is a betrayer. In the fear of the Lord one has strong confidence, and his children will have a refuge (Prov. 14:25-26).

Can it be true that a third or more of the world's population will go to bed hungry tonight? And will another third suffer from chronic malnutrition? And can it be that for the next 20 years, maybe more, food shortages and hunger may be the most pressing problem the world faces? And right now, in some parts of the world, will thousands upon thousands die of starvation if immediate help cannot reach them? Yes, it is true.

It is hard, almost impossible, for us to have this disaster sink in. We have never really had to be hungry. The question for us is simply what foods we like best, or what restaurants serve the best meals. Most of us have never had to worry about where our next meal may come from. There has always been something, bread and butter, if nothing more.

We are more likely to be worried about energy. Will there be enough gas for us to make our vacation trip? Will we have enough fuel to be comfortable, or will we in the winter have to turn our thermostats down to 65 or even 60, and in the summer may we have to "suffer" in 80 or 90 degrees in our homes? Will food costs force us to give up on steaks, and even occasionally on hamburger? Are any of us worrying about whether there'll be food at all?

There are people who worry about that—and with good reason—hundreds of millions throughout the world. There may be pockets in our own communities where people have this anxiety, especially old people on scant Social Security to pay for their food, their housing, and their medicine. In our land if people worry, it isn't because the supermarkets are not full of food. It's because we lack the will or the wisdom to provide proper distribution. In vast parts of the world there isn't food to distribute.

It is an awesome thing to be a Christian in a country like ours and know these facts. The Lord gave hunger and food top priority. He taught us to pray for daily bread. He identified himself with the hungry and said, "I was hungry, and you gave me food."

World hunger may seem such a staggering problem that we despair over doing anything at all about it. We may turn to our well-supplied tables, and try to forget. *We must not forget.* If we do nothing else, we can support our congress in every effort of foreign aid—other than arms. We can give generous checks to the hunger funds of our churches. We *can* do something!

If a brother or sister is ill-clad and in lack of daily food, and one of you says to them, "Go in peace, be warmed and filled," without giving them the things needed for the body, what does it profit? So faith by itself, if it has no works, is dead (James 2:15-17).

Solitude is not loneliness. It is to retreat from the bustle of the hour and to reflect on life, on God, on oneself. In his book, *Out of Solitude,* Henri Nouwen speaks about what we may discover.

In solitude we can slowly unmask the illusion of our possessiveness and discover in the center of our own self that we are not what we can conquer, but what is given to us. In solitude we can listen to the voice of him who spoke to us before we could speak a word, and who healed us before we could make any gesture to help, who set us free long before we could free others, and who loved us long before we could give love to anyone. It is in this solitude that we discover that being is more important than having, and that we are worth more than the result of our efforts. In solitude we discover that our life is not a possession to be defended, but a gift to be shared. It's there we recognize that the healing words we speak are not just our own, but are given to us; that the love we can express is part of a greater love; and that the new life we bring forth is not a property to cling to but a gift to be received.

In solitude we become aware that our worth is not the same as our usefulness. We can learn much in this respect from the old tree in the Tao story about a carpenter and his apprentice:

A carpenter and his apprentice were walking together through a large forest. And when they came across a tall, huge, gnarled, old beautiful oak tree, the carpenter asked his apprentice: "Do you know why this tree is so tall, so huge, so gnarled, so old and beautiful?" The apprentice looked at his master and said, "No, why?"

"Well," the carpenter said, "because it is useless. If it had been useful it would have been cut long ago and made into tables and chairs, but because it is useless it could grow so tall and beautiful that you can sit in its shade and relax."

In solitude we can grow old freely without being preoccupied with our usefulness, and we can offer services which we had not planned on. To the degree that we have lost our dependence on this world, whatever world means—father, mother, children, career, success or rewards—we can form a community of faith in which there is little to defend but much to share.

And he said to them, "Come away by yourself to a lonely place, and rest a little (Mark 6:31).

Every day the newspapers list fatalities on the highway. I usually scan the names *and* their ages. My heart is heavy; usually more than half are our youth. It is not especially sad when someone in ripe years surrenders life, but there's something tragic about a young man or woman, boy or girl, having to leave this earth, whether by illness or accident. Our family has not been untouched. A nephew died at 14, a niece at 19, our son at 24, and my cousin's son, 17. All were promising young people, who could have made significant contributions to this earth.

I suppose we too often think of youth only as a time of preparation. Preparation for what? For running the farm, for taking over the business, for going into a profession, for mothering a family, for managing the government? It is all that, but more.

Youth is not a preparation for life at all. Youth is life itself. There is no time for rehearsal. The great play is on. Every day is another block of time in which to live—to love, to serve, to weep, to laugh. We cannot employ today only to set the stage for tomorrow. There may be no tomorrow.

Long years ago a youth of 33 writhed to his death on a cross. Across the centuries this young man summons other young men and women to join him, and to give him the vibrant, aspiring years of their youth. These years may be the only ones that can be given, for there may be no more.

And what years they are! Exuberant, warm, sensitive, and strong years! If the Lord can have these years, he may have captured the best. Perhaps these are enough for him.

Many of us who have reached our later years discover that we yearn for the faith and hope and outgoing love of our youth. Far from increasing and strengthening our faith, and broadening the scope of our love, the years have eroded the zest we once had. We understand a little of the Lord's meaning when he said, "Unless you turn and become like children, you will never enter the kingdom."

George Macdonald, who lost a son in the early years, addresses him across the gulf:

Gleam-faced, pure-eyed, strong-willed, high-hearted boy!
Thou, child and sage inextricably blent,
Will one day teach thy father in some heavenly tent.

Remember also your Creator in the days of your youth, before the evil days come, and the years draw nigh, when you will say, "I have no pleasure in them" (Eccles. 12:1).

When somebody says that the most powerful thing in the world is love, we make a skeptical mental note, "How nice, but you don't know the world as it is." A celebrated economist has said that even we who know capitalism to be a better system than socialism or communism must admit that its driving forces are greed and envy. Yet, only within capitalism, said Eric Hoffer, longshoreman philosopher, can there be freedom.

Quite apart from the relative values in economic or political systems, in the lives of individual people, is love stronger than hate or greed or envy? Jesus says yes. In fact, it is the only force powerful enough to change people. When someone said, "I invite you to a one-man revolution, the only kind of revolution that's coming," did he have in mind the radical effect of love in a person's life? I think so.

If someone hates you, you don't change. You hate back, and that only increases hatred. But if someone loves you, and keeps on loving you however much you rebuff him, you will change. It's like the unrelenting rays of the sun on ice. You can't keep on hating him, pushing him off, turning from him—with the warmth of love pressing in on your spirit.

The love we have in Christ is like that. Like the sun that just keeps on shining, Jesus keeps on loving. The leaders, who in fear and hatred plotted his death, couldn't stop him, nor could Pilate, who sentenced him. And from the cross he faced the taunting, raucous crowd and cried, "Father, forgive them." What can you do with a love like that?

You can try running away from it, as far as you can, but it will be there. You can pull the shade and keep the sun's rays from reaching you, but you can't stop the sun from shining. You can't stop God from loving you. And if, for even one fleeting moment, you have caught the full warmth of that love, try to shut it out as you will, it will haunt you. Let it reach you, and it will change you as no other power ever could— whether hatred, greed, envy, or fear. This is indeed the power above all powers.

Love is patient and kind; love is not jealous or boastful; it is not arrogant or rude. Love does not insist on its own way; it is not irritable or resentful; it does not rejoice at wrong, but rejoices in the right (1 Cor. 13:4-6).

There are reasons to believe that the earliest Christian confession was the simple affirmation, "Jesus Christ is Lord." Edgar Carlson, for many years president of Gustavus Adolphus College, in his book, *The Classic Christian Faith,* discusses what Christ's lordship means:

> If we did really take it seriously, this simple affirmation that "Jesus is Lord," would come to us with the impact of the crack of doom—and the crack of dawn. For what is really asserted is that Jesus Christ is Lord in a sense which has no earthly parallel. He is "Lord of lords."
>
> All the authorities and dominions which we know in this world can exercise only a limited lordship. For instance, they are limited in duration. They last for a while only. We are under parents, but we will grow up and no longer be under their authority. . . . We may be under political tyranny now, as many Christians around the world are, but some day we shall be free. . . . But you never grow up out of the dominion of Christ. You can't get rid of his Lordship by growing old, not even by dying! For death is precisely the place where the controls of life move out of your hands—into his. . . .
>
> These early dominions are limited in scope, too. You can move outside of their jurisdiction. You can leave home, quit school, move out of the country. This freedom gives a kind of veto power which stands over against the power of the rulers. But you can't move outside of the dominion of Jesus Christ. . . .
>
> These earthly dominions are limited, too, in how much of us they can command. They may tax our purses, they may govern our time, they may control our actions, but they cannot govern our wills. They may discipline our outer man, but they cannot command our spirits. We will think what we want to think, we will believe what we want to believe. . . . But if you have encountered Jesus at all, you know that he will have none of that. It is precisely there, at the center of our selves, that he would rule.
>
> From all earthly dominions there is an appeal. . . . But there is no appeal above and beyond the Lordship of Jesus Christ. The Father has committed all judgment into his hands. To him has been given *all* authority in heaven and on earth.

Therefore God has highly exalted him and bestowed on him the name which is above every name, that at the name of Jesus every knee would bow, in heaven and on earth and under the earth, and every tongue confess that Jesus Christ is Lord, to the glory of God the Father (Phil. 2:9-11).

Obedience makes sense when you understand that disobedience will get you into trouble. You obey the speed limit, when to disobey may get you arrested. You observe the IRS regulations; if you don't, you pay a fine. It can be demonstrated that to disobey the commandments, "Thou shalt not kill," "Thou shalt not steal," "Thou shalt not commit adultery," is to invite all sorts of unpleasantness.

There's another kind of obedience that does not rest on understanding at all. It rests on trust. This is the kind God asks of us. We don't honor God very much by not killing someone; it simply doesn't pay. But when we obey God in matters that we cannot understand or that have every chance of giving us trouble—that's obedience out of sheer trust. We honor God most by this kind of obedience.

When they were small, my boys were quite different. One, when I asked him to do something, would irk me by asking, "Why?" The other didn't bother to ask; he simply went ahead and did it. I suppose I should have been pleased with the curiosity and caution of the first son, but I confess I was more pleased with the second—with his obedience in trust.

God cannot be displeased when his children try to find out why they ought to do something he has asked. But he has asked us to do many things for which there are no obvious reasons. I think of Baptism, for instance. Who can explain to anyone's satisfaction what occurs in Baptism? To be sure, we speak of the washing of regeneration, the grafting of a child into Christ, the gift of faith. But these are "explanations" that at best satisfy only the believer. We baptize, simply because Christ asks it. We obey in trust.

What do I receive through the bread and wine of the Lord's Supper? I am told that my sins are forgiven and that I have communion with my Lord. The more the churches have tried to give theological explanations for what the Lord's Supper means, the more separated from one another they have become. Most of us may agree with C. S. Lewis that it is enough that the Lord has told us to come, and we come!

How many missionaries have gone to far countries with no assurance that they would succeed in winning the world for Christ. They went, they obeyed—in trust.

For I am a man under authority, with soldiers under me; and I say to one, "Go," and he goes, and to another, "Come," and he comes (Matt. 8:9).

The United States ambassador in London is not a citizen of England or of the United Kingdom. He only lives and works in London. His citizenship is in the United States of America. His job is in London, but his orders come from the President of the U.S.

God invites us to be his ambassadors on earth. If we accept the assignment, we no longer take our orders from the rules and standards of earth. We are under orders from God and from his eternal Kingdom. Our job is on earth, of course, but the job description is given us by God.

There is a hymn which says, "I'm but a stranger here; heaven is my home." This is but another way of saying that we belong to a wider and bigger empire. As ambassadors, we are more than gypsies or wandering strangers on the earth. We are assigned work to do here.

It makes a big difference. If you are but a citizen of the earth, you need only get along as well as you can during the swift years you have here. Get by! Avoid pain and enjoy pleasure. But if you are an ambassador, you have a mission. You represent the interests of another. You cannot simply get by. The ambassador's task may not always be pleasant. If his country's interests clash with the actions of the foreign country, he may need to take a stern and hard line. He may be quite unpopular. But he has no choice. He must represent his own country, cost what it will.

God has created us to be more than high-grade animals. The tiger in the jungle adapts himself to the life of the jungle. The fish of the sea adapt themselves to the life of the sea. But man has a higher role than simply to adapt himself to life on the earth. He must conform himself to the life of the Kingdom of God, and this may sometimes give him trouble in adapting himself to the ways of the world. As a citizen of earth alone he might conceivably get by (illegally, of course) and grow rich in the smuggling racket, but as an ambassador of God he would have to clash with the whole rotten business. He might have to take a hard line sometimes against the practices which are tolerated (even legal) in industry and labor and government. He may lose friends; he may forfeit power and wealth; he may get hurt. He may even be killed, like many ambassadors before him. But he will have the only job on earth that yields nobility and glory.

So we are ambassadors for Christ, God making his appeal through us (2 Cor. 5:20).

An immigrant on the prairies a hundred years ago had some rather elementary needs. He needed shelter (a sod hut); he needed food (grain ground by hand); he needed clothing (probably one warm outfit). And he needed a dream and a faith. He had them all.

His inventory did not include a home with central heating and air conditioning, nor a guaranteed income with Social Security and pensions, nor telephone, radio, and TV, nor vacation and travel. His needs did not include many which we think of as basic—and which we spend a lifetime trying to get and keep.

The Lord's caution, "A man's life does not consist in the abundance of his possessions," was probably spoken to people who did not need his warning as much as we do. We have a whole index of deceptive and exaggerated needs. We live in a time when nations boast of their greatness in terms of the gross national product. We are caught in an economic system that can exist only if people buy what they don't really need. To take the Lord's words literally, even seriously, becomes very difficult for us.

There is at least a partial solution for each of us. Not all, even in our affluent society, have what they need. If we have more than we need (and measured by our immigrant forebears, don't we all?), we may be on the alert to seek out those who have real needs. In almost every community there are pockets of poverty and stark need, despite all the private and governmental programs assigned to help. Also, through our churches, we may give gifts for the aid of these people, here and abroad, and no agency administers these as efficiently as do the church agencies. Writing a check may seem a cold and impersonal way to reach out the hand of compassion to help, but it's one of the real ways open to us to feed the hungry and care for the stranger and help the sick.

It will take imagination and compassion and will to do it. First, we must reexamine the inflated lists of what we've thought needful for ourselves and then return a bit closer to the inventory of our grandparents. When some of our excesses have been pared off, we need the will to distribute this to others.

It is just possible that if we make some headway doing this, we will discover or rediscover the wonderful truth of the kingdom, "It is more blessed to give than to receive."

Not that I complain of want; for I have learned, in whatever state I am, to be content. . . . I have learned the secret of facing plenty and hunger, abundance and want. I can do all things in him who strengthens me (Phil. 4:11-13).

Paul told the Christians at Philippi, "I am sure that he who began a good work in you will bring it to completion at the day of Jesus Christ" (Phil. 1:6).

What is that *good work?* Certainly healing—the healing of soul and mind and body. God has set out to restore us to the wholeness which he intended for us from the beginning. But he will not be able to finish the work until death has released us into the fulness of the kingdom on the other side. Until then, we will struggle against those forces that seek to destroy us.

The Scriptures speak of some ultimate healing on a grand scale. Paul intimates that creation itself is "groaning" and longing for deliverance, and that there will be a "new heaven and a new earth." What this means is difficult to envision, but it points to a consummation when, with tragedy and sin and pain and death gone, healing will be complete.

Until then, our God is at work with healing. Through the Holy Spirit he works to clear our minds of error and doubt, to rid our bodies of the enemies of health, to keep our souls against the attacks of the devil.

He uses both ordinary and extraordinary means for healing. He heals our minds by the slow, often tedious, disciplines of education. Generation after generation, people have been at work to push back the frontiers of ignorance, and to bring people's minds into the light of reason and knowledge. In this work, the church has had a major role throughout the centuries. Its field is not primarily biology and physics, although it has encouraged science to a free exploration of the Lord's universe. Its field is truth, values, the world of the spirit, the kind of knowledge upon which all knowledge must rest and rely in order to be healing.

The remarkable advances in medical science are God's gifts. Our day has seen a revival of interest in God's extraordinary or miraculous healing, but those who reject God's way through medicine must sadden the Lord who has offered us so much through research.

Not our minds alone, nor our bodies, but our souls must be kept for him and grow in grace. Under the healing work of the Spirit, especially through the Word and sacraments, this gracious work toward wholeness goes on.

He will wipe away every tear from their eyes, and death shall be no more, neither shall there be mourning nor crying nor pain any more, for the former things have passed away (Rev. 21:4).

Many years ago Bruce Barton, a popular author, chose out of all the people who have ever lived the men he would like to have invited to a dinner—Socrates, Dr. Samuel Johnson, Samuel Pepys, Montaigne, and Abraham Lincoln—and gave reasons for his choice.

If I were to assemble a group around the table from the people of the Bible, I know the ones I'd choose. They would all have had this in common: in spite of their having failed or disobeyed God in tragic and shameful ways, God had used them.

Abraham, who to save his skin in Egypt, told Pharaoh that Sarah was his sister and let her become a part of Pharaoh's household, perhaps in his harem.

Jacob, who tricked his twin brother Esau out of his inheritance and later tricked his father-in-law, Laban, out of his flocks.

David, who committed adultery with Bathsheba, and plotted successfully to have her husband, Uriah, killed while fighting in his armies at the front.

Peter, who on that fateful night of Jesus' arrest, lost his nerve, and fearful for his own life, three times swore that he had never known Jesus.

Paul, who participated in the stoning of Stephen, the first martyr, and who later used all his zeal to eradicate the Christian faith.

The list could be enlarged to include many more, perhaps you and me. If God were limited to using only those whose lives had been without disobedience and shame, he probably would have an empty table. We may not have sinned in as passionate or dramatic a way as these, but we would be there. Nor is it to our credit that we've been unimpressive sinners. For want of courage, we may have dabbled in what seems trivial wrongs. But no wrong is trivial with God.

The great, good news of the gospel is that God forgives, forgets the past, gives us his Spirit for a new and amended life, and counts us on his team. We are all the loved and the forgiven ones. Around his table, neither Abraham nor Peter, nor the others, would regale one another with their achievements. Their conversation would center on the wonder of the love of God that, despite their defections, had honored them with service in his kingdom.

But the Lord said to [Ananias], "Go, for [Paul] is a chosen instrument of mine to carry my name before the Gentiles and kings and the sons of Israel; for I will show him how much he must suffer for the sake of my name (Acts 9:15-16).

In the Old Testament there are some fascinating stories of how God turns a bad situation into unsuspecting good. Take Joseph, for instance. Kidnapped and sold into slavery by his envious brothers, in Egypt he shows an aptitude for interpreting dreams, which wins him the top spot in Pharaoh's government. Later, during a widespread famine, his brothers come to Egypt to buy grain. They are terrified when they identify their brother. Joseph says, "It was not you who sent me here, but God; and he has made me a father to Pharaoh, the lord of all his house and ruler over all the land of Egypt." So Israel was saved from famine.

Then, there is the Book of Esther. A remnant of Jews were exiled under King Ahasuerus, among them Mordecai and his beautiful young cousin, Esther, who becomes the king's queen. A plot to exterminate the Jews, under the wicked Haman, was discovered by Mordecai, who urged Esther at great risk to intercede with the king. (Anyone, even the queen, who entered the king's presence without being summoned was sentenced to death.) Mordecai said to Esther, "And who knows whether you have not come to the kingdom for such a time as this?" Esther goes; Haman is foiled and killed; Mordecai is elevated to honor next to the king; and the Israelites are saved.

In the Book of Ruth, this Moabite woman marries a Jew, the son of Naomi. When he dies, his mother prepares to return to her own land, the land of Judah. She encourages Ruth to remain and marry a Moabite. Out of love for her mother-in-law, Ruth pleads, "Entreat me not to leave thee, . . . where you go I will go, and where you lodge, I will lodge; your people shall be my people, and your God my God." In the land of Judah she marries Boaz, becomes the mother of Obed, the grandmother of Jesse, the father of King David, and thus she becomes an ancestor of Jesus.

Then Daniel. Brought into exile by Nebuchadnezzar, Daniel defies the law to worship the king, is thrown into a den of lions, and through God's miraculous deliverance is spared, to become one of the most honored of the king's people.

Not only in the Scriptures, but in the lives of most of us, there are instances where God has turned what seemed disaster into a blessing.

We know that in everything God works for good with those who love him, who are called according to his purpose (Rom. 8:28).

RIGHTEOUSNESS, THEN LOVE February 4

Is God's purpose with us to make us more loving, more truthful, more fulfilled? All these, and much more. But, as P. T. Forsyth points out, he starts with righteousness.

Christianity, as the religion of holy love, has for its ruling idea neither light nor truth—in the Western sense of such words at least. It came to meet neither our darkness nor our error, our passion neither for illumination nor for knowledge. It was neither for the imagination nor for the intelligence in chief, rich as it was for both. It came to the heart, and above all, the conscience. It came in the name of righteousness, and not of culture nor of cultus in the first place. It came to man neither as dull nor as sick, to cure neither spiritual ignorance nor spiritual disease. For those purposes would have been required the gift either of fresh knowledge to dispel the dark, or some fresh essence to restore vitality enough to cast off our disease. But such was not the trouble, and such was not the boon. The lack was neither vision nor vitality. It was love's holy righteousness. Christ came to redeem us from our last strait; and this deep distress was neither blindness nor sickness of spirit—it was guilt. The difficulty was not our attitude to love alone—it was not coldness needing warmth—it was our treatment of *holy* love, or holy love's treatment of us. The redemption Christ brought was not from our stupidity, nor from our feebleness—it was from our sin. And the question, the cry, he met was, "How shall a man be just with God?" or "How shall God seem just with man?"

Christ came to make Christendom seek before all else the Kingdom of God and its righteousness, which would increase and multiply all these other good things in tail. Can it be doubted that the pains (in both senses of that word) which the church has spent during all these centuries upon its theologies would have made a very different world today, and one much nearer the Kingdom of God, had they been spent on God's righteousness, as much as upon light, truth, or sentiment? . . . The revival of the passion for righteousness at any price is the mark of the true aristocracy which divides the Kingdom of God from all those egoist democracies that seek, however piously, a whole skin, a full purse, and a good time in a well-warmed world, and then put on moral side in the name of peace.

But seek first his kingdom and his righteousness, and all these things shall be yours as well (Matt. 6:33).

Do you remember the time when the disciples awakened Jesus? When a sudden storm arose, the boat was in danger of being swamped. Jesus was dozing, apparently oblivious to the peril. Awakened, he chided them for their fears. One might ask, why should they have been worried about the ship and the storm when he was aboard?

Sometimes the church is likened to a ship (you may have the symbol in some stained-glass window in your church). One might ask, does the church carry Christ, or does Christ carry the church? There are frightened voices that predict that the church cannot survive this age of science and secularism. They see the storms that buffet the ship, and the ship seems too frail a craft to withstand the fury of the winds. But all the while, the important thing is that Jesus is aboard. If he is confessed as Lord and Savior, if he is given the obedience of people's hearts, then the church need not fear. Its foes are not as strong as its Lord.

The Bible, too, is sometimes likened to a ship, more often as a cradle, bearing the Lord. But in a profound sense, it is the Lord who carries our Bible. If in our use of the Bible we let Jesus Christ be exalted, we need not fear for the book. He who comes to us in and through the book, also carries the book—and he carries us. We need not marshal our forces of scholarship in frantic defense of the Bible. Whenever the church has done this, it has ended up looking ridiculous. It has confused its people and has left the world outside indifferent. No followers have been won by thrusting the book at them. We witness best when, not the book, but the Lord of the book comes into view. We need only to let the Bible cradle us as it cradles our Lord. In and through its pages we need only to nestle close to him in faith.

Isaiah taunted the people who shaped gods out of wood and metal to carry. He invited them to the God who could carry them. Even for us who do not have idols sitting around in our homes, the temptation to carry God is a real one. It is never easy to rest back into the everlasting arms, confident that no storm can dislodge us from the love of God that is in Christ Jesus. The storms may rage, as indeed they do, but he will never forsake us.

And the men marveled, saying, "What sort of man is this, that even winds and sea obey him?" (Matt. 8:27).

DO YOU FEEL POWER? February 6

I once wandered through the debris of a village in western Minnesota that had been ravished by a tornado. More than 40 people had been killed. Among the many evidences of the storm's freakishness, I saw a straw driven like steel into a telephone pole. Now, no longer empowered by the storm, it was again a fragile bit of straw.

God is power, titanic and majestic. This is obvious from his creation, all the way from the swirling galaxies to the mysterious atom. It is not as obvious in the lives of his children. We are assured that if we are caught up in God, we who in our own strength are no more than straw, take on a power that is not our own. Drifting out of God's reach, we become frail and fragile, and are driven like chaff in the wind.

One of our central confessions is, "I believe that I cannot by my own reason or strength believe in my Lord or come to him, but the Holy Ghost has called me by the Gospel. . . ." We have neither faith nor power on our own. It is the work of our gracious God that we are drawn into the field of his mighty acts for us and in us. We rest back into a tornado of power when we rest back in God.

I admit that I am uncomfortable when people speak of the power of God in their lives, probably because I feel the absence of any surging power. I rarely, if ever, feel a burst of spiritual energy driving me on to battle a horde of demons or a world of injustice. I know I should, but I resist having such power take over. Where will it carry me? Far beyond the limits of the conventional and safe, I fear.

The hurricane is there, I know. Its center is the cross of Jesus Christ. It swept into our world with the power to save. It surges all around us, especially in the Word and sacraments. It threatens to draw us into its vortex, to fill us with new longings and yearnings, new courage and power. It did that for Paul, for Augustine, for Luther, and for countless others. How much it has done it for me, I must leave to God to determine. Not enough, I know.

The comfort is that even if our faith be fragile, and our performance feeble, if we do not run from the winds of the spirit that blow, we are counted as his. We must pray that we have the courage to let his power in, to carry us where it will.

All authority in heaven and on earth has been given to me. Go therefore and make disciples of all nations . . . and lo, I am with you always, to the close of the age (Matt. 28:18-20).

43

The human being has always tried to find fulfillment by skirting both duty and obedience, which alone are the paths to the abundant life in God. David F. Swenson, once professor of philosophy at the University of Minnesota, and a Christian, speaks of man's glory and crown:

For duty is the eternal in a man, or that by which he lays hold of the eternal; and only through the eternal can a man become a conqueror of the life of time. It is in the moral consciousness that a man begins truly to sense the presence of God; and every religion that has omitted the ethical is in so far a misunderstanding of religion, reducing it to myth and poetry, having significance only for the imagination, but not for the whole nature of man as concrete reality. The moral consciousness is a lamp, a wonderful lamp; but not like the famous lamp of Aladdin, which when rubbed had the power to summon a spirit, a willing servant ready and able to fulfill every wish. But whenever a human being rubs the lamp of his moral consciousness with moral passion, a Spirit does appear. This Spirit is God, and the Spirit is master and lord, and man becomes his servant. But this service is man's true freedom, for a derivative spirit like man, who certainly has not made himself, or given himself his own powers, cannot in truth impose upon himself the law of his own being. It is in the "Thou must" of God and man's "I can" that the divine image of God in human life is contained, to which an ancient book refers when it asserts that God made man in his own image. That is the inner glory, the spiritual garb of man, which transcends the wonderful raiment with which the Author of the universe has clothed the lilies of the field, raiment which in its turn puts to shame the royal purple of Solomon. The lilies of the field cannot hear the voice of duty or obey its call; hence they cannot bring their will into harmony with the divine will. In the capacity to do this lies man's unique distinction among all creatures; here is his self, his independence, his glory, and his crown.

While he was still speaking to the people, behold, his mother and his brothers stood outside, asking to speak to him. But he replied to the man who told him, "Who is my mother, and who are my brothers?" And stretching out his hand toward his disciples, he said, "Here are my mother and my brothers! For whoever does the will of my Father in heaven is my brother, and sister, and mother" (Matt. 12:46-50).

The whole world is the scene of broken fellowships. We were created by God to live in fellowship with him, and, as his children to live in fellowship with each other. We are one big family. But we break up— into nations, into races, into ideologies. We build walls to keep each other at bay, not only as nations and races, but as individuals within a community, congregation, even a family. How to break down walls and have people and nations cooperate with each other may be the most critical question of our century.

There are people who believe fear can do it. If nations and people are afraid enough of each other, they will behave. Children may cooperate in the tasks of the household because they fear punishment. Nations may cooperate in the work of the family of nations because they fear the strength of one member. But fear breeds resentments, suspicions, and at last a reckless bravado.

Other people believe that if nations and people are sufficiently educated to the fact that all parts of society ultimately lose or gain together —if they really know and understand this—there will be a life together.

A third proposal is that people and nations should learn to know one another better, and if they do, they'll like being together. There's an old refrain, "The more we get together, the happier we'll be." The fact is, of course, that there are some people you may like less the better you know them. You may think your neighbor next door quite a decent chap until, knowing him better, you discover that he beats his wife and robs his child's piggy bank.

All these proposals may have value, but the problem of human estrangement has deeper roots. It is at this point that Christianity enters with a revolutionary idea for communal life on the earth, whether as nations or as people one-by-one: people can get together in their common home—and with their common Father. When we remember that, all differences aside, we are all human beings before we are anything else, and when, knowing this, we are drawn into vital and personal fellowship with God, then walls begin to crumble and the signs of the bigger family appear.

He is not very far from each one of us, for "In him we live and move and have our being" (Acts 17:27-28).

INDEPENDENT, DEPENDENT, INTERDEPENDENT
February 9

Most of us applaud independence because we associate it with freedom. Those who have "made it" are free to buy what they want, travel anywhere, and retire with security. We respect them—and perhaps envy them.

Such independence is a bit phony, of course. With money or status, no one is safe from cancer or a stroke or from some economic crisis. The wise, despite the fawning world, will have the grace and the sense of humor to know that they are profoundly dependent beings.

This is a grace that comes especially with Christian faith. It is by the sheer favor of God, a loving God, that we have anything—our brains, our opportunities, our holdings. If we have been given good minds, health, friends and have lived in a land where the doors of opportunity are open to those who will work, whatever accumulation of this world's goods we may have attained, we will hold them in trust. We are God's, and whatever is in our hands is God's.

Nor should we be unaware of the vast interdependence by which we live. Every person is dependent on a network of other people for the simplest needs. How many people have been involved in providing the foods of the market? Who provides the fuel for our cars, heat for our homes, clothing for our bodies? What a vast army of people man our government, our schools, our communications—services we take for granted?

The world itself is one small, terrifyingly interdependent place. No nation can go it alone. The old adage that if one suffers, all suffer, is ominously true in our day. Our independence and our freedoms can be maintained only if they do not rob any other part of humanity of its independence and freedom. The nuclear age has made interdependence no longer an option. It is a grim necessity, if any part of the world is to survive.

Nor should the option be thought a grim one. Our Lord created us to be a family, to be free from those passions that rob others of freedom, free to care for one another, free to accept one another as brothers and sisters, free to thank one another for the services that we need and have. Dependent on him for everything, we use whatever independence we may have to contribute to a delightful *interdependence* of the family of man.

But God said to him, "Fool! This night your soul is required of you; and the things you have prepared, whose will they be?" So is he who lays up treasure for himself, and is not rich toward God (Luke 12:20-21).

William Stringfellow, attorney, author, lecturer, is one of our most perceptive lay theologians. In his book, *Count It All Joy,* he says:

> The unique character of the Christian faith, as distinguished from the religions . . . is reflected in the practice of the Christian life as contrasted with the practice of religion. It is, as it were, that the principle of sacrifice common to religion of all sorts is turned upside down in the Christian faith. In religion sacrifices in one form or another must be offered to establish relationship with the deity and to please or appease the deity. A fatted calf must be placed on the altar, fasting or similar pietistic regulations must be observed, certain moral behavior is prescribed, conformity or belief is required. All these and similar ritualistic, moralistic or dogmatic exercises are the specific forms of sacrifices made to the idea or image that takes the place of God.
>
> In the Gospels, however, the principle of sacrifice is, so to speak, reversed. The emphasis there is upon the sacrificial gift God makes of his own life for all men. To be fastidious about it, there is really no such thing as a martyr in the Christian faith, for the true sacrifice has been made in behalf of men by God and it is his sacrifice that saves the world; to his sacrifice nothing whatever can be added by any man and by his sacrifice are all men freed from making any sacrifices. The man who has died in Christ, lives in Christ, and if that man now is killed because he is a Christian, though he dies, he lives in Christ and his death is no sacrifice for him. . . .
>
> The Christian offering, far from resembling religious sacrifices, is the offering of oneself as a sinner and as a representative of all other men as sinners in confidence in the mercy of God's sufficient sacrifice for all men. For *all* men: that part of it is very important . . . If certain sacrifices can and must be made to secure divine approval and favor, then salvation extends only to those who have the stamina, wit or opportunity to make the prescribed sacrifices. The weak, uninformed or absent are doomed.

O Lord, open thou my lips, and my mouth shall show forth thy praise. For thou hast no delight in sacrifice; were I to give a burnt offering, thou wouldst not be pleased. The sacrifice acceptable to God is a broken spirit; A broken and contrite heart, O God, thou wilt not despise (Psalm 51:15-17).

IS RELIGION SLIPPING?

I'm not an historian, but I suspect that in every century there have been gloomy voices predicting the decline of religion. We are not without them today.

Were I to judge today's world by the small South Dakota community of my childhood, I might join them. Everyone was baptized, confirmed, and went to church. When the weather was bad, my grandfather marshalled the family around the living room and read what to me was an interminably long sermon. It was easy for me to conclude that all immigrants were pious, churchgoing people.

It was years later that, with a shock, I learned that at the time of the American Revolution only about 6% of the colonial population belonged to a church, and that even by 1850 less than 25%—compared with well over 50% in the mid-20th century. The good old days were not refreshingly good for religion.

I don't want to disparage my forebears. The immigrants that came to the Dakotas in the late 1800s did build their churches almost before they built their homes. They had come to improve their economic future, but they did not leave God and the church behind. At great sacrifice they established congregations and schools, to educate their children and keep them in the faith.

While the statistical picture for the established churches is not as impressive in the last quarter of the 20th century as during the burgeoning 1950s, there is probably more "spiritual" ferment in our day than we've had for many decades.

I plead that we do not let our confidence in God or in the church rise and fall with each Gallup poll. We cannot program God, nor can we predict his activity. The history of Christendom these centuries has many periods when the casual observer has all but given up on the church, and suddenly with no apparent cause, there has been a resurgence of the Spirit. His kingdom is in our midst, and he has assured us that not even hell with all its fury shall be able to dislodge it.

As the mountains are round about Jerusalem, so the Lord is round about his people, from this time forth and for evermore (Psalm 125:2).

I had never heard the term "identity crisis" until after I was 50. Very early I knew who I was. My father, though kind, never let me forget that I was under his authority and care as his son. My four brothers and sister, in one way or another, reminded me that I belonged to them. Sunday after Sunday in church I was told that I was a child of God, whatever terror or comfort that might bring. In any event, I knew who I was, son, brother, child of God. The pastor, who didn't overlook man's sinfulness, didn't let me forget that inside I was a mess, and needed God, both for judgment and mercy. It gave me comfort to read Margaret Halsey's column in *Newsweek:*

> The false idea is that inside every human being, however unprepossessing, there is a glorious, talented and overwhelmingly attractive personality. This personality—so runs the erroneous belief—will be revealed in all its splendor if the individual just forgets about courtesy, cooperativeness, and consideration for others and proceeds to do exactly what he or she feels like doing.
> Nonsense.
> Inside each of us is a mess of unruly primitive impulses . . . there is no such thing as a pure, crystalline and well-organized "native" personality, though a host of trendy human-potential groups trade on the mistaken assumption that there is.
> "I don't know who I am." How many bartenders and psychiatrists have stifled yawns on hearing that popular threnody for the thousandth time?
> But this sentence has no meaning unless spoken by an amnesia victim, because many of the people who say they do not know who they are, actually *do* know. What such people really mean is that they are not satisfied with who they are. They feel themselves to be timid and colorless or to be in some way or other fault-ridden, but they have soaked up enough advertising and enough catch-penny ideas of self-improvement to believe in universal Inner-Wonderfulness. So they turn their backs on their honest knowledge of themselves—which with patience and courage could start them on the road to genuine development—and embark on a quest for a will-o'-the-wisp "identity."

My little children, I am writing this to you so that you may not sin; but if any one does sin, we have an advocate with the Father, Jesus Christ the righteous" (1 John 2:1).

Suppose we were asked to receive someone into our home, not for a day or for a week, but to stay. And suppose this person were a stranger, and not a very attractive one at that. If we had said yes, this person would no longer be a stranger. She or he would become a member of our household, perhaps later even taking our name.

You have known people who have done just that, and so have I. A pastor and his family who lived near a large prison took paroled prisoners into their home. He said, "They have no place to go but the tavern." He added that his children had a more interesting assortment of uncles than you could imagine. Not long ago I read of a family that had across the years received 60 foster children into their home.

Most of us stand off to the side as spectators. We admire people who do this, but we are mildly frightened at the prospect of doing it ourselves. What radical changes would we have to undergo in our orderly and comfortable routines? And what risks would we be taking? We are relieved to think that no such strangers have sought our door. We excuse ourselves by saying that we've never been asked.

But we have been asked, by no less a person than our Lord himself. He may not have asked that we take some specific person into our homes permanently, but he does ask that we take all people into our hearts permanently. And this is of no less importance than having them in our homes.

It's easy to receive those we love, or those we find attractive. But our Lord makes no distinction. His large family is made up of all people everywhere.

If we are to try obeying him, the first step will be to remember that we ourselves are the "received ones." With all our shortcomings, all our sins, all our wretchedness, we have been received by our Lord. He does not sort us out, saying, "This one I find attractive; he can come." He receives us all by grace through faith.

We are the loved ones, the forgiven ones, the accepted ones, the received ones. It is we who are to carry on this glorious infection of loving and receiving. To receive one another, Christ says, is the only channel open to us to receive him. Nor are we to receive one another grudgingly, with a heavy heart, but rather with the joy of finding that those whom we thought to be strangers are indeed our brothers and sisters.

He executes justice for the fatherless and the widow, and loves the sojourner, giving him food and clothing. Love the sojourner therefore; for you were sojourners in the land of Egypt (Deut. 10:18-19).

WHEN THINGS GO WRONG

Dietrich Bonhoeffer, brilliant young theologian, was imprisoned by the Nazis for conspiring against Hitler, and was executed. During his concentration-camp days he was a spiritual leader for other prisoners. His writings during those dark days have inspired millions. These notes are from his *Letters and Papers from Prison.*

"Houses and fields and vineyards shall again be bought in this land" proclaims Jeremiah (32:15), in paradoxical contrast to his prophesies of woe, just before the destruction of the holy city. It is a sign from God and a pledge of a fresh start and a great future, just when all seems black. Thinking and acting for the sake of the coming generation, but being ready to go any day without fear or anxiety—that, in practice, is the spirit in which we are forced to live. It is not easy to be brave and keep that spirit alive, but it is imperative.

It is wiser to be pessimistic; it is a way of avoiding the disappointment and ridicule, and so wise people condemn optimism. The essence of optimism is not its view of the present, but the fact that it is the inspiration of life and hope when others give in; it enables a man to hold his head high when everything seems to be going wrong; it gives him strength to sustain reverses and yet to claim the future for himself instead of abandoning it to his opponent.

It is true that there is a silly, cowardly kind of optimism, which we must condemn. But the optimism that is will for the future should never be despised, even if it is proven wrong a hundred times; it is health and vitality, and the sick man has no business to impugn it. There are people who regard it as frivolous, and some Christians think it impious for anyone to hope and prepare for a better earthly future. They think that the meaning of the present events is chaos, disorder, and catastrophe; and in resignation of pious escapism they surrender all responsibility for reconstruction and for future generations. It may be that the day of judgment will dawn tomorrow; and in that case, though not before, we shall gladly stop working for a better future.

I want you to know, brethren, that what has happened to me has really served to advance the gospel, so that it has become known throughout the whole praetorian guard and to all the rest that my imprisonment is for Christ, and most of the brethren have been made confident in the Lord because of my imprisonment, and are much more bold to speak the word of God without fear (Phil. 1:12-14).

We are equal, but we are different. Man and woman are both created in the image of God. Both are loved by God. Both have the same eternal worth. They were created for each other, to complement and fulfill the other. When God said, "It is not good that the man should be alone; I will make him a helper fit for him," he did not create another man. Nor by the term *helper* did he mean a slave or some second-class citizen.

It is obvious that in our more primitive struggle with nature, the man, physically stronger, should play the dominant role. In modern society, the necessity for physical strength has diminished. Many opportunities are now equally open to both men and women. But this does not erase their differences, nor make them independent of each other. Nor does it thrust them into the same roles in society.

Our age speaks much about masculine and feminine qualities. It is popular to point out that a man has both qualities, as does the woman. It is a bit more difficult to define precisely what those qualities are. Is tenderness a feminine quality? If so, I have known men who are more tender than some women. A friend of mine, a bank president now retired, is loved throughout the community for the 'heart" with which he administered his bank all those years. Is heartlessness a masculine quality? History is replete with queens and empresses who for sheer cruelty could not be matched among men.

I become a bit impatient with trying to sort out feminine and masculine qualities, and especially impatient when some extremists are troubled about having God be masculine. Roman Catholics perhaps have the better of both worlds, with God the father and with their honor to Mary as mother. But the issue has little bearing on the essential roles and tasks given to men and women in society.

And the new opportunities for women may have little to do with equality. In her traditional role as wife and mother, woman has probably exercised more power in a quiet and subtle manner than she will ever know. We may always have been more matriarchial than patriarchial. To say, "I am only a wife and mother," is to abdicate the center of power. The family is the prime institution of power, and in a singular way women have been directors and teachers in this place, in the long run more important than parliaments.

Then the Lord God said, "It is not good that man should be alone; I will make him a helper fit for him" (Gen. 2:18).

When, during the French Revolution, the prison doors of the Bastille were battered down, the prisoners were free to leave. Many, long imprisoned and accustomed to the routine of their cells, were afraid to leave.

This is the plight of humanity. In the imagery of the Bible, man had been imprisoned by the Enemy, brainwashed to love darkness more than light, and had become accustomed to a life in the shadows. In the vagaries of the prison, they pursue money that could buy everything but happiness, power that could control everything but their own desires and appetites. Differences between good and evil, right and wrong, were lost in the dimness of the prison.

The great good news of the gospel is that Jesus came to overcome the Enemy, to shatter the doors of the prison, and to fling wide the doors of the Father's house—and freedom! Huddled in their cells, people often refuse to believe that the doors are really open. Or believing, they lack the courage to part with the strange security of the prison, to accept freedom, and to embark on a life of responsibility and accountability.

The warden of this spiritual prison is a cunning foe. His public relations officers do an admirable job of deluding the prisoners that they are free—free to indulge their appetites, free to pursue their selfish ends, free to crush their rivals, free to amass phony wealth, free to swagger in the pride of power. There is but one absolute restriction: they are not to see the light. In the light, they would discover that freedom is freedom to turn from the anarchy of their egocentric ways to embrace the ways of God, to accept responsibility for the care of the earth and for one another. And this is a gigantic and terrifying turn-about.

On the cross our Lord engaged the Enemy in a last-ditch stand and overcame him. The great deceiver, the devil, the prince of liars, the cruel warden, is stripped of his power, and his prison has lost its doors. Man is free to leave.

Nor did our Lord leave the matter there. Through the quiet work of his Spirit, he lures man into the light and goes on to groom him to a new life of real freedom. This he does primarily through the means of grace, his Word and sacraments. After all, it would be senseless to enter the Father's house with self-pity and self-indulgence still crippling the freed-one from enjoying the liberty of the kingdom.

For freedom Christ has set us free (Gal. 5:1).

C. F. W. Walther is a legend in American Lutheranism. Pioneer pastor and theologian, he led his church through days when "pietist sects" were luring people away into an emotionalism which he considered destructive of the comfort God's Word clearly offered. Himself a deeply pious man, he reminded his people that their peace lay in the clear promises of God. These are paragraphs from his widely read book, *The Proper Distinction Between Law and Gospel:*

When the Pietists had brought a person to the point where he considered himself a poor, miserable sinner, unable to help himself, and asked his minister what he must do now, the minister did not, like the apostles, answer him: "Believe on the Lord Jesus Christ, and thou shalt be saved," but, as a rule, they told him the very opposite. They warned him against believing too soon and against thinking that, after having felt the effects of the Law he might proceed to believe that his sins had been forgiven. They told him that his contrition must become more perfect, that he must feel contrite, not so much because his sins would call down upon him God's anger and hurl him into perdition, but because he loved God. Unless he could say that he felt sorry for having angered his merciful Father in heaven, his contrition was declared null and void. He was told that he must feel that God was beginning to be merciful to him; he must get so far that he could hear an inner voice telling him: "Be of good cheer; thy sins will be forgiven thee; God will be merciful to thee." He must continue struggling until his agony was over, and having rid himself of the love of sin and having been thoroughly converted, he might begin to take comfort.

Now, this is an awful method. The truth is, we are not to be converted *first,* and after that *believe;* we are not to have a sensation first that we are in possession of grace. But without any feeling we are to believe that we have received mercy, and after that will come the feeling of mercy, which God apportions to each according to his grace.

But now the righteousness of God has been manifested apart from the law, although the law and the prophets bear witness to it, the righteousness of God through faith in Jesus Christ for all who believe. For there is no distinction; since all have sinned and fall short of the glory of God, they are justified by grace as a gift, through the redemption which is in Christ Jesus (Romans 3:21-24).

Knowledge is important. Our world has seen a veritable explosion of knowledge in all areas. Who could have dreamed a few short years ago that we would conquer smallpox, place men on the moon, and live with the magic of the computer?

But it's not knowledge that provides life with ultimate meaning. It is faith. We must have something—or someone—to believe in. Knowledge is made up of a vast assortment of pieces, like a jigsaw puzzle. It is faith that can assemble the pieces into a picture of the whole. Until the picture emerges, everything is a jumble.

Knowledge has made our world incredibly rich, but with glaring limitations. It has nothing to say about the nature of values. It gives us power never dreamed of—power to build cities and power to destroy them with a blow, power to travel at the speed of sound but with no clear destination. It has given us skills—skills to lengthen life but no word about why one should live to be 90, skills to exploit nature for its resources but no feeling for nature as a friend to be cared for. It has given us insights—insights into the social and political structures of nations but no word of duty beyond the need to survive, insights into the biology of the body but no clue to the hidden glories of the soul, insights into the billions of galaxies but silence about a God beyond the stars.

God has offered us a picture, to be received by faith and not by knowledge. It is a staggering pattern. The Bible's 66 books contain it. Beginning with the bracing lines, "In the beginning God created the heavens and the earth," and moving toward the climactic promise of a new heaven and a new earth, the picture has breathtaking dimensions.

In this drama God and man are the central figures, with the universe itself the stage, with nations and civilizations as props, with time the prompter. What happens between God and man is the eternal plot. Nor is man the buffoon or the porter. Man, in this drama, is "a little less than God." For man is a son of God, a prince in the royal household. Only with man having this high station would the climax of the play, the death and resurrection of God the Son for him, make any sense whatsoever.

This is the picture, received by faith, which can pull together the fragments of knowledge, and make of the jumble a design of meaning and beauty.

Now faith is the assurance of things hoped for, the conviction of things not seen (Heb. 11:1).

Socrates, who lived in Athens 400 years before Christ and was considered the wisest and noblest of the ancients, has been immortalized through Plato's *Dialogues*. He was sentenced to death for "corrupting the youth" of Athens; he refused escape, and died drinking the hemlock. These are his last words to his friends, recorded in the *Phaedo*.

"We should use every endeavor to acquire virtue and wisdom in this life; for the reward is noble, and the hope great. . . . Since our soul is certainly immortal, this appears to me most fitting to be believed, and worthy of the hazard for one who trusts in its reality, and it is right to allure ourselves with such things, as with enchantments. . . . On account of these things, then, a man ought to be confident about his soul, who during his life has disregarded all the pleasures and ornaments of the body as foreign from his nature, and who knowing that they do more harm than good, has zealously applied himself to the acquirement of knowledge, and to having adorned his soul not with foreign but its own proper ornament, temperance, justice, fortitude, freedom and truth, this waits for his passage to Hades, as one who is ready to depart whenever destiny summons him. . . . Now destiny summons us, as a tragic writer would say, and it is nearly time for me to betake myself to the bath; for it appears to me better to drink poison after I have bathed myself, and not to trouble the women with washing my dead body."

When he had said thus he rose, and went into the chamber to bathe. "It is certainly both lawful and right to pray to the gods, that my departure hence thither may be happy; which therefore I pray, and so may it be." And as he said he drank it off readily and calmly. . . . Shortly after he gave a convulsive movement, and the man covered him, and his eyes were fixed, and Crito, perceiving it, closed his mouth and eyes.

"This," said Phaedo, "was the end of our friend, a man, as we may say, the best of all of his time that we have known, and moreover, a most wise and just."

For the Lord gives wisdom, from his mouth come knowledge and understanding; he stores up sound wisdom for the upright; he is a shield to those who walk in integrity, guarding the paths of justice, and preserving the ways of his saints (Prov. 2:6-8).

We please God first when we acknowledge that he is God and that he calls the signals. He does not come under our command; we come under his. He has every right to judge us; we have no right to judge him. He is not on trial by man; man is on trial by God. And it should be a most encouraging thing that he, the great God, bothers to judge us and to punish us. Suppose he cared so little that he was totally indifferent, that he couldn't care less what we did or did not do. The judgment of God is profoundly a part of the good news about God. He cares.

We please him further when we drop all our phony pretenses at having measured up to his standards and law. This is not easy for us. We'll do our best to show God that we're measuring up reasonably well. We'll point out that we're not bad parents, that we have not embezzled, never mugged anyone, never committed adultery, never falsified our IRS reports. Moreover, we've taught Sunday school, sung in the choir, we've been a deacon and a member of the school board. We may be silent about the paltry sums we've given, rarely a modest 10%. But all in all, we've not done too badly. More than likely, of course, if we keep our eye on Jesus, our defense may whimper to a stop. We know, we all know, that by the standards of his kingdom—total unselfishness, total love, total righteousness—any defense we may try collapses. We please him by letting them collapse.

We please him by throwing ourselves on his mercy alone. The cry of the publican, "God be merciful to me a sinner!" is pleasing to God, for with God there is mercy. Mercy swallows up justice. The heart of the Christian faith lies here. Jesus Christ, true God and true man, dying on a cross for the sins of the world, is the guarantee of God's endless mercy. In him we have forgiveness of sins and the promise of a life everlasting with God.

We please him by lives of gratitude and love. Never doubting the mercy that receives us and holds us, come what may, we turn to thank him. And he tells us that the only real way we can thank him is to love and serve our brothers and sisters. We can do nothing directly for God; he is neither hungry nor sick. But he has proxies all over the place, near us and to the uttermost parts of the world. We please God supremely by serving others.

Come, O blessed of my Father, inherit the kingdom prepared for you from the foundation of the world; for I was hungry and you gave me food, I was thirsty and you gave me drink. I was a stranger and you welcomed me, I was naked and you clothed me, I was sick and you visited me, I was in prison and you came to me (Matt. 25:34-36).

We can deny our oneness. But, like it or not, we are one.

We are one, great, human family. Each human being on earth has one heart, one brain, two lungs, two eyes, two feet. We are all created by the same God who already has claimed us all as his children. We all occupy the same home, the planet earth. That which gives the greatest joy and the deepest sorrow is the same for a mother in India as for a mother in America, for a father who is rich as for a father who is poor, for a white as for a black. We can deny that we are one, and we do. We divide into races, into nations, into groups of all kinds. This denial is futile, for we are created to be one.

We who have allowed Christ to capture us are another group, his body on earth. We are his church. As a smaller circle rests within a larger, the Christian church lives within the larger circle of humanity. We do not lie alongside the rest of humanity. We are at once human and Christian.

Within the smaller circle, we have our own problems with oneness. Though we have but one Lord, we separate ourselves into denominations, often with reluctance to accept one another in the same family. Our coming from various cultures and traditions may give richness to the family if we are not all jammed and conformed into one unambiguous mass. We may even be excused for having some regimental loyalties, if we remember that we have but one leader and a common foe, and that we war not against each other. The scandal of Christendom has been the centripetal forces that have driven us apart.

The luxury of being separate disappears in a crisis. A tornado, a typhoon, or a flood suddenly brings all into a fellowship of danger and suffering. In a disaster a rich man's son and a poor man's son, a black man and a white man, coping side by side, become friends, their economic and racial gulfs forgotten. Even within the church, on the foreign field for instance, missionaries have forgotten their denominational banners to march together under the one flag of Christendom.

The variables that separate us are the accidents of our existence—birth, fortune, color, nationality—to a certain extent, even creeds. Overarching all our diversity, and pervading them all, is the fact and the blessing of a great oneness!

Praise the Lord, all nations! Extol him, all peoples! (Psalm 117:1).

In 1920 Clarence Day published a book describing memories of his home and especially of his father under the title *Life with Father*. This excerpt portrays a man who, though hardly pious, nonetheless takes God with some seriousness:

They [father and mother] both insisted strongly, for example, on our going to church, but they didn't agree in their reasons. It was the right thing to do, Father said. As a rule, non-church-goers were not solid, respectable citizens.

My mother put it differently to us. She said we owed it to God. Church to her was a place where you worshiped, and learned to be good. . . . My mother once wrote in my plush-covered autograph album, "Fear God and keep His commandments"; but the motto that Father had written on the preceding page, over his bolder signature, was, "Do your duty and fear no one."

When Father went to church and sat in his pew, he felt he was doing enough. Any further spiritual work ought to be done by the clergy. . . . As to his mental picture of God, I suppose that Father was vague, but in a general way he seemed to envisage a God in his own image. A God who had small use for emotionalism and who prized strength and dignity. A God who probably found the clergy as hard to bear as did Father himself. In short, Father and God, as I said, usually saw eye to eye. . . . They had perfect confidence in each other—at least at most moments. The only exceptions were when God seemed to be neglecting his job—Father's confidence in Him was then withdrawn, instantly. . . .

He usually talked with God lying in bed. My room was just above Father's and he could easily be heard through the floor. On those rare nights when he failed to sleep well, the sound of his damns would float up. . . . At the peak of these, God would be summoned. I could hear him call "O, God" over and over with a rising inflection, as though he were demanding that God should present Himself instantly, and sit in the fat green chair in the corner, and be duly admonished.

Then God answered Job out of the whirlwind . . . "Where were you when I laid the foundation of the earth? Tell me, if you have understanding" (Job 38:1-4).

The days of Jesus were unbelievably full—with healing the sick, traveling from town to town, and preaching from synagogue to synagogue. Yet, in the middle of his rushed life, we find these words, "In the morning, a great while before day, he rose and went out to a lonely place, and there he prayed." Jesus matched involvement with withdrawal, action with contemplation, togetherness with solitude, noise with silence.

We, too, need a lonely place in our lives. Without silence, words lose their meaning; without listening, speaking no longer heals; without distance, closeness cannot cure.

We are a world of action. From morning to night, we hurry to do something. It may be worth doing. But unless we are on guard, we may be exhausted by doing, and have no time left either to examine our direction or recoup our strength. Even when on our leisure we turn to play, the recreation itself may leave us spent.

We may pray, but we pray in bits, and then by habit—and hurriedly. Few of us take the time to cultivate the inner presence of God. The art of meditation is almost alien. We regard with suspicion Eastern cults that urge meditation. We need to remember that solitude and meditation, prayer, and communion with God were at the very center of our Lord's life on earth.

St. Augustine of the fifth century has these beautiful words: "You have made us for yourself, O Lord, and our heart is restless until it rests in you. . . . Too late have I loved you. . . . Behold, you were within me while I was outside; it was there that I sought you, and rushed headlong upon these things of beauty which you have made. You were with me, but I was not with you."

It requires deliberate discipline of a high order to be able to withdraw, to listen, to meditate, to pray, to sit in silence. God has given us this world and one another. We dare not retreat from the care of either. But he has also given us himself. In quiet communion with him, we may recharge our flagging spirits with his gifts: forgiveness, peace, courage, and joy.

And this will not be a retreat from the surging responsibilities of life. We will then learn to live *in* the world without being *of* it. In our quiet place we recover both freedom and power.

Now when Jesus heard this, he withdrew from there in a boat to a lonely place apart (Matt. 14:34).

If you are not a Christian and do not confess Jesus as Lord, have you any part of him? The two or three billion people of the earth who follow other faiths or disavow any religious faith, are they altogether excluded from him? Stated another way, has he who is Lord of all limited his work and blessings alone to those who explicitly receive him as Savior and who belong to his visible body, the Christian church? These are puzzling questions.

No one who has been captured by Christ and his spirit can possibly wish anyone to be excluded from him. We are under orders to make him known to everyone and to extend his invitation to all; and the love which he has awakened in us will hope that somehow, someway, he is not limited to our faltering efforts in winning the world for himself. D. T. Niles, noted Christian evangelist from Ceylon, once said that Christians must realize that Jesus Christ was there in Asia and Africa before the missionaries arrived. We dare not be so audacious as to think that the Lord of the universe has but one strategy in reaching his children.

Can it be that Jesus, *incognito* in the best of non-Christian religions and cultures, draws people into his kingdom? Whether Moslem, Hindu, Buddhist, or whatever—if they are moved to awe and wonder and to a love of the brother beyond race or creed, is this the work of Christ in their hearts? Who knows? Every person who lives in the love of God must hope so.

It is also true, however, that no serious follower of Jesus can let him be only one among other religious leaders of the world. He stands alone, "full of grace and truth." This inclusive and exclusive claim must be made. He is the savior of the world.

Let me try an illustration. Suppose during wartime a large group of refugees are at the seaport waiting to embark for the United States. They long for something better. They have no money, but are told that someone has paid their passage, and they board the ship. At sea they try in vain to discover the identity of their benefactor. When they land in New York, a voice over the loud speaker informs them that the man in the white coat on the pier is the one who paid their way.

Inadequate as the analogy may be, for me it provides a partial answer to the riddle. Somehow and in some way, all the great spiritual and moral qualities of the human race come from him who became incarnate in Bethlehem and who, whether his name is known or not, is the giver of all good and perfect gifts, including life everlasting.

He that is not against us is for us (Mark 9:40).

Why don't people say "By Joseph" instead of "By God"? Or "Abraham Lincoln" instead of "Jesus Christ"? Why do people swear and curse using the name of God?

A person's name is not just another word. In a deep sense, your name is you. The way people use your name shows how they feel about you. If people love you, they will speak your name with tenderness. If they fear you, they will say your name with respect. If they adore you, they will speak your name with a kind of reverence. If on the other hand, they hate you or despise you, they will probably talk about you sneeringly, with scorn and contempt.

When people throw God's name around carelessly or are indifferent about his will, they show that they hold God in something less than respect or love. They may not intend to despise God, but they certainly do not show that they fear or love or honor him.

Søren Kierkegaard has a disturbing analysis of why even people who want to be known as Christians are careless about God's name.

It is not very epigrammatical that profane swearing was not customary in paganism but is quite at home in Christendom; that paganism generally uttered the name of God with a certain awe, with a dread of the mysterious, whereas in Christendom God's name is the word which occurs most frequently in daily speech and to which altogether the least significance is attached, because the revealed God, poor fellow (because he was so lacking in shrewdness and foresight that he became revealed instead of keeping himself hidden as superior persons always do), is the one personage out of the whole population who has become all too well known, upon whom one confers an exorbitant favour when one goes to church once in a while, where one gets praised for this by the parson, who thanks one on behalf of God for the courtesy of the visit, honours one with the title of pious, and takes occasion to sneer a bit at the man who never shows God the courtesy of going to church.

Could it be that Kierkegaard is right, and that even we who are Christian have lost the sense of the majesty and the wonder of God? Have we heard so much about his mercy and love, and so little about his awesome judgment, that we have reduced him to some indulgent and senile grandfather who basks in the trivial honors we condescend to give him?

You shall not take the name of the Lord your God in vain; for the Lord will not hold him guiltless who takes his name in vain (Exod. 20:7).

DO I REALLY NEED FORGIVENESS?   February 26

Let me say at the outset that I don't always *feel* the need to be forgiven. I *believe* I need to be; I *know* I do, because the Scriptures say very clearly that I do. But what do I need to be forgiven for? Like the rich young ruler, I have obeyed the commandments. I have not murdered or committed adultery. I'm not a thief, not even a minor shoplifter. I've tried to be honest with IRS. I may have stretched or withheld the truth at times, usually to avoid hurting someone's feelings. What's so terrible about a little lie? Certainly not terrible enough to drive Jesus to a cross for my sins.

If I want to understand myself, and if I want to understand Christ's love for me, I am told that I must find myself in the corner of bad people who need, more than anything else, the forgiveness of sins. The question haunts me. Is there in me, and in all people, some evil so subtle and pervasive and destructive (like a hidden cancer) that unless it is dealt with, any progress toward spiritual health (honesty, joy, love, hope) will be an illusion? And does it take a therapy so radical that only the death of Jesus will do? Our Christian faith says that it cost him a cross.

You may be initially drawn to Jesus by his miracles of mercy, by his penetrating parables, by his indignation against sham and oppression. Before long, as Jesus grows upon you, and you stand watching him die, you will know a strange uneasiness. You don't belong in the same company with him. Like Peter, you'll feel like crying out, "Depart from me, for I am a sinful man, O Lord." Somehow the yawning gap between you and Jesus will have to be bridged. Your most noble efforts won't do it. The only bridge is repentance and confession, and being caught in the tide of his forgiving love which sweeps all your sins away.

Forgiveness has tended to slip out of the vocabulary of secular man. If we believe that there is no God at the center to be accountable to and that the universe is but a vast machine, forgiveness is meaningless. If man is but a cog in the machine, driven by his appetite and his chemistry, forgiveness is nonsense. If we are but helpless pieces of some cosmic game, why ask us to repent and be forgiven? You don't forgive a dog for stealing a bone, nor a tornado for levelling a village, nor a river for overflowing its banks. But we are created children of God, with holiness the expectation and demand, and as utter failures to meet the demand, there is no door but forgiveness for our return to God.

He said to the paralytic, "Take heart, my son; your sins are forgiven" (Matt. 9:2).

More than 150 years ago, in a far simpler age than ours, Henry Francis Lyte wrote the hymn, "Abide with Me," with these lines:

Change and decay in all around I see,
O thou who changest not, abide with me.

Since then, changes have rushed upon us with ever increasing speed, until we wonder if anything from the past has a chance to survive. In all fairness, we must be glad for much of change. Who wants to travel by ox cart or farm with the hoe? Much has been to our gain, but we may be giving up on eternal values which alone can keep life worthwhile. At the moment there is abroad a lurking cynicism that gives up on all order and meaning. Charles S. Anderson, professor of theology and college educator, points to the absence of form in art and music as symptoms of this loss and the resulting chaos:

Go to an art museum and make a tour. As you enter the gallery given over to modern, contemporary art, you will see a commentary on our age. The concern for order and symmetry, the interest in nature and its beauty, and the representation of life in meaningful symbols have been left in the galleries devoted to former ages. The great screaming message of much of our art seems to be that there is no meaning at all. The tangled lines and indiscriminate blobs of color, the sculpture made of old automobile parts and bathtubs, which is timed to blow up as part of the show, these and other examples all point to a definite view of man and the world. Now, I admit that I am a rank amateur in art history and appreciation, but the conclusion to which I have been driven is not mine only. The form of art today, or the lack of it, is in itself symptomatic of a general mood.

Much of modern music expresses the same feeling of discordance and meaninglessness. The world pictured by these art forms and by much of contemporary literature is an ugly place of discord and lack of meaning.

"Thou who changest not, abide with me," is a cry from all of us. We must have some place to stand as the world swirls around us. There must be changes, but we cannot live with change alone. We must have God, and the unchanging truths of his way of life.

Thy faithfulness endures to all generations; thou hast established the earth, and it stands fast (Psalm 119:90).

THE SILENCE OF GOD February 28

"Why doesn't God do something about it?" Who hasn't uttered this anguished cry when things go utterly wrong—when a madman plunges a world into war and burns six million Jews, when no one seems to know how to stop a senseless war in Vietnam?

Silence is the title of a novel from Japan by Shusuku Endo. The story is the persecution in 17th century Japan of Jesuit missionaries and Christians which virtually wiped Christianity from the land. Again and again, the young missionary from Portugal, Sabastian Rodrigues, watching his flock tortured and killed, cried to God to break his silence. The Japanese magistrate used a bizarre device to pressure Rodrigues to renounce his faith in Christ. Within earshot of the missionary, he suspended Christians by their toes into slimy pits, and told Rodrigues that only if he would apostatize would he spare them from death. Rodrigues finally capitulated, believing that Jesus himself would, in love, have taken such action to spare his people. The book ends with the question still haunting the missionary, "Why doesn't God break silence?"

We may reassure ourselves in the words in Hebrews 1, "In many and various ways God spoke of old to our fathers by the prophets; but in these last days he has spoken to us by a Son." But there are times when even this reassurance doesn't break the terrible silence that haunts us when disaster strikes. Sometimes the whole world seems careening to catastrophe, with alcohol, drugs, crime, military madness fueling the jet that can't be stopped. We cry in desperation for God to do something about it before his children perish. And it's not enough to have some good counsel from the parables of Jesus. We want him to thunder his presence. Why, oh why, does he keep silent?

There is no easy answer, that's for sure. We may quote comforting Scriptures to each other, and remind one another that if the whole world blows up, in Christ do we have a dwelling place not made with hands. But we want him around, here and now, to do something about the madness of his children.

Hundreds of thousands of people have asked the question, as we did when our Paul at 24 was suddenly struck down on a city street. Why didn't God remind him to turn his head toward the oncoming traffic and avoid the truck? What's God up to anyway, if he doesn't bother to help his children in the day-by-day issues of life? I have some tentative answers, but we'll have to wait for larger ones. Meanwhile, in the darkness and in the silence, we trust him.

Though he slay me, yet will I trust him; I will maintain mine own ways before him (Job 13:15).

It has occurred to me that instead of extensive "scientific" studies on death and dying, we might be better served by the poets. They lift us out of the melancholy moods, and without letting us escape into sheer romanticism, direct us to the themes of death and life. I like the lines from William Cullen Bryant's "Thanatopsis":

So live, that when thy summons comes to join
The innumerable caravan, which moves
To that mysterious realm, where each shall take
His chamber in the silent halls of death,
Thou go not, like the quarry-slave at night,
Scourged to his dungeon, but, sustained and soothed
By an unfaltering trust, approach thy grave,
Like one who wraps the drapery of his couch
About him, and lies down to pleasant dreams.

And the lines from Tennyson's "Crossing the Bar":

Sunset and evening star,
And one clear call for me!
And may there be no moaning of the bar,
When I put out to sea.

But such a tide as moving seems asleep,
Too full for sound and foam,
When that which drew from out the boundless deep
Turns again home.

Twilight and evening bell,
And after that, the dark!
And may there be no sadness of farewell,
When I embark.

For tho' from out our bourne of Time and Place
The flood may bear me far,
I hope to see my Pilot face to face
When I have crossed the bar.

Verses such as these, born out of the biblical faith, point us beyond death to an endless life with our Lord.

Behold, the dwelling of God is with men. He will dwell with them, and they shall be his people (Rev. 21:3).

Who has not pondered the mysteries of life and found no clear answers? Why does God leave so much of life beyond our sight and understanding? Why does he let us walk in darkness? Gerhard Frost, in his book, *The Color of the Night*, reflects on the life and sufferings of Job:

> The spearpoint of Job's many questions is this: Why so much mystery? Why must I travel blind?
>
> This is one of the most profound levels of pain. Job's outcry is more than protest against the anguish of isolation and the loss of his supporting community. It is the supreme agony that comes from trying to make sense of that which lies beyond the reach of logic. It is a crisis in meaning. Job feels himself to be in the grip of ultimate nonsense. His cry is qualitatively above the *whys* of intellectual inquiry. It is a religious outcry, a protest against life's unyielding absurdity, against the incoherence of his situation.
>
> We are meant for this reflective warfare. This is our dignity. We are exploring, probing, searching, and reaching creatures. We are God's hurting ones. Amid the magnificence of Who? What? How? Where? and When? is the ennobling Why? It must never cease to be asked.
>
> We must raise our *whys*. And we will, whether we wish to or not. The mind can no more contain its whys than the body can hold its breath. But there are many ways of asking why. It can be whined or cursed or snarled or pouted. But it can also be prayed.
>
> A why can be a child's empty cup, held up to the love and wisdom of our gracious God. Our Lord doesn't fill it to the brim, but he satisfies each person's need. He is too kind to drown us in all the knowledge we crave. He doesn't give more than we can hold; sometimes we must wait to be made larger cups. Our present questions may be the wrong ones. Then he helps us outgrow them and prompts us to move to better ones.
>
> God knows that the road we must travel would overwhelm us if we could, in a single moment, see around every bend. He gives us a candle rather than a floodlight—and he promises to be there. He asks us to remember that mystery is one form of his mercy. His aim is not to keep things from us, but to keep things—the best things—for us.

Why is light given to a man whose way is hid, whom God has hedged in (Job 3:23).

"Let love be genuine," said Paul. Don't be a phony. Don't simply pretend to love. Love is too wonderful for games.

Love, after all, is more than good manners or courtesy. These may be coverups for the very opposite of love. You may say, "I'm sorry," and not really be sorry at all. You may say "Thank you" in all the proper places and never really be grateful at all. You may greet a person, "How nice to see you," and wish you were a hundred miles away.

God wants from us an elemental honesty. He asks for integrity. His love for us is so genuine, so real, that in Christ Jesus he went to a cross in death. This was more than good manners. This was the real thing. He asks that we make a serious try for the same quality of love.

It is never easy—this kind of love. It stretches our stubborn, indifferent natures out of shape. We will never be the same again.

We may have to start with going through the motions of love when we don't feel like it at all. If this is done, not to deceive someone into thinking that we love, but in a genuine desire to learn how to care, then we're on the Lord's side. We need not wait for a surge of love to begin meeting someone's needs, even if that someone is repulsive to us. In our doing for him, the Lord has a chance to nudge us into the world of real love.

Only he can do it. His Holy Spirit, working through Word and sacrament in a silent, ongoing revolution, can do it. No other power can. Even the Holy Spirit will have trouble getting it done. We are deeply self-centered, and we don't give up easily.

But it does happen. And when it does, the glory of God and heaven break through. The world would be a dreary place if it did not happen. You know people for whom the miracle has occurred and who do reach out to others in a graciousness that brightens all of life. Perhaps you are one of them.

If you are one of them, you may be unaware of it. At least, if someone were to say, "What a loving person you are!" you would be embarrassed. If you have made progress in getting outside of yourself to enjoy people and to find pleasure in helping them, you will know how far you yet have to go before you can remotely match the depth of the love of God. Your greatest joy will still come from the wonderful awareness that you are nestled in the love of the Lord.

. . . not anything else in all creation will be able to separate us from the love of God in Christ Jesus our Lord (Rom. 8:39).

History has dark chapters when Christians have destroyed each other over their differences. Why should it be so difficult for Christians to engage in discussion and have serious disagreements without becoming estranged from one another?

When St. Paul exhorts his people to speak the truth in love, he must have known that there would be times when they might have serious differences over truth itself. If my friend feels keenly that his opinion is the truth, and I feel that the opposite is the truth, it will take patience for both of us to keep love for one another alive. Each of us will be tempted to absolutize our "truth."

During the Vietnam war, for instance, there were earnest young men who for conscience sake refused to serve in the armed forces and were dismissed as "yellow-bellied traitors" by people who, also for conscience sake, felt that obedience to the law of the land was the duty of every Christian. And many people were enraged by the civil disobedience of Martin Luther King Jr., even though nonviolent. Christians today are divided over the nation's military build-up, over laws regulating abortion, over attitudes in race relations.

And what of theological differences? Whole denominations have been torn apart for want of patience and charity, and because each side claimed a direct line from God for its "truth." Meanwhile the love which the Lord had died to give his children fled, and suspicion, distrust, and even hatred, took the field. And truth itself, real truth, wept.

Sometimes in congregations people who long have been drawn together in affection are separated over issues far less important than either patriotism or theology. Budgets, membership on boards, selection of a pastor, a new order of service—matters of judgment and taste and not of truth—have driven joy from the family of Christ. Only when people are again captured by God's grace, with a fresh invasion of repentance and forgiveness, can joy return. The Lord has to remind his people that their allegiance to truth needs the leaven of charity and a sense of humor, if love is to live.

In the terrible days of the Inquisition, the church executed people who didn't have the right kind of "truth." Today we don't execute, we only exclude, we only separate. Jesus, who told us to love even our enemies, looks on in sorrow.

Rather, speaking the truth in love, we are to grow up in every way into him who is the head, into Christ, from whom the whole body, joined and knit together . . . makes bodily growth and upbuilds itself in love (Eph. 4:15-16).

THE DEATH OF SELF-PITY

For 14 years Carroll Luther Hinderlie directed the shaping of a unique retreat-center in an abandoned copper mine village in the Cascade Mountains of Washington. Holden Village became a community dedicated to claiming for the Christian the whole of God's creation, "the visible and the invisible." In the words of Hinderlie:

All that is Christ's has become ours. The Holy Spirit has been given to make our awareness continuous that we are sons and daughters of God, no longer slaves of fear. Self-pity is the shape of this demonic fear in our life, and its power has been broken by the exuberance of praise that we are sons. . . .

What happens to men who do not own all things in Christ? Those who cannot possess this morning's sunrise or enter into the sense of belonging to one another in our glad company as fellow kings under the King of Kings? Because they do not accept God's promise that they are somebody, they must ever be restless to be something. They cannot relax from the "grab-race." When you do not know you are a son in the Beloved, your life will be twisted and knotted with your striving to grab your place in the sun. You have to count, because you have not been counted as one of the heirs of God, a co-heir with Christ to suffer with him, instead of suffering over your own slights and your own gains. Because you do not own everything, you must grab all you can get while the grabbing is good. You are a victim of man's tragedy so well put by Pascal, "More, more, is the cry of the mistaken soul. Less than *all* cannot satisfy a man."

When you own everything, that is when you are a Christian. "You belong to Christ." Then all things belong to you. This world is yours and all the worlds to come! In your "Thanks, dear Father," the power of demonic self-pity is broken; the whole universe is yours as sons and daughters of God. This is what Holden Village is saying to you by just being there. Every son is called to be a poet and painter, a geologist and economist, a theologian and a man of letters—nothing human is foreign to you when God's promise gives himself as our Father in baptism. You are joined to the whole human race and the whole earth is the Lord's—and you are Lords without the apostrophe when you have let that little possession mark become your baptismal ring of freedom.

. . . and if children, then heirs, heirs of God and fellow heirs with Christ, provided we suffer with him in order that we may also be glorified with him (Rom. 8:17).

There's no standard more disturbing to me than the Lord's words, "Every one to whom much is given, of him will much be required." No matter how I try to escape, the finger of God singles me out. I have been given incredibly much. So have you.

I can hear and I can see; thousands can't. I can read; millions can't. I have enough food; a third of the world is hungry. I live in a country where no bombs have fallen, no enemy crossed our borders; hundreds of millions in this century have been killed or driven from their homelands. I've had work to do; millions are unemployed. What's more, I've had loving parents and family, my health has not collapsed, my mind has not slipped cogs and now, reviewing the inventory of my years, I have little time to recoup the debits of wasted opportunities.

If nations come under the judgment of God, what country in all the long history of the world can compare with the prodigal assets given to us? Quite apart from the fact that, though 6% of the world's population, we possess 40% of its wealth, what civilization can compare with ours in the freedoms we have—freedom of speech, of press, of assembly, of religion? Before the high court of God, or the tribunal of history, our nation, more than any other, must stand uneasy before the court's standard, "Every one to whom much is given. . . ."

If the Lord were primarily a judge, we would be undone. But we have met him at the cross, and have heard his prayer, "Father, forgive. . . ." We are caught in the surging tide of his mercy.

But the standard is still there. In the midst of our joy over mercy and forgiveness, it calls us to repentance, and to a fresh try at obedience.

What the judgment of God may be upon our nation we cannot know. To nations, too, God shows mercy, but the price of our national indulgence doubtless has to be paid. The Scriptures tell us that God is not mocked; what is sown shall be harvested. History itself is replete with stories of nations that have lost their values in selfish pursuit of power and pleasure; they inherited the whirlwind and sunk into oblivion.

The great comfort for each of us is that whatever storms may come, the Lord does not abandon us. We may have to suffer trials, the fruits of our selfishness and of our nation and of the world, but he will not let us be destroyed if we rest back in him.

Every one to whom much is given, of him will much be required; and of him to whom men commit much they will demand the more (Luke 12:48).

Greek mythology gives us the story of the handsome youth, Narcissus, who turned away from the love of all others, including Echo, the nymph, who loved him dearly. He fell in love with his reflected image in a pool of water, and died loving the image alone.

Speaking to our modern preoccupation with self, David W. Preus, president of the American Lutheran Church, expresses a warning:

> Two popular contemporary attractions are narcissism and individualism. Both are popular, both are destructive. Sound Christian doctrine summons us away from both of them. Yet both continue to exercise enormous public appeal. The Christian church has a responsibility to identify them, warn of them, and present the biblical alternatives.
>
> Narcissus was fascinated by his own reflection. . . . All of us are faced with the same temptation. We lose healthy contact with the rest of existence because we are so concerned with ourselves.
>
> God's ongoing effort, and that of his church, is to get us beyond ourselves, to get our eyes off ourselves onto God. Our hope, our help, our center is in him, not in ourselves. That is why Jesus said, "Follow me," and not "Investigate yourself." Christian doctrine makes it very clear indeed that self-centeredness is sin, a betrayal of our Father, a sure way to destruction.

Also, speaking about how individualism reflects itself in worship when people get their inspiration from television and radio alone, without active participation in the life of a congregation, Preus continues:

> God has made us for a life with him and with his people. We are made for *koinonia*, for fellowship. We miss what life is about if we isolate ourselves and do not live as members of God's family. It is not only that we need the family of faith, the family also needs us. Loving, caring, sharing, burden-bearing, justice-seeking people must be people who live with and for others.
>
> The church as a household of God, the family of God, is one of the rich biblical pictures of the church. We are baptized into the family to live as children of the heavenly Father and as brothers and sisters to each other. The doctrine of the church directs us beyond individualism, beyond ourselves, to a life in the family of God.

When the day of Pentecost had come, they were all together in one place (Acts 2:1).

If visitors from outer space were to reach the earth, which of the races would they likely judge most attractive? Most likely not the pallid, bleached-out white race. Probably the olive beauty of the Oriental, or the bronze of the Latin American, or the rich ebony of the Black. Years ago, after a week in Mexico City, it suddenly dawned on me that we, the whites, were quite bland compared with the rich blend of Indian and Spanish skins of our neighbors to the south.

We make a great deal of differences, whether in skin or status. To our Lord, who gave us this delightful variety, we are all equally beautiful. It's fascinating, for instance, in a volume of *Who's Who*, to read of people who have distinguished themselves in the world of education, art, science, industry. You'll look in vain for the name of some neighbor who, his life through, has poured out his life for his family, church, and community with never a name in a newspaper headline. To our Lord no unselfish service, heralded or not, is ever unnoticed or lost.

How easily we let some point of view, some unfounded bias, shape our judgment and values. As Christians we know that all people are equally dear to the Lord. But we have prejudices that distort our behavior. Not until our children adopted three multiracial "grandchildren" did it occur to me that I, too, had racial problems. And not until our fine grandson, who has more white blood than black, had to register himself in school as black, did it occur to me how arrogant and biased we white people are. Now, I am told, the blacks, grown more proud of their heritage and roots, have begun to be equally disdainful of the white blood that flows in my grandson's veins. To what race does he belong?

The Lord knows. He belongs to the human race, a child of Adam and Eve, as we all are. And like the rest of us, he is ticketed by grace for the same eternal home.

But our prejudices die hard. Our points of view don't shift easily. There was a day in our village, an island of Norwegian immigrants, when to mix Norwegian with Irish or German blood, even with Swedish, was looked upon with suspicion. The twentieth century has seen vast changes, of course. God has used this shrunken world and the mobility of populations to force us out of our ghettos. There are still those who dig in instead of yielding, and rear walls even higher. The Lord must weep to see his children rob themselves of the excitement and love of the larger fields of his kingdom.

And he made from one every nation of men to live on all the face of the earth (Acts 17:26).

In twentieth-century England there gathered a cluster of brilliant Christian writers—Charles Williams, C. S. Lewis, Dorothy Sayers, J. R. R. Tolkien—all of whom at one time or another wrote fantasies to convey deep truths of the Spirit. Some of these writers were inspired by an elder "father" in fantasy, George Macdonald, whose writings C. S. Lewis credited with leading him to the faith.

Lewis once said that fantasy or the fairy tale is the only effective medium to penetrate the modern, flat language of science with the great Christian truths. In reading fantasy, the reader who joins the writer in a search for the hidden meanings will be rewarded with fascinating and unsuspecting discoveries.

For instance, in Macdonald's *At the Back of the North Wind* a boy whose name is Diamond has adventures with Lady North Wind (a kind of angel who lives in the world of the spirit), whose companionship with the little boy gives him the delightful quality of goodness without his really being aware that he is good. Here is an excerpt from the book:

> To try to make others comfortable is the only way to get right comfortable ourselves. Our Selves will always do pretty well if we don't pay them too much attention. Our Selves are like some little children who will be happy enough so long as they are left to their own games, but when we begin to interfere with them, and make them presents of too nice playthings, or too many sweet things, they begin at once to fret and spoil.
>
> "Why, Diamond, child!" said his mother at last, "You're as good to your mother as if you were a girl—nursing the baby, and roasting the bread, and sweeping up the hearth! I declare a body would think you had been among the fairies."
>
> Could Diamond have had greater praise or greater pleasure? You see when he forgot his Self his mother took care of his Self, and loved and praised his Self. Our own praises poison our Selves, and puff and well them up, till they lose all shape and beauty, and become like great toadstools. But the praises of father or mother do our Selves good, and comfort them and make them beautiful. *They* never do them any harm. If they do any harm, it comes of our mixing some of our own praises with them, and that turns them nasty and slimy and poisonous.

For whoever would save his life will lose it, and whoever loses his life for my sake will find it. For what will it profit a man, if he gains the whole world and forfeits his life? (Matt. 16:25).

Most children will say "daddy" or "papa," rarely "father." It would seem strange if in the Lord's Prayer we were to address God as "Dad," but scholars tell us that the word the Lord used was an informal address, more like "Daddy" than a stern, formal "Father." We are his children, confident of his love and understanding, and in the Lord's Prayer we come to him spontaneously in trust.

But our Father is a being of infinite power. He is a judge of unrelenting righteousness. He is not a dad who, to get chummy with his children, plays their games. He does join them, but not in touch football. He joins them in their sorrows and guilt, their fears and hope. He became flesh and dwelt among us, said John, and "we have beheld his glory, glory as of the only Son from the Father."

The ancient Jew was taught that God was so exalted and holy that a mere human being ought not even utter his name. He is "high and lifted up," in Isaiah's words, awesome in power and majesty.

It was Jesus who brought him into view as Father and Friend. "My Father and I are one," said Jesus. In coming to earth he had emptied himself, so that the power with which he created and sustains the universe was hidden, and so that we could the better see the divine heart of love. In Christ, God became a servant, a friend, a father.

Even in our warmest and most intimate moments, we cannot quite face God as we would a friend across the table. Instinctively we know that we are talking to an all-knowing, all-powerful, all-holy, and every-where-present being. He is Friend, but much more than a friend. He is Father, but much more than a father. He is King and Judge.

Through profound study and experience Luther learned that the face of God was not of anger but of love, and that we are received by him not because we have satisfied the demands of righteousness, but because he is a forgiving God of infinite mercy. But Luther never forgot that as a sinner he stood in awe over against the majesty and holiness of his heavenly Father.

It may be that in our day we have lost the awareness of God's fierce wrath against all unrighteousness, and in consequence have made him a Lord of sentimental love—a kind of indulgent father who is neither angered nor grieved by our sinfulness. This is to lose the profound depth of his compassion. He is our God, who in his Son went to his death to make us his own again. In radical gratitude, we pray "Our Father."

Pray then like this: Our Father who art in heaven . . . . (Matt. 6:9).

Until the bombs dropped on Hiroshima and Nagasaki, the world had seemed a relatively secure place for me. But then we had in our hands something that could end civilization.

Visiting Europe in 1952, I had seen how quickly Germany was rebuilding its cities, but I was haunted by the prospect that a World War III would leave nothing to build with. My cousin, a colonel in the Air Force, said they spoke quietly about the possible "two-hour war" that might come. If Russia and the United States were to unleash their nuclear attack, in two hours there would be nothing left.

What has happened since 1952 gives me no comfort. I'm told that in addition to missiles, we now have among other forms of attack 31 Trident submarines, each capable of wiping out 160 Soviet cities. And each year the military budgets of these two giants keep growing, to the serious neglect of much that each nation could do for its people.

I once visited Charles Malik, Christian statesman from Lebanon, then chairman of the United Nations Assembly. "No one wants war," he said. Every leader of state of whatever country works for peace. If so, I have wondered, what demonic trap keeps us deluded into thinking that war is a solution? After World War II, suddenly Germany and Japan, our enemies, became our allies, and we gave them billions; and Russia, our ally, overnight became the enemy.

Occasionally I wonder what would happen if, for instance, our president should have the daring to propose that we reduce our arms budget 5% each year for 10 years, and simply challenge Russia to do the same, without getting any previous assurance that they would. Would our citizens support the president? Would Russia join the venture, and be relieved to turn to its domestic issues? Naive though such a proposal may be, the alternative seems certain catastrophe.

With pious resignation, I may say that "heaven is my home," and that if the earth blows itself up, I have a dwelling place, eternal, not made with hands. But the earth is the Lord's, and we've been given management of it, and until he himself decides to usher in a new one, we can't give it up. So we pray, we hope, and we give whatever support we can to every effort for peace.

Woe to those who go down to Egypt for help and rely on horses, who trust in chariots because they are many, and in horsemen, because they are strong, but do not look to the Holy One of Israel or consult the Lord! (Isa. 31:1).

I have found few "instructions" on suffering more helpful than Leslie Weatherhead's brief summary:

A doctor challenged me one day that the church had never worked out a philosophy of life which would sustain a sufferer. I am sure this has often been done, but I will summarize my own point of view:

1. The will of God is perfect health of body, mind, and spirit for all his children. No artist could *desire* imperfection in the created object.

2. Through the ignorance, folly or sin of the sufferer or, what is more likely a member of the human family to which he belongs, the individual may suffer.

3. God is always eager to restore to health, but He has ordained that He will do so usually in cooperation with man. Otherwise divine omnipotence would abolish man's understanding and skill.

4. Those working to heal should ask and answer the all-important question: "How can we best cooperate with God—from whom alone all healing derives—in the case of this person?" The answer may be surgery, medical treatment, psychiatry, prayer, or the little known radiaesthetic energy or "odic force" which men like Mr. Harry Edwards possess. *Not one of these is a cure-all.* Prayer may comfort and sustain, and even make illness seem unimportant, but God does not allow man, by putting a prayer in the slot and drawing out a cure, to escape the burden of research, skill and hard endeavor.

5. If a patient is healed, the will of God is done—though some hymns about "Thy will be done" would suggest the opposite. If the patient is unhealed, God is only *temporarily* defeated. . . . If the Cross, devised by evil men, could be turned into a victory which redeems the world, then even cancer, whatever its cause, cannot finally defeat God's plan in the life of any of his children.

6. Suffering has no power to make a saint, but courage, faith, and prayer can help the patient make such a reaction to suffering as to turn liability into asset.

7. Let us never look on suffering and say, "This is the will of God," since a *man* who deliberately thus wrought his will would be sent to prison or a mental hospital. Let us labor to end the causes of suffering, and to help God weave what we cannot remedy yet into spiritual victory, as Christ did when he accepted the Cross.

A thorn was given me in the flesh, a messenger of Satan, to harass me, to keep me from being too elated. Three times I besought the Lord about this, that it should leave me: but he said to me, "My grace is sufficient for you" (2 Cor. 12:7-9).

When a person is "born again," what happens? If at birth he was color blind or tone deaf, does the new birth help him see color or sing on pitch? When Jesus told Nicodemus, "That which is born of flesh is flesh, and that which is born of the Spirit is spirit," he had no intention of having Nicodemus enter into his mother's womb and return to life with a whole new set of "natural" qualities.

To be born of the Spirit is to have something new "superimposed on" or "permeate" that which already is given. It is not a denial of the wonderful equipment or drives which the Lord gives at birth. We will not lose the love of eating or of sex. The person born with one intellectual "talent" will not have a brilliant five. Nor will a person naturally uncoordinated suddenly become a ballerina.

When and how the "new birth" comes is not easily charted. Nor can anyone claim to give the new birth in ten easy lessons. Jesus, in his talk with Nicodemus, left him with the mystery, "The wind blows where it wills." Here, and later, the Lord did identify the mystery with baptism. For that reason, the whole Christian church has been obedient in holding the Sacrament of Baptism in great honor. And at least 95% of Christendom has given the gift of baptism to infants, long before they could consciously understand.

May it be that the gift of the Spirit, being "born again," is given to the child, and that the church's task is to have the child know that the gift is his, to lay claim to it, and to use it? If upon the birth of a child, a rich uncle deposits $100,000 in trust to the child, it would be a pity if no one informed him of the gift and he'd go through life in poverty, when indeed he was rich. Maybe this is like the gift of the Spirit. It's there at baptism, and needs only to be claimed and used.

There are people who, oblivious to their wealth, are suddenly awakened to know Christ, and how rich they are! For them, it's almost as if they've been in a dark cave and suddenly burst out into the sunlight. For others, the "awakening" is a lifelong process, like sitting on a hillside from 4 a.m. to 8 a.m., and having darkness gradually give way to light.

Whatever the birth of the Spirit may be, it's real. It is as real—more real—than the birth we celebrate on our birthdays. It lasts longer—throughout eternity!

Truly, truly, I say to you, unless one is born anew, he cannot see the kingdom of God (John 3:3).

God never stops loving us, but we may blunder along and miss him in our whole lives through. He seeks us, but in a profound sense he cannot find us until we begin to seek him. He calls us, but his voice doesn't reach us until we call for him. God does not force himself upon us. He pleads with us through the Holy Spirit and waits eagerly and patiently for us to *do* something.

He asks that you call upon him, that you seek him. That's all. And if you do, all heaven can break open for you.

Among the many cruel and demonic devices hatched in this 20th century is the scientific and systematic *brainwashing* of people. Men's minds are twisted like plastic into something utterly unnatural. Men become worse than animals.

Brainwashing is an old trick of Satan, long before the age of science. He did it with Adam and Eve in the Garden; he did it with King Saul. He plants evil thoughts, wicked appetites, false ideas, and distorted passions in the minds and hearts of men. Day by day, almost unnoticed by him, man's whole being is wooed and enticed away from truth and righteousness and God. Man turns a deaf ear to the call of God. He drifts out beyond the orbit of God's pull. And the time may come when he never again can call upon God or seek him.

It is through his Word and sacraments that God continues to reach out to us. We who sit in the church pews on Sunday are within the arena of God's call. Even in the pews, we may fail to hear him and neglect to call upon him. But we need not.

Nor are we beyond the reach of Satan in church. Because we sing hymns, have our feelings stirred by a good sermon, pray the right prayers, and leave the church with the good feeling of having done the right thing, the deceiver can lull us to sleep in self-satisfaction or in pride, the most insidious of sins. To be in the presence of God is to be ushered into the world of indescribable comfort, but it also is to dispatch us into a world of need. When the Holy Spirit moves us to reach out for God, we had better be aware of the glorious and frightening consequences. But let us give him ear as he calls!

And the great dragon was thrown down, that ancient serpent, who is called the Devil and Satan, the deceiver of the whole world—he was thrown down to the earth, and his angels were thrown down with him (Rev. 12:9).

WHAT'S WRONG, LORD?

It's six years since I've retired from my desk. I was told that I would have a terrible time dropping responsibility, and that each morning I would awaken and groan to remember that someone else was at my old desk. It hasn't happened. Should it, Lord?

When friends asked me what hobbies I had developed to cushion the emptiness of retirement, I was hard pressed. I don't work with wood, I don't golf, bowl, or collect coins or stamps. They seemed to feel sorry for me. I usually told them that for the first three months I'd gaze at Nora, a delight I'd too often neglected, and after that I'd try to be a good grandfather. With 13 grandchildren, I seemed to have a career. Do you think I should take up knitting, Lord?

To be frank, I do keep doing some of the things that I did when I was employed, like writing and preaching when I'm asked. But I don't always feel that I have a duty to say yes to every invitation. Is that wrong, Lord?

My reading is now the unproductive kind. No longer do I read to prepare for a paper or a speech. You might say, I read for fun. And it's fun to let the author talk to me without wondering what I can "steal" from him. Is that a waste of time, Lord?

And speaking of time, I wonder if I may not now be more in tune with you, for whom a thousand years is as a day. The clock becomes our master, and we have a rough time with patience. Impatience may be the scourge of our years. I think I'm learning from you who does not hurry the seasons nor the rising of the sun. Each day I thank you for another 24 hours, and remember with the Preacher in Ecclesiastes that there is a time to be born and a time to die. That's good, isn't it, Lord?

When people remind me that there are people who have had very productive years after 70, like Pablo Casals, Albert Schweitzer, Sigmund Freud, Frank Lloyd Wright, Karl Barth, or Roland Bainton, I'm more depressed than cheered. I'm not in their class, after all. And do I have to measure my worth by being "productive"?

You've assured me, Lord, that if I were altogether unproductive (like a severely retarded child), I'd be equally dear to you, and that your forgiveness covers even my unproductiveness—and, measured by your standards, there's much of that in my life. I'm glad that you will take me as I am.

For a thousand years in thy sight are but as yesterday when it is past, or as a watch in the night (Psalm 90:4).

Who hasn't asked, or been asked, "What's heaven like?" The Scriptures are filled with picturesque language—streets paved with gold, a place of no night or darkness, myriads of angels around a throne. It may be enough to know that our Lord will be there and we with him. C. S. Lewis in his *Letters to Malcolm* "plays" with a fascinating analogy:

> I do *not* think that the life of heaven bears any analogy to play or dance in respect of frivolity. I do think that while we are in this "valley of tears," cursed with labor, hemmed round with necessities, tripped up with frustrations, doomed to perpetual plannings, puzzlings, and anxieties, certain qualities that must belong to the celestial condition have no chance to get through, can project no image of themselves, except in activities which, for us here and now, are frivolous. For surely we must suppose the life of the blessed to be an end in itself, indeed The End: to be utterly spontaneous; to be the complete reconciliation of boundless freedom with order—with the most delicately adjusted, supple, intricate, and beautiful order? How can you find any image of this in the "serious" activities either of our natural or of our (present) spiritual life? Either in our precarious and heartbroken affections or in the Way which is always, in some degree *a via crucis?* No, Malcolm. It's only in our "hours-off," only in our moments of permitted festivity, that we find an analogy. Dance and game *are frivolous,* unimportant down here, for "down here" is not their natural place. Here they are a moment's rest from the life we were placed here to live. But in this world everything is upside down. That which, if it could be prolonged here, would be a truancy, is likest that which in a better country is the End of ends. Joy is the serious business of Heaven.

There are other writers, too, who have described life even here at its best to be a life of freedom in Christ, where spontaneity and fun and merriment have replaced discipline and duty and obedience, where "holy hilarity" has made even sacrifice a joy. At such moments, when in following Christ and doing his will we are lifted out of ourselves into a strange happiness—at such moments we have a fleeting taste of freedom and bliss, as a kind of "heavenly game."

Thou hast turned for me my mourning into dancing; thou hast loosed my sackcloth and girded me with gladness, that my soul may praise thee and not be silent. O Lord my God, I will give thanks to thee for ever (Psalm 30:11-12).

At some time or another, most of us will pass snap judgment on an act, without knowing much about the person or circumstances. Paul Scherer tells of a sermon in which the preacher "was rebuking that kind of do-less religion which pins its faith to God and never has a single, reckless fling of its own for love and justice and mercy and decent human life." Who was it, the preacher asked, who wrote "in the Cross of Christ I glory"? Sir John Browning!

Then the sermon went on to tell that Sir John was the British governor general of Hong Kong at the time when the British Empire was forcing the opium traffic on China. What the preacher didn't know, or what he ignored, said Scherer, was that Sir John was a man of great philanthropies, reforms, and that he had helped countless people.

The same sermon went on to point out that the man who wrote "How sweet the name of Jesus sounds in a believer's ear," was John Newton, who ran a slave ship between Africa and the slave markets of the western world. Every Sunday he read the church liturgy to his crew twice, in the morning and at evensong, with the moans and the stench of a doomed humanity boiling up into his ears and nostrils out of the ship's hold. But the sermon omitted something. After a long struggle with his vicious self, Newton had become a minister of the Church of England, and it was 21 years later that he had written the hymn. His epitaph, which he himself wrote, records his own story:

> John Newton, Clerk
> Once an Infidel and Libertine
> A servant of slaves in Africa
> Was by the rich mercy of our Lord and Saviour
> JESUS CHRIST
> Preserved, restored, pardoned
> And appointed to preach the Faith
> He had long labored to destroy

God alone knows the secrets of the heart. It is for us to use great caution, much patience and charity, as we pass judgment on another. It is far better to be too kind than too severe. Luther, speaking about the Lord's command against false witness, says that we must be vigilant not to slander anyone, "but apologize for him, speak well of him, and put the most charitable construction on all that he does." And doesn't Jesus say something about the beam in our own eye, and the speck in our brother's eye?

Judge not, that you be not judged. For with the judgment you pronounce you will be judged, and the measure you give will be the measure you get (Matt. 7:1-2).

BEING WEALTHY March 17

There's nothing in the Bible that says it's wrong to have wealth or power. Much is said about the temptation to get them by fraud, to rely on them, or to misuse them; but God, who is the author and giver of wealth and power, is not so absent-minded as to denounce them. In talking about the New Testament figure of Zacchaeus, the man of wealth who climbed into a sycamore tree to see Jesus, Theodore Heimarck, a long-time pastor in Minneapolis, said:

Jesus, penetrating the surface of things, saw the man's loneliness and fears and invited himself to the home of a despised "publican and sinner." Christ entered the miserable and disappointing world of a "rich" man, who was the victim of the lure of the world's prizes of power and riches, in order to bring him into Christ's world of "at-one-ment" with the source of life.

This is really Christianity's perennial and mysterious attraction that is given the name "grace." It is a great word. We keep misunderstanding it. Every generation is feverishly concerned about reaching up to him. And all the while, so experience shows, it is characteristic of our God that he is reaching down to us. He asks only that man's life be opened to his love, manifesting it by accepting the friendship proffered in Christ. This is the "good news"; that in total disregard of who we are, or what we are, or what we have been, his offer is the offer of friendship. Zacchaeus gladly took him to his home, and it meant for him the beginning of a new life. . . .

In the company of Jesus, Zacchaeus was forced to think life's intentions through again. He was rich, so we are told, and yet he was being instructed by one who became poor in order to make us truly rich. How could this be? Certainly it cannot be said that the riches themselves prevented life's fulfillment. Let others say that— and I understand some are saying it. We, however, must not forget the blessings of wealth; it secures the conveniences as well as the necessities of life; it gives opportunity to alleviate the distress of the neighbor, as witness our schools and hospitals and dozens of other benevolent institutions; it enables a man to help equip the great enterprises of the kingdom of God, for it builds churches, prints Bibles, and sends missionaries. . . . Of course riches cannot purchase the deepest satisfactions of life. They cannot purchase health, or friends, or love, or even loyalty. And, strangely enough, one almost has to be rich before full realization of its limitations comes. These limitations Zacchaeus knew from bitter experience. This was the *beginning* of wisdom.

If riches increase, set not your heart on them (Psalm 62:10).

Do you remember the fable about the north wind and the south wind, and the argument about which was the stronger? The test was which could compel a man to remove his coat. It was the warmth of the south wind and not the fury of the north wind that won the match.

Love is stronger than hate. It is love that makes the world go round, not hate—however cold and ruthless the world may seem.

I can stand up to hatred. You hate me; I hate you. I clench my fists, firm up my fortress, and hold you at bay. But if you insist on loving me, day in and day out, regardless of my indifference or resentment—this I cannot stand. My defenses weaken, and the walls begin to crumble. How can I hold you off when you insist on loving me?

The kingdom of God is the kingdom of love. Jesus said that this kingdom would be a leaven, a yeast, a salt that slowly but relentlessly would affect and change the whole. It would not storm the walls. It would creep up almost unnoticed. It would seep through, like osmosis.

If someone hates you, what do you do—hate him in return? This will change nothing. But if in return for his hatred you meet him with patience and love, you will threaten the whole situation. You will bring to bear on him the power of God. He will be less than human to hold out against you.

Hundreds of millions have known this strange power in their lives. In our generation perhaps the most publicized instance is the life of Martin Luther King. Giving his life for the rights of his black people, meeting cruel and violent resistance, he again and again reminded his followers never to give way to hating—that hatred, whether in blacks or whites, was always a destructive, and ultimately, a defeated force. It was said that St. Francis in 13th-century Italy returned to his monastery one day to find that the monk he had left in charge had driven away some robbers with angry words. Francis sent him out to find the robbers and ask their pardon. All three robbers were thus brought to the Lord. The supreme instance is Jesus himself who never gave way to hatred, even as he was dying on the cross.

Obviously the way of love is not always easy, but it is the way of God. And because it is the way of God, it is the way of power.

But I say to you, Love your enemies and pray for those who persecute you, so that you may be sons of your Father who is in heaven (Matt. 5:44-45).

CONVERSION

Samuel M. Shoemaker, Episcopal priest, was one of the most fascinating churchmen of the mid-20th century. Discussing conversion, he said:

Conversion, the initial Christian decision, must not be tested by any psychological pattern; it must be tested on rather a broad basis by its fruits. We are not set to put people through certain psychological hoops; we are set to help liberate them from themselves into "the glorious liberty of the children of God." Some have been "converted" who would wholly repudiate the word, and heartily deny that they were so good as this implies. But the test is in its effects. Where there is emerging victory over self-centered habits, where faith and its practice grow stronger, where the whole life bears a new tone, where human relationships come straighter, where work is better and more happily done, and where the Spirit of Christ affects one's relationships and affairs, there you have the footprints of Christ's wonderful work in conversion. . . .

All this, I must point out, is essentially a religious and not merely a psychological experience. Psychology has scarcely any counterpart to it. Psychology knows certain sudden, sometimes lasting, changes in the human psyche, and let us be thankful for everything that helps men upward. But it knows nothing of forgiveness, yet forgiveness is the only real break between us and the past. We cannot find in psychology anything approaching atonement, though psychology itself must recognize how deep in human beings is the longing for something to *make up for* their sins as they certainly cannot do for themselves. The "good life," however good and however much we want it, has no drawing power in it like the love of God. And no study or understanding of the laws of psychology can possibly offer us anything of the help that is indicated by the word "grace." Therefore, while psychology can describe the experiences of religion, it cannot offer the dynamic to produce them.

Create in me a clean heart, O God, and put a new and right spirit within me. Cast me not away from thy presence, and take not thy holy Spirit from me. Restore to me the joy of thy salvation, and uphold me with a willing spirit (Psalm 51:10-11).

I wish there were an abridged version of Christ's parable of the prodigal son. If I were to write it, I'd make a slight change in the plot. I would have him go to the far country with his inheritance. But instead of having him squander it, I'd have him invest it in the best stocks and bonds of the country and let him become the richest man in the land.

Then, one evening, when his fellow citizens threw a big banquet for him, and with everyone fawning over him, I'd have him "come to himself." I'd have him say, "What am I doing here? I don't belong here. I'll go to my father and say to him, 'I have sinned against heaven and against you, and don't deserve longer to be your son, but let me come home and work on the farm with the other workers.'"

The reason I like this plot is simply that the point of Jesus' parable wasn't how the son botched up things in the far country. The point was that he went to the far country. He left his father's home! Whether he succeeded or failed by the standards of the far country was incidental. In fact, to succeed, he might very well have had to abandon the principles of his father as much, perhaps more, than in failing.

The abridged edition would fit many of us. By the standards of the world many of us are successful. We get along, because we have relaxed the standards of our Father's house. We don't tell big lies, but we tell little, polite ones to keep out of trouble. We don't rob banks, but we cut corners here and there and compromise with the world's style of life. We'll stay away from groups that seem too eager for justice for all. We'll work harder for the favors of the world, promotions and rank, than for the care of our wives, husbands, or children. We may take more seriously our membership in a union or a service club or a political party or a bridge club or a bowling team than our membership in our church. There are all sorts of little things that give us away; we're really trying to make it in the far country, with little thought of the Father's house.

The parable doesn't say what the father had him do on the farm. Only this, that he was back as a *son*—not as a common laborer—with all the rights of a son, and under no period of probation to see if he had really sloughed off the ways of the far country.

We are back, through the sheer mercies of our Father. The chapter in the far country can be behind us—its successes or failures—and we can press on to serve and enjoy the few swift years we have in the Father's house here, and on the other side, forever.

". . . for this my son was dead, and is alive again; he was lost, and is found." And they began to make merry (Luke 15:24).

NO MYSTERY LEFT? March 21

Paul Scherer, one of America's distinguished preachers from 1930-1960, a voice I heard each week over national radio in my early ministry, wrote of mystery in life:

"The most beautiful thing we can experience," writes Albert Einstein, "is the mysterious"; and nobody I suppose will question his right to speak, as he calls back to us from where he stands and tries to tell us what he sees. "The man to whom this emotion is a stranger," he goes on, with a hush in his voice, "the man who can no longer pause to wonder and stand rapt in awe, is as good as dead; his eyes are closed." Jesus, with a finger to his lips, spoke softly of the wind stirring in the treetops, how it blows where it will, and one hears the sound of it, but cannot tell whence it cometh, and whither it goeth. Since then, among other things, we have made a study of the wind. No sooner does it begin to tiptoe through the forest, setting all the leaves of the poplar agog with the witchery of its whispered confidence, than somebody from the U.S. Weather Bureau shatters our dreams by calling for an anemometer to measure its velocity. Then, what with geodetics and barometrics, he tells us exactly where it comes from, and in tomorrow's paper, in the upper right-hand corner, exactly where it's going—maybe! It's very distressing, how much we know about everything. . . .

I can't tell how it is with you, but I am thirsty—my lips are dry and parched, for one long, deep, cool draught of ignorance, to help wash down this arid desert of analysis and statistics which I am supposed to swallow and call it knowledge. . . .

No, it isn't knowledge that banishes God, it's the conceit of it; it's this scientific Babbittry, with never in its busy, noisy days a worshipful silence, nor anywhere on its barren landscape a place to kneel and hear the sweep of wings and feel the fleeting touch of a cool hand like the peace of God. . . .

Life holds her mysteries still; and when I turn from that world without to this world within, I am face to face with the greater mystery of my own selfhood, lifting up its head with a strange sense of its high inheritance, and the redeeming fellowship of a Nazarene setting his feet steadfastly toward a glory that both daunts it and cries it on.

The wind blows where it wills, and you hear the sound of it, but you do not know whence it comes or whither it goes; so it is with every one who is born of the Spirit (John 3:8).

There are two kinds of power: there is the power to change things, and there is the power to endure things that do not change. God gives both.

We live in a day of change. Many people fear that these changes are not something we have either planned or can control, but that they will become a tidal wave which one day will sweep over us and destroy us. It may be. Forces may be unleashed which are beyond our power to change or direct. We may have to endure them.

I knew a home where the father was an alcoholic. Try as he would, he failed to overcome the affliction. He died an alcoholic. Again and again, his wife was urged by her friends to leave him. Her simple reply was, "Then I would only have to worry about him the more." She stayed with him to the end and inspired her children to forgive. She did not have the power to change him, but she had the power to endure.

We must always entertain the hope that things can change and that we may be given power to effect change. God himself is on the side of changing. He would never have bothered to send his own Son to die on a cross and to establish an eternal kingdom in our midst if he had settled for the status quo.

The world today is in danger of a new cynicism, a capitulation to doom. People groan as if neither God nor man has any resource to make a better world. There is power abroad, titanic power, for change. Our grandchildren could conceivably live in a world far better than any age has ever known. Technology itself may be one of God's great gifts. We may conquer hunger and disease, even war.

Come what may, however, we have the rights to an eternal kingdom. Nothing can take that away from us against our wills. We can have the power to endure all things in this triumphant hope.

Be faithful unto death, and I will give you the crown of life (Rev. 2:10).

As a young pastor in Moorhead, Minnesota, Fredrik A. Schiotz wrote a book, *Release*. In its preface he says:

> All over the world today there is evidence that society is in a state of dissolution. Dissolution precedes death. Death may mean the *loss* of life, but it may also be the *forerunner* of life. It is significant that the seasons of dissolution and social rebirth have been God's moments. Christianity's vitality has been most evident in the days when men have beheld a crumbling of material values.
>
> There is in the world an awareness that postwar years have been lean years. We have knelt before strange altars and find ourselves hungry. For those who will lift up their eyes, it is clear that God has much work to be done.

In the next forty years Fredrik Schiotz's life was caught in a maelstrom of work. He was summoned from his Minnesota parish to pioneer the work among Lutheran students on state university and college campuses. After a brief interlude in a Brooklyn parish, he was "drafted" to oversee American aid to missions throughout the world which had been cut off from European aid during World War II. This work completed, in 1954 he was elected president of the Evangelical Lutheran Church, later of the American Lutheran Church. He served as president of the Lutheran World Federation, and was active in the Central Committee of the World Council of Churches. Ever since he was nine, he said, he knew that his call was to be a pastor or a missionary. It was doubtless the vision he had of the nature of God's grace that held him fast and that spurred him on. Of this he speaks in his early book:

> A love that seeks nothing for self, that seeks everything for the one who is loved, that seeks its object over a span of years without tiring or giving up hope, that sorrows but accepts rebuff without protest, that does not become offended because men reckon Him among sinners, that is accused of deviltry without hating in return—this is the marvel of the ages, this is the love of God in Christ. . . . It is the glory of Christ that he always has a sufficiency out of which to give—and that He never refuses to those who seek. It is the privilege of those who hunger constantly to be refilled.

Let us not be weary in well-doing: for in due season we shall reap, if we do not lose heart (Gal. 6:9).

There are many of us "good" fathers who have made our homes the highest shrine; we assuredly deserve some praise for the love and pride and care and money we lavish upon our families. But this shrine is a half-way altar. Emile Cammaertes says:

My religion was neither disciplined, nor selfish. After a few years of spiritual exaltation, following my baptism and confirmation, I became irregular in religious observances and I felt more and more inclined to consider the Church as a benevolent mother whose mission it was to help my individual efforts, instead of the Kingdom of God on earth whose laws, as a good citizen, it was my duty to obey. . . .

On the other hand, my life became more and more absorbed in my home, and I was inclined to limit the number of my acquaintances, in order that the family circle should not be broken. I fell into the trap opened under the feet of many "good" fathers who believe that they have fulfilled their responsibility, because they have sacrificed their personal pleasures or ambitions to their wife and children. I deluded myself in thinking that my love for them was unselfish, while I derived an unlimited selfish pleasure in finding myself the center of their attention. This new worship or mutual worship was certainly real, and was not tainted with the humanitarian idealism which had marred my worship of nature, art and "mankind," but it was by no means innocent. It is not sinful to love one's wife and children, but it is sinful to love them to the exclusion of other people, and it is still more sinful to allow this love to divert one's attention from the love of God.

My faith was too superficial to thrive on happiness alone. Life, with me, although deeply real, remained one-sided. I loved my work, took delight in my leisure, and was relatively free from money problems. I could even afford to give my children what is supposed to be a sound education, and what is certainly a very expensive one. God, I thought, blessed my efforts, and because he blessed them, I rashly assumed that they deserved to be blessed. I supposed that I had reached the end of my journey and that I could soon rest in security and contentment. Such delusion may be compared to that of an inexperienced climber who thinks he has reached almost the top of the pass after emerging from the woods which cover the slopes of the mountain, while he has still to face the longer and steeper part of his climb, among the desolation of rocks and snow.

You shall love the Lord your God with all your heart, and with all your soul, and with all your mind (Matt. 22:37).

LEARNING TO LOVE March 25

Can we learn to love? If God is the teacher, yes. Otherwise, perhaps not. One of the fruits of the Spirit is love. And Paul says, "The greatest of these is love."

The kind of love Christ talks about is hardly the love filling most of our romantic ballads. It is of sturdier stuff. When Christ says, "Love one another as I have loved you," he gives us a most difficult command. I might very well reply, "Lord, that's easy for you to say, but have you seen the kind of people I live with and work with? They're not very easy to like." To which he might well reply, "I didn't ask you to like them. I asked you to love them, to meet their needs. Whether you like them or not is quite irrelevant. I'm having my troubles liking you too, the way you are, but I gave my life for you."

To love someone is never the same as liking someone. Jesus made that point very clear when he said, "Love your enemies and pray for those who persecute you, so that you may be sons of your Father who is in heaven. . . . For if you love those who love you, what reward have you?"

The radical character of God's love is the kind that gives and gives and gives without limit and without demanding a responding love. It may hope for a response, but failing to elicit any, it goes on loving nonetheless. It is drawn to the object of love because of need. Someone is hungry—like him or not, feed him; someone is lonely, he repulses you—go to him; someone is sick, he reeks—visit him; someone is in prison, he deserves it but he needs a friend—go to him; someone hates you, and his hatred is embittering his life—try to free him from his hatred by seeing him.

There are people we instinctively dislike. Remember the nursery rhyme:

I do not like thee, Dr. Fell,
The reason why I cannot tell,
But this I know, and know right well,
I do not like thee, Dr. Fell.

And it could be that the better you know him, the less you will like him. But, if he has needs, and you obey the Lord by trying to meet his needs, the miracle could happen. With greater understanding and with the subtle change that comes in him from your concern and love you might learn also to like him. But remember, the test is not whether you like him; the test is in your helping him. For this is the language of love.

Love bears all things, believes all things, hopes all things, endures all things (1 Cor. 13:7).

As a young pastor I was more fascinated and moved by Paul Scherer than by any other preacher. In one of his sermons, speaking about how people whose lives were in shambles gladly heard Jesus, he says:

Dr. Joseph Fort Newton tells a true story of the history of Tennessee. An Indian band had raided a pioneer settlement, and after murdering nearly everybody had carried off some little boy with them into the forest. Years passed, and in a skirmish with the Indians some of their warriors were taken prisoners, among them a few men with faces almost white. Two of the mothers came to see if they could find their lost boys. They walked along the line peering into the wild faces in vain. Suddenly an officer asked if they remembered any melody they used to sing to the boys. . . . One of the mothers began singing a crooning lullaby. The effect was startling. All at once a stalwart figure broke from the line and came cautiously toward her. They looked at one another for an instant, she still singing, until the wild man fell on her shoulders and cried for joy.

If that's what the world's like, Someone walking along the line, bringing love back, and dreams on the wings of a song—then there is no fear. "Either what women having ten pieces of silver, if she lose one piece doth not light a candle, and sweep the house, and seek diligently till she find it?" What is there left then, in all this world, to be afraid of? Certainly no blind fate that overtakes a man and leaves him stranded, like a dime in a dusty crack.

And so, as he went on speaking that morning, the future came alive in their eyes. He saw it, and the joy of it must have been like the joy of the angels of God—to see hope born that way, as though a hand had swept over their faces changing them. They drew nearer, and he smiled. It reminded him of the day in Nazareth when the younger son of the old farmer came home. He told them of it: the father who had waited so long every morning as twilight fell, and the neighbors who shook their heads as they passed in the dusk. And then of how after years of it the little town was all agog one night. Somebody had seen the lone, silent watcher throw open the gate, and uttering a weird cry run into the arms of a ragged tramp all dusty from the road. And now the house was full of lights and hurrying figures. He said something like that was going on in heaven, and they would find themselves, these restless, timid folk, at home again, for all the sorrows they had known, and the pain, and the loneliness; and they would be better for it, and richer. . . .

While he was yet at a distance, his father saw him and had compassion, and ran and embraced him and kissed him (Luke 15:20).

It wasn't as if we had never heard of Copernicus or Galileo, but four centuries after their shocking disclosures about the universe, in the South Dakota village of my childhood I think we still found the three-story universe the more comforting—the earth the center, with a canopy of sun and moon and stars, and God "up there" somewhere. Visiting a planetarium is breath-taking, but I never leave without a wistful longing that I still could say, "Twinkle, twinkle little star, How I wonder what you are," and have my old universe intact.

It was hard enough for the psalmist: "When I consider thy heavens, the moon and the stars which thou hast ordained, what is man?" Man was dwarfed even then, but with billions of bodies in billions of light years of space, where does that leave us?

I try to get it all into a new perspective, with time and space and numbers quite irrelevant. If a father has 12 children, can he not know them all and love them all? Our heavenly Father, with billions of children, being infinite, can't he know and love them all? Or, does a father who owns five acres of land necessarily love his children more than a father who owns 5000 acres? Our heavenly Father who owns an estate of billions of galaxies, is he less able to love us than if he presided over only our cozy three-story universe?

That he loves us and cares for us at all, whether in a small universe or a vast one—this after all is the wonder. Space has nothing to do with this amazing biblical story. And amazing it is, so amazing that to believe it at all is sheer miracle. Luther spoke for us all when he said, "I believe that I cannot by my own strength or power believe. . . ."

Every time we pray, we leap over the reaches of time and space to have this great and good God nearer than the air we breathe. Whether as a child or as a learned scientist, when we pray:

> Now I lay me down to sleep,
> I pray thee, Lord, my soul to keep.
> If I should die before I wake,
> I pray thee, Lord, my soul to take,

we are in fact defying the whole astronomer's universe to nestle in a love that is as comforting as it is baffling.

Behold the Lord God comes with might, and his arm rules for him; behold, his reward is with him, and his recompense before him. He will feed his flock like a shepherd, he will gather the lambs in his arms, he will carry them in his bosom, and gently lead those that are with young (Isa. 40:10-11).

Few of us in this jet age can comprehend what our immigrant fore-bears must have felt as they left their European homelands to pioneer this new land. A young woman, Linka, became the bride of Herman H. Preus, who as pastor in Spring Prairie, Wisconsin, served also as the president of the newly formed church among Norwegians for 32 years. Linka kept a diary, which records her prayer on board ship as they were to embark in 1851:

> Our gracious Father, we are always in Thy keeping. Thou art our sure defense. Keep us throughout this journey under the pro-tection of Thy mighty wings, and in all that we undertake let Thy will be done! O Lord, I am now altogether surrounded by stran-gers. Thou *alone*—yet not alone, for Thou art very *great*—Thou, my Father, art near, and also Herman. Do not forsake me, O my God! I know Thou wilt never leave me. Hinder Thou that I should ever turn aside from Thee. It is my firm resolve, O God, daily to pray Thee that I may never go astray; that my earthly life may at all times be pleasing in Thy sight. Help me to be a good wife, that in me Herman may find the one he thought could bring him happiness. O gracious Father, let Thy Spirit so endow Herman with power that he may be able to fulfill the ministry to which he is dedicated. Our strength and help is in Thee; do Thou abundantly supply it.
>
> Hand in hand we go out into the world! Be Thou ever near; we always need Thy help. Father of all mercies, hear Thou my prayers for the sake of Jesus Christ.
>
> Now to bed. Still the ship lies quietly in the harbor. Will this be the last night I sleep in Norway? Thou on high alone knowest, and only Thou canst tell whether my eyes again shall look upon the mountains of Norway. Indeed, to know the future would not even be good for me. Great changes may take place before that could come to pass; and would the knowledge of that be good for me? Indeed, it would not.
>
> Good night, my sisters and my brother and all my loved ones. May the Lord keep you all under His protecting wings! Good-bye, may life be good to you. I know you will remember your Linka.

Mrs. Preus died at the age of 51. Two of her sons became pastors, six of her grandsons, seven of her great-grandsons, and seven of her great-great-grandsons.

Now the Lord said to Abram, "Go from your country and your kin-dred and your father's house to the land that I will show you. And I will make of you a great nation, and I will bless you, and make your name great, so that you will be a blessing" (Gen. 12:1-2).

When Darwin's *Origin of Species* ushered in the idea of evolution, the church was uneasy. If our origins were tucked far back into the unknown past, what of the great story of Genesis? Most Christians came to terms with the theory, concluding that the Genesis story could very well be God's great epic poem instead of a newspaper account of what happened, and that no matter what the beginnings were like, God had to be the author and creator.

In recent years we have been far more agitated by questions of the *end*. When will the Lord come again? Or, when life ends for any of us, what's on the other side? I confess that now, with my parents and grandparents and my son having gone over to the other side, I can be more intrigued by heaven than by the doctrine of creation.

When he was a high school senior, I once asked my son, Andrew, if he had given much thought to death and heaven. He replied, "Not really. There is so much to do right here and now. And I know that when death comes I will be in the hands of God." Perhaps we need not ponder or speculate too much on how things got started nor on how things will end. Perhaps God is satisfied to have us put both the beginnings and the end in his hands and turn to do his work right now, the work at our very elbows.

Jesus said, "I am the alpha and omega, the beginning and the end." It would be well if we took him at his word. Can you think of anyone else or anything else—some philosophy or theory—that you would rather trust with any of the mysteries of life, including the beginning and the end of all things? We know him. He was, and is, one of us. He died on a cross for us. He assured us that he has a place prepared for us, and that when death overtakes us, he'll be there to take us by the hand and usher us into the home prepared for us from the foundation of the world.

In the exquisite sadness of the *Rubaiyat,* Omar Khayyam speaks of the futility of trying to probe these mysteries:

> Myself when young did eagerly frequent
> Doctor and Saint, and heard great argument
> About it and about, but evermore
> Came out by the same door as in I went.

Mysteries they are, but in our Christian faith we have Someone to whom we can trust them, and go on to fill our days with the riches of a kingdom he has already given us.

Let not your hearts be troubled; believe in God, believe also in me. In my Father's house are many rooms . . . I go to prepare a place for you (John 14:1-2).

Jesus said of John, "Truly, I say to you, among those born of women there has risen no one greater than John the Baptist."

What's so great about John? He wasn't rich, he wasn't powerful. He had little formal education. He had a following for awhile, but they left him, and in his early thirties he was beheaded through the whim of a vengeful woman.

Very simply, he got himself out of the way. He deflected the loyalists and power that he might have had, so that Jesus might take the stage. By his own testimony he was a voice crying in the wilderness, alerting people to a kingdom and a king who was at hand. For a moment he held the stage and cried, "Repent, for the kingdom of heaven is at hand," and then one day, as Jesus passed by he said, "Behold the Lamb of God that takes away the sin of the world." And the story continues, his followers left him to follow Jesus. John had gotten himself out of the way. That was his greatness.

And isn't this the greatest tribute that can be paid anyone—that he drew people's attention away from himself to something greater than he? That he became a window, a transparent window (not an artglass window that attracts attention to itself), through which people could see beauty and goodness on the other side!

The story is told of a railway section hand who had died. Leaving the cemetery, a man who had worked at his side through the years said to a companion, "Hans had a great God." Wouldn't it have been too bad if he had said, "Hans was a great guy," or even "Hans was a great Christian?" This man had seen through Hans to the God who had given Hans his own greatness.

This kind of "renunciation" is most difficult for a person who has admirable qualities and who, quite unintentionally, may draw attention to himself. The tempter may lead him to enjoy the approval and praise of others, and to let himself be an art-glass window.

The corrective is to remember that everything we are, everything we have achieved—everything, including life itself—is a pure gift from him who gave us minds and hearts and who inspired us to whatever goodness we may have. To him be the glory!

If I speak in the tongues of men and of angels, but have not love, I am a noisy gong or a clanging cymbal. And if I have prophetic powers, and understand all mysteries and all knowledge, and if I have all faith, so as to remove mountains, but have not love, I am nothing (1 Cor. 13:1-2).

ENJOYING GOD March 31

We all know that life is serious business and that religion is not to be taken lightly. But seriousness is not the opposite of joy. We have all known people with a delightful sense of humor who at the same time have been highly sensitive and responsible people.

In answer to the question, "What is the chief end of man?", the Westminster Shorter Catechism says, "Man's chief end is to glorify God and to enjoy him forever." We need not wait to enjoy him until we reach heaven; we begin here and now.

The thought of enjoying God was strange to the religions that prevailed at the time of Jesus. This struck me with some force when I first read Homer's *Odyssey*, the account of Odysseus, the hero of Troy, and his perilous journey back to his home in Ithaca. The gods and goddesses harried him every step of the way. Calypso "did her best to keep me yonder in her cave"; Zeus "meant the worst to me" by sending terrible storms; "my ship was wrecked by Poseidon"; Cyclops "filled his belly with human-flesh," Odysseus's men; Circe drugged the others and "drove them off and penned them in pig-sties"; Scylla and Charybdis and Sirens, with their enchanting music, tried to lure them to destruction. How could people enjoy gods and goddesses who with envy and caprice were a constant threat to their happiness?

It is not so with the God of the Bible, the Father of our Lord Jesus Christ. He created all things for the sheer joy of creating them. And it must have been a high moment for him when he made us in his own image. He intended to enjoy us, and he intended for us to enjoy him.

To be sure, things turned out rather badly. We turned from him, became afraid of him, and plunged into all sorts of sin and pain. But that did not end it for God. He sent his only Son to suffer, die, and be raised again. He had created us for joy, and he could not be diverted.

Through Jesus Christ we are restored to God, to his creation, and to one another and are on the path of enjoying him again. He has forgiven us; he has given us the Holy Spirit to usher us again into the kingdom. In his kingdom, he leads us into the arenas of joy—and chief among the joys is God himself!

Rejoice in the Lord, O you righteous! Praise the Lord with the lyre, make melody to him with the harp of ten strings! Sing to him a new song, play skillfully on the strings, with loud shouts (Psalm 33:1-2).

He had none of the credentials worthy of the historian's research. He was not rich, he was not learned, he belonged to no royal family. He was a carpenter's son in a small town. He became an itinerant preacher (there were many in those days); he attracted a small following (12 untutored men); and his life was snuffed out one Friday for disturbing the peace. That was all, measured by the usual canons of history.

For two thousand years he has haunted the world. Other great men have taken their quiet places in the shelves of libraries and no longer trouble the world—Alexander, Genghis Khan, Nero, Napoleon. But not Jesus of Nazareth.

Every other leader of men has had minor and local allegiances compared with his. Hundreds of millions of people throughout the centuries have lived and died for him. He simply does not fit in the long parade of the world's great. And today, in this 20th century, he bids to be the only candidate for the loyalty of the whole world. There is none other.

The church that bears his name is the most international movement of the day. It does not win the applause of men everywhere. The church has been, and is, under attack. But not the Lord of the church. Pilate's verdict, "I find no fault in him," has been the unqualified verdict of the world ever since he lived among us. It is still the verdict of the world today. It is said of Gandhi, a Hindu, that he had but one picture on his wall—Jesus of Nazareth. The growth of the Christian movement has been largely westward from Jerusalem, it is true, but Jesus is the universal cosmopolitan. He is white, he is black, he is yellow.

If any other part of the biblical story is to become credible at all, we will have to let the life and person of Christ be the clue. He walked the earth. There are four biographies left to us: Matthew, Mark, Luke, and John. Read them as if you had never read them before. Let this man become your companion as you read. Let the full force of his person strike you. It will dawn upon you that if any man ever represented what man in the fullness of his humanity ought to be, Jesus is that man.

And the Word became flesh and dwelt among us, full of grace and truth; we have beheld his glory, glory as of the only Son from the Father (John 1:14).

HOW CAN IT BE BOTH? April 2

Religion is full of contradictions or paradoxes. Two truths seem to cancel out each other, yet both are true. How can the Lord's Supper, for instance, be both bread and wine and body and blood? How can the Bible be both the Word of God and the words of men? How can Jesus be both God and man?

Paul, in speaking of Christians, uses several such contradictions: "as unknown, yet well known," "as dying, and behold we live."

The strangest figure in the pages of history is Jesus of Nazareth, conceived by the Holy Ghost, born of the Virgin Mary. You simply can't say, he was like this man or that man. You may say, "Hitler, like Napoleon, was a dictator," or "Teddy Roosevelt, like Lincoln, was a great commoner." Jesus has no parallel. He, of all historic characters, is the world's unknown. And yet millions of people have within their hearts known this Jesus more intimately than their own mothers or children. An old German schoolmaster, whose rooms were lined with the volumes of Goethe and Schiller, had this inscription above the door of his home: "Here dwell Goethe and Schiller." Of course, they did not live there; they were dead and gone. But when Paul said, "I live, yet not I; Christ lives in me," he was testifying to a knowledge more fixed than the stars. You may be sustained in trial and testing by the knowledge or memory of a devout mother; but her presence can never have the reality that the presence of Christ can have in your hearts. We, his followers, are sometimes called the strangers of the earth, for by faith we live and move and have our being in a God whom we've never seen or touched. But who is the more strange, the man of faith who walks strong and kind and fearless among the perils of life, or the so-called normal man driven hither and yon by passion and pressure until he has no soul to call his own?

"As dying, and behold we live." What is that must die? Not appetite for food, surely. Not sex drives. Not even the possessive instinct. There is something deeper. Sin! Sin invades the core of a person, especially in the form of pride. Pride puts us in nasty competition with one another. Pride refuses to rejoice with those who rejoice. Pride turns compassion into condescension, love into pity. Pride destroys fellowship. It is when pride dies that we begin to live. The "old man" dies, the new man in Christ lives!

We are treated as imposters, and yet are true; as unknown, and yet well known; as dying, and behold we live . . . as sorrowful, yet always rejoicing . . . as having nothing, and yet possessing everything (2 Cor. 6:8-10).

GETHSEMANE

When I first met Hanns Lilje in 1952, he was bishop of Hannover. I had read his book, *The Valley of the Shadow*, the account of his imprisonment by the Nazis. He had escaped execution by a day when the American troops entered Nuremberg. He recalls one of the last nights in prison, when death seemed imminent, and speaks of a remarkable friend:

> Suddenly and silently, both the bolts of my cell door were pushed back; very quietly the door was opened, a very little way. There stood Freiherr von Guttenberg; he signed me to be silent. When everything was quite quiet round us, we carried on a short conversation, in a low whisper. He said to me: "Don't you think that those of us who are in this situation understand the story of Gethsemane better than ever before?" He was not the only one in this building who knew and loved Pascal's incomparable meditation upon the story of Gethsemane; so we talked together for a little while about the comfort that this part of the New Testament brought us in our present situation. I shall never forget this scene; it might have come straight out of a Dostoevsky novel; the dark and gloomy building; the din of bursting shells and whistling bombs, outside; and within, the whispered conversation about the Son of God, who on that night on the Mount of Olives lifted the horror from every other human night; henceforth he is forever with those who suffer and struggle and pray in the darkness. Nor shall I ever forget this man: he was one of those who was never so absorbed in his own fate that he forgot the fate of his people. . . . He had retained a complete capacity for thinking of others; and the reason for this was the simple fact that he was a Christian. His example showed us that kindness and courage are mysteriously related. Genuine kindness is the privilege of great and fearless souls. Most human beings cannot be kind in this way, because they are afraid. Who but a fearless man could have exercised this quiet kindness which he gave us during those nights of danger? . . . If this man had ever been caught in his act of simple and courageous humanity, the consequences for himself would have been disastrous. But he lived in that spirit of kindness that springs from holy fearlessness. He is one of those who kept alight in this building the pure, clear flame of human dignity and greatness.

I tell you, my friends, do not fear those who kill the body, and after that have no more that they can do (Luke 12:4).

WHAT LANGUAGE SHALL I BORROW?

In the great Lenten hymn, "O Sacred Head, Now Wounded," we pray the refrain, "What language shall I borrow to thank thee, dearest friend?"

It is as if, standing at the cross, we say, "Lord, you have done so much for me, what can I do for you? Can I offer you prayers an hour each day or sing your praises an hour each day?"

He may well say, "It's all right to pray and to sing, but if you really want to thank me, I will tell you what language to use. I have no needs. But my children, many of them your neighbors, many of them the world around, have great needs. They are lonely, discouraged, sick, hungry, homeless, in prison. The only way to do for me is to do for them."

I'm taken aback. I had hoped that the Lord and I could have had a cozy time, a nice private party, a rendezvous, just he and I. And now he spoils it all by bringing with him his whole family.

But there's no escape. Charles W. Colson, once called Nixon's "hatchet man," was converted and wrote his story in the book, *Born Again*. In his seven months in prison he discovered that never again could he settle for a "private party" with the Lord, but that the Lord was calling him to do something about the "stinking, rotten holes of utter, pervasive bitterness and despair," where 300,000 of God's children lived within "the barbarous hollowness of prison life." In his efforts for prison reform, Colson had found a language to use in thanking his Lord. Others had found the language before him: Sir William Wilberforce in his battle against the slave trade in Britain; William Booth, founder of the Salvation Army; Jane Addams, founder of Chicago's famous Hull House.

For every Christian there are moments of solitude with God, when retreating from the world, we have the joy of his "private" presence. But make no mistake, his family is hovering near. He will not maroon us on an island, alone with him. For the Lord does not abandon his family, and if we are to be with the Lord we will find ourselves in the thick of his family—where he is.

For most of us the sins of omission cry to high heaven. We may defend ourselves by reminding God that we have not killed or stolen or abandoned our families, that we have prayed and supported his church. We are respectable, law-abiding, decent people. But the eloquent language of thanks will always be what we do for those in need.

As you did it to one of the least of these my brethren, you did it to me (Matt. 25:40).

G. A. Studdert-Kennedy has written a poem entitled "Indifference":

When Jesus came to Golgotha they hanged him on a tree,
They drove great nails through hands and feet, and made a Calvary;
They crowned Him with a crown of thorns, red were His wounds
   and deep,
For those were crude and cruel days, and human flesh was cheap.

When Jesus came to Birmingham they simply passed Him by,
They never hurt a hair of Him, they only let Him die;
For men had grown more tender, and they would not give Him pain,
They only just passed down the street, and left Him in the rain.

Still Jesus cried, "Forgive them, for they know not what they do,"
And still it rained the wintry rain that drenched Him through and
   through;
The crowds went home and left the streets without a soul to see,
And Jesus crouched against a wall and cried for Calvary.

Maybe for us, too, indifference is the cruelest blow of all. To be loved or to be hated is one thing; to be passed over as *nobody* is quite another. A woman might say, "If he can't love me, I wish he would hate me." To be politely ignored is to lose all hope.

Love and hate belong to the world of passion, and passion is life. Indifference is death. Judas loved Jesus, but when Jesus failed to grasp the opportunity for power, his love turned to bitterness, and bitterness to hate, and hate to betrayal. Then, like the winds that shift suddenly from north to south, the heart of Judas swung to love again. And on that fateful Friday, when he flung his 30 pieces of silver with the cry, "I have betrayed innocent blood," it was the one open vote in defense of Jesus (the other disciples had fled or were silent). His cry, in Paul Scherer's words, was "a Te Deum from Hell."

The apostasy of the church, or your apostasy and mine, will not come from our hatred of God, but from our indifference to him.

I know your works; you are neither cold nor hot. Would that you were cold or hot! So, because you are lukewarm, and neither cold nor hot, I will spew you out of my mouth (Rev. 3:15-16).

There is much talk these days about the end of the world. Two great wars, and some lesser ones, plus two astonishing bombs, have made such conversation commonplace. Whether you read the Book of Daniel or the *New York Times,* the thought of some catastrophic end will reach you.

Man has always had to face his own life's ending, of course. In ancient Greece the average life span was 39 years; in 1800 Massachusetts, 35; as late as 1890, the age was 43. Medical advance has pushed it beyond 60, but every ache and pain are warnings that there is an inevitable end. Why become so preoccupied with a corporate end?

I like the temper of this story about John Quincy Adams. At 81, he was walking down the path one day when a friend greeted him with, "And how is John Adams today?" Mr. Adams replied, "John Adams is very well, thank you. But the tenement he has inhabited these many years is in a sad state of disrepair. It sags in the corners, its roof leaks, and when the winds blow it creaks and groans in every joint. I suspect that John Adams will soon be forced to seek other quarters. But John Adams himself is very well, thank you." It is more than likely that John Adams had grasped the sweep of the apostle's words, "For we know that if the earthly house of our tabernacle be dissolved, we have a building from God, a house not made with hands, eternal, in the heavens."

Here in this life you have on your hands a losing struggle with housing; these frail walls of flesh and blood do not stand up to the oncoming winter weather. At last the roof caves in, and out you go. But not to homeless wanderings. You rub your eyes and see before you the open doors to mansions in an eternal city. It is your home, forever and ever.

I cannot see how life here can be tolerable at all unless it is tied up to this other-worldly hope. From the moment we are born, the forces of destruction are fighting a winning battle within these bodies of ours. In Longfellow's words,

Art is long, and time is fleeting,
And our hearts, though stout and brave,
Still, like muffled drums, are beating
Funeral marches to the grave.

The Lord may give you many years or few, but he beckons you to a sound and gallant mood, holding before you the promise of a life that will never end.

For this perishable nature must put on the imperishable, and this mortal nature must put on immortality (1 Cor. 15:53).

Jesus was visiting at the home of Simon the leper when a woman with an alabaster jar of ointment, pure nard, very costly, broke the jar and poured it over Jesus' head. The disciples thought, *What waste! It could have been sold to feed many poor.* But Jesus said, "She has done a beautiful thing to me." Paul Tillich comments:

Who can blame the disciples for being angry about the immense waste this woman has created? Certainly not a deacon who has to take care of the poor, or a social worker who knows the neediest cases and cannot help, or a church administrator who collects money for important projects. Certainly the disciples would not be blamed by a balanced personality who has his emotional life well under control and for whom it is worse than nonsense, even criminal, to think of doing what this woman did. Jesus felt differently, and so did the early church. They knew that without the abundance of the heart nothing great can happen. They knew that religion within the limits of reasonableness is a mutilated religion, and that calculating love is not love at all. Jesus did not raise the question about how much *eros* and how much *agape*, how much human passion and how much understanding was motivating the woman; He saw the abundant heart and He accepted it without analyzing the different elements in it. . . .

The history of mankind is the history of men and women who wasted themselves and were not afraid to do so. . . . They wasted as God does in nature and history, in creation and salvation. . . . Luther's God, who acts heroically and without rules—is He not the wasteful God who creates and destroys in order to create again? . . . . There is no creativity, divine or human, without the holy waste which comes out of the creative abundance of the heart and does not ask, "What use is this?" . . .

We know that lack of love in our early years is mentally destructive. But do we know that the lack of occasions to waste ourselves is equally dangerous. . . . People are sick not only because they have not received love but also because they are not allowed to give love, to waste themselves.

The Messiah, the Anointed One, must waste Himself in order to become the Christ. The Cross . . . is the most complete and most holy waste. . . . It is the fulfillment of all wisdom within the plan of salvation.

But Jesus said, "Let her alone; why do you trouble her? She has done a beautiful thing to me" (Mark 14:6).

Christ arose from the dead! This is not an allegory, or a myth, or a parable. It happened! It is a solid event in history, unlike any other event, but an event! He died . . . he rose again.

Nor did he suffer and die to teach a lesson—like how to be brave, or how to be loyal to your convictions. He suffered and died and rose again to overcome the enemy, Satan, and in some strange way to pay for the sins of the world. He suffered and died and rose again to redeem the world, to recover mankind, to restore that which had been lost, to free the imprisoned, to save the world.

It is not strange that we rub our eyes and say, "How can this be so?" Whoever heard a claim like this before?

The wonder is that we can believe it at all. This itself is a miracle of God. Most of us have heard of the event since we were children. The wonder of it may have been lost in the repetition. But it is the world's greatest wonder. Stepping on the moon is a trifle compared with it. After all, to say that the God who holds the universe in his hand would demean himself to become man and die for us—now think, is this not a truth more fantastic than anything the world has ever heard?

I never enjoyed preaching the Easter sermon. It always seemed to me that the theme had become too big for words, and probably belonged only in the soaring setting of an oratorio. Fortunately God has given his people just such music, including a hymnody that carries the spirit far beyond the eloquence of mere sentences. I think of the hymn ascribed to Martin Luther:

Christ Jesus lay in death's strong bands,
For our offenses given;
But now at God's right hand he stands
And brings us life from heaven. . . .

It was a strange and dreadful strife
When Life and Death contended;
The victory remained with Life,
The reign of Death was ended.

The cross and the empty tomb are the measure of God's love. Unless we can accept this radical love of God, both Jesus' death and resurrection become impossible to believe. Such love can never seem reasonable, but it is glorious beyond imagination.

For God so loved the world that he gave his only Son, that whoever believes in him should not perish but have eternal life (John 3:16).

Peace and good will may not necessarily go together. In fact, when that which is good confronts that which is evil, peace is gone. A war is on.

We put a high price tag on getting along with people. A father may say, "My son is getting along famously. Everyone likes him. He's getting promotions and making good money." This may, or may not, be a tribute to his son. If his son is on a corrupt police force, for instance, he's probably gotten both their good will and the promotions by conforming to their standards. The highest goal is not for us to be well adjusted to our society, but to be well adjusted to God's kingdom— which, at times, may put us in conflict with our society.

Jesus did not make peace with the Pharisees or with the Roman Empire. They simply could not stand him. They put him to death.

To say of Jesus, or for that matter of any thoroughly good person, "He is so good, why should anyone be against him?" is to misunderstand the nature of evil. Evil cannot stand goodness, and the world has its share of evil. A good man may suffer precisely because he is good. Even though he does not try to correct evil people, his very presence among them is a reproach to them, makes them uncomfortable, and leads them to plot against him. At best, they elbow him out of their company; at the worst, they persecute him in one way or another.

Jesus warned his disciples that this would be so. Why should they not expect to suffer if he suffered? He even told them that they would be blessed in this kind of suffering and rejection.

Most of us have not known this kind of suffering, probably because we associate with rather good people, or—more likely—because we are not good enough. We come to terms with evil. We compromise when we should take a stand. In fact, even we who regard ourselves as essentially good have a hard time with people who become vitally concerned with justice and mercy and become a bit "militant" in trying to achieve justice. We may label them as "do-gooders" and have as little to do with them as possible.

Let us pray that we may grow in goodness, even if this costs us the peace that a more limited goodness may give us.

Blessed are you when men revile you and persecute you and utter all kinds of evil against you falsely on my account. Rejoice and be glad, for your reward is great in heaven, for so men persecuted the prophets who were before you (Matt. 5:11-12).

It was the first Easter. Jesus had been raised from the dead. Some of his followers had seen him and heard him. That afternoon, walking toward Emmaus, he joined two of his followers in conversation. Later he sat down to eat with them. Not until then, when he broke the bread, did they recognize him. Strangely enough, it was when he *did* something, that they knew him.

Perhaps it is not strange, after all. May it not be that we know our Lord most deeply by what he has done for us, and not principally by what he has said to us? He died for us! That is the towering message of the Bible. The Sermon on the Mount and the parables are among the most exalted literature in the world. They are words, however, not deeds. His death for our sins—this is the deed to dwarf all deeds. Now we know he loves us.

The Lord asks us to be his witnesses. This certainly means that we must use words to tell about him. But it means more. Because we are his followers, we are to reach out to people in love as he did. Every one of us is moved more deeply by acts of love than by words of love. We need not preach eloquent sermons or write theological essays about Jesus to be his witnesses.

The dear Lord's best interpreters are humble, human souls.
The gospel of a life is more than books or scrolls.

The opportunity for witness lies in the most commonplace situations. Someone is lonely, and we write a letter or make a phone call. Someone has lost a job, and we help him find another. Someone is old and lives alone, and we bring a warm meal. Someone is lied about, and we defend her. Someone is in jail, and we go to him.

We are common people. We remember that Jesus was too. He was a young carpenter from a small town. Yet he was God come to earth. But he used all sorts of common places to reveal himself and his love, deeds of mercy which finally brought him to the crowning deed, a death for our salvation.

And he took the blind man by the hand, and led him out of the village; and when he had spit on his eyes and laid his hands upon him, he asked him, "Do you see anything?" (Mark 8:23).

In his book, *The Color of the Night,* Gerhard Frost uses the Book of Job to reflect on God's way with man in the hours of suffering. He says:

As a very young child, my greatest fear was of darkness. At times it even kept me awake. My father's study was just across the hall, where often he would be at work at my bedtime. In a moment of panic I would cry out, frantic for a response. And the response always came: "Go to sleep, I'm right here!" With this assurance, I would rest.

My father didn't bring a light—I would have liked that—but he gave me something better, the assurance of his loving presence. A light would have left me alone. In real need, it couldn't satisfy. Presence, loving presence, is what I craved.

Job would have liked a light in his darkness, a ready answer to his terrifying questions. Instead he is given caring Presence. Baffling as the barrage of unanswerables must have been, he couldn't fail to get the larger message, "I'm right here!"

"I'm right here, Job, rejoicing in my creation, loving every part of it, except its pain. I'm in its struggles, Job, even the struggle of the desert flower that grows in that cracked rock. I love the lone, scraggy tree that bends with the wind. I care for each blade of grass. And I care for you, Job, especially in your need.

"I walk in the wastelands, for I made them. Vastness doesn't mean abandonment. I'm right here in this 'forsaken' place, and I'm with you."

The Lord reminds Job of his love-pledge even to the unpeopled wastelands, offering this as a double guarantee to Job, his costlier creature. Here the Lord's voice from the whirlwind calls across the centuries and blends with the voice of Jesus Christ: "If God so clothes the grass of the field, which today is alive and tomorrow is thrown into the oven, will he not much more clothe you, O men of little faith?" (Matt. 6:30).

In the Book of Job, one of the greatest in all literature, Job batters at the door of God for some answer to the catastrophic sufferings that have come upon him, and there is no answer but the one Dr. Frost finds: God says, "I'm right here, Job." Job probably wanted more, and you and I want more. But where there is no answer to the riddle of suffering, it yet is of comfort to know that God never forsakes us.

Who has cleft a channel for the torrents of rain, and a way for the thunderbolt, to bring rain on a land where no man is, on the desert in which there is no man; to satisfy the waste and desolate land, and to make the ground put forth grass? (Job 38:25-27).

I have moments when I can well understand that an atheist may find comfort in having no God. To have the universe be an enormous machine, everything geared together in amazing precision and I only another cog in the machine—this lets me off. I have no responsibility. Every turn in my life is determined for me. I only spin.

This "comfort" has never been described as beautifully as it was penned by the Persian poet, Omar Khayyam, in his *Rubaiyat:*

The moving finger writes; and, having writ,
Moves on: nor all thy piety nor wit
Shall lure it back to cancel half a line,
Nor all thy tears wash out a word of it.

And that inverted bowl we call the sky,
Whereunder crawling coop't we live and die,
Lift not thy hands to it for help—for it
Rolls impotently on as thou and I.

Shakespeare's Macbeth expresses it with less beauty, and with the note of despair which is the outcome of a life or a world in which God and meaning have been lost:

Tomorrow, and tomorrow, and tomorrow,
Creeps in this petty pace from day to day,
To the last syllable of recorded time;
And all our yesterdays have lighted fools
The way to dusty death. Out, out, brief candle!
Life's but a walking shadow, a poor player
That struts and frets his hour upon the stage
And then is heard no more: it is a tale
Told by an idiot, full of sound and fury,
Signifying nothing.

All's not right with the world, but God is in his heavens, and in Christ he has come into our lives to save, to lead and to rule. What greater comfort than that?

Fear not, little flock, for it is your Father's good pleasure to give you the kingdom (Luke 12:32).

The Allied forces overcame Hitler in Central Europe. Hundreds of thousands of German troops were still in Norway, Denmark, and the Low Countries. Let us suppose that they had elected to dig in and continue their dominion of these small countries. We would then have had the strange situation of the vanquished ruling the victors—the victors suffering discomforts, buffetings, and persecutions at the hands of the power which already had been defeated and undone.

This is a parallel of our situation since the defeat of Satan by Christ on the cross. Christ emerged the victor in the decisive battle for this world. And in the interval of centuries that have followed, while we await the final mopping-up action by the return of Christ, the people of God find themselves in the strange situation of being molested, enticed, threatened, persecuted, and sometimes crushed by a world of evil and intrigue, the defeated enemy. Despite Christ's assurance, "I have overcome the world," a world of evil, the defeated power, puts repeated roadblocks in the way of righteousness and goodness.

It is simply not true that if we are decent, fair, industrious, honest, and God-fearing, we will automatically prosper. It would be true only if the forces (both within us and without) that dislike honesty, integrity, righteousness, and purity were already annihilated or were so emasculated that they could marshal no protest. To say glibly that this is God's world and that if we go God's way we shall surely be at ease is to ignore the stubborn fact that we are fallen beings and live in a fallen world.

Our fiercest battle against the foe may be within our own hearts and wills. Each of us has a self to be resisted and a self to be honored and obeyed. We are "the old Adam" and "the new man in Christ." The new man is actually Christ living within us, and although by his grace we are already victors, we will battle against the old Adam in fear and trembling until death releases us to receive the crown.

We are not contending against flesh and blood, but against the principalities, against the powers, against the world rulers of this present darkness, against the spiritual hosts of wickedness in the heavenly places (Eph. 6:12).

After all, what can one person do? Against the tremendous odds that a complex society presents, most of us sit back and conclude that nothing but a vast coalition of forces can do anything. It's not the first time people have felt like that.

When God addressed Moses at the burning bush and told him to reenter Egypt and free his people, Moses countered, "Who am I that I should go to Pharaoh?" God told him that with God at his side he could more than match the power of Pharaoh.

History has many instances where one person, unaided by committees and even opposed by them, set out alone to follow a vision. It was against the counsel of everyone that Florence Nightingale set out to heal the wounded in the Crimean War. A mother, when her six-year-old boy came home with a note from the teacher saying he was too stupid to learn, replied, "I'll teach him myself," and she gave us Thomas A. Edison.

We have become obsessed in this country with the idea that we can't work alone—only in organizations. Decisions must be group decisions. Work must be done through committees. This idea has two devastating effects: it lets the individual off, and it paralyzes initiative —and it usually is far less efficient.

More profoundly, it isn't God's way. He doesn't commission committees. He doesn't array groups before his throne for judgment; we appear before him one by one.

I recall with some amusement and pride, an instance out of World War II. We lived in Mason City, Iowa. Every evening at 10 the eastbound Milwaukee stopped for 15 minutes, and the soldiers on the train poured out into the nearby tavern for a breather. My wife, who had two brothers in the army and who felt that it was a shame for the city not to have anything better for the boys, called on Mr. Ingrahm, the train's executive, and offered to provide coffee and doughnuts on the depot platform every night. He said, "Who do you represent, and where is your committee?" She told him that she could marshal all the churches in the city behind such a service and that she wanted no committee. She'd do it alone. Well, she did it, much to the surprise and delight of Mr. Ingrahm, and for more than a year thousands of GIs enjoyed the warmth of coffee and friends in that Iowa town.

But Moses said to the Lord, "Oh, my Lord, I am not eloquent, either heretofore or since thou has spoken to thy servant, but I am slow of speech and of tongue." Then the Lord said . . . "Now therefore go, and I will be with your mouth and teach you what you shall speak" (Exod. 4:10, 12).

An intelligent and successful businessman once said to me, "I think it's good for me to come to church Sunday after Sunday to hear the same thing." Obviously he didn't think my sermons were so good that he'd like them repeated each week. I knew what he meant. He needed to hear, over and over again, the old, old story of Jesus and his love.

Once, at the seminary, the unmarried men of the dormitory sent a committee to learn if they could have the morning mail before their 8 o'clock class instead of at 8:50. Unfortunately, the branch post office couldn't release it in time. Knowing the nature of their urgency (I had once been a student too), I nonetheless asked what mail might be so important than an hour made a difference. I supplied the answer myself. "You're waiting for a daily letter from some girl, and it's a very repetitious kind of letter. You have but minor interest in the books she's been reading or the movies she's seen. What you want to hear is the same thing she wrote yesterday and the day before and the day before that, 'I love you.' And, you'll just have to be impatient an extra hour."

Maybe all the worthwhile things of life are repetitious. When someone greets you with "What's new?" he's just making talk.

My father had a general store in a South Dakota village until he died. For 45 years he walked the same two blocks from his home to the store, turned the same key in the same lock, served largely the same customers, lived with the same wife, and for 32 of those years had the same pastor. One might have concluded that it had been a dreary, treadmill life. After his death all sorts of people told me things about him: how he had helped them through hard times, how he had never sent them a bill. Like a family doctor or pastor, he had touched almost every area of their lives.

We come to hear the same great Word, we sing hymns that have been sung for centuries, we confess our faith in words that have been used for 2000 years. We do not come for novelty, but for repetition. We are entertained by novelty, we live by repetition. Our God is the same yesterday, today, and forever.

Lord, thou hast been our dwelling place in all generations. Before the mountains were brought forth, or ever thou hadst formed the earth and the world, from everlasting to everlasting thou art God (Psalm 90:1-2).

The saddest and strangest quality of the human being is his deep inclination to run away from God. We, who were made to live with him, turn from him. Like branches cut from the tree, we wither and die without him, yet we cut ourselves off from him. Dying of hunger, we refuse food; routed in battle, we refuse reinforcements and victory; troubled and distraught, we refuse peace; condemned and dying, we refuse pardon and life. There is no more tragic spectacle than people refusing God.

The obvious reason for this flight from God is the suspicion that he is an angry God. And he is. But, would we have him be otherwise? What sort of being would he be if he had no capacity for indignation and wrath? There is a time for mercy, and there is a time for wrath. The capacity for the one implies a capacity for the other.

We often hear people say, "If there is a God, why does he allow wars?" This is really the same as saying, "Why doesn't God let the world get by with its greed, selfishness, indifference, and lust?" The fact is that if he is God, he can't let unrighteousness go unpunished. And wars are a corporate punishment for the corporate wrongs of people. Would we want a God who is a sleepy old dullard who chuckles and thinks it amusing when Cain kills Abel or when Jesus is nailed to a cross? We want an angry God!

We run away from God not because he is angry, but because we are sinful. The secret of our running lies not in the nature of God, but in the nature of people. A little boy does wrong, and tremblingly awaits the punishment of his father. He may try to hide in the closet or under the bed. When he appears before his father, his eyes are filled with both fear and pathetic love. He is torn between running away and flinging his arms about his father. After the spanking, his only comfort is to cling tightly to his father as he sobs himself into peace. He knows intuitively that the hand that spanked him is the hand that loves him.

If I take the wings of the morning and dwell in the uttermost parts of the sea, even there shall thy hand lead me, and thy right hand shall hold me (Psalm 139:9-10).

Laurence N. Field, pastor, bishop, teacher and poet, has a delightful little book, *Whimsy*, describing episodes out of his life as bishop in Montana. It must have been on a depot platform during a Western night that he was led to pen these words:

Once upon a time a beam of light leaped from a star—an intangible, infinitesimal, mysterious something without substance that defies definition and comprehension! Boldly out into space it leaped, straighter and swifter than thought, 186,000 miles a second, and more! It was a long time ago, as we think of time, as long before Christ as we are living after him. At that moment Abraham was just finding his way down the pass into the Promised Land. On and on it sped. And all around it hurtled, revolved, and spun untold myriads of star bodies, bigger than our solar systems, smaller than my thumb —suns, asteroids, comets, meteors, star dust, gases—keyed up to millions of miles per second, and yet even the largest of them geared so closely and accurately that, after a trillion-mile circuit, they would complete their orbit right on the split second. So much so, indeed, that when men, peering through telescopes from a faraway fragment called Earth, noted the slightest abberation in arrival, they would say, not, "It is late this time," but, "We have made an error in our calculations," or, "Our instruments must be faulty."

On and on it flew! Kingdoms rose and fell, civilizations were born, flourished, waned, and died! Joseph, David, Alexander, Nero, Peter the Hermit, Luther, Bismarck, William the Second, Hitler, you and I! Finally, after 4000 years of this terrific speed, this wee, incomprehensible something of a light-ray lit upon one of the very tiniest and most out-of-the-way little clods of all in that vast infinity, namely, our own Mother Earth. Unobstructed and like a flash, it leaped through a large, thick plate-glass window in a certain city, on a certain campus, on a certain continent. And this is what it saw: a couple of two-legged miniscules known as Professor So-and-so and Doctor Thus-and-thus. They have just put their mighty doddering heads together and decided: *There is no God!*

The heavens are telling the glory of God; and the firmament proclaims his handiwork (Psalm 19:1).

We had guests. There were six of us at the table. When someone asked, "What time is it?" five people looked at their watches. I said, "Let's take count. How many watches or clocks do we have among us and in this house? There were two electric wall clocks, one radio clock, three alarm clocks, three wristwatches lying on a shelf (two needing repairs), one lovely Waltham given me by the faculty which I use only on my travels or in the pulpit to help me stop. There were at least 11 in running order. I suspect most American homes may not be far behind.

How can we compare ourselves with the people of any other period in history, or, for that matter, in almost any other part of the world?

We can accumulate more things, both in variety and quantity, than was every dreamed of in earlier periods of history. In fact, we are virtually flooded with items, large and small. Like ours, the average home has more clocks than are ever needed to learn the time of day.

If we should be deluded into thinking we have found the secret of life by our command of things, we are being misled. It may even be that the abundance of the material may rob us of life. We may have to unload in order to live. The cargo of our abundance may keep us fastened to earth. We may never see the stars nor scale the heights.

The people of Jesus' day never had a chance at abundance. Yet even they were beguiled by the struggle for that which they could hold in their hands, however meager. Jesus warned them that something more was needed.

There is a faith, a love, a joy, a hope that has relatively little to do with things. These are qualities of the heart, often of a heart that is not encumbered by things. These come directly from God. No automobile or snowmobile can be a carrier. They grow in a heart grateful for the simple, but overwhelming, truth that God loves us, that in Christ Jesus and the cross he forgives our sins and claims us as his own, and that he has prepared a place for us that even death cannot destroy.

The riches of the spirit or the heart will never come from listing an inventory of the things we possess. Such riches may be ours even if we have no list at all.

Do not lay up for yourselves treasures on earth, where moth and rust consume and where thieves break in and steal, but lay up for yourselves treasures in heaven, where neither moth nor rust consumes and where thieves do not break in and steal. For where your treasure is, there will your heart be also (Matt. 6:19-21).

T. F. Gullixson, in his book, *In the Face of the West Wind,* was an astute observer of how the hardships of the immigrant West both ennobled and destroyed people:

> The glow of northern sunshine lurked in her golden hair. The freshness of Baltic springtime was in her face. A song as out of mountain waters lived in her heart. Echoes of church bells hid themselves in her soul. . . .
>
> In the Maytime of life she came to America—she and her husband. They made a home on the prairies.
>
> The song in her heart might have stayed with her, for the prairies also know the music which the morning stars sang together, and they sing yet to those that are not deaf. But her ear attuned itself to the cackling of hens just off their busy nests, to the lowing of cows with udders full, to the lazy grunt of pigs ready for the packer's price; and she listened for a refrain to the barnyard medley in the jingle of coin in a purse and the rustle of currency in hand. The song in her soul was muted.
>
> There were times when the echoes of old church bells made her restless, calling in answer to church bells here; just as a sleepy instinct in puddle ducks cries out to the wild mallards going over above. But the echoes grew dim and dimmer, until finally the comforting noises of the hen house and cowshed stilled them forever. . . .
>
> Her body failed. The years collected their toll. She could no longer tend the chickens and feed the cows and slop the hogs and keep watch over all. They took her to the city away from her pens and her yards; but her heart stayed with its treasure. Life's center was gone. Reason too went.
>
> She was mad—gently, harmlessly mad; restlessly, tirelessly, pathetically mad, as she tramped the city streets looking for those cows, those pesky, straying cows; those cows always just ahead but never caught. She died one day, still looking for her cows.

What happened to this girl of the golden hair is not the story of most immigrants. But it is a chronicle of what can happen to any of us who becomes obsessed by possessions. Christ keeps calling us to find our treasure in God and his kingdom.

Riches do not profit in the day of wrath, but righteousness delivers from death (Prov. 11:4).

Why do two people promise to live together until death parts them, when you know that over a third will break the promise? Wouldn't it be realistic, perhaps more ethical, for the church to scratch this business about a promise? I've known some fine young people who have written their own marriage service and left it out. But without intending to, by eliminating the promise, they have robbed their marriage of the component of *duty* without which their love has little chance of flowering.

In the delightful book about her childhood, *From This Good Ground*, Edna Hong, speaking of her father and mother, says, "God saw the opposites in their nature when they themselves were love-blind to them. He was not an enemy of their erotic attraction and romantic love. As a matter of fact, he was so much a friend that he placed this natural love of theirs in bond, guaranteeing that this love shall be preserved in marriage. . . . It was preposterous even to think that the conflict between father's easygoing nature and mother's devotion to duty and strict regime would or could ruin their marriage, so neither father nor mother gave it a thought. One does not fear what is not anticipated. . . . So, without shaking the foundation of their marriage, without father being emasculated or mother oppressed, the opposites were worked into a common ground. . . . Had they allowed their incompatibilities to break their union, their powerful natural attraction to each other would never have become a cherishing love, a preserved and persevering love—that is, conjugal love."

She goes on, "Theirs was a Christian conjugal love, for they had made a sacred and solemn vow to the Christian God before Pastor O. A. Bue in Bloomfield Church, Ostrander, Minnesota, and were sincerely convinced that their marriage thereby was armed against any foe."

Most marriages have rocky stretches when the early flush of love needs the buttressing of a promise. To leave out the promise deliberately, for fear that it may be broken, is to eliminate the cornerstone of a building for fear that it may erode. Marriage is a merger of love and duty, of desire and promise. When love is wounded, God makes promise be the healer. And this goes on so long as they both shall live!

Have you not read that he who made them from the beginning made them male and female, and said, "For this reason a man shall leave his father and mother and be joined to his wife, and the two shall become one"? So they are no longer two but one. What therefore God has joined together, let no man put asunder (Matt. 19:4-6).

An emcee at any banquet is never the principal guest nor the main speaker. As master of ceremonies, he is in fact only an announcer. He introduces someone, and then steps aside. There are good emcees, and there are poor ones. The poor ones get in the way of the speaker; the good ones succeed in focusing on the speaker.

John the Baptist was history's most notable emcee for Jesus. He announced him; he introduced him. Then he succeeded in the greatest art of all; he succeeded in getting himself out of the way. His followers left him to follow Jesus. He moved off the stage into Herod's prison, and Jesus became the center.

We too are on the program as announcers. We are to be the Lord's witnesses. We succeed to the degree that all eyes center on Jesus, on God. To God be the glory. We fail to the degree that we get in the way.

We may not intend to get in the way, but it is always a lurking temptation. If someone says of us, "She is a wonderful Christian," or "He is a great guy," or "He is an eloquent preacher," we may unintentionally have replaced the Lord as the center. And, self-centered as we all are, we may be more pleased with the accolade than we should be. We may have failed to make the introduction and then leave the Lord alone to receive the glory.

Churches have always been concerned about programs or techniques for evangelism, even courses of study to train emcees. Programs and techniques, I must confess, leave me uneasy. I'm reminded of the mice who devised a sure plan to outmaneuver the cat. They'd tie a bell around his neck, and thereby be warned of his approach. It was a fine plan, but "who'll bell the cat?" Any plan for bringing Christ to the nations or to people, one by one, depends on finding people who are willing to try to present him.

Sometimes when we think we have bungled the introduction and we retreat in confusion, the Lord finds it easier to emerge as the center. In any event we are the emcees, and we must make the announcement of his coming and his lordship. Nor need it always be in words. People may find the Lord looming up through some humble, selfless service that we give, which, like a finger, points to him.

But you shall receive power when the Holy Spirit has come upon you; and you shall be my witnesses in Jerusalem and in all Judea and to the end of the earth (Acts 1:8).

Roy A. Harrisville, New Testament scholar and poet, speaking in chapel at Luther Seminary, took issue with the notion that the secret of life is to be found in probing "the self." Referring to Socrates's "Know thyself," he goes on to say:

> And here we are more than 2000 years later, still nursing the conviction that the "I," the self, is the be-all and end-all, our language, our behavior shot through with the notion that we are all self-contained, and that the "I," the self, needs protecting, like an egg with a weak shell hatched by a diseased hen. We talk of "getting in touch with ourselves," or "self-image," and if we should happen to hear we must love our neighbor as ourselves, we turn such talk 'round to read we must first learn to love ourselves.

> The irony, of course, in all this talk of getting next to the self is that we've become a nation of moral burglars. . . . We are among the most self-conscious people on . . . earth, and, whether as a consequence or by accident, we are among the most disoriented.

> But what if the entire affair should be a myth? What if the self should have no definition apart from some other thing, some other one? Then, to pay less attention to ourselves than to something else, to look beyond ourselves to someone else would do the trick. And what if that continuity in the self, preserved, or so we think, when we move from here to there, should be something given by another?

> If that's so, then the question can only be: Who or what shall give definition to our existence; who or what shall make us what we are; who or what shall hold our peculiar collection of atoms, perceptions, and conceptions together so they don't fly apart? Some mythical self? "Not I," says Paul. And not as though the "I" standing alone, existing alone, like John Wayne on a palomino, silhouetted against the gnarled trunk of a tree in a B Western, not as some self, conscious of itself alone, were any alternative "Not I." But who or what then? Adam, law, flesh, sin, death—or Christ? And nothing in between, no No-man's land for sale for some fabled self between. . . . That which gives definition to life is Jesus Christ. We were crucified with him . . . Christ our consciousness, Christ the unity in all the confusion battering our senses, Jesus Christ, because he loved us and gave himself for us! Dear God in heaven, what is there left to say?

I have been crucified with Christ; it is no longer I who live, but Christ who lives in me; and the life I now live in the flesh I live by faith in the Son of God, who loved me and gave himself for me (Gal. 2:20).

THE BUSINESS OF FAITH

Almost everything you do, you do on faith. You say, "Next week I'm going to Chicago," but you do not know that you will be alive next week. You plan in faith that you will be. You marry, in the hope, or at the risk, of finding happiness. You do not know for sure. You marry by faith.

When you stake your whole life on the unknown, on the existence of God, you have really plunged into the world of faith. There is no proof that there is a God; conversely, there is no proof that there is no God. You choose, on faith.

Jesus invited you to go a step farther, "You believe in God; believe also in me." When you do, you stake your life on the God that Jesus revealed and that Jesus Christ is. G. A. Studdert-Kennedy, British chaplain in World War I, essayist and poet, speaks of this plunge:

How do I know that God is good? I don't.
I gamble like a man. I bet my life
Upon one side in life's great war. I must,
I can't stand out. I must take sides. The man
Who is a neutral in this fight is not
A man. He's bulk and body without breath,
Cold leg of lamb without mint sauce. A fool.
He makes me sick. Good Lord! Weak tea! Cold slops!
I want to live, live out, not wobble through
My life somehow, and then into the dark.
I must have God. This life's too dull without.

If you have gone this far—better still, been *taken* this far by the Holy Spirit—you have plunged into a way of life which will dominate everything you think and do. You rest in a strange peace which nothing else in the world can give you. You stand on the solid ground which is still there if the planet blows up.

But you are caught in a whirlpool, too. You are fastened to God. Where God goes, you go. It is as simple, as dangerous, and sometimes as unpleasant as that. Perilous as this may be, it is your only claim to glory.

Indeed I count everything as loss because of the surpassing worth of knowing Christ Jesus my Lord. For his sake I have suffered the loss of all things (Phil. 3:8).

No light reading has given me as much amusement and pleasure as the Don Camillo series by Giovanni Guareschi, over 200 episodes in the duel between two friends, the priest, Don Camillo, and Peppone, the communist mayor in an Italian village. In one episode Peppone is made to be the devil's advocate against Lungo who had just said, "The fact is that God does not exist; he's merely a priest's invention. The only things that exist are those that we can see and touch for ourselves. All the rest is sheer fantasy."

Peppone replies, "If a man's born blind, how is he to know that red, green and the other colors exist, since he can't see them? Suppose all of us were to be born blind; then within a hundred years all belief in the existence of color would have been lost. And yet you and I can vouch for it. Isn't it possible that God exists and we are blind men who on the basis of reason or experience alone can't understand his existence?"

There's always been a great deal of talk about God. What does this mean? That man knows God? That he longs for him? That he secretly wants to destroy him? Or that man simply likes to talk?

One thing is sure: there is a great difference between what a man on the inside (a believer) may say about God and what a man on the outside (an unbeliever) may say about him. And it may just be that the man on the outside has no right to talk about God at all.

A man who has never loved—has he a right to talk about love? A man who has never tasted meat—has he a right to talk about meat? Perhaps he has a right, but what he says about love or meat can hardly be taken seriously.

Jesus said, "If anyone wants to do God's will, he will know." That is, if I really want to get on the inside and become involved in God and his enterprises, then God will let me in on the "know" about himself. If, on the other hand, I want to stand on the outside as an observer, detached and objective, I don't have a chance to know. You cannot know as an observer, as you do in a laboratory; you know as a participant.

This good news of God is for us all. We need not be experts in theology to know. God may be able to break through to a humble, unlettered person with genuine knowledge about himself more easily than to a highly educated person who has no desire or disposition to worship or follow him. It is the heart and the will that open the door to God.

We have beheld his glory, glory as of the only Son from the Father (John 1:14).

Following the death of his wife after but three years of marriage, C. S. Lewis in his book, *Grief Observed,* reflects on the whole range of death and grief. Following are fragments from his book.

And poor C. quotes to me, "Do not mourn like those that have no hope." It astonishes me, the way we are invited to apply to ourselves words so obviously addressed to our betters. What St. Paul says can comfort only those who love God better than the dead, and the dead better than themselves. If a mother is mourning not for what she has lost but for what her dead child has lost, it is a comfort to believe that the child has not lost the end for which it was created. And it is a comfort to believe that she herself, in losing her chief or only natural happiness, has not lost a greater thing, that she may still hope to "glorify God and enjoy Him forever." A comfort to the God-aimed, eternal spirit within her. But not to her motherhood. The specifically material happiness must be written off. Never, in any place or time, will she have her son on her knees, or bathe him, or tell him a story, or plan for his future, or see her grandchild.

It's not true that I'm always thinking of H. Work and conversation make that impossible. But the times when I'm not are perhaps my worst. For then, though I have forgotten the reason, there is spread over everything a vague sense of wrongness, of something amiss. Like in those dreams where nothing terrible occurs—nothing that would sound even remarkable if you told it at breakfast time— but the atmosphere, the taste, of the whole thing is deadly. So with this. I see the rowan berries reddening and don't know for a moment why they, of all things, should be depressing. I hear a clock strike and some quality it always had before has gone out of the sound. What's wrong with the world to make it so flat, shabby, worn-out looking? Then I remember.

How wicked it would be, if we could, to call the dead back! She said not to me but to the chaplain, "I am at peace with God." She smiled, but not at me.

And I heard a voice from heaven saying, "Write this: Blessed are the dead who die in the Lord henceforth." "Blessed indeed," says the Spirit, "that they may rest from their labors, for their deeds follow them!" (Rev. 14:13).

Is the policeman a friend or an adversary? Friend, of course! He is engaged by us to protect us. Even when we are in the wrong, he has the gracious task to stop us in our tracks so that we do not harm ourselves or others. But how many of us, driving on the highway and hearing the siren, stop to greet the patrolman with a cheery, "Hi, friend?" Immediately I think of him as my adversary. I have often been shamed by the friendly way he has warned me, even when he has done his duty by giving me a ticket.

As we walk along the street, do we see in each stranger a possible "mugger" or a potential friend? For every mugger there are a thousand possible friends.

I have been amused, at myself and at others, for regarding our government, especially the Internal Revenue Service as the adversary. On occasion I have been pleasantly surprised to have its office inform me that I have overpaid my tax. The office was my friend, after all. People employed in government sometimes fail us, and forget the trust we have put in them, but this does not make our representative government a rival that we must outmaneuver. Government, unless it is totally corrupt, is a gift from God to us.

Let us be frank with ourselves. We all do have a perverse twist in our natures. We are suspicious, untrusting, and easily shift people out of the ranks of friends into the ranks of enemies. We may be doing it in our own homes—husband and wife, brother and sister, parent and child.

Evil is abroad and is to be found in every human being. But good has been placed here too—by God. And God is on the side of goodness. Every time we trust, we engender trust in others; every time we love, we stir love in others; every time we are honest, we encourage honesty in others; every time we are friendly, we invite friendship from others.

It's easy to give up on the human race, and conclude that everyone is on the alert all the time, openly or subtly, to help himself at the expense of others. But this is the cynic's way. It is not God's way, nor the way of the Christian. There are all sorts of people who rise above the temptation to have people be their adversaries and to have them be their friends. It is from such people that joy and goodness come into our lives.

Repay no one evil for evil, but take thought for what is noble in the sight of all. If possible, so far as it depends upon you, live peaceably with all (Rom. 12:17-18).

A statesman in India, welcoming a group of American churchmen said, bluntly, "Give us your friendship and your skills, but keep your religion to yourselves." Franklin Clark Fry, eminent Lutheran leader, who headed the group, replied to this candid greeting, "We want to be your friends, and as your friends we must offer you the best we have, which is Jesus Christ."

It is the very nature of the church of Jesus Christ to reach out to others with the gift of faith. William Temple, former Archbishop of Canterbury, said that the Christian church is unique among all human institutions because it alone is chiefly concerned with those who are outside of its own life.

The church is no cozy club. It is not an association of like cultural and political convictions, leagued together against people of different interests. The church is not essentially an institution at all. It is a mission. It has been sent to those who yet are outside of the faith. And it has been sent to capture them and to change them. It has been sent to offer a gift—the gift of the love of God. In the body of Christ we each have our own role to perform in the offering of the gift to others.

We are a restless people, therefore. It is not enough for us to find a congregation of like-minded people to burrow in to a safe and comfortable fellowship. If we are a congregation really touched by Christ, we will be living with an eye to those who yet are in no congregation, in no fellowship of believers. It may seem presumptuous for us to "interfere" with our neighbors who have no association with a Christian church. It may seem arrogant to cross oceans to "impose" our faith on cultures and religions that do not know Christ. But if we feel uneasy about this, we may not yet have discovered for ourselves the staggering dimensions of the love of God in Christ. How can we be complacent about those who don't know the joy and peace or resting themselves in the love of God?

It is not necessarily wrong for the church to be concerned about increased memberships or even with bigger budgets, if these are not barometers of its passion to convey the love of Christ to people. If these become ends in themselves, then the church is no different from a political party or a labor union which strives to increase its numbers, resources, and power. The church longs and yearns that all people may know the love and peace of God.

May the God of hope fill you with all joy and peace in believing, so that by the power of the Holy Spirit you may abound in hope (Rom. 15:13).

Normally we are warned against pretending to be something or somebody we are not. A man who deals habitually in pretense we call a hypocrite, a deceiver, a fraud. But Paul called on his congregation in Ephesus to pretend that they are like God. "Be ye imitators of God!" Though you are sinful human beings, try behaving as if you were God.

Of course, it makes all the difference in the world why you imitate or pretend. If you do so deliberately to deceive, with no intention of becoming any different from what you are, then it's shameful business indeed. But if you do so in the scant hope that you may grow to be more and more like the object of your pretense, then your enterprise is honorable.

The fact is, most of us engage in the wrong kind of imitation of God. God is all-powerful—and how we strive for power! History is full of instances where great rulers, becoming more and more powerful, at last could not be satisfied with this world alone, but began claiming divine right and power and arrayed themselves among the gods. Our modern dictators have been smitten with the same absurd mania. Not only dictators, however. Every Tom, Dick, and Harry along the street struts like a puppet god, and with his "bless you" or "damn you" pretends to have heaven and hell at his disposal. We are all imitators and little rivals of God for power. Then there is this little matter of judgment. In gossip or slander or idle chatter we pass judgment on people and events as if, like God, we knew all things.

One thing is sure: when Paul invites us to imitate God, he does not point to a lot of little thrones and urge us to clamber into them to try running or judging the world. We can be equally sure that Paul did not speak flippantly when he called on us to become imitators of God. After all, this all-powerful and all-wise God had appeared in a very accessible form. From Bethlehem to Calvary he had left a pattern for people to follow and to imitate. John said that the Word, which was God, had become flesh and dwelt among us, and we beheld his glory. The eternal Creator, who wheels his throne on the rolling worlds, had walked the dusty roads of Judea and fried fish along the sea of Galilee. This Jesus, the Son of God and the Son of Man, we are called on to imitate in spirit and in truth so that day by day we might become more like him.

Therefore be imitators of God, as beloved children. And walk in love, as Christ loved us and gave himself up for us, a fragrant offering and a sacrifice to God (Eph. 5:1).

"Most of the legal systems of the world are religious or quasi-religious in origin," observes Arthur Larson, director of the Rule of Law Research Center at Duke University and former under-secretary of labor. The center had enlisted the services of fifteen of the greatest legal scholars from the different legal systems and subsystems of the world, beginning with the Anglo-American tradition, and including a former chief justice of Japan, an Indian high court judge, and authorities on Islamic, Jewish, Chinese, and Soviet law.

The focus of the study was the thesis that nations can, without sacrificing an undue amount of the sovereignty they now realistically have, achieve the amount of world order that the world realistically needs to keep the peace. The alternative, the study affirms, is the bleak fact that there will be no future for the civilized world. Every legal system in the world, from earliest times down to the latest post-war constitutions, has accepted the idea that the sovereign is not above the law. He is within law. The next step is to have nations themselves accept the idea that they too live under the law—world law.

Behind this conclusion is the awareness that ultimately law is not the making of man, whether one man or a majority of people. Whether one talks about the moral law, the universal law, the law of equity, or the law of God, there is a recognition that man's law must be measured against a law higher than man.

Larson calls attention to an instance in 1 Kings 21. Naboth was an ordinary man whose vineyard was contiguous to King Ahab's castle. The king tried to talk him into selling or trading for one of equal value. But Naboth, the commoner, stood up to Ahab the King and said, "The Lord forbid that I should give you the inheritance of my fathers." Though angry and sullen, that was the end of the matter as far as the king was concerned. But Jezebel the Queen taunted the king for his weakness, arranged the murder of Naboth, and confiscated his vineyard. The judgment of God was swift. "In the place where dogs licked up the blood of Naboth shall dogs lick your own blood." Sovereignty belonged to God.

The sovereignty of kings, presidents, parliaments—and nations too—is held under a higher law. This truth, reaffirmed by the Center's research, is the hope for a new day of world law and world peace.

I am the Lord your God. . . . You shall have no other gods before me (Exod. 20:2-4).

YOU ARE NOT TRAPPED April 30

Sometimes I feel trapped. I am caught by existence itself; I did not choose to be born, but here I am. However, I am fastened to a family, a father and mother whom I did not choose. Step by step I get involved in things that will not let me go. The years creep on, and doors keep closing. The path narrows, and my memories may be full of dreams and plans that never opened themselves for me.

There is one path that never narrows. It is as wide as the world and as high as the heavens. This is the path of the disciple. To follow Jesus Christ and to be commissioned in his kingdom is to have a great job to do until the very end. The job is of the same splendid dimensions whether you are poor or rich, young or old, married or unmarried, sick or well.

If you are trapped in poverty—too bad, perhaps. The Lord numbers many of his most gallant and noble managers among the poor. If he ever publishes a *Who's Who*, it is more than likely that the distinguished list will include more poor people than rich. (Of course, he has more of them to choose from.) You may whine and pity that you never became rich, but God doesn't. He is less likely to pity your poverty than fear your wealth. Poor or not, you may be his instrument to inspire hope and faith and love among rich and poor alike.

You may be trapped in what seems continued loneliness. You had hoped to marry and be surrounded by children and grandchildren, and you have had to settle for nephews and nieces, cousins and friends. My only sister married late and had to settle for 18 nephews and nieces, but for them and for her brothers she has been a fountain of love and care. Many unmarried people have "adopted" scores of children and have influenced their lives for good, sometimes providing inspiration that parents have been unable to give.

Or sickness may come and hold you fast. Or old age. But the magnificent field of intercessory prayer is not closed to you. And who knows how much good flows into the life of the world because of the quiet, continuing praying of people who care.

We are not trapped. The Kingdom is ours. This is our employment, to the end.

Has not God chosen those who are poor in the world to be rich in faith and heirs of the kingdom which he has promised to those who love him? (James 2:5).

THE SERVANT CHURCH

I was a pastor for 20 years. If one day a member had said to me, "I know a man whom we ought to have in our church; meet me tomorrow at 12 and I'll introduce him to you," I probably would imagine that he'd be someone who was attractive, perhaps a good tenor for the choir, had money and station, and would be an asset to the church. At the appointed hour my friend took me to the jail, and showed me a petty thief, picked up for drunkenness, shoplifting, and child abuse. It would have taken me some moments to recover and realize, "Yes, of course, that's precisely the kind of person we ought to interest in the church. He needs us."

On the other hand, I ought not be thought crass and self-serving when I seek to win for the church someone who has native strength and charm, skills and money. The church can use such a person, not primarily to build its budget and prestige, but as significant resources to minister to the world, including the weak and the poor. Was there anything wrong about enlisting a St. Francis, a Luther or a Wilberforce, people of strength and extraordinary ability? Moreover, the gifted and the rich are as much in need of the ministry of the church as others.

The Christian faith seeks to serve instead of being served, and every church ought to reflect this. The more spectacular exceptions to this goal today are not the more established congregations, but many of the popular "religious" TV programs. Under the leadership of some engaging person, they reach into the homes of millions of people with appeals for money, which rarely, if ever, flows out to help the poor or win disciples.

The heart of the Lord's work will always lie with smaller groups, congregations, drawn together to edify one another and to reach out to serve the world. A cozy tryst before a TV screen may be entertainment, but hardly enlistment in Christ's mission for the world.

But when you give a feast, invite the poor, the maimed, the lame, the blind, and you will be blessed, because they cannot repay you. You will be repaid at the resurrection of the just (Luke 14:13-14).

God put Abraham to the severest test of all. He made him choose between two loves, both honorable and noble. One was the love of his only son, Isaac, the other was the love of God. It was a fierce choice, because it was not a choice between evil and good. It was a choice between the high and the highest.

That which tears at the heart is not the choice between the base and the noble; life's profoundest pathos is the need of choosing between a lesser and a greater good. When our love of Christ involves the neglect of our nearest and dearest, we experience the most poignant pain and the deepest joy.

When during those terrible 30s in Germany, Martin Niemöller elected to enter a concentration camp rather than compromise or deny his Lord, he also elected to leave his wife and eight children defenseless against the probable torment of the Gestapo. It was not that he loved his family less; it was that he loved truth, justice, and his Lord more. When missionaries had to leave their wives and children behind in this country if they were to return to their posts—and they chose to go —they gave up the happy and honorable duty of being with their dear ones to obey the higher mandate of bringing the gospel to a dying world.

To choose between honesty and dishonesty, between devotion to family and attachment to illicit love, between unselfishness and greed are easy decisions compared with those that pit two obvious goods against one another.

When Luther wrote those fearful words, "Let goods and kindred go, this mortal life also; the body they may kill . . . ," you dare not suppose that he did not love his little girl Magdalena or his little son Hans—not if you have read his letters to them.

In many circumstances, far less threatening than that of Abraham or Niemöller or Luther, we may be faced with such decisions. A man runs for office. By ferreting out some old scandal about his opponent, he may win the election, but he will do grave injury to his opponent's family. Or, a man needs his job to support his family, but his employer involves him in questionable practices. If he disobeys his employer, he loses his job. Is the care of his family a higher good than protesting the practice of his boss? We all face decisions between two goods, two rights. May God help us to find our way.

Blessed is the man who walks not in the counsel of the wicked . . . but his delight is in the law of the Lord (Psalm 1:1-2).

In recent years the subject of death has become almost an obses-sion, with courses of study offered in colleges and even high schools, and with all sorts of books in the field. It has puzzled me why it should be so, when years ago I can't recall any similar attention given it. Is it because we are reminded so often that the bomb, exhaustion of natural resources, the pollution of air and water may end life for us all? Or may it be that with modern health care people no longer die in their homes, surrounded by family, and are whisked off to a cemetery or a crematorium before the public "memorial service"—so that the phenomena of death becomes a strange, unknown mystery?

Oliver Wendell Holmes, in his essay, "The Autocrat of the Break-fast Table," describes what at one time was a common introduction to death:

> The great Destroyer, whose awful shadow it was that had si-lenced me, came near me, but never so as to be distinctly seen and remembered, during my tender years. There flits before me the image of a little girl, whose name even I have forgotten, a school-mate, whom we missed one day, and were told that she had died. But what death was I never had any very distinct idea, until one day I climbed the low stone wall of the old burial ground and mingled with a group that were looking into a very deep, long, narrow hole, dug down through the green sod, down through the brown loam, down through the yellow gravel, and there at the bottom was an oblong red box, and a still, hard, white face of a young man seen through an opening at one end of it. When the lid closed, and the gravel and stones rattled down pell-mell, and the woman in black, who was crying and wringing her hands, went off with the other mourners, and left him, then I felt that I had seen Death, and should never forget him.

In the average Christian home a half century ago, a dying grand-father or brother most likely was cared for in the home, with family coming and going during the days of approaching death. When death came, the body lay in state in the living room until the church service, and all assembled at the grave for the last farewell. Most important, the service pointed beyond the grave to heaven, where now the dear one was with the Lord and with all the blessed.

Death is swallowed up in victory. O death, where is thy victory? O death, where is thy sting? (1 Cor. 15:54-55).

THE ISLAND May 4

We humans have always sought for meaning, but more poignantly today than ever. In this vast universe of billions of light years and billions of stellar bodies whirling in space, we seem dwarfed virtually into nothing. The cry comes, "Who am I?" The Scriptures give us a bracing picture of our place in the universe. It is as if God addresses each of us:

My child, out in the seas of space I have an island. I place you there for awhile. You will have longings for the home kingdom, I hope. I want you to visit this colony of mine. Nor is it to be a vacation—nor for that matter, a sentence. I have work for you to do. I want you to transplant some of the justice and truth and love of the home kingdom to that island. The task will not be an easy one. Many of your brothers and sisters already there have forgotten about me and the task I have also given them. They will tell you that it doesn't matter what you do. "Get what you can when you can," they will say. But remember that it does matter, a very great deal, to me. You see, I love that island. Otherwise I should not have created it, and certainly I would not have sent my Son to die to redeem it.

I count on you. I have no one else. I could have sent my angels to do this work, but I send you, my sons and daughters, instead. If you do not work for justice, the earth will never know justice. If you do not love, no one there will know love. If you are not loyal to the truth, all will be error. If you fail me, war and debauchery and crime and boredom will overrun the earth.

I will not leave you alone. I will be with you, even to the end. In my church I will come to you through the Word and the sacraments. Love them and use them. When your tenure on the island is over, I will take you by the hand and lead you across the border, and we'll go on together forever.

All thy works shall give thanks to thee, O Lord, and all thy saints shall bless thee! They shall speak of the glory of thy kingdom, and tell of thy power (Psalm 145:10-11).

Years ago in some parts of rural America there would be a "hiring day" in the spring when farmers came to town to meet with men who wanted to hire out for the summer. The story is told that after visiting with several men, a farmer hired a man despite the fact that he answered all questions with a curt yes or no, and that he gave as his qualification the puzzling statement, "I can sleep on a windy night."

Weeks went by and he found no fault in his man. One night the farmer awakened with a start. There was a terrible gale blowing. He quickly pulled on some clothes, and dashed out to the yard to check: first on the windmill, it was securely fastened; then the chicken coop, all windows firmly latched; then the barn, all doors closed—everything ship-shape. Returning to the house, and finding his hired man sound asleep, he suddenly understood the cryptic statement, "I can sleep on a windy night."

Obviously a person cannot be prepared for all the emergencies and storms of life. But there are certain commonsense precautions we all try to take. We are responsible human beings, after all.

Jesus did tell us of something that is coming, and he said, "Be ready." He is coming! At some unknown and unsuspecting time the Great Day will come, "like a thief in the night," and the glory that has been largely in hiding—even when he was on earth—will burst upon us.

It is a pity if we look for our Lord's return with fear, or with indifference. Even though we find life on his earth filled with enough joy not to want to leave it, there ought to be within each of us a quiet longing for the day of fulfillment, when we shall see him face to face.

Making ready for that day should be no different from making ready for his coming into our lives, day by day. His presence will be no more real when we see him in his full glory than his unseen presence is right now. He stands at the door and knocks every day. He is as near as the air we breathe every day. Our joy at seeing him in his glory should be much as the joy of a mother whose long-awaited son surprises her at the door.

For most of us perhaps, the day may be before his great appearing, the day when death is done with us and we are on our feet again before him in his eternal home.

Therefore you also must be ready; for the Son of man is coming at an hour you do not expect (Matt. 24:44).

The memory of a good father and mother is one of the dearest, if not the dearest, treasure that a person may have. A number of years ago I heard a juvenile judge say to a group of men, "Rather than divorce your wife and let your children feel that you have abandoned them, it would be better if you had died and given your children a chance to build a legend of a caring father." These were harsh words, and certainly not true in all instances, but in a day when many homes are broken, it is well to ponder the really marvelous heritage of a loving mother or father.

In *Leaning on the Everlasting Arms* by William Saroyan there is a conversation between two GIs on a troop train, Tobey (who never knew who his parents were) and Marcus, dreaming of coming back to his home:

> Marcus said, ". . . I want you to meet my family. We're poor, always have been—my father was a *great* man. He was not a successful man. He didn't make any more money than we needed—ever. . . . He worked in the vineyards, in the packing houses, and in the wineries. He did plain, ordinary, everyday work. If you saw him in the street you would think he was nobody. . . . He was my father and I know he was great. The only thing he cared about was his family—my mother and his children. He saved money for months and made a down payment on a harp—yes, a harp—I know nobody plays a harp any more but that's what my mother wanted, so my father saved up money and made a down payment on a harp for her. It took him five years to pay for the harp. It was the most expensive harp you could buy. . . . Then he bought a piano for my sister—that didn't cost so much. I thought everybody was great like my father—until I got out and met some of the rest of the people. They're all right, they're fine—but I don't think they're great. Well, maybe they are and I just don't know them very well. You've got to know people real well to know whether they're great or not. A lot of people are great that nobody ever thinks are great."
>
> "I wish I could have known a man like your father," Tobey said. ". . . I guess I'm lucky in a way, not knowing who my father was, because, not knowing, I can *believe* he was great, just like your father."

I the Lord your God am a jealous God, visiting the iniquity of the fathers upon the children to the third and fourth generation of those who hate me, but showing steadfast love to thousands of those who love me and keep my commandments (Deut. 5:9-10).

133

Often a person finds it hardest to believe what he most eagerly wants to believe. A lover may be like that. Doubts trouble him. "Can it be possible that she loves me?" A mother whose son is reported safe and returning from the war may say, "I can't believe it until I hold him in my arms."

It was that way with Thomas, called Didymus. The other disciples said, "We have seen the Lord." Thomas said, "Except I see in the hands the print of the nails . . . I will not believe!" Thomas was no cynic; he was an ardent lover and follower. It was he who had once proposed to the band of disciples that they not abandon Jesus, but follow him to Bethany and to Jerusalem, even if it meant death for them all. The tragedy for Thomas was not his lack of love or faithfulness; the pity for this good man was that for eight days he lived in the anguish and uncertainty of doubt. The reason? He had stationed himself in a place other than the place Jesus appeared. The disciples were together, and Thomas was not with them.

It is a simple truth that what happens to us in most instances depends on where we have stationed ourselves.

To station ourselves in a worshiping company on Sunday morning may seem a casual thing. It may not be that at all. The decision to go to church is itself of significance, almost the first act of worship. You cross the threshold of the church, and you are in the orbit where God has promised to be. Through the hymns, the confession, the prayers of the people of God, the proclamation of his Word—through it all you are cradled in an unseen presence, the presence of God.

The supreme issue of life is to be touched by God. Life may touch us with many of its variables, wealth or poverty, health or illness, fame or obscurity. We were created for him, to belong to him, to live with him—come what may.

The legend of Thomas is that he was the first missionary to India, and that he was faithful to the end.

Thomas answered, "My Lord and my God" (John 20:28).

In Lincoln's words, the American ideal is "government of the people, by the people, and for the people." This is not the ideal of the Kingdom of God. His rule is not a democracy. He was not elected by popular vote, whether of angels or people. If all the people of the world should vote to impeach him, he would be ruler still.

It may seem quite unnecessary, even indelicate, to review his credentials for being the ruler. He hardly needs an attorney for his defense, but it may be reassuring for us to take a hard look at why he should be the ruler.

Anyone who can create from nothing the heavens and the earth, and who can synchronize the billions of these plunging bodies in the universe so that they do not collide and bring everything to chaos—such a being does have some impressive credentials.

Moreover, he presides over a court of absolute fairness and justice. All other courts, even at their best, are often riddled by fear, envy, pride, arrogance, ignorance, and partisanship. Who should be God but One who in his wisdom sees all, knows all, and renders a just verdict with all the data at hand?

There is still more.

He should be the ruler who allows all his subjects to lean on him, count on him, and who cares for them with infinite concern. This is the God who is revealed to us in Christ Jesus, to whom all power in heaven and on earth has been given. His claim to rulership through power and wisdom is dwarfed by this supreme claim: *He loves.*

Our 20th century has had unhappy experiences with rulers of power. The totalitarianism of our age has made us skittish about surrendering autonomy to any one person. But we need not hesitate to give our all to this King, Christ, the ruler of all. He became the servant of all, he gave his life for us all. And he *invites* us—not commands us—to turn over to him our hearts, minds, and wills, precisely in order that he may give us freedom. The very gift which all dictators deny to their people, this ruler gives to all his people. The obedience he asks is the free, glad obedience of sons and daughters to their loving heavenly Father.

My son, give me your heart, and let your eyes observe my ways (Prov. 23:26).

Whatever confidence I have for the tomorrows will have to come less from my reliance on the ingenuity of men and more from my trust in God.

I know he wants me to have a future. And he wants it to be full and rich. He is far less concerned about the additional gadgets I may command than about the inner quality of my life, however. And I know that if death overtakes me, or overtakes the planet itself for that matter, it is not the end. God has a trump card. He has other islands in this vast archipelago where he will have me take up life again, and on a far more exciting scale. There are eternal tomorrows for me.

But I do not give up on the planet too easily. Until the Lord comes himself to usher in the consummate new order, I believe he has prospects of unpredictable possibilities on this earth. The earth is the Lord's. This is my Father's world. He has not abandoned it, nor does he intend to do so. In unseen but powerful ways, he is still in command. He will keep seedtime and harvest, spring and fall, day and night going on schedule. He will keep the stage set for the drama of man's inner life.

In his incomparably beautiful *Rubaiyat* Omar Khayyam says,

> Ah, Love, could thou and I with Fate conspire
> To grasp this sorry Scheme of Things entire,
> Would we not shatter it to bits and then
> Re-mould it nearer to the heart's desire?

It has been shattered to bits with the coming of our Lord and the ushering in of the kingdom of God. Into our present and into our future there has come a new dimension. Never again can we reckon the future without the miracle of God's presence. He is in our midst, nudging, prodding, and luring us on into a newness of life which alone makes any future desirable. The future is wide open. It is gloriously unpredictable, because our Lord is there.

He who did not spare his own Son but gave him up for us all, will he not also give us all things with him? (Rom. 8:32).

No matter how excellent an educational system we may achieve, it will still be true that the family, father and mother and children together, is the primary institution to convey to future generations the values of the past. This is true for values in art, in morals, in religion, in attitudes toward life. As mothers and fathers go, so goes the world.

In the past, and even today, mothers have probably played the dominant role in the home, certainly in terms of time. Fathers have been breadwinners, sometimes working long hours, and in modern society often away from home. Fathers, therefore, have been more visible in business, science, government, and the professions.

This doubtless is changing. Only in notable instances in the past have women won distinction in the world of science, government or business—often, however, in the world of education and the arts. One might remember Pierre and Marie Curie as exceptions, both eminent physicists and chemists, awarded jointly the Nobel Prize in physics in 1903. Upon Pierre's death at 47, Marie carried on in research for another 28 years, being the only person to receive the Nobel Prize a second time, in 1911.

When the mother of Arthur and Karl Compton was awarded an honorary doctor's degree by the College of Wooster in Ohio, the citation was simply "Mother of Comptons." Arthur, physicist and Nobel Prize winner, was professor and chancellor of Washington University, St. Louis, and Karl, also a physicist, was president of Massachusetts Institute of Technology.

A legend from pagan antiquity tells how the gods once summoned to Olympus the mortals, telling them to bring with them their highest gifts and achievements. The one who brought the greatest gift was to receive the crown. The artist brought his paintings, the sculptor his statues, the husbandman the fruits of his field, the poet his poems, the inventor his machines. But among them came also an old woman with nothing in her hands. The gods asked her, "Why are you here with nothing in your hands?" The woman answered, "I am here just to look on. I merely wanted to see who received the crown. These are all my children."

Then the judges said, "Give her the crown, for she has trained and inspired them all."

Train up a child in the way he should go, and when he is old he will not depart from it (Prov. 22:6).

Mahatma Gandhi stood the British Empire at bay with simple, non-violent resistance. Many people in the Western world have little faith in nonresistance. From a practical point of view (and we are practical people), must not violence and power be met with violence and power? John and Mary Schramm in their book, *Things That Make for Peace*, invite us to rethink the whole matter:

> It is a great disservice to give people the idea that to be truly Christian we must renounce power and become powerless people. Nothing could be farther from the truth. Rollo May states so clearly that power does not result in violence. Rather violence springs as a noncreative reaction to a feeling of impotence.
>
> Power in its root meaning simply means "to be able." Any productive and fulfilling life must flow from this "capability." Jesus promised us power with the coming of the Holy Spirit. This gift is still promised, and to reject power is to reject God's gift and intention for us.
>
> The unique Christian insight comes at the point of the definition and understanding of power. The world pictures force, brute strength, money, muscle, tanks, bombs, tyranny, monopolies—the list goes on and on. The Christian pictures the cross. In the "foolishness" of this symbol of power the Christian senses a radically different kind of power. It is a new way of being "capable." A picture of this different definition would be Jesus standing in front of Pilate. Pilate represents all the power of the great empire of Rome. Jesus appears to be one lonely, solitary, impotent man. It is clear through the eye of faith, however, that the real power is incarnate in the solitary figure.

John Howard Yoder, a Mennonite scholar, wrote:

> When he called his society together, Jesus gave its members a new way of life to live. He gave them a new way to deal with offenders—by forgiving them. He gave them a new way to deal with violence—by suffering. He gave them a new way to deal with money—by sharing it . . . He gave them a new way to deal with a corrupt society—by building a new order, not smashing the old.

For consider your call, brethren; not many of you were wise according to worldly standards, not many were powerful, not many were of noble birth; but God chose what is foolish in the world to shame the wise, God chose what is weak in the world to shame the strong (1 Cor. 1:26-27).

Melanchthon once said that his first question upon reaching heaven would be how Jesus could be both God and man at the same time. We live with this mystery, but its implication for us and for the world is profound. Michael Rogness says:

> The depth of this conviction is not just in explaining Christ's presence in Communion, but in realizing how fully God incarnated himself in our world and how fully he united himself with our human nature in Christ. This colors our whole understanding of Christ's relationship with the world, and his relationship with us, and in turn our relationship with the world. If we were to be content with a so-called "spiritual" presence of Christ in the Sacrament, then our spirituality in general could very well become one of becoming more spiritual in this sinful world. But to comprehend how Jesus is so much a part of our nature and our world is to eliminate a false spirituality which would lead us as disciples to become more "spiritual" and less "worldly" in an escapist sense.

> Precisely the opposite is true: because Jesus became so much one of us, we too should immerse ourselves in the needs and concerns of those around us. Our life as Christians is not to be elevated piously into some spiritual never-never land, but to live with Christ in the full breadth of experiences in this world. The whole range of human life is under the Lordship of Jesus Christ, because he became a part of the whole range of human life. We can be confident of his presence in joy and suffering, health and pain, happiness and grief, company and loneliness, beauty and ugliness, and, yes, in sainthood and sinfulness.

> This view of Christology, with its affirmation of both the human and divine natures of Christ, reinforces the First Article of the Apostles' Creed as well, because since the incarnation is such a concrete union of the two natures, we cannot help but take seriously both the spiritual and the physical dimensions of life, simply because Jesus did.

> This insight into Christ, and other great teachings in our tradition from the 16th century, are tailor-made for our churches today. We ought to draw them out and make them sing again.

And the Word became flesh and dwelt among us, full of grace and truth; we have beheld his glory, glory as of the only Son from the Father (John 1:14).

There are three kinds of people: those who play life scrupulously by the rules, those who play short of the rules, and those great people who play way out beyond the rules.

Unfortunately, there are many people who play short of the rules. They observe rules only if it pays them. They are self-centered, they befriend people only if they can use them to advantage, they weasel out from any community responsibility. They are waste cargo, parasites on society. The world would have been better had they not been born.

Then there is the person who plays strictly by the rules, the utterly fair person, who always carries his corner of the load. If there are ten bags of cement to be carried, he will uncomplainingly take his five, if you carry your five. If there are eleven men on the team, he will take his one-eleventh share to win the game. He marries, and he will go fifty-fifty with his wife to make the home right. If he belongs to a congregation, and the Lords asks them to send out a missionary, he sharpens his pencil and figures out the fraction that should be his fair share and remits it in the next mail. You have known him—this careful, cautious, timid, frightened man of the rules.

He wonders why he does not care much for football, or why he is not very happy at home, or why religion doesn't excite him. He is not a shirker nor a cheater; he is just and fair. He obeys the laws, he plays by the rules—no more and no less—and lives out his days in boredom, wondering why he never gets paid off with happiness.

Fortunately, there are men and women who play way out beyond the rules, who never pause to figure out what is their fair share. God and the high call of duty and the splendid commission to love all combine to set before them a task. And they give themselves to the task, in delightful abandonment. They haven't time to be irked by the stragglers and grumblers.

What would the world do without these people? That which makes them tick is *gratitude*. They are thankful to be alive, to have work to do, to be blessed with family and friends, and thankful to God for his love and salvation. They count it an honor to undertake causes for justice and mercy. They give themselves gladly and uncalculatingly to their work, to their home, to their congregation and community. They leave the rules far behind. They know the freedom and joy of the kingdom.

You lack one thing; go, sell what you have, and give to the poor, and you will have treasure in heaven (Mark 10:21).

I had quoted Luther's explanation of the Second Article of the Apostles' Creed in a sermon at Rockefeller Chapel at the University of Chicago. After the service, a lady said, "I'm an Episcopalian. Where did you find that? It's the finest summary of the faith I've ever heard." Many of us, having memorized the Small Catechism long ago, have forgotten how simple and comprehensive these short paragraphs are. I quote them here:

I believe in God the Father: I believe that God has created me and all that exists. He has given me and still preserves my body and soul with all their powers. He provides me with food and clothing, home and family, daily work, and all I need from day to day. God also protects me in time of danger and guards me from every evil. All this he does out of fatherly and divine goodness and mercy, though I do not deserve it. Therefore I surely ought to thank and praise, serve and obey him. This is most certainly true.

I believe in Jesus Christ, his only Son: I believe that Jesus Christ —true God, Son of the Father from eternity, and true man, born of the Virgin Mary—is my Lord. At great cost he has saved and redeemed me, a lost and condemned person. He has freed me from sin, death, and the power of the devil—not with silver or gold, but with his holy and precious blood and his innocent suffering and death. All this he has done that I may be his own, live under him in his kingdom, and serve him in everlasting righteousness, innocence, and blessedness, just as he is risen from the dead and lives and rules eternally. This is most certainly true.

I believe in the Holy Ghost: I believe that I cannot by my own understanding or effort believe in Jesus Christ my Lord, or come to him. But the Holy Spirit has called me through the Gospel, enlightened me with his gifts, and sanctified and kept me in true faith. In the same way he calls, gathers, enlightens, and sanctifies the whole Christian church on earth, and keeps it united with Jesus Christ in the one true faith. In this Christian church day after day he fully forgives my sins and the sins of all believers. On the last day he will raise me and all the dead and give me and all believers in Christ eternal life. This is most certainly true.

I am reminded of your sincere faith, a faith that dwelt first in your grandmother Lois and your mother Eunice and now, I am sure, dwells in you (2 Tim. 1:5).

For a quarter century in the editorials of *Saturday Review,* Norman Cousins has provided our age with penetrating insights and incisive criticism, but always with a note of hope. His continuing concern has been for the nations in this nuclear age to find an order of international law and save us from mass suicide. I quote excerpts from his editorials:

If I believed that peace could be achieved only at the expense of principle, I would be against peace. If I believed that peace meant surrender to evil, I would be against peace. I say this though I have seen an atomic bomb explode 16 miles away, though I have seen dozens of dead cities, their insides hollowed out by dynamite and fire, though I have seen the faces of the dead in war and the faces of the damned whose bodies but not whose minds survived.

The issue is not whether one side can impose its will on the others but how we can keep both sides from fusing inside an atomic incinerator.

Man is completely daring and inventive about the feasibility of a world holocaust but absurdly unresourceful about the making of a world community. He denies the oneness of hope but asserts the oneness of despair. Unity of spirit is resisted, unity of defeat is pursued.

The easiest way for a nation to destroy itself is to make national security the highest value. People are never more insecure than when they become obsessed with their fears at the expense of their dreams, or when the ability to fight becomes more important than the things worth fighting for.

In the making of moral judgments, the humblest citizen in the nation stands on even ground with a president.

When world law was first mentioned, people said that it was too soon. Now when it is mentioned, they say it is too late. It is neither too soon nor too late. If we have a voice and an idea behind it, and if what we say makes sense, the time is just right.

All things are possible once enough people realize that the whole of the human future is at stake.

Unless the Lord watches over the city, the watchman stays awake in vain (Psalm 127:2).

There are several directions toward which you may fix your gaze, and with varying degrees of profit.

You may look *around* you. It is not an altogether pleasant panorama. You will see a world of greed, envy, suspicion, and fear. Distractions shriek at you from every conceivable advertising and communications medium. A babble of voices fills your ear. There may be little around you to give you courage and hope.

You may look *behind* you. A long look at history, with its rise and fall of civilizations, its debt of the past clamoring for payment, its cargo of opportunities missed welling up with a great tide of remorse —this backward look is not at all reassuring.

You may look *before* you. However gallant you try to be about the future, the rolling clouds that dim your vision and block out the tomorrows offer little solace.

You may look *within* you. Taking refuge within yourself, in a type of psychological monasticism, is a popular 20th-century avocation, but hardly a successful one. No person has really succeeded in "getting away from it all" by the inward look, because you yourself are a composite of past, present, and future, with all the environmental and hereditary ills packed into that self of yours.

A world that is glutted with the grim news of contemporary events, a world that probes history for some pattern of value and progress, a world that plans furtively for the future with a fever for vast social dynamics, a world that seeks refuge in new cults of psychology to eke out some peace from the jig-saw jumble of appetites, urges, and frustrations—this world has largely forgotten the *upward* look.

The vast reaches of the starry heights will not whisper of the love of God, and looking into its twinkling mass you will fail to be overwhelmed by the love of God—unless (and this is a big unless) you have found his love in him who came down from heaven to become one of us, who after dying and rising for us, ascended on high, and who will one day return in glory. Lift up your eyes to him!

And as they were gazing into heaven as he went, behold, two men stood by them in white robes and said, ". . . this Jesus will come in the same way as you saw him go into heaven" (Acts 1:10-11).

WHERE MEANING CAN BE FOUND   May 17

A much discussed play of the mid-century is T. S. Eliot's *The Cocktail Party*. Celia goes off and becomes a missionary, and is crucified by the natives on an anthill. Her companions, the cocktail crowd, upon hearing it, begin to feel that Celia's fate has made meaningful both her life and death. They are haunted to find something to give their lives a meaning higher than a round of parties.

What is it that points up your life? Are you willing to work during the day, because when the day is over there will be a party? What makes you carry on over the dreary spots? It is the money you get at the end of the trail? For many a person the only bright spots looming up ahead are a mug of beer before the tube, an unexpected letter in the next mail, or the visit of a friend. We are often like people driving unseeing through the mighty sequoia forests, missing altogether their beauty and majesty because the only thing occupying our minds is the menu for the next meal.

You can try tying life together with a menu or a fishing trip or a mint of money, but your life will be bleak and meaningless. You will need something stronger and more comprehensive to hold it together. Christ said that nothing short of the kingdom of God would do it.

We were made to live and die, if not heroically, at least with meaning. We were not made just to live and die, even if we could live without want and die without pain. It would be a tragedy, wouldn't it, if we were to build a church to worship the living God and have our children use it to store grain? It is a greater tragedy when God creates us to be the dwelling place of his Spirit and kingdom, and we become mere containers for good food on the inside and surfaces for cosmetics and fabrics on the outside.

The glorious fact is that God has not doomed us to find meanings simply within the borders of this world's goods. He has established a kingdom on earth. He has made a beachhead and set up on these far shores a matchless, though invisible, kingdom, and he invites us in.

If we come seeking, in the repentance and faith which his Spirit works within us, we shall find and be ushered in. And within this kingdom new vistas of meaning will unfold which we had never suspected existed.

Fear not, little flock, for it is your Father's good pleasure to give you the kingdom (Luke 12:32).

144

Occasionally Christians wonder why all people do not come running to the Lord. Don't they want hope and courage and love—the very qualities that give life its meaning?

There is another side to the coin of discipleship. We are given the status of sons and daughters, by grace alone to be sure. We need not finish a course in discipleship before the Lord invites us in. We are told to come as we are, sins, doubts and all. Nor is there any fine print, as if, once into the kingdom, we find that God does indeed require us to "pay" for our rights as sons and daughters.

But, as sons and daughters, we do get caught with the whole, marvelous life of sons and daughters. There is a *noblesse oblige*, an expectation, an honor, so high that we may feel uneasy. As a child has the impulse to retreat when suddenly he bursts in on the staggering sights of the carnival tent, so we may, upon seeing the enormous implications of Christian living, have an almost irresistible desire to back off.

Søren Kierkegaard, warning against overlooking the "offense" or demands of Christian life, says,

> Christianity has been spread too thin. The zeal for extension must be checked, in favor of a deeper intensity. It might be better if the Gospel were taken from us until we should learn to appreciate it. . . .
>
> I could be tempted to make another proposal to Christendom. Let us collect all the New Testaments there are in existence, let us carry them out to an open place or upon a mountain, and then while we all kneel down let some one address God in this fashion: Take this book back again; we men, being such as we now are, are no good at all for dealing with a thing like this which only makes us unhappy. Such is my proposal, that like the inhabitants of Gadars we beseech Christ to "depart out of our coasts." This is an honest and manly way of thinking, quite different from that disgusting, hypocritical, preacherfying fudge about life being of no value to us apart from the inestimable blessing of Christianity.
>
> A man's whole life is worldliness. . . . At the same time, naturally, he is a Christian. This is just as ludicrous as when savages adorn themselves with a single piece of European clothing—for example, the savage who comes on board stark naked except for the epaulets of a general on his shoulders.

O the depth of the riches and wisdom and knowledge of God! . . . *For from him and through him and to him are all things. To him be glory forever* (Rom. 11:33, 36).

At the great dinner, where do you expect to find your place card? The Divine Host, the all-knowing and all-seeing God, will check the list of guests and arrange the seating. If by grace you are among them, where will you start looking for your place? Will you mutter to yourself that most likely your name is up there at the head table and edge up to the center, or will you start looking down at the foot somewhere?

If you start down at the foot, you will jostle into some rather interesting people. Paul will be elbowing his way to find the place for sinners, of whom he said he was the chief. Peter, the man who denied his Lord, will be down there overjoyed to find his name there at all. John the Baptist, who did not count himself worthy to unloose the sandals of the Host, will be there too. And Isaiah, the man who wept over his unclean lips.

Where at the table the Lord will have put your card, only he knows. But it is very revealing to know where you intend to start looking.

Nor is it likely that you will change your habits much at the last great dinner, the heavenly banquet of the Bridegroom. If you have been blundering around the head tables your life through, you probably will be the same comic figure at the end too.

If during your lifetime you have been sneering at your drunken neighbor, or if you have whispered about your stupid associates, or looked down your nose at the less prosperous, the less disciplined, the less intelligent, and the less ambitious, you probably will strut your stupid social behavior right into heaven and be brought up with a most embarrassing jolt as you blush your way down toward the celestial kitchens to eat with the cooks.

Over against God who knows all, how honorable, sincere, unselfish, kind, pure, and patient have our motives been? The great question is, do we have a right to be at the table at all?

In the liturgical service of many churches we open with a confession of sin: "Almighty God: we poor sinners confess unto thee that we are by nature sinful and unclean, and that we have sinned against thee by thought, word and deed." And we continue, "We flee for refuge to thine infinite mercy." It is by his favor, his mercy, his grace, that any of us will be at the table. For which we thank and praise him forevermore!

When you are invited by any one to a marriage feast, do not sit down in a place of honor . . . . go and sit in the lowest place, so that when your host comes he may say to you, "Friend, go up higher" (Luke 14:8, 10).

God can be angry, and so can his children.

If you consult a Bible concordance, you will find that the word *wrath* appears throughout the Old Testament, but hardly at all in the New. It does appear in the same chapter as John 3:16 (John 3:36), once or twice in the letters of Paul, and several times in Revelation. The fact that it is not often used to describe God does not mean that the God of the New Testament is an indulgent grandfather or grandmother who never gets angry. In fact, the wrath of God is one side of the coin. His love is the other.

Can you imagine a wise and good father who would not have fierce anger against those things and those people who are destroying his child?

In his charming book, *The Letters of Luke,* Canon Lloyd has Luke writing to his friend Theophilus from Antioch. Luke says that in all that wicked city he has found only one group of people, a little colony of Jews, who register any indignation over the corruption and wretchedness there. He tells Theophilus that he has joined them. The Jews worshiped a God who could be angry. They knew him as a God of wrath.

When our son was killed in an accident, I found myself angry that a promising young man of 24 should have his life snuffed out before he could be of service to the world. I asked myself, "Angry at whom?" Not at the truck driver, surely. And not at God, because I did not believe that God arranges accidents or disease. I found myself angry at this sorry state, this "fallen order," where sin and tragedy and pain and death can damage the lives of people. Suddenly it occurred to me that God, too, is angry at this, and I found it a comfort to be joining God in his anger. It would be hard to worship a God who sits serenely by, untouched and sweet-tempered when things go wrong for his children.

God's wrath is obviously directed more at the things that can destroy a person's soul or a nation's integrity, such as the miscarriage of justice and the absence of mercy, than it is aimed at accidents or diseases that cut short the span of life. His greatest stake is to win us and the world for his kind of life, and not simply to extend a person's years on earth.

We can understand, too, that this quality is what he wants in us. It is said that when, as a young man, Abraham Lincoln visited New Orleans and saw an auction of slaves, his anger was aroused and he vowed that if he ever had a chance to strike at this evil, he would strike hard. We need not fear a God of wrath; we need to emulate his wrath!

The wrath of God is revealed from heaven against all ungodliness and wickedness of men (Rom. 1:18).

How we envy people who can enjoy the moment, who are absorbed in the tasks at hand, with minimal anxiety for what may come tomorrow! They go about with a relaxed step, they find merriment and beauty, they spread cheer.

What is their secret? Not stupidity, certainly. Not indifference. Not insensitivity. Nor self-confidence.

More than likely, their secret is God. They have a towering confidence in his love and care. They entrust the tomorrows to him. They accept the tasks and the joys of the moment as assignments and gifts from him. They believe that the outcome of life is in his hands.

William James, great American psychologist, speaks of this quality:

> The transition from tenseness, self-responsibility, and worry to equanimity, receptivity, and peace, is the most wonderful of all those shiftings of inner equilibrium, those changes of the personal center of energy, which I have analyzed so often; and the chief wonder of it is that it so often comes about, not by doing, but simply relaxing and throwing the burden down. This abandonment of self-responsibility seems to be the fundamental act in specifically religious, as distinguished from moral, practice. It antedates theologies and is independent of philosophies. . . . Christians who have it strongly live in what is called "recollection" and are never anxious about the future, nor worry over the outcome of the day. Of Saint Catharine of Genoa it is said that "she took cognizance of things, only as they were presented to her in succession, moment by moment . . . when the duty that was involved in it was accomplished, it was permitted to pass away as if it had never been, and give way to the facts and duties of the moment which came after."

If we pray for this grace, it will be necessary for us to be willing that the Lord take care of tomorrow. Most of us find this exceedingly difficult to do. We worry about all sorts of possibilities (most of them never materialize), when we might very well have laid this burden down at his feet.

Consider the lilies of the field, how they grow; they neither toil nor spin; yet I tell you that Solomon in all his glory was not arrayed like one of these. But if God so clothes the grass of the field, which today is alive and tomorrow is thrown into the oven, will he not much more clothe you, O men of little faith? (Matt. 6:28-30).

The last one hundred and fifty years have witnessed a veritable explosion in technology. Century after century life had remained essentially the same. For thousands of years in transportation the fleetest conveyance was a horse on a dry track traveling about 35 miles an hour. Then came the steam engine, and today we fly to the moon at incredible speed. In this century alone we have witnessed the coming of the airplane, radio, television, electronics, atomic energy, the computer. Suddenly nature is yielding her secrets. What tomorrow may bring baffles the imagination.

It is not strange that we humans oscillate between pride and bewilderment. What has the mind of man wrought! We can travel faster, see farther, and hear more than ever before. With new sources of power we can produce goods a hundredfold in variety. We humans have been enormously successful.

But our success is toward limited, and often questionable, goals. At the very moment when we ought to be elated over our triumphs and have unlimited hope for the future, we find ourselves wondering, in fact, often despairing. When in the early days of the telephone, Thoreau of Walden Pond was informed that people of Boston had spoken to the people of Texas, he responded with the question, "But did the people of Boston have anything to say to the people of Texas?" There are goals other than power and speed, in fact, goals that power and speed may jeopardize.

Strangely enough, we moderns are harassed by feelings of guilt. Eloquent evidence of this is to be found in writers of fiction and drama as well as in the case histories of psychiatry. At the very moment when former canons of right and wrong are abandoned and society has become "permissive," the sense of guilt has become an almost universal symptom of human plight.

It cannot be denied that God has drifted off to the edges of daily life and perhaps for many has disappeared altogether. With God gone, the category of authority disappears. Then we are left alone without a sovereign and without law, or we become victims of all sorts of fraudulent claimants for authority. We who were made for obedience find no one to obey. We are left to create moral order in a universe that has no transcendent basis for order. We cry for a judge, but the bench is empty.

I am the Lord your God. . . . You shall have no other gods before me (Deut. 5:6-7).

Most of us fear courtrooms, certainly if we are defendants, on trial and waiting a verdict. It is inevitable, however, that we are on trial to be judged in four courts.

The first of my courts is *you*, my contemporaries. This is the lowest court, and the one I should fear the least, and often the one I fear the most. It is the lowest court because it is the one which makes the most mistakes. Socrates, for instance, was accused by his fellowmen of corrupting the morals of the Athenian youth and was sentenced to drink the hemlock. History has reversed the decision and has pronounced him one of the greatest of ancient men. John Hus was burned at the stake for heresy, and history has given this Bohemian a place among the immortals of those who championed truth. Joan of Arc died on the fagots for treason, and later France elevated her to the station of savior of her country. And Jesus himself! "Crucify him, crucify him," shouted the jury. Think of the 2000 years of reversal of that verdict. And yet, I tremble before this court. I worry about what people will say. I want acceptance so badly.

The next court is *history*, the future. When I am dead and gone, when people have had a better chance to assess me dispassionately, when more of the facts are in, then a more sober verdict may be given. But even this court can err. Marc Antony offered this cynical observation in his eulogy of the dead Caesar:

The evil that we do lives after them,
The good is oft interred with their bones.

To be sure, many of the names that make the headlines today—rock singers, athletes, and others—will be forgotten, and some obscure Pasteur or Einstein will fill the pages of history books. But think of the truly great, some quiet mother or friend, who may go unnoticed in both courts.

Then the third court: *myself*. I may trick you, I may even deceive history, but I have a harder time deceiving myself. It is a solemn thing to take matters before my own heart and conscience. But even here I may find fraudulent, extenuating reasons to let myself off.

Paul, reviewing these courts, concludes, "It is the Lord who must examine me." After all, only he knows the inner recesses of the heart, the deep inner motives which even we cannot identify. This is the fourth, and most terrifying court, the all-knowing court. Here, stripped of all pretenses, we cry, "God, be merciful." And there is mercy!

The steadfast love of God is from everlasting to everlasting upon those who fear him (Psalm 103:17).

There's a lot of talk today about the end of the world. People are frightened, often virtually paralyzed for any noble work. Some give up and turn to drink and drugs. Others give themselves frantically to short-range goals, like money and pleasure.

Of course the world will end; Christ has assured us of a great day when he will return. Meanwhile, the end may come individually to all of us; we'll trickle out of hospital beds.

When Jesus said, "We must work the works of him who sent me, while it is day; night comes when no one can work," was he talking about his own death, the death of his disciples, or the death of the present order? Perhaps about all. There is a time to work—to live, to love, to do the tasks at hand. Gerhard Forde, professor at Luther Theological Seminary, speaks to this issue:

> The usual "religious" sort of reaction to the nearness of the end would be to leave off doing "earthly" things and do instead something terribly pious to impress God when he shows up. But that is only because of our built-in tendency always to attempt to go "up to heaven." The point is that the nearness of God's kingdom ought to make us more down to earth—more concerned that God's will be done here on earth. . . .
>
> If God is coming, a man ought to be found living as God intended him to live: taking care of this earth. That, after all, was his charge to the first Adam. The point is that hope in the world to come does not lead us to *divide* our allegiance between this world and the next. On the contrary, since that world is God's entirely free gift, since it comes by his will alone, we are freed to give ourselves entirely to this world, to set about seeing to it that his will is done "on earth as it is in heaven." . . .
>
> The world to come does not mean the destruction of what is good in this world, but its fulfillment. The world to come does not therefore compete with this world for our affections. Because the hope of the world to come is sure, we are enabled to enter into, rejoice in, and care for this world. . . .
>
> Hope in the gift of the world to come is hope strong enough to enable us to turn from our fruitless quests for a heaven above and look to God's creation, to receive it back again, to enter into it, and struggle to see that God's will be done—that true justice, peace, and love are established . . . and to wait with patience.

Forgetting what lies behind and straining forward to what lies ahead, I press on toward the goal for the prize of the upward call of God in Christ Jesus (Phil. 3:13-14).

Do you have your priorities straight? That is, in the list of things you count important in life—family, friends, making money, winning elections, health, beauty, God, education, travel, recreation—in what order do you have them?

Looking at the collection God would remonstrate, "Just a minute. I'll have nothing to do with your list. Read me out of it. I must be *all*—or nothing."

Jesus speaks of the kingdom of God in those terms—a pearl of great price, a treasure so valuable that a person can rightly sell all he has to buy it. And it's true. The greatest treasure of life is not an accumulation or a multitude or a vast variety. It is not plural, it is singular. It stands out as the one thing needful. To have it, you must renounce all, not only that which is sinful and wicked, but even father and mother, wife and child. It asks all, and if you do not risk all, you get nothing.

Every person, deep down, yearns and longs to find some one thing so valuable that you'd let everything else go, if need be, to have it. Jesus says that there is such a treasure, and Paul says that he has found it, "the surpassing worth of knowing Christ Jesus my Lord."

You take your whole list of priorities, pile everything on the counter, and push it all over to God in exchange for a life with him. Most likely he'll give it all back to you, now to manage *for him*.

I knew a man who had the one treasure. Within his heart he had sold all that he had, to have God. God blessed the work of his hands, so that he grew wealthy, but wealth was to him only something to handle for God. It was incidental to his life, like a box of candy sitting on a table when lovers are together. It could be there or not, it made no great difference. I knew a dear old lady who had found the treasure. As a young girl in Norway she had waited for the letter from her lover who had emigrated to this land to prepare for her coming. When she arrived, he had married another. Alone, in a foreign land, her years were spent working in a laundry, until old and bent and gray she could work no longer. But early in life she had found the treasure; and when I knew her, living in one little room with her scant belongings, she was one of the most serene and radiant souls in the parish. She had found him; she had the pearl of great price.

The kingdom of heaven is like a merchant in search of fine pearls, who, on finding one of great value, went and sold all he had and bought it (Matt. 14:45).

In the foothills of Montana's Rockies a little stream is born. It trickles its fitful path down the hillsides, and flows into the plains. Growing broader and deeper, it becomes a river, the Missouri.

Montana says, "River, you're mine." But on it flows, declining to be cradled long by its parent state. Coursing on through the sister Dakotas, it hears again the claim, "River, you're ours." Heedless, it pushes on, angling its way between Nebraska and Iowa, but not before each of these neighbors has reached out for possession, "River, you're mine." Like a restless eel, it slips away, down to join the great Father of Waters, the Mississippi. And as it joins its flow with the larger, the Mississippi says, "At last you have come to me; now you're mine."

Still it flows silently on. At last its currents become slower, fuller, until down into the great Gulf of Mexico it comes to rest in the bosom of the ocean. In the rhythmic heaving of the deep, it hears the ocean's whisper, "River, you're mine. You've always been mine. It was I who sent the storm clouds into the mountains to give you birth. It was I who pulled you steadily, irresistibly away from all others back to me. From me you came, to me you return. Only I can really say, 'You're mine.'"

Into a home a little girl is born. Bending tenderly over the cradle, a mother whispers, "Baby, you're mine." The years go on, and soon the baby has become a lady. And a lover takes her by the hand, and a deeper voice echoes the mother's whisper, "Sweetheart, you're mine." Then one day she stands looking into the deep eyes of her own baby, and her mother ears seem to catch the unspoken claim of her child, "Mother, you're mine." But the years refuse to linger, and all too soon her hair becomes silver. Life grows fuller, deeper, slower, and one day she glides through the narrows into Eternity's ocean. There, in the bosom of her heavenly Father, she hears the voice of God, "My child, you're mine. You've always been mine. It was I who gave you life. It was I who drew you, through my redeeming love in Christ, drew you away from all others back to me. From me you came, to me you return. Only I can really say, 'You're mine.'"

Then one of the elders addressed me, saying, "Who are these, clothed in white robes, and whence have they come? I said to him, "Sir, you know." And he said to me, "These are they who have come out of the great tribulation; they have washed their robes and made them white in the blood of the Lamb (Rev. 7:13-14).

The conviction that there is life after death has been strong in every age and among every people. The Roman Cicero (106-43 B.C.) writing *Of Death and Old Age* expresses these longings in language which, though pre-Christian, is not unlike the clarion refrains that we find, for instance, in the Apostle Paul. Cicero says:

I would not, my children, that you should think, when I am departed out of this life and gone from you, that I shall be nowhere or brought to nothing. . . . My mind shall remain as before, although you see it not visibly. . . .

Every good and wise man dieth willingly, and rejoiceth therein exceedingly, taking death to be a joyful messenger to summon him to endless felicity. . . . I have a great desire to see and behold your fathers, whom I entirely loved, and had for their singular virtue great admiration.

And when I am in my journey to them (which I so greatly desire) there should no man bring me back again, though he would and also could; neither to make me to retire to the place from whence I came, like to a ball which tennis players toss and strike to their counter players, and they again to the other side, yea, though he would undertake to renew my youth again. . . . I will say more, if God would grant me now in this age to return again to my infancy and to be as young as a child that lieth crying in his cradle. I would refuse and forsake the offer with all my might; neither would I when I have already in a manner run the whole race and won the goal, be again revoked from the end marks to the lists, or place where I took my course at the first setting out. . . .

I depart out of this life as out of an inn, and not out of a dwelling-house. For nature hath given to us a lodging to remain and sojourn in for a time, and not to dwell in continually. O lucky and blessed day wherein I shall take my journey to appear before the blissful troop and convocation of happy minds, and leave this troublesome world, being the vale of all misery and the filthy sink of all mischief. . . . For I shall not only go to those worthy men, but also to my dear son Cato, who was a man of such sanctity and goodness as none more.

What no eye has seen, nor ear heard, nor the heart of man conceived, what God has prepared for those who love him (1 Cor. 2:9).

In the southern part of Russia is a small body of water, the Sea of Azov. If you were sailing there and wanted to reach the larger body, the Black Sea, you would have to navigate your craft through a small neck of water joining the two. If you desired even larger waters, the Mediterranean, you'd have to steer your boat through other narrows, the Bosporus and the Dardenelles. If after the Mediterranean, you'd long for even more spacious reaches, there'd be another narrows, the Straits of Gibraltar, into the Atlantic. And if you'd want the freedom of the almost limitless Pacific, you'd have to navigate the Straits of Magellan (in pre-Panama-Canal days). Each time you would earn the greater freedom by paying the price and taking the risks of navigating some narrows.

I've thought of life like that. You can drift in the cozy waters of an Azov, but if you are to possess the greater freedoms—and responsibilities—that lie beyond, there will be the pain and the risk of *decision*. No one drifts to greater and greater freedom of the spirit.

Life presses these moments of choice upon us.

They may be moments of good fortune, unexpected prosperity, and happiness. Will you drift about, simply cherishing your good luck, even thinking you might have deserved it, becoming a bit proud, perhaps even priggish and haughty? Or, will you take stock of where you are, steer your soul into the broader waters of gratitude and greater commitment in service to God and your fellowmen?

They may be moments of ill fortune. Things go against you. Someone lets you down. You lose a job. Someone dear to you is run down by a drunken driver. Your child gets leukemia. Now, what do you do—let yourself be blown about by bitterness, remorse, guilt, a sense of failure? Or do you take a hard look at God, at Jesus who died for you without bitterness on a cross, and let him take his place by your side at the wheel while you navigate into new waters of gratitude, patience, cheerfulness?

God gave human beings the gift of choice. He gave us a wheel and a rudder. Our craft need not drift. We never need be helpless in a storm; we can steer into it and through it. And on the other side of every narrows are the broader waters of life abundant.

Choose this day whom you will serve . . . but as for me and my house, we will serve the Lord (Josh. 24:15).

G. S. Studdert-Kennedy, a British World War I chaplain, tells of visiting a captain who was recovering from what had seemed certain death. He said, "Padre, tell me what God is like. Whenever I've been transferred from one regiment to another, my first question has always been, 'What's the colonel like?' because I've discovered that conditions in the regiment will be what the colonel makes them. Before the war, when taking a position with a new firm, I'd always ask, 'What's the boss like?' Now I'm told that I'll recover and live, and I must know what the Big Boss of life is like."

We need not *guess* what he's like. He has been among us. Jesus is the "Big Boss" of life. "All authority in heaven and on earth has been given me," he said. He is the ruler of the universe. In the language of the Nicene Creed he is "God of God, Light of Light, very God of very God."

Sometimes Jesus is called our high priest, sometimes our prophet, sometimes our king. In the Old Testament the high priest offered the sacrifices for the sins of the people. Jesus, as high priest, offered up himself as the one great sacrifice for the sins of the world. Also, in the Old Testament there were prophets who were teachers, telling of God and his will. Jesus, as prophet, not only taught us about God and his will, but he revealed God to be himself, endless in love and mercy.

Jesus is not like other rulers, hidden within some well-protected office. He is at our elbows, nearer than the air we breathe, always ready to hear us and help us. He is at once ruler and friend. But let us not forget that he is the ruler, the king, of everything. He is the king who has come down into the created universe, down to humanity, and come up again in his resurrection, pulling us up with him.

The story is told of a young king who made a tour through his kingdom. In one of the villages, his eye caught the eyes of a beautiful peasant girl. Back in the palace, he could not forget her. He had fallen in love with her. Now, what should he do—go back to the village and ask her to be his wife, to become the queen? He didn't dare do that. He thought to himself, "She'll be shocked, overcome in awe, perhaps fear." But he didn't want her awe or fear. He wanted her love. So, he disguised himself, returned as a peasant, and won her love. Only then did he tell her that he was king.

Jesus came as one of us, won the love of the world—and rules the world.

For in him the whole fulness of deity dwells bodily, and you have come to fulness of life in him, who is the head of all rule and authority (Col. 2:9-10).

On Memorial Day millions of graves will receive their annual care. The dead, often forgotten during the long year, will have their day for a moment. There is a sense in which the graves should be forgotten. A person who lives only in the past may grow melancholy and morbid. No one should bury the zest for living and the hopes for the future in some sentimental grave.

On the other hand, there are good reasons for spending much thought with the graves. We ought to have a past tense. Memories should be precious. The heritage which the fathers and mothers gave us should be carried with thankfulness. Then, too, we ought not to shy away from the sobering fact that some day we too will rest in some grave. Life is a bird on the wing that has but a little way to flutter. Many of the anxieties and ambitions we coddle would assume their proper place and seem trivial if we kept before us the nearness of the grave. Moreover, the bodies that rest in graves remind us that death is not the end, and that he who raised up Jesus will raise us up, too.

While Memorial Day has become the occasion for remembering all the dead, the day originally was set aside to remember the heroic dead of war. Since all war seems so futile, it is easy to become cynical and conclude that these dead have died in vain. The fact that we live as we do now, with the freedom of representative government, makes of their deaths more than stark tragedy.

It is important that we remember that they did not die in order that we might live. Just to live is not enough. Their lives were too great a price to pay just so that we might eat and make love and grow fat. There is no logic in asking a young man to give up his life in order that an old man might grow rich. They died that we might be free— free to live lives of honor and justice and mercy.

In all candor, and with utter shame, we must confess that for millions of Americans freedom means simply the opportunity to do what they please. That sort of freedom is not worth one life in Iwo Jima or Bataan or Korea or Vietnam. If freedom means the right of a business man to make excessive profits or a professional man to exact unjust fees, then our economic freedom is a new type of economic tyranny. Our heroic dead died in order that we might live and freely do what we *ought* to do.

Woe to you . . . hypocrites . . . you have neglected . . . justice and mercy . . . are full of extortion and rapacity (Matt. 23:23-25).

When you look at the foibles and pretenses of the human race, your own and others, you may have one of three reactions—sadness, anger, or humor—perhaps a mixture of all three. A sense of humor, the ability to laugh, is God's gift to us. Reinhold Niebuhr regards laughter as a companion of faith:

> Laughter is a sane and healthful response to the innocent foibles of men; and even to some which are not innocent. All men betray moods and affections, conceits and idiosyncrasies, which could become the source of great annoyance to us if we took them too seriously. It is better to laugh at them. . . . There is, in the laughter with which we observe and greet the foibles of others, a nice mixture of mercy and judgment, of censure and forbearance. There is judgment, therefore, in our laughter. But we also prove by the laughter that we do not take the annoyance too seriously. However, if our fellows commit a serious offense against the common good, laughter no longer avails. . . .
>
> There were those who thought that we could laugh Mussolini and Hitler out of court. . . . But laughter alone never destroys a great seat of power and authority in history. Its efficacy is limited to preserving the self-respect of the slave against the master. It does not extend to the destruction of slavery. . . .
>
> The sense of humor is even more important provisionally in dealing with our own sins than in dealing with the sins of others. . . . This means that the ability to laugh at oneself is the prelude to the sense of contrition. Laughter is the vestibule to the temple of confession. But laughter is not able to deal with the problem of the sins of the self in any ultimate way. . . . There is furthermore another dimension of genuine contrition which laughter does not contain. It is the awareness of being judged from beyond ourselves. "For me it is a small thing to be judged of men," declares St. Paul, "neither do I judge myself; for I know nothing against myself; he who judges me is the Lord." . . .
>
> The sense of humor remains healthy only when it deals with immediate issues and faces the obvious surface irrationalities. It must move toward faith or sink into despair when the ultimate issues are involved. That is why there is laughter in the vestibule of the temple, the echo of laughter in the temple itself, but only faith and prayer, and no laughter, in the holy of holies.

The kings of the earth set themselves, and the rulers take counsel together, against the Lord. . . . He who sits in the heavens laughs (Psalm 2:2, 4).

A MAN OF UNDERSTANDING June 1

Perhaps the greatest moral teacher of China, Confucius, who died in 479 B.C., left a collection of words of wisdom, many of them parallel with the biblical book of Proverbs, and some of them not unlike the words of Jesus. Here is a selection:

Someone asked Confucius, saying, "Master, what think you concerning the principle that good should be returned for evil?" The Master replied, "What then will you return for good? No: Return good for good, for evil, justice."

A disciple having asked for a rule of life in a word, the Master said, "Is not *Reciprocity* that word? What you would not others should do unto you, do not unto them."

A plausible tongue and a fascinating expression are seldom associated with true virtue.

A youth should be filial at home, respectful abroad. He should be earnest and truthful. He should overflow in love to all, but cultivate the friendship of the good. Then, whatsoever of energy may be left to him, he should devote to the improvement of his mind.

Learning without thought is labor lost. Thought without learning is intellectual death.

You! shall I teach you in what true knowledge consists? To know what you do know, and to know what you do not know—that is true knowledge.

He who offends against God has none to whom he can pray.

Riches and honors are what men desire; yet except in accordance with right they would not be enjoyed. Poverty and degradation are what men dread; yet except in accordance with right these should not be avoided.

Rare are they who prefer virtue to the pleasure of sex.

A disciple having asked for a definition of charity, the Master said, "Love one another!" Having further asked for a definition of knowledge, the Master said, "Know one another!"

Chi Wen thought thrice and then acted. The Master said, "Twice will do."

Those who know the truth are not equal to those who love it; nor those who love it to those who delight in it.

Wisdom abides in the mind of a man of understanding, but it is not known in the heart of fools. Righteousness exalts a nation, but sin is a reproach to any people (Prov. 14:33-34).

As Jesus went from village to village, more and more people trailed after him, until there were thousands. They were enrapt by his teaching and healing. After one long day they made no move to go home. Night was falling. Where would they go for food? It was then that Jesus multiplied five loaves and two fish to feed them all.

What lesson is to be drawn? Is it the fact that he performed an unprecedented miracle? He had performed greater ones. He is God the Son, "by whom all things were made." Feeding the thousands, after all, was trivial compared with creating the heavens and the earth.

A more profound lesson is that our God is a God of infinite compassion for the sick, the hungry, and the poor. Could it be that when he told his disciples that they would do greater works than he, he was telling them that within his kingdom of compassion they would carry on the feeding of the hungry and the care of the sick in ways which he had only begun?

This the church has done. There is no institution or movement in all history to rival even remotely the works of compassion that have been initiated and carried on by the Christian church. No one else in those early centuries seemed to care. It was left to Christ's followers to establish institutions for the care of orphans and widows, the poor and hungry, the sick and aged. Even in our day, in the average city, most hospitals have been begun by churches. Now that the government (shaped by the gospel quietly at work as yeast in the culture) is widely active in these tasks, churches are still the government's strongest ally to alleviate human suffering both within our land and reaching out across oceans to other lands.

I remember well at the Lutheran World Convention Assembly in Hannover in 1952, when Bishop Eivind Berggrav of Norway discussed what the church's future would be in the emerging welfare states. He declared that whatever restrictions these governments might place on the church, the church would have to insist on two rights: right to teach and preach the gospel, *and* the right to carry on works of love for the poor and the sick. These two mandates of Christ are intrinsic to the very life of the church.

Christ's kingdom is a spiritual kingdom, to be sure, but a kingdom in which the plain, ordinary, physical needs of people are taken in utter seriousness—as they were by the Lord himself!

Come, O blessed of my Father, inherit the kingdom prepared for you from the foundation of the world; for I was hungry and you gave me food . . . I was sick and you visited me (Matt. 25:34-36).

No Christian can really be satisfied with the measure of his disciple-ship. We are all haunted by falling far short. But the danger is that we still settle for a conventional, even calculating, form of discipleship. Søren Kierkegaard wrote an allegory entitled "The Tame Geese."

Suppose it was so that the geese could talk—then they had so arranged it that they also could have their religious worship, their divine service. Every Sunday they came together, and one of the ganders preached.

The essential content of the sermon was: what a lofty destiny the geese had, what a high goal the Creator (and every time this word was mentioned the geese curtsied and the ganders bowed the head) had set before the geese; by the aid of wings they could fly away to distant regions, blessed climes, where properly they were at home, for here they were only strangers.

So it was every Sunday. And as soon as the assembly broke up each waddled home to his own affairs. And then the next Sunday again to divine worship and then home again—and that was the end of it. They throve and were well-liking, became plump and delicate—and then were eaten on Martinmas Eve—and that was the end of it.

That was the end of it. For though the discourse sounded so lofty on Sunday, the geese on Monday were ready to recount to one another what befell a goose that had wanted to make serious use of the wings the Creator had given him, designed for the high goal that was proposed to him—what befell him, what a terrible death he encountered. This the geese could talk about knowingly among themselves. But, naturally, to speak about it on Sundays was unseemly; for, said they, it would then become evident that our divine worship is really only making a fool of God and of ourselves.

Among the geese there were, however, some individuals which seemed suffering and grew thin. About them it was currently said among the geese: There you see what it leads to when flying is taken seriously . . . they become thin, do not thrive, do not have the grace of God as we have who therefore become plump and delicate.

Man also has wings. . . .

Then Jesus told his disciples, "If any man would come after me, let him deny himself and take up his cross and follow me. For whoever would save his life will lose it, and whoever loses his life for my sake will find it" (Matt. 16:24-25).

The really exciting things have always been mental and spiritual. The adventures of the mind in the field of ideas and visions are far more breathtaking than the perils of the body with dragons and typhoons. It must have been thrilling for Columbus in 1492 to catch sight of land, but the really dramatic incident in his life was the moment when his mind and spirit were captured by a vision of a westward passage to the Indies. Dr. Grenfell's years on the Labrador coast constitute an epic of the unusual and unexpected, but back in his quiet student days when he resolved to seek the medical practice of greatest need, wherever that would take him, at that time, perhaps at some lonely unobserved moment, then and there the world-shaking climax came for him.

The poverty of our age reveals itself most clearly in man's furtive and futile search for excitement in some novel use of the body, a new dish or drink, a new gadget or machine, a new night spot, a new joke, a new wife or husband. Made for the stars, he worms along in stock quotations. The life that should have been of such epic sweep in ideas and dreams bogs down in the marshes of cosmetics and salary schedules.

We can escape this treadmill only by being captured by a great controlling vision and passion. And the only vision capable of lifting life to such a level is the belief that we are on earth for one towering purpose: to serve God by serving others. You are not an accident. There will never be another you. In the mind of God you are different, unique among the billions who have been born and will be born. If you miss the lines, God has no understudy waiting in the wings to take your place.

You are on earth not to collect your earnings, but to pay your debts. You are not to set out each day to defend your rights; in the strictest sense, you have no rights. Nothing that you have is essentially yours. Every capital asset you have, you have been given. Even your ambition, your industry, and your sense of duty you owe to God, and through him, to others.

There is no other great idea or vision, revolutionary enough to lift our lives from the doldrums of boredom, weariness, and futility.

Wherefore, O King Agrippa, I was not disobedient to the heavenly vision (Acts 26:19).

Before her death in 1582, St. Teresa of Avila, Spain, had reestablished the Carmelite rule and founded 17 convents and 15 monasteries. This period in Spain was marked by a remarkable flowering of spiritual life, and includes names such as John of the Cross, Luis of Granada, Ignatius Loyola, and others. St. Teresa's *The Interior Castle,* with its "seven mansions" is one of the spiritual treasures of the period. In it she speaks of prayer:

A man is directed to make a garden in a bad soil overrun with sour grasses. The Lord of the land roots out the weeds, sows seeds, and plants herbs and fruit trees. The gardner must then care for them, and water them, that they may thrive and blossom, and that the Lord may find pleasure in the garden and come to visit it. There are four ways in which the watering may be done. There is water which is drawn wearily by hand from the well. There is water drawn by the ox-wheel. . . . There is water brought in from the river, which will saturate the whole ground; and last and best there is rain from heaven.

Four sorts of prayer correspond to these. The first is a weary effort with small return; the well may run dry; the gardener then must weep. The second is internal prayer and meditation upon God; the trees will then show leaves and flower-buds. The third is love of God. The virtues then become vigorous. We converse with God face to face. The flowers open and give out fragrance. The fourth kind cannot be described in words. Then there is no more toil, and the seasons no longer change; flowers are always blowing, the fruit ripens perennially. The soul enjoys undoubting certitude; the faculties work without effort and without consciousness; the heart loves and does not know that it loves; the mind perceives, yet does not know that it perceives. If the butterfly pauses to say to itself how prettily it is flying, the shining wings fall off and it drops and dies. The life of the spirit is not our life, but the life of God within us.

Thus, when you give alms, do not sound the trumpet before you, as the hypocrites do in the synagogues and in the streets, that they may be praised by men. Truly I say to you they have their reward. But when you give alms do not let your left hand know what your right hand is doing, so that your alms may be in secret, and your Father who sees in secret will reward you (Matt. 6:2-4).

Love is not the means to an end; love is the end itself. If you use it to achieve some other end, you destroy it.

Not even God uses love to manipulate or change people. Whether we return his love, whether we are grateful for his love, whether we in turn love anyone—he keeps on loving us. This is the biblical picture of God, the God revealed in Jesus Christ.

Suppose a bee returned to the hive with a great discovery: "Man loves the bees, not because we provide him honey, nor because we pollinate his flowers. He loves us, even when we sting him." The bee was utterly wrong. We have affection for bees, if at all, chiefly because they give us honey.

But God loves us even when we hurt him, as we do with our ingratitude and willfulness. This is the staggering message of the Christian gospel.

Jesus died on a cross, not in order to save us, but because he loves us. God did not sit around speculating how best to recover us for his heavens, and finally conclude that only the spectacle of love would work. He did not decide to love, *in order* to lure us into his kingdom. If love were but his strategy, and if the strategy failed, he would stop loving.

But he doesn't stop. It is his nature to love. If love fails utterly to win us, he loves still. He has no other nature but love.

Nor does his love have any partiality. He has the same love for the prodigal who squanders his inheritance as for his brother who dutifully manages the farm, the same love for a Paul who rejoices his heart as for a Nero who breaks his heart, the same love for a St. Francis who helps people as for a Hitler who destroys people, in a sense, the same love for his lost children in hell as for his jubilant children in heaven.

God's deepest wish for us is that we may catch on to this kind of love and have it become our way of life. Only a few great souls have reached this grace in any large measure, but whenever we are able to reach out to others with no thought of gain, no purpose of changing anyone, but simply to love as we have been loved—then we touch the secret of the Kingdom.

Love your enemies and pray for those who persecute you, so that you may be sons of your Father who is in heaven; for he makes the sun rise on the evil and on the good, and sends rain on the just and on the unjust (Matt. 5:44-45).

I invited him to join our church. Thirty years earlier, as a student, I had known him as a rising young community leader. Having returned as pastor of one of the city's churches, I renewed our acquaintanceship. He now was one of the most important voices in the city, and most respected for integrity.

"I can't join your church," he said, "because I'm no longer able to believe in God as I was taught as a child." Somewhere, somehow, through the years he had lost the serenity of faith that once had been his, and doubts had taken the field. Wistfully he told me he wished that he could believe. "I would like to believe in God, but I can't. Does that make me an unbeliever?"

"Only God can answer that," I replied.

I wondered if the fact that he wanted God was evidence that God was with him? What is faith, after all, but a wish and a leap in the face of doubt? I think it was Browning who said, "This Christianity, it may be so or it may not be so, but will you have it be so if it can?"

God is never immediately in evidence, like the nose on your face. He is both the hidden one and the revealed one. Every believer clings to God in the face of swirling doubt. The Holy Spirit does give an inner assurance, "witnessing with our spirits that we are children of God," but the assurance is the kind that does not come from laboratories. When the father cried to Jesus, "I believe, help my unbelief," was he not speaking for many of us?

A man once flippantly said, "You might as well play safe and believe. If it's not true, you've lost nothing; if it is true, you've got insurance." This man misunderstood both the pathos of faith and its frightening and glorious consequences. For, after all, to put your faith in someone is to trust and to follow that someone. Life will be different.

I've always had deep sympathy for those who stand at the borders of the Kingdom wishing they could cross over. There are many such fine people in the world. How to help them remains one of the tasks of the church and of every Christian. To cross over is to find life, with its joy and peace.

The time is fulfilled, and the kingdom of God is at hand; repent, and believe in the gospel (Mark 1:15).

Blaise Pascal, born in France in 1623, is one of Christendom's great theologians and mystics. The *Pensees* consist of a mass of notes which Pascal had accumulated with the idea of writing an apologia for Christianity. The following passage is from this collection:

Man is nothing more than the weakest of all reeds, but he is a reed that can think. The whole universe need not arise in wrath to overwhelm him. A fume, a drop of water, is enough to end his life. But even should the whole universe crush him, man would still be nobler than his slayer, for he is conscious of death; and what recks the universe of its power over him? Thus, all our dignity consists in the faculty of thought. It is from that point that we must raise ourselves, not from space or time. Let us strive after right thinking. There lies the first moral principle.

It is perilous to make man aware of his affinity with the beasts unless at the same time he is made aware of his own greatness. It is perilous likewise to make him in his low estate, overconscious of his greatness. Yet more dangerous is it to leave him ignorant of either. But it is well to show him both.

Let man value himself at his true worth. Let him think well of himself, since there is in him a nature capable of goodness; but, because of the lower side of that nature, let him not think too well. Let him despise himself, because this capacity of goodness fails of its effect; but let him not despise the capacity itself for that reason. Let him both love himself, and hate; he has within him the faculty of apprehension and of happiness; but he has not truth within him, neither absolute nor all-sufficing truth.

To me they are equally blameworthy who choose to exalt man, and who choose to belittle him, and who choose only to make sport for him. Only can I approve them who pursue their quest with groans. The Stoics said, "Withdraw into yourselves, there you will find peace." But it is not so. Others say, "Go forth, and seek happiness in pastimes"; and that is not so. Evils come upon us; happiness is neither within nor without; it is in God and in ourselves.

For I know that nothing good dwells within me, that is, in my flesh. I can will what is right, but I cannot do it. For I do not do the good I want, but the evil I do not want is what I do (Rom. 7:18-19).

SWEET MELANCHOLY June 9

A strain of music, long forgotten, will do it. Suddenly something out of the past will surface, creating a mood of joy and sorrow—sorrow because it is in the past and beyond reach, joy because there was gladness in its time. One of Longfellow's verses does this for me.

> I see the lights of a village
> Gleam through the rain and the mist;
> And a feeling of sadness comes o'er me
> That my soul cannot resist.

> A feeling of sadness and longing,
> That is not akin to pain,
> And resembles sorrow only
> As the mists resemble rain.

I'm not sure why I memorized these lines, nor why they insist on pushing up into my mind at unsuspecting moments. But when they do, they lead me to my grandfather's farm a mile from my home village on a drizzly evening. I slip into a mood of melancholy, but a melancholy so pleasant that I resist having it go. My childhood and youth are wrapped up in the blurred lights of the village. Rarely do I begin to sort out events and people. The mood is rather a composite of my past, a bouquet of assorted memories. I find myself wanting to stay there, with my mind's eye resting on the lights and shadows of home.

The spell is broken if I begin an inventory of events and people—my father and mother, we six children from one to eight, milking the cow in the barn, huddling around the glowing coals of the hard-coal heater in winter, wandering to the lake with our bamboo poles in summer, church each Sunday. These, and a hundred other memories, flow together into an indistinguishable whole to give me that enchanting melancholy.

I often wonder what Longfellow's lines would do for me if my childhood had been miserable—if I had not been surrounded by caring and understanding people, if sorrows had not been cradled in love and trust, if hope had been crushed by cynicism, if the quiet ministration of the Christian church had been denied me.

The Lord is my chosen portion and my cup; thou holdest my lot. The lines have fallen for me in pleasant places; yea, I have a goodly heritage (Psalm 16:5-6).

On February 20, 1943, a Mexican farmer, Dionisio Pulido, saw a thin column of white smoke curling up snake-like from his field. As he went forward to investigate, he heard a muffled report. The column of smoke grew thicker and suddenly seemed to be driven skyward by a tremendous force. Then an earthquake! Seismographs in New York, 2250 miles away, recorded it. Leaping flames were shooting into the sky, and masses of stone, white-hot, were being hurled a thousand feet through the air.

This was the birth of a volcano, the first since 1759 in the Western hemisphere. One day life was routine in this farming village, but underneath in the bowels of the earth gigantic forces were building up that finally burst the earth's crust, demolished an area of 100 square miles, and dislocated 8000 people. Now the new volcano, Paricutin, 180 miles west of Mexico City, towers 1200 feet above the quiet countryside.

There are historians who think of the history of nations and of the world as huge, repetitious cycles, and conclude as the writer in Ecclesiastes, "What has been is what will be, and what has been done is what will be done; and there is nothing new under the sun."

Other historians see history as an ascending plateau, each successive generation inheriting the experience and wisdom of the preceding one, each rising a bit higher than its antecedents. Still others see history as a series of upheavals, each with catastrophic power, each followed by widespread changes in human life. Life runs on in uneventful order for years. Only the most perceptive can hear the rumblings underneath the surface. Then suddenly there is eruption. Old values and traditions lose their hold; governments topple; the seams that had held the fabric together weaken and tear; new shapes yet unformed are in the making. History is in disarray and disorder.

Our twentieth century has been one of upheavals. Wars and revolutions have convulsed many parts of the world. Old orders are gone and new ones in the making. The question haunts us. Are there greater catastrophes yet to come?

We dare not give way to paralysis. The earth is the Lord's. He has placed us here in charge. In selfishness and fear, we may fuel new upheavals. If they come, the Lord is still here, and he has the power to have us endure the changes and to use us to bring about a new and better day.

The nations rage, the kingdoms totter; he utters his voice, the earth melts. The Lord of hosts is with us; the God of Jacob is our refuge (Psalm 46:6-7).

For over a quarter of a century the voice of Walter A. Maier reached millions, perhaps hundreds of millions, over the *Lutheran Hour* radio. Speaking on the Lord's words from the cross, "Father, forgive them, for they know not what they do," he said:

> For whom particularly did Jesus intercede? Not for his mother . . . not for the godly women . . . not for His disciples. . . . It is easy to plead for those who love us—a mother for her son, a wife for her husband, a pastor for his flock; but here Jesus intercedes for the soldiers who are crucifying Him. Was there ever love like this? Recall, by contrast, the hatred of Tamerlane, Oriental conqueror, said to have made a pyramid of 90,000 human heads on the ruins of Baghdad. Genghis Khan killed more than 18 million human beings in China alone. Review the hatred practiced in the name of religion! . . . Yet at Calvary, Jesus, suffering in the vilest miscarriage of justice, appeals for his enemies and pleads not merely that their penalty be reduced, not that the Lord instead of striking them dead on the spot, would grant them some consideration; but by the highest, deepest, widest love even God could show, He begs that they be entirely forgiven, completely pardoned, their sins altogether removed, the charge of murder wholly canceled. . . .
>
> From that high altar where Jesus was being sacrificed as the final offering for the sins of the world, He appealed for all who had despised and rejected Him, for every sinner in the ages yet to come. Above all, however—and this is the personal message of the Lenten season, the warning and comfort of Christ's cross—He pleaded, "Father, forgive them," because He was thinking of you and your transgressions, because even the agony of the crucifixion could not make Him forfeit you nor keep Him from beseeching His Father to remove your iniquities. . . .
>
> Christ did far more than pray for you. In his matchless mercy and endless grace He died to seal your pardon with His blood. Amazing grace: the sinless Savior crucified for sin-filled mankind; the pure and holy Redeemer suffering for an impure and vicious race; the glorious Son of God offered as a living and dying sacrifice for all the selfish sons of men; the almighty Lord of lords slain for His depraved, degenerate creatures; Jesus Christ delivered into death for you!

And Jesus said, "Father, forgive them; for they know not what they do" (Luke 23:34).

It's possible to be a cynic and be thankful to no one. "Why should I be grateful to my folks; I didn't ask to be born, and they've had as much pleasure from me as I have from them." "Why should I be grateful for my country? Don't I pay taxes? And how about the mess the country makes of corruption, crime, and war?" In this frame of mind, the cynic would be hard-pressed to find anything to be thankful for.

One thing is sure: such a person would be hard to live with. You wouldn't want to go fishing with him, or have him marry your daughter.

He's in the minority, fortunately. Most people do feel gratitude, at least now and then. And there are those rather remarkable people whose life-tone is one of gratitude. Without being naive, or blind to the wretchedness of life, they don't waste their energies on complaining and griping, but keep their eyes on the good things of life. One may not be as adept at this as the little old grandmother who at the Thanksgiving table took her turn in singling out one thing for which she was grateful. With a twinkle in her eye, she said, "I'm thankful that the two teeth I have left meet."

It's possible—perhaps—to be thankful without being thankful to anyone in particular. More than likely, however, we will want *someone* to thank. It isn't enough to enjoy the gift; we turn to thank the giver. If at Christmastime you receive a package, but there's no card, even before you open the box you search to find a clue to the giver. If you find none, the gift loses some of its charm, and you're haunted. "Who thought enough of me to give me this?"

I wish I had memorized the lines of a bit of verse, "The Atheist's Wail." I have searched in vain for it. Its lines were something like this: "I can stand to writhe on a bed of pain, and I steel myself, and I don't need God. I can stand at the open grave of a loved one, and steel myself, and I don't need God. But when the autumn leaves are in full color, and the sun is shining brightly, and I'm walking through the woods with my beloved's hand in mine, it's a terrible thing not to have anyone to thank."

It *is* a terrible thing not to have anyone to thank!

I will give thanks to the Lord with my whole heart; I will tell of all thy wonderful deeds. I will be glad and exult in thee, I will sing praise to thy name, O Most High (Psalm 9:1-2).

I quote from the pen of Dr. Martin L. Kretzmann, who had a long and distinguished career as a missionary leader:

"Servants' Entrance." Those were the words on a simple piece of metal tacked to a door. But this door opened from the inside of an urban church directly to the sidewalks of the city. It was the last message the worshipers saw when they left the building.

It would take a lifetime of reflection and study to fathom the meaning and purpose of those two words in that particular place. But, just for starters . . .

I am reminded that "the Son of Man came to serve, not to be served." "Who would be great among you must be your servant." "He took the form of a servant." "It is enough for the servant to be like his master."

The words mark the death of triumphalism. I enter the world to serve, not succeed. I have no personal successes to offer, no panoply of self-glory, no self-righteousness, nothing deserved. Even my servanthood is a gift of grace alone.

"Servants' Entrance." This is a starting point—no, the *heart*—of a theology of the church. If the reality of the church is in being the Body of Christ, then the Body is true to its nature only when it is ready to lose its life for the sake of the world, as he did.

Can an institution renounce self-preservation as a goal and diligently seek the kind of self-effacement characteristic of good servants? If our theology of the church starts from this point, questions regarding who will be first and greatest will not bother us much. Maybe we will even learn to laugh again about things that caused endless controversy among the servants.

"Servants' Entrance." This is also a starting point for a theology of the world. When Christ's body leaves the church by that exit, it affirms the reality of the world and His concern for everything that goes on there. This isn't easy for us who have been programmed to think that religion is exercised within the building walls. But an entrance is more than an exit.

Have this mind among yourselves, which you have in Christ Jesus, who, though he was in the form of God, . . . emptied himself, taking the form of a servant, being born in the likeness of men (Phil. 2:5-7).

Of all the leaders of the early church, St. Augustine, Bishop of Hippo in Africa until his death in A.D. 430, has most influenced the thought of Christendom. His *Confessions* and *The City of God* have been determinative in every century. It is in his *Confesions* that he reveals his struggle from a life of sin to a life with God. One day he had been interrupted from his reading in one of the epistles of Paul when he heard a voice saying, "Take up and read." Augustine says:

> I snatched it up, opened it, and read in silence the chapter on which my eye first fell: "Not in rioting and drunkenness, not in chambering and impurities, not in strife and envying: but put you on the Lord Jesus Christ, and make no provision for the flesh, in its concupiscence." No further wished I to read, nor was there need to do so. Instantly, in truth at the end of this sentence, as if before a peaceful light streaming into my heart, all dark shadows of doubt fled away.

The *Confessions* contain many insights into the inner life of this man, among them the following:

> You have made us for yourself, O Lord, and our heart is restless until it rests in you.
> Too narrow is the house of my soul for you to enter into it: let it be enlarged by you. It lies in ruins; build it up again.
> Too late have I loved you, O Beauty so ancient and so new, too late have I loved you. Behold, you were within me while I was outside; it was there that I sought you, and rushed headlong upon these things of beauty which you have made. You were with me, but I was not with you. They kept me far from you, those fair things which, if they were not in you, would not exist at all. You have called to me and have cried out, and have shattered my deafness. You have blazed forth with light . . . and have put my blindness to flight. . . . I have tasted you and I hunger and thirst after you. You have touched me, and I have burned for your peace.

As a hart longs for flowing streams, so longs my soul for thee, O God. My soul thirsts for God, for the living God. When shall I come and behold the face of God? (Psalm 42:1-2).

MOTIVES AND ENDS June 15

If your reason for doing something is unworthy, does that make the results bad? Obviously not. If I shovel the snow off my invalid neighbor's sidewalk because I want his vote in the next election, my motive may be less than praiseworthy, but his clean sidewalk is good. If a man pays his workers well, if he produces a good commodity, and if he sells it for a fair price (in order to build up a profitable business), quite apart from his motives, the results are good.

Moreover, even the most noble motive may have a mixture of something less noble. One might ask, has a person ever done a purely unselfish act? Perhaps. If you see someone drowning, and without a single thought to whether he's a stranger, enemy, or friend, you plunge in to rescue him, you come near the ultimate selfless act. Even so, the act may later be tarnished by the pride which people's praise creates.

I'm not sure that the Lord bothers much with pure motives. "Go, help your enemy," he said. "You may not like to, but that's beside the point. He's in trouble, help him." The Lord may add, "Remember, I gave my life for you—unattractive as you are."

To be sure, God works to purify our motives, so that what we do will have a touch of selfless service. But he's got stubborn stuff on his hands. We will be lured into finding ways to use "selfless" acts to feed our egos, to enhance our pride. I am a preacher. To preach the gospel is to point beyond myself to the One who should have all the glory. In all frankness, however, I must admit that to have a hundred or a thousand people sitting rapt before me, listening to me, does fuel my sense of importance. When I say, "I like to preach," do I describe a pure motive? However, if I do succeed in exalting my Lord, is this not a laudable end? And why worry too much about sorting out the mixed bag of motives?

A woman who devoted her life to rescuing "fallen girls," discovered during psychological analysis, that her dynamic motive was sexual curiosity. She then felt that she must give up her work. But if she had done so, sexual curiosity would not have ceased to plague her, and she might have found a less socially valuable outlet. Mental health probably lies in recognizing as well as we can—or need to—*all* our motives, and directing them to an end which is of help to others.

If your enemy is hungry, feed him; if he is thirsty, give him drink (Rom. 12:20).

For over a quarter of a century president of Augsburg College, then professor of theology at Luther Seminary, Bernhard Christensen has had the soul of the mystic and poet. Though plagued for years by debilitating arthritis, he has remained alive to the cultural movements of our time and has been a warm and understanding friend of people from all walks of life. In his book, *The Inward Pilgrimage,* he surveys the spiritual classics of the centuries, from Augustine and St. Francis to Evelyn Underhill and Bonhoeffer. I quote from the preface:

"There is a river whose streams make glad the city of God." This beautiful metaphor from Psalm 46 suggests the place of the spiritual classics in the life of the Christian church. . . . Every age of the church has produced examples of treasures of spirituality. With the passage of time, however, and with the rise of divisions within the church, even some of the finest of the classics have come to be neglected. . . . If it is a good thing to cultivate the fellowship of contemporary spiritual Christians, it is an equal enrichment, by means of the printed page, to "walk through the centuries" in the company of good friends of God.

Such a walk leads inevitably to a vision of the manifold variety of spiritual experience. As the colors of one spectrum of light can blend into numberless patterns of beauty, so the one light of faith reveals itself in a multitude of varying life-patterns, all beautiful. The gifts and graces of the Spirit have come to expression in widely different forms in different ages of the church, but an essential unity pervades them all. The piety of an English Baptist differs from that of a Scandinavian Lutheran; an American Quaker's prayer life will not be the same as that of a Spanish Catholic. Yet the widely divergent patterns of faith all reflect the one life in Christ. And learning to know the spiritual life as it has been lived among men and women of other cultures and other churches can add immeasurably to our own inner pilgrimage.

There is a river whose streams make glad the city of God, the holy habitation of the Most High (Psalm 46:4).

It isn't true that nature is the healer. When in August 1960 our son was killed and could not join us at the lake, the pine and the birch which should have been the canopy for our tryst only haunted me with his absence. Something deeper than nature had to speak to my soul.

All the poets notwithstanding, birds and sky and hills say nothing about the love of God. The galaxies that whirl in their orbits, the migration of birds and fish, the rising and the setting of the sun—all this speaks of order, amazing order, but the voice of love and mercy is muted.

During the 1930s in the Dakotas, when year after year the crops were burned in the fields, no farmer in his right mind would have wakened to another unclouded sky and rhapsodized, "God is good; he lets the sun shine."

If there are sins to be forgiven, guilts to be eased, hopes to be revived, inner conflicts to be resolved, a source other than nature will need to be found. In his great anguish, Job cried, "Where shall wisdom be found and where is the place of understanding?" The deep said, "It is not in me," and the sea said, "It is not with me."

It is nature's God who heals. While he reveals his majesty and power and order through nature, he reveals his love supremely in his Son, Jesus Christ. If we dismiss Christ as only another in the long parade of teachers and martyrs, we will be without the one penetrating clue to God as a God of love.

Finding a God of infinite mercy in the face of Jesus, we can then see signs of his love in the myriad voices of nature. Even so, its voice will be garbled. There is "tooth and claw"; the lion and the lamb do not lie down together. Out of the heavens that declare the glory of God come the tornado, the typhoon, the blizzard. The gentle rains swell into floods and sweep property and life to destruction.

To be sure, we can thank God for springtime and harvest, for forests that become houses to give us shelter. Out of his love, he has given us nature as a home. But to discover his love, we peer above and beyond nature to find a God who died on a cross for us. Nothing in all nature, said Paul, can separate us from the love of God which is in Christ Jesus.

I lift up my eyes to the hills. From whence does my help come? My help comes from the Lord, who made heaven and earth (Psalm 121:1-2).

It was in 1925, before the day of "miracle drugs," and I was working for my board and room at Moe Hospital in Sioux Falls, a small hospital-clinic. A boy of 12 had been brought in, his leg riddled with shotgun pellets. Gangrene had set in. I'll never forget the face of the father as the doctor gave his grim counsel. "Either we remove the leg or he will die." The father wanted neither option. He didn't want his boy to go through life with one leg, and he did not want his boy to die.

Life is full of choices that have to be made between alternatives that we don't want. We believe that there is a right and a wrong, but sometimes, in a given situation, the lines between them are blurred. A choice may not be altogether right, or altogether wrong.

No story in the Bible is filled with such pathos of choice as when God ordered Abraham to sacrifice his son Isaac. Abraham did not want to disobey God; he did not want to kill his son. He had to choose. We may never quite understand God putting Abraham to such a test. Every father faces some such pain when his son is drafted into the army during wartime. He wants his son to be a loyal citizen and obey his government; he does not want his son to be killed.

In less dramatic situations, parents often have to choose between letting their teenage child do something, or not. What the child wants to do is full of risk, risk of character and perhaps life. Shall they say no, and stifle the child's growing independence, or shall they say yes, and risk the perils?

A friend applies for a job and asks you to provide recommendations. You know the pressures of his home situation made him fail his last job, and you fear that if you include this information, he won't get the job. Should you, or should you not? A house is on fire. The husband can save himself, but he cannot possibly save his invalid wife. She begs him not to leave her. Should he stay and die with her?

We are left without absolutes, except in broad sweeping principles. When you have marshaled all the wisdom you can and have siphoned off as much self-interest as possible and you make the choice with every good intention, you may still have to be tentative enough to add a little prayer, "Forgive me, Lord, if I have misjudged what you wanted me to do." He forgives!

Thou hast commanded thy precepts to be kept diligently. O that my ways may be steadfast in keeping thy statutes! (Psalm 119:4-5).

I'M AFRAID TO MEET GOD June 19

My friend called me to ask if I could drop by. When I came, he said, "Al, I've just been to my doctor. I have cancer, and he tells me I have six months. I'm not afraid to die, but I'm afraid to meet God, and you'll have to help me." He told me that only the three of us should know, the doctor, he and I. He lived alone.

When I tried to tell him how God dealt with us in mercy, how Jesus had taken our sins to himself, and how we, in faith, could appear before God as if we had never sinned, he became indignant. Trained as a jurist, he said, "Al, that's not fair. It isn't even decent. We would never deal with wrongs and offenses in the lowest court of the land in this shabby way. I've never believed in purgatory, but I know God has to clean me up before he can take me."

That the guilty should get off scot free offended his sense of justice, and to have the penalty of the guilty leveled against the innocent (Jesus Christ) was intolerable. He said, "The whole system of law is destroyed, and we are left with moral anarchy."

I had not thought of the "offense of the gospel" precisely in those terms before. Through the juridical mind of my friend I understood better. It dawned on me that the law is never offensive. Everyone knows that the guilty should be punished and the innocent acquitted. This makes sense the world over. But that the innocent should suffer, and the guilty be set free—this is to destroy all law and order. To be set free from the law, as Paul says we are, is this not to bring on utter chaos?

I will always be thankful to my friend for helping me see that grace is such a radical departure from law. I think I understand better why there had to be a cross. The sins of men could not be glossed over by an indulgent Grandfather-God, nor could they be pushed aside in the high court as midemeanors. Someone had to be given a sentence. That Jesus took the sentence for us and paid the just penalty of the court for us—this violates every canon of justice and decency. But that's the way of the gospel.

And when this great truth dawned for my friend, it was a new day!

Likewise, my brethren, you have died to the law through the body of Christ, so that you may belong to another, to him who has been raised from the dead in order that we may bear fruit for God. . . . But now we are discharged from the law, dead to that which held us captive, so that we serve not under the old written code but in the new life of the Spirit (Rom. 7:4-6).

Whenever I preach in Singsaas, my grandparents' church on the Minnesota-South Dakota border, my eye wanders through the window to see the gravestones nestled around the church with its white spire pointed heavenward. Sleeping there are five of my great-grandparents, my four grandparents, many uncles and aunts and cousins. In another prairie cemetery a few miles away my parents and our son rest side by side.

There have been many changes since 1870 when the immigrants established their church. My grandparents' homesteads are in the hands of other farmers, and the grandchildren are scattered. The only piece of this earth that the family now occupies is the graveyard. I find nothing melancholy about having them there. Here the rich past and the promise of a glorious resurrection come together.

When my cousin's son at 17 was killed, his parents, remembering a chance remark he had once made about resting in the Pacific, arranged a service at sea and had his ashes dropped into the great waters. I remembered that Mahatma Gandhi had asked that his ashes be given to the life-giving Ganges of his land, and that Jawaharlal Nehru had ordered his to be taken into an airplane and scattered across his beloved India. I find nothing distasteful, but even something beautiful, about such expansive resting places.

But I'm glad I can wander around the graveyards of my family. My grandchildren love to go from marker to marker, listen to the recollections and legends I have to tell about their forebears, and be carried back into the roots of their histories. And while I don't then preach a sermon on the resurrection, I know their young minds move from these dead to the celebrated company that awaits them.

Rarely now are people allowed to know death at first hand. No longer does a family live with the labored breathing of death in the next bedroom; no longer do the dead lie in state in the living room; rarely does a whole community assemble for the funeral. So death, such an integral part of life, is smuggled out and hidden from view.

At Singsaas, the cemetery's sober reminder that death is real is matched by the pulpit's clarion word of a resurrection.

But we would not have you ignorant, brethren, concerning those who are asleep, that you may not grieve as others do who have no hope. For since we believe that Jesus died and rose again, even so, through Jesus, God will bring with him those who have fallen asleep (1 Thess. 4:13-14).

For 300 years the early church was persecuted. Pagan governments feared the strange revolutionary power of this new faith. It wasn't until Emperor Constantine in the 4th century made it virtually the religion of the state, with protection and patronage, that persecution ceased.

The 20th century has again seen the spectacle of the state fearing the church and persecuting it. Hitler's Nazi state did it. Russian Communism tries either to eliminate it or emasculate it. Albert Einstein paid high tribute to Christianity as the only power that effectively protested the brutalities of Nazi Germany.

Søren Kierkegaard found fault with the 18th century church in Denmark for being too friendly and accommodating to the prevailing culture and values of the state, and no longer deserving persecution. In all fairness, the church in every century, ours included, is uneasy over this charge, and vigilant that it be not so. Here are Kierkegaard's words:

> Take a picture. When a cabman, for example, sees a perfectly splendid horse, only 5 years old and without blemish, the very ideal of what a horse should be, a fiery, snorting steed such as never before was seen—than says the cabman, "No, that's a horse I can't bid on, nor can I afford to pay for it, and even if I could, it wouldn't be suitable for my use." But when some halfscore years have gone by, when that splendid horse is now spavined and lame, etc., then the cabman says, "Now I can bid on it, now I can pay for it, and I can get so much use out of it, or what is left of it, that I can really take pleasure in spending a little to feed it."

> So it is with the State and Christianity. With the proud air Christianity had when it first entered the world—"No," every state might say, "that religion I cannot buy; and not only that, but I will say, Good Lord deliver me from buying that religion, it would be certain ruin to me." But then as Christianity in the course of some centuries had become spavined, chest-foundered, bungled, and generally made a mess of, then said the State, "Yes, now I can bid for it; and with my cunning I perceive very well that I can have so much use and profit out of it that I can really take pleasure in spending a little to polish it up a bit."

If you were of the world, the world would love its own; but because you are not of the world, but I chose you out of the world, therefore the world hates you. . . . If they persecuted me, they will persecute you (John 15:19-20).

In James Russell Lowell's poem, *The Vision of Sir Launfal,* the knight rides forth with high purpose in search of the Holy Grail, the legendary cup of the first Lord's Supper. At the castle gate is a beggar, and with revulsion tosses him a coin. Years later, after an unsuccessful search through many countries and many years, Sir Launfal returns, poor and weary. At the gate is the same beggar. A surge of compassion sweeps through Sir Launfal, and he shares with the beggar his last crust of bread. Then he hears a voice, "softer than silence":

> Lo, it is I, be not afraid!
> In many climes, without avail,
> Thou hast spent thy life for the Holy Grail;
> Behold, it is here—this cup which thou
> Didst fill at the streamlet for Me but now;
> This crust is My body broken for thee,
> This water His blood that died on the tree;
> The Holy Supper is kept, indeed,
> In whatso we share with another's need;
> Not what we give, but what we share,
> For the gift without the giver is bare;
> Who gives himself with his alms feeds three,
> Himself, his hungering neighbor, and Me.

What is a gift without the giver? Well, you say, it is something after all. If every day you were to receive $50 in the mail, month after month, year after year, and never know who sent it, you could still use the money. But you would be missing a great deal, you would be haunted by not knowing the giver. How could you thank anyone? Moreover, what sort of strange person would be so guarded as to give gifts and withhold himself?

All life is a gift. Day after day, year after year, we accept our hearts and brains, eyes and ears, the world of color and sound, our opportunities and earnings, often as if God were not there, and therefore with no one to thank. Remember too, that he gives himself, supremely in Christ and the cross. If we forget that, we may in turn be led to give gifts, but without ever really giving ourselves. And the gift without the giver is bare!

For the Son of man also came not to be served but to serve, and to give his life as a ransom for many (Mark 10:45).

On the farm we had to milk the cows even on Sunday—twice in fact. But the day was set aside. Work was minimal. An aura of reverence pervaded the day. We did not pray all day, but God hovered over it, giving us rest from the tedium of the week. And the church bells were heard across the prairies, summoning us to assemble for thanksgiving.

Our complex industrial society has robbed us of the enchantment of this day. Not altogether, however. There is respite from routine. There are visits to friends and family. There is recreation.

Leisure and play, healing as they are, may in themselves become destructive. We may have to return from an exhausting weekend to find rest in routine again. And what is worse, the preoccupation with recreation may distract us from any thought of God.

One historian has said that the old Germany was destroyed by Hitler when he initiated his Sunday programs for youth, taking them away from the churches. Disobedience to the commandment, "Remember the Sabbath day, to keep it holy," changed the character of the nation. If God's day can be wiped out, God can be forgotten.

It will take individual and personal disciplines for us to recover Sunday. It may be quite futile to roll back to the day when all stores were closed, all tractors silent, whole communities finding their way to churches, traffic on the highways at a minimum. The best we can do is to resist the tempo by self-discipline. Most important, certainly for people who profess faith in God, is to find our way to a church for worship. Other disciplines may be optional. In my childhood community, some practices that should have been optional became law. We were not to play ball on Sunday, nor dance, nor attend a theater, nor sing songs other than hymns. Religion was a somber affair, and mirth was to be relegated to the other six days of the week.

In one of my churches was a man who had not missed a Sunday service in 32 years. Why this self-imposed discipline? Certainly not because church services were always so edifying. And not because he feared that God would punish him for any lapse. The reason was quite clear: he had resolved that he ought to set aside at least an hour a week to thank God in company with others who gathered to thank him.

When someone says, "I feel better when I've been to church," don't dismiss him as a romantic or a fanatic. He may very well be on to something profoundly great!

Remember the Sabbath day, to keep it holy (Exod. 20:8).

Shakespeare has his Hamlet reflect on the nature of man:

What a piece of work is man! How noble in reason! how infinite in faculties! in form and moving, how express and admirable! in action, how like an angel! in apprehension, how like a god! the beauty of the world! the paragon of animals! And yet, to me, what is this quintessence of dust?

These are words uttered long before scientific man had staged his spectacular display of knowledge and power. Don't we now, far more than in an earlier day, have a right to strut? After all, do we not fly like birds, fling our voices around the world in seconds, burst the boundaries of space to explore the moon and planets? What mighty works indeed!

Even so, they are trivial sideshows compared to the billions of wheeling stars, the rising and the setting of the sun, the fabulous architecture of an insect. The big tent is still God's show.

We are created in the image of God, to be his companions and, if not co-creators, at least partners in this universe. All the galaxies put together cannot rival the wonder of man himself. This universe is but the stage on which God and man play out an eternal drama.

And this drama has to do with our heart and spirit. Can we be like God in justice, in mercy, in charity, in righteousness? Can we be shaped up to take our place in the eternal kingdom?

We have been dwarfed by the stars. Are we now also dwarfed by our technological achievements? Is the airplane more wonderful than the people who designed it and the pilots that guide it through the sky? Is the computer more fascinating than the minds that conceived it? Has the stage become more interesting, and even more important, than the players?

When death comes, we are done with the planet. The brief interlude of threescore years and ten is over. Now we shift scenes. We go on to the next act in the drama. God and we are not done. His mighty acts— the maneuvers to win us and to keep us forever—will never end.

Yet, thou hast made him little less than God (Psalm 8:5).

There is a vast difference between freedom to do willy-nilly what one *wants* to do and freedom to do what one *ought* to do. In fact, freedom to do what one wants to do is not freedom at all, but yielding to the variables of our impulses. To do what one ought to do is freedom within the structure of law—or the will of God. Often this appears simply as enduring what must be or what ought to be.

In a charming story about Father Andrea, Pearl Buck has the missionary-priest speaking to his class:

"My sons, I will tell you a thing. You think, when you are children, that you will break away from the bondage of your parents and that when you go to school you will be free of them. In school you dream of manhood, when there will be no more teachers for you to obey. But you can never be free! When your immortal souls took on flesh, they became even as the Son of Man was—bound. No man is free—we are not free of one another—we can never be free of God.

"The thing is, not to cry futilely after freedom, but to discover cheerfully how to bear the burden of bondage upon us. Even the stars in heaven are not free. They too must obey the paths of order in law, lest by their wantonness they wreck the universe. You have seen the shooting stars in the sky in summer. They seem beautiful in freedom, a burst of light and splendor against the clouds. But their end is destruction and darkness. It is the stars marching steadily on in their appointed ways which endure to the end."

The story ends with one of the boys, years later as a revolutionist, confronting his old teacher with a cocked gun.

"We are revolutionists," he cried. "We have come to set everyone free!"

"Set everyone free?" said Father Andrea slowly, smiling a little. He stooped to pick up his cross from the dust.

But before his hand could touch that cross, the boy's finger moved spasmodically upon the trigger, and there was a sharp report, and Father Andrea fell upon the ground, dead.

He who looks into the perfect law, the law of liberty, and perseveres, being no hearer that forgets, but a doer that acts, he shall be blessed in his doing (James 1:25).

If you are a mother and a professional woman, what keeps you going? Why do you work hard? What really are your goals? You may think of professional goals, like excellence of performance, acceptance by your peers, advancement. If one day, while in the office, a telephone call tells you that your husband and children have been killed in an accident, suddenly you realize that you have been thinking of secondary goals. It was they, those you love, their future and welfare, that gave even your professional goals their primary meaning. You had been living for them.

Most of us are far more attached to, and reliant on, family and friends than we know. This is as it should be. But family and friends may also be too small a group.

We have all known families that are tightly knit, that love one another, indulge one another, and have only casual interest in others. They turn in on themselves; they are too tightly knit. As a family they slip into a selfishness that ultimately robs the family itself of merriment and joy. Family selfishness can be as destructive as individual selfishness.

We have also known people, unmarried or without children, who have gathered into their orbit an expansive "family" of friends to whom they give their affection and concern.

We belong first and eternally to the family of God, which means all people. God put us into the smaller family (father, mother, children) as a laboratory to learn the lessons of love which then would equip us for living in the larger family.

It is exhilarating to meet a family, fond of each other, who have been set free for the larger family. The children make friends with each other easily; father and mother are involved in a net-work of activity touching the lives of a host of people; conversation around the table roams a world of interesting people and events. Nor is it curiosity alone that propels them into the lives of others, but rather an extension of the compassion they have learned in the schoolroom of their own home.

The setting of Jesus' life was not a cozy circle around Joseph and Mary, good as that must have been, but a multitude of people who discovered in him a brother and friend. We are of that multitude, and he invites us to join him, not in rejecting our smaller families, but in opening the doors to let all sorts of people, people in need and people not in need, across the threshold of our hearts. When we do, we will discover a new fulness.

For this reason I bow my knees before the Father, from whom every family in heaven and on earth is named (Eph. 3:14-15).

On the wall of one of the catacombs, the burial tunnels under the city of Rome, is the faint inscription of a man with a cross, and underneath are these words, written no doubt in derision and scorn, "Alexos worships the Christ." Gone now is the glory that was Greece, the splendor that was Rome. Forever stilled are the marching feet of Caesar's columns. But the Christ whom Alexos worshiped is enthroned in the hearts of millions of people, and his cross crowns thousands of stately cathedrals and village chapels. This Jesus is the one unique figure in all history. He is God the Son, come to earth to be the atonement for the sins of the world.

It is because of this that he could say in truth, "I am the way." It is in him that life for us has meaning here in time, and a glory hereafter in eternity. Neither theologies, philosophies, nor ideologies have the power to give us that.

Ideas do have persuasive powers. The teachings of Karl Marx, for instance, grew legs and led a whole people into revolution. For us, the idea that representative government is the best instrument for giving freedom and opportunity to a maximum number of citizens has been a guiding force.

Ideologies, however, do not control us as profoundly as do people. A man does not become a good husband and father by believing in monogamy and by understanding the sociological importance of the family. *People* make him a good father—a wife and children whom he loves and who love him and count on him.

As Christians we may know the church's doctrines and be persuaded that no teaching about life and the universe can compare with Christianity. Deep down, however, we know that behind whatever we believe *about* the faith, there is the magnetic, commanding, and comforting person of its Lord, Jesus Christ. We are drawn to him, as to no ideology or theology. If someone asks us, "What is the way of the Christian?" we really have but one answer, "The way is Christ himself." We are not saved by embracing an idea; we are saved by Christ.

Attached to him, I become attached to his church and to the people he died to redeem—all people. I can sing "My church, my church, my dear old church, my fathers' and my own," with full heart. But it is Jesus himself, God come into view, with his tenderness and strength, with the love that drove him to the cross for you and me—it is Jesus that is the "way," the fountain head of all other worthy loves.

There is no other name under heaven given among men by which we must be saved (Acts 4:12).

To become aware of the love of God, the kind of love that dies for those he loves, is to feel one's own unworthiness. A sense of unworthiness in turn leads to sorrow over being unworthy, or repentance, which in turn points to the central passion of God's love—to forgive our sins and to claim us as his own. Forgiveness of sins, then, becomes God's most eloquent language of his love for us, and that which provides us radical healing.

Søren Kierkegaard speaks of the forgiveness of sins:

> Just as the first expression of a true and deep experience of human love is the feeling of one's own personal unworthiness, so the longing after the forgiveness of sins is the evident sign that a man loves God. But no man by himself can hit upon the thought that God loves him. It must be proclaimed to man. This is the Gospel, Revelation. But just because no man of himself can hit upon the thought that God loves him, just for this reason can no man of himself conceive how great a sinner he is. The Augsburg Confession consistently teaches that it must be revealed to a man how great a sinner he is. For without a divine scale to measure with no one is the great sinner (that he is only . . . before God).

> But both sides correspond to one another: when a man does not conceive how great a sinner he is, he cannot love God; and when (in response to the proclamation how highly God loves him) he does not love God, he cannot conceive how great a sinner he is. The inwardness of the consciousness of sin is the passion of love. For it is true that the Law makes one a sinner—but love makes one a far greater sinner. It is true that one who fears God and trembles feels himself a sinner, but he who truly loves feels himself a still greater sinner. . . .

> Essentially this is the everlasting comforting thing about the doctrine of the forgiveness of sins: Thou shalt believe it. For when the anxious conscience begins to employ itself with heavy thoughts and it seems to one as if in all eternity it would be impossible to forget— then the word is, Thou shalt forget, thou shalt stop thinking about thy sin, thou hast not only a right to stop . . . no, thou shalt forget, for thou shalt believe that thy sin is forgiven.

For the law of the Spirit of life in Christ Jesus has set me free from the law of sin and death (Rom. 8:2).

Is there any institution that can take the place of the church? If it fails, who will pick up its mission for the world?

From the time of Christ, the church has been commissioned to tell the story of God. Its mission is to bring man into responsible and grateful fellowship with God. Its task is to put man under the command of God and to nestle him in the care of God. Neither government nor labor unions nor any other institution in society is dedicated to this task. If the church does not do it, it will not be done.

Moreover, what institution so singularly champions the qualities of kindness and justice and righteousness? If man's relation with man are to be ruled by mercy, where but from the Word of God is the powerful imperative for mercy to come? In the long history of man we find little evidence that nations treat nations in mercy. Man is pitted against man, tribe against tribe, race against race—usually in a selfish and often ruthless pursuit of advantage and gain.

Into this callous struggle the gospel of our Lord comes to turn man from his indifference and greed to a compassionate concern for the needs and rights of his brothers. The gospel is the story of God's way. God created man to live with him and to live in love with one another. He sent his only Son, Jesus Christ, to die on a cross for the sins of men. This he did, not for gain but out of a radical and strange love for man. He counted on this story to change the hearts of men and to change the structures of society.

The year 1787 is a watershed for the church's responsibility. For 13 centuries, ever since Emperors Constantine and Theodosius made Christianity the religion of the Roman state, in almost every European country the king, or queen, or emperor (the state) had assumed responsibility for having the faith taught to the people. With the adoption of the U.S. constitution, the state set the church free from governmental control, support, and responsibility. Now it has become clearly up to the church alone to assume responsibility for the faith. We dare not fail our Lord or his children. With the approval or disapproval of the state, with its support or against its opposition, we pick up the original commission, "Go therefore and make disciples of all nations."

Then it seemed good to the apostles and the elders, with the whole church, to choose men from among the brethren and send them to Antioch with Paul and Barnabas (Acts 15:22).

John Steinbeck, in his book, *Travels with Charlie,* tells of drifting into a Vermont church one Sunday morning:

> The service did my heart and I hope my soul some good. It had been long since I had heard such an approach. It is our practice now, at least in the large cities, to find from our psychiatric priesthood that our sins aren't really sins at all but accidents set in motion by forces beyond our control. There was no such nonsense in this church. The minister, a man of iron with tool-steel eyes and a delivery like a pneumatic drill, opened up with prayer and reassured us that we were a pretty sorry lot. And he was right. We didn't amount to much to start with, and due to our own tawdry efforts we had been slipping ever since. Then, having softened us up, he went into a glorious sermon, a fire-and-brimstone sermon. Having proved that we, or perhaps only I, were no damn good, he painted with cool certainty what was likely to happen to us if we didn't make some basic reorganizations for which he didn't hold out much hope. He spoke of hell as an expert, not the mush-mush hell of these soft days, but a well-stoked, white-hot hell served by technicians of the first order. . . . I began to feel good all over. For some years now God has been a pal to us, practicing togetherness, and that causes the same emptiness a father does playing softball with his son. But this Vermont God cared enough about me . . . to put my sins in a new perspective. Whereas they had been small and mean and nasty and best forgotten, this minister gave them some size and bloom and dignity. I hadn't been thinking very well of myself for some years, but if my sins had this dimension there was some pride left. I wasn't a naughty child but a first-rate sinner, and I was going to catch it. I felt so revived in spirit that I put five dollars in the plate, and afterward, in front of the church shook hands warmly with the minister and as many of the congregation as I could.

If we confess our sins, he is faithful and just, and will forgive our sins and cleanse us from all unrighteousness. If we say we have not sinned, we make him a liar, and his word is not in us (1 John 1:9-10).

THE WORLD OF ENDLESS FASCINATION

In the world of things the extraordinary quickly becomes the commonplace. It is only the world of spirit that has the power to continue in mystery and fascination. I can remember the first automobile that came to our town, the first airplane I saw at a county fair, the first faint sounds from a radio. The first time I flew in a jet, from Chicago to Los Angeles, I was exhilarated with our torpedo rise into the sky, but in a short time I fell asleep. I concluded that my grandfather would have been as excited about a new horse. After we broke into space and reached the moon, space flights were hardly mentioned in the press. I take the miracle of the computer for granted every time I am at an airport or a bank. Even the terrifying bomb I'm able to push back somewhere into the commonplace.

There *is* a world far more fascinating. That world is the kingdom of God. It can intersect, penetrate, invade, permeate everything we see and touch—and glorify it, if we will but let it. We can block it out of our consciousness. We can escape it altogether. God has given us the power to close the door or to let it swing open. We can remain blind and see no form. We can remain color-blind and see no color. We can live within the narrow walls of touch and measurement, or we can invite God to give us the gift of faith and have an incredibly rich world open to us.

We were created for both worlds. We can love the winds that sing in the treetops. We can love the lavish hues of a prairie sunset. We can love the soft touch of a grandchild's hand. A beautiful world yields its riches to our eyes, ears, and hands. Even the roar of the turbine may cheer us with the awareness of what man's science has achieved.

But there is another, a more fascinating world, beyond our eyes and ears. There is a God we have never seen or touched or heard. He has established a kingdom in our midst, and, through Christ, has given us the right to enter. We face this world with awe and wonder. Its mysteries stagger the imagination.

This world comes to us principally through the Bible. It tells of a God who in love created us, who in love redeemed us, who in love holds us fast, who in love will usher us at last into his eternal kingdom. In this story the Holy Spirit lures us into this altogether fascinating world. Be glad we can be citizens of both worlds.

He has delivered us from the dominion of darkness and transferred us to the kingdom of his beloved Son, in whom we have redemption, the forgiveness of sins (Col. 1:13-14).

The church has two mandates. It is to bring the world into the church, and it is to bring the church into the world. It gathers, and it scatters. It is a rendezvous with God; it is an army in battle for God. It is not *of* the world, but it is *in* the world.

It has a triple strategy to fulfill its mandates. It *evangelizes*, it *infiltrates*, it *confronts*.

Christ's last recorded command (Matthew 28) is that we go into the world and make disciples. We are to win followers. We are to bring them *in*—into the fellowship of the believers, the church. We bring to the world the great story, the gospel. We evangelize.

While its avowed and open mission is to evangelize the world, the church also has the subtle but powerful role of infiltrating the world. It is a leaven, a yeast, a salt, touching every area of the world's life. The gospel converts people, and through converted people it penetrates all the orders of creation—the family, government, education, industry, communication, labor, science, the arts. Think of the people who in each of these arenas have had integrity and mercy, discharging their day-by-day responsibilities as followers of their Lord. They are the unseen leaven. They are the salt. They are the adhesive that holds the structures of life together.

There are times when the church, as an organization, a visible body, must confront and collide with the world. With prophetic clarity, it must call the age to justice and mercy. As an organization, the church is a focus of power, and there may be times when it must use this power to confront other centers of power.

In the past two decades there has been a clamor for the church to become bold and speak out on the issues of the day. Should we not throw the organized weight of the church for legislation dealing with pollution, armaments, traffic in drugs and alcohol, injustice for minorities, abortion, homosexuality, and an assortment of other issues affecting the lives of people? The troublesome question is, can the church ever agree and speak with a unanimous voice on a specific piece of legislation? Probably not. But each of us, as a member of the church, is under mandate from our Lord to use whatever prophetic insights the Lord gives us to confront centers of error and evil.

We evangelize, we infiltrate, we confront!

You are the salt of the earth; but if salt has lost its taste . . . it is no longer good for anything except to be thrown out and trodden under foot by men (Matt. 5:13).

All sorts of arguments can be found for the futility of prayer. Why pray to a God who already knows what we need? He loves us, his children the world over, even when we ignore him. Certainly he cannot withhold his blessings until we remind him or press him.

There have been times when I've thought that he has told us to ask for things, all sorts of things, even for trivial things, because he wants us to talk to him. After all, it would be strange for members of the family never to communicate at all with their father.

So, I pray. I ask for health, my own and for my dear ones. I've got a long and assorted catalog—safety, security, guidance. On a Sunday morning I join the congregation's prayers: ". . . defend thy church, give it pastors according to thy Spirit . . . preserve our nation in righteousness and honor . . . take from us all hatred and prejudice . . . sanctify our homes . . . comfort all who are in sorrow and need . . . bless seedtime and harvest . . . the arts and culture of our people . . . keep us in fellowship with all thy saints." I assume that God wants all these values for us long before we ask for them. I also assume that he will not, in some sort of pique, let these blessings lie in his celestial warehouse undelivered unless we ask for them. Yet we pray.

There are other difficulties. We pray for health, and health doesn't come. We pray for safety, and a dear one is struck down in the streets. We pray for the end of the war, and the war grinds on.

I must remember that what I ask for may not be good for me, and that in his love he cannot humor me by giving it. "My thoughts are not your thoughts," he reminds me.

I dare not put limits on God. What he may do, or be able to do, in the wake of my prayers, I leave to him. A friend of mine, more cautious than I, said, "Prayer does not change things, it changes you." Of course it changes me. I am in God's presence when I pray, and am therefore exposed to him and to the powers that surge from him. But I must disagree with my friend. I believe that in some mysterious way, prayer also changes things—maybe the chemistry of cancer, the hearts of people I pray for, the turn of events, even the shape of history. How this can be, I cannot know. But I pray.

There is one kind of prayer that raises no questions: the prayer of thanksgiving! And what a prayer that can be for the person who is sensitive to all the blessings that God gives. The list can be endless!

Blessed be the Lord! for he has heard the voice of my supplications (Psalm 28:6).

The singular task of the church is to enlist people for our Lord's eternal kingdom. This is commonly called evangelism, to win people for Christ.

Arthur Larson, Christian layman, Director of the Rule of Law Research Center at Duke University, former Undersecretary of Labor, and eminent jurist, points out that the church has also a direct mandate from the Lord to be deeply concerned with the evil and madness of war. In a sermon preached in his home church, First Lutheran, Sioux Falls, he asked,

> Does the Christian, surrounded by a world of seemingly endless war, widening polarization of group mistrusts and hatred, of deepening alienation and even desperation among young people; of endemic violence, law-lessness and brutality ranging from mindless private killings to the most ruthless use of kidnappings and murder as a calculated political device, of accelerating problems of overpopulation, pollution and poverty, while over all hangs the threat of an uncontrolled nuclear arms race that could lead to the ultimate obliteration of all life on the earth in a nuclear holocaust—does the Christian, I ask, turn away from all this and say: "This is not the concern of Christianity; this is a job for the politicians?" I think not.
>
> The beginning point of Christianity is the sanctity of human life, the infinite, unmeasurable preciousness of the life of every single one of God's human children. If you really believe that—and you must if you are a Christian—you simply cannot accept the kind of policy that uses mass killings as an instrument of pursuing national goals.
>
> The most poignant affirmation of this Christian conviction I have ever seen was on a television program some time ago when an eager TV commentator was trying to get some kind of heroic statement from a desperately tired American soldier in Vietnam who had just returned from a superhuman performance on the battlefield. He got the heroic statement alright. The soldier, with eyes on the ground, said almost inaudibly: "It ain't right to kill people."
>
> Christianity is the fountainhead both of the modern civilized view of the worth of the individual human being, and of the modern sophisticated realization that really important causes in this world are advanced by means other than bloodshed.

Thou shalt not kill (Exod. 20:13).

IT ISN'T FAIR

The elder son muttered, "It isn't fair." And it was not fair. His brother had left home, squandered his inheritance, lived a life of shame, and now upon his coming home, the father swept him back in favor with no questions asked. Moreover, he arranged a big party for him, which he had never done for the elder brother.

Little wonder that he protested. Is not faithfulness and obedience to be rewarded, and is not delinquency to be punished? Is it right to let mercy get in the way of justice? Right or wrong, it is God's way with men. This is the point of the story of the prodigal son, as Jesus told it. No matter who we are, no matter what we have done, God receives us in mercy—if we come repentant. He asks no questions, makes no demands, lets the past be forgotten, and throws wide the doors of his kingdom for us.

Who wants to quarrel with God's way? Would you and I want to appear before him and his high court and plead for justice: "God, be fair with me. Give me what I have coming, no more and no less." We may be audacious enough to ask this of some human court and engage an attorney to see that we do get justice. But not before God. If we are at all honest, we will join the publican who cried, "God, be merciful to me a sinner!" In the presence of God there is only one plea to make, the plea for mercy.

And what of the younger son? Would he have been rehabilitated more surely if the father had punished him by putting him on probation for a year, given him the scurviest jobs on the farm, had him checked every week for faithfulness? This probably would have been fair. Whatever the outcome, it wasn't the father's way. And it is far more likely that the son, overwhelmed by his father's love and mercy, would in gratitude spend his life in faithfulness and service.

We have a God who doesn't deal in probation and measurements as qualifications for our being his. He is lavish with mercy. He is not fair. He goes far beyond fairness and sweeps us up in love. This is the sublime lesson of the cross of Christ. There we receive forgiveness, restoration, reconciliation, and love without end.

And he arose and came to his father. But while he was yet at a distance, his father saw him and had compassion, and ran and embraced him and blessed him. And the son said to him, "Father, I have sinned against heaven and before you" (Luke 15:20-21).

No one is an aggregate of deeds alone. Deeds are windows. Through them we form an image of people as they really are, good or bad, generous or selfish, trustworthy or devious.

When I remember my mother, now gone over 30 years, it is not an inventory of the things she did that comes into view. The deeds fade, and an image emerges, the image of a tender, humble, lovable person with willowy strength. I don't ever remember her saying, "Alvin, I love you." Words were unnecessary; deeds spoke with eloquence. Now, when her children recall her, we do talk about her qualities—for instance, that we can't remember her saying an unkind thing about anyone, that she had a serenity and uncommon patience. Without deeds, of course, we could not have known that she loved us. Deeds let us see into her heart. And it's that great heart we now remember.

It is often said that what a person *is* is more important than what a person does. True as this may be, what a person does is the clue to what a person is. What one does at a given moment may also of itself be most important.

I am drowning. My friend stands on shore. For him to call to me, "I love you," is not enough. What he does is now more important than what he says. As he leaps into the deep to rescue me, I have the double gift—the gift of his love and the gift of rescue.

It is not enough for God to say that he loves me. I am drowning. I need rescue. At great cost to himself, this is precisely what he has done. In Christ Jesus, his only Son, God came down to become involved in my plight. He went to a cross in death, in some strange way to provide rescue for me. It was not only a lesson in love; it was an event of rescue.

The language of the Bible stretches itself almost out of shape to tell me this. It declares that I was in the prison of the enemy and God overcame the enemy and set me free. It says that I stood before the high court condemned, and he took my sentence upon himself and gave me acquittal. It says that I was blind, and he gave me sight. And it goes on to say that it cost him his life to do this. God did not only tell me of his love; he loved me to the death. It is not by accident that the message of the Bible is primarily a story, and not a philosophical system. It is the moving story of God entering our history, our world, to do something important for us. He came to save, not to lecture.

He who believes in him is not condemned (John 3:18).

Christian faith draws on imagination and intuition, as do fairy tales. Unlike fairy tales, the faith is anchored in an historical figure and historical events, Jesus Christ, his cross and his resurrection. G. K. Chesterton, eminent Christian essayist, writes of the place of fairy tales in his essay, "The Logic of Elfland":

> My first and last philosophy, that which I believe in with unbroken certainty, I learned in the nursery.... The things I believed most then, the things I believe most now, are the things called fairy tales. They seem to me to be the most entirely reasonable things. They are not fantasies; compared with them other things are fantastic....
>
> I deal here with what ethic and philosophy come from being fed on fairy tales. If I were describing them in detail, I could note many noble and healthy principles that arise from them. There is the chivalrous lesson of "Jack the Giant Killer"; the giants should be killed because they are gigantic. It is manly mutiny against pride as such. There is the lesson of "Cinderella," which is the same as that of the Magnificat—*exaltavit humiles*. There is the great lesson of "Beauty and the Beast"; that a thing must be loved before it is lovable. There is the terrible allegory of the "Sleeping Beauty," which tells how the human creature was blessed with all birthday gifts, yet cursed with death; and how death also may perhaps be softened to a sleep. But I am not concerned with any of the separate statutes of elfland, but with the whole spirit of its law, which I learnt before I could speak, and shall retain when I cannot write. I am concerned with a certain way of looking at life, which was created in me by the fairy tales, but has since been meekly ratified by the mere facts.

He goes on to deplore that "flat" language of science, where we describe nature in terms of "law" and "necessity" and "order" and "tendency," and adds,

> The only words that ever satisfied me as describing Nature are terms used in the fairy books, "charm," "spell," "enchantment." They express the arbitrariness of the fact and mystery. A tree grows fruit because it is a *magic* tree. Water runs downhill because it is bewitched. The sun shines because it is bewitched.

In many and various ways God spoke of old to our fathers by the prophets, but in those last days he has spoken to us by a Son (Heb. 1:1).

A Christian congregation is no ordinary grouping of people. It has its beginnings far back in the heart of God. He created them in love, and he can not let them go. This gives him his trouble, and this gives us our glory. We are attached to him, not by dint of our own will nor by the excellence of our performance. We are the created ones, the redeemed ones, the called ones, the gathered ones. We are the people being reshaped into the beings he intended us to be from the beginning. Through Word and Sacrament the Holy Spirit broods over us, penetrates us, disturbs us, condemns us—and then captures us by the incredible love revealed in Christ Jesus. Little wonder that we are, deep down, a peculiar people.

A congregation may seem very much like any other organization made up of all kinds of people. They are of many occupations. They have widely different tastes in music, art, and fashion. They have varied political and economic views. And they have all the weaknesses that plague the human race—prejudice, hatred, indifference, fear, even despair. But these are the kind of people Jesus came to call. It was for this sort he died. Theirs are the ills the Holy Spirit is at work to heal.

One might wonder if God thinks it all worthwhile. The change in people is often not spectacular enough to create any rhapsody. Read the Old Testament to catch some of the pathos of God. He had chosen a people to be his own. Time and again, they turned from him. It is a wonder that his patience held out. Why did he not let them go, once and for all? He was "stuck" with them—because he could not stop loving them. He kept on their trail through the prophets, a long line of them. Finally, he sent his only Son. This was, and is, the measure of his love.

These two thousand years, since the coming of our Lord and the establishing of his kingdom on earth, have not been an epic of unabridged glory for the church. It will take more than a casual analysis to discover the glory of God in the people of God. We fail him again and again, in every generation. But we are nonetheless a peculiar people. The love of God in Christ has touched us. And we are never again the same. Within our hearts, deep within, something is at work. The kingdom is within us and in our midst, even if neat, discernible criteria may not be found to pinpoint its presence. We live by faith, and the works of God can often be seen only with the eyes of faith.

You are a chosen race, a royal priesthood, a holy nation, God's own people (1 Peter 2:9).

SINNERS IN THE HANDS OF AN ANGRY GOD   July 9

This is the title of the celebrated sermon preached by Jonathan Edwards in his New England church during the Great Awakening in colonial times. Edwards, an eminent scholar and preacher, became the first president of what now is Princeton University. This sermon, with its terrifying title, really speaks of the patience and mercy of God which stays his wrath and his hand of judgment:

> Your wickedness makes you as it were heavy as lead, and to tend downwards with great weight and pressure towards hell; and if God should let you go, you would immediately sink and swiftly descend and plunge into the bottomless gulf, and your healthy constitution, and your own care and prudence, and best contrivance, and all your righteousness, would have no more influence to uphold you and keep you out of hell, than a spider's web would have to stop a fallen rock. Were it not for the sovereign pleasure of God, the earth would not bear you one moment; for you are a burden to it; the creation groans with you; the creature is made subject to the bondage of your corruption, not willingly; the sun does not willingly shine upon you to give you light to serve sin and Satan; the earth does not willingly yield her increase to satisfy your lusts; nor is it willingly a stage for your wickedness to be acted upon; the air does not willingly serve you for breath to maintain the flame of life in your vitals, while you spend your life in the service of God's enemies. God's creatures are good creatures, and were made for men to serve God with, and do not willingly subserve to any other purpose, and groan when they are abused to purposes so directly contrary to their nature and end. And the world would spew you out, were it not for the sovereign hand of Him who hath subjected it in hope. There are black clouds of God's wrath now hanging directly over your heads, full of the dreadful storm, and big with thunder; and were it not for the restraining hand of God, it would immediately burst forth upon you. The sovereign pleasure of God, for the present, stays his rough wind; otherwise it would come with fury, and your destruction would come like the whirlwind, and you would be like chaff of the threshing floor.

Now when they heard this they were cut to the heart, and said to Peter and the rest of the apostles, "Brethren, what shall we do?" And Peter said to them, "Repent, and be baptized every one of you in the name of Jesus Christ for the forgiveness of your sins; and you shall receive the gift of the Holy Spirit" (Acts 2:37-38).

How do you bridge the gap between what a man is and what he ought to be, between what he does and what he ought to do? This is the supreme ethical question. It becomes the supreme religious question. God demands holiness; man is unholy. God demands love; man is unloving. God demands perfection; man is imperfect.

That yawning gap is the focus of man's elemental uneasiness, his deep anxieties, his destructive guilts. It splits his being in two. It drives him to a life of pretense. It makes him a fraud. And it may drive him to despair, as it did Ibsen's Brand, who after a lifetime of trying to fulfill God's law to the letter was completely undone.

How shall we be justified in the eyes of God? Not by works, says God. For even the most intense effort and the most complete adherence to law will only make us more aware of the impossible width of the chasm. The apostle Paul, after such effort, cried, "I do not do the good I want, but the evil I do not want is what I do. . . . Wretched man that I am! Who will deliver me from this body of death?"

There is no bridging the chasm through *forgiveness*, the overarching forgiveness of God himself. "If thou, Lord, shouldst mark iniquities, O Lord, who shall stand?" cried the psalmist, and adds, "But there is forgiveness with thee." And forgiveness is the center of the work of Christ on the cross and the doorway to the life abundant.

Among the many ways in which the Bible tells of our Lord's work for us, the forgiveness of sins is central. But there are others. Christ is a *window*, for instance. In and through him we understand that God is more than a mighty sovereign or lawgiver. Christ reveals him as a Father of love. And we have the image of *warfare*. Christ, as the Lord of hosts, wages war against the enemy who holds us in his prison, and on a cross overcomes him, batters down the doors of the prison and sets us free. We are victors in Christ.

But the profoundest image is the *court*. We are not only blind, needing revelation (the window), nor are we only defeated and imprisoned, needing victory and freedom (the warfare). We are disobedient, rebellious, needing forgiveness. We hardly need to feel guilty over being blind or being defeated, but we do have guilt at being disobedient. And we are all disobedient. We all fall short and need mercy. And Jesus, the judge of all, steps down from the bench to take our place, assume our sentence, and go to his death for us. Now the gap is bridged!

There is now therefore no condemnation for those who are in Christ Jesus (Rom. 8:1).

We often hear that "money talks," implying that men's lives are ruled by money. Even more crass and cynical is the phrase, "every man has his price." I have met many people for whom money is not an end in itself at all, but merely a means to an end—sometimes a good end, like service to others, sometimes an unworthy end, like pride.

The Lord never explicitly said, "Give me your money." He did say, "My son, give me your heart."

I have a hard time with my heart. My longings, my aspirations, my affections, my desires—these are all included in "heart." I have less difficulty with the control of my money than with the control of my heart. I can write a check even when I don't feel like writing it, out of a sense of duty or shame; my heart simply is not in it. To yearn for God, to send my spirit in praise of him, to give my service or money spontaneously in glad gratitude to him—this often is too much for me.

A good question might be, "Does my money follow my heart, or does my heart follow my money?" If from a sense of duty I take a plunge with my money, give to the Lord and his church more than I feel like giving—perhaps, just perhaps, my heart will latch on to the gift and tag along. Is that what the Lord meant when he said, "Where your treasure is, there will your heart be also"?

During a drive for our church's building fund I called on a man for his gift. He asked me to suggest a sum. I proposed $1000. He replied that he felt like giving $300, and then he said, "Pastor, if the Lord wants me to give $1000, he'd make me feel like giving $1000, wouldn't he? And I feel like giving $300." What could I say? I thanked him for his $300 and on leaving said, "John, I wouldn't be surprised to have the Lord make you feel like giving $1000." I began getting his checks through the mail, $100 a month, until he had reached $1300. His heart had apparently been trapped by his checks.

Another man, on leaving a generous check with me, said, "I have learned that it's more fun to write checks than to get them." Strange as it seems, our Lord, like a wise fisherman, may use our money as a "lure" to have our hearts "bite" and be captured by him.

Truly, I say to you, this poor widow has put in more than all those who are contributing to the treasury. For they all contributed out of their abundance; but she out of her poverty has put in everything she had, her whole living (Mark 12:43-44).

By common consent Walter Lippman has been the most astute observer and widely read commentator of our 20th century. His most noted book is probably *Preface to Morals*. The following excerpts, though published in 1929, are, if anything, more germane now than then:

By the dissolution of their ancestral ways men have been deprived of their sense of certainty as to why they were born, why they must work, whom they must love, what they must honor, where they may turn in sorrow and defeat. They have left to them the ancient codes and the modern criticism of these codes, guesses, intuitions, inconclusive experiments, possibilities, probabilities, hypotheses. Below the level of reason, they may have unconscious prejudice, they may speak with a loud cocksureness, they may act with fanaticism. But there is gone that ineffable certainty which once made God and His Plan as real as the lamp-post.

We should not forget that the religions which have dominated human history have been founded on what the faithful felt were undeniable facts. These facts were mysterious only in the sense that they were uncommon, like an eclipse of the sun, but not in the sense that they were beyond human experience. . . . The modern man uses the word "supernatural" to describe something that seems to him not quite so credible as the things he calls natural. This is not the supernaturalism of the devout. They do not distinguish two planes of reality and two orders of certainty. For them Jesus Christ was born of a Virgin and was raised from the dead as literally as Napoleon was Emperor of the French and returned from Elba.

I am not enough of a logician to say that I am quite sure that I understand what it means to say "God is not concrete, but He is the ground for concrete actuality." There have been moments when I imagined I had caught the meaning of this, but there have been more moments when I knew I had not. . . . For while this God may satisfy a metaphysical need in the thinker, he does not satisfy the passions of the believer. This God does not govern the world like a king nor watch over his children like a father. He offers them no purposes to which they can consecrate themselves; he exhibits no image of holiness they can imitate. He does not chastise them in sin nor console them in sorrow. . . . For the purposes of religion he is no God at all; his universe remains stonily unaware of man.

Fear not, for I have redeemed you; I have called you by name, you are mine. When you pass through the waters I will be with you (Isa. 43:1, 2).

Often someone will say, "The Bible does not speak to my situation," by which is meant that there are no specific instructions for overcoming mental depressions, loneliness, a rocky marriage, drug addiction, or unemployment. These ills may not be labeled, but resources for all these, and many more, are to be found within its pages.

Few passages in Scripture can match the bracing comfort of these words from Isaiah:

> Comfort, comfort my people, says your God. Speak tenderly to Jerusalem and cry to her that her warfare is ended, that her iniquity is pardoned, that she has received from the Lord's hand double for all her sins (40:1-2).

First, the war has been won. Our Lord has met the enemy and has conquered him. Man's spirit no longer needs to be captive to dark powers. They may still molest him, but they need not enslave him or destroy him. Man may still lose some battles against them, because they're still around to harrass him. But the victory has been won by our Lord, and in him, we, troubled still, are already victors.

Second, our sins are forgiven. Their guilt has been taken away, as far as the east is from the west. How many of the problems that trouble us have their roots in the gnawing guilt that paralyzes us for joy and hope and courage? Shame and remorse and failure block out the sun, and the path into the future seems dark. We can't erase the past, and some of the hurt will remain, but in the forgiveness of God there is a strange power to free us from the crippling burden of haunting memories. At the very heart of life, with God, we can stand as if we had never sinned.

Nor is it the past alone that is dealt with in God's comfort. We have received from the Lord's hands *double* for all our sins. There's grace enough for the wretched past, and there's grace to send us fresh into the morrows. There's enough to clear out the debris of yesterday's wreckage and enough to build over again. Not only are our debts paid; we have new capital. The past is covered—and also the future. We are in business again, in the business of life, with the lavish capital he provides day by day.

It may not always be a simple matter to translate this kind of sublime comfort into the specific issues of loneliness, depression, and a sense of failure. But the stuff is all there, with God eager to help us use it.

The Lord lifts up the downtrodden (Psalm 147:6).

Classified in biology, the human is an animal, a mammal, a biped. Picking up on this definition, sociologists and anthropologists discuss what kind of biped and what makes humans tick. The following are general descriptions:

We are *eating* animals. Our elemental drive is for food. Give us security, a full dinner pail today, and the guarantee of a full dinner pail for the tomorrows, and we will be happy. Deny us food for 36 hours, and we will be unmanageable. This is the presupposition of Marxist economics. Not only armies, but civilizations too, move on their stomachs, and wars are always economic wars.

We are *fighting* animals. What makes us tick is our rivalry with others for power, prestige, preeminence, acceptance. To be rejected, to lose face, is far more frightening and destructive than to lose money or security. Wars are political, not economic; nations, like people, dare not lose face.

We are *mating* animals. Sex is the driving force, as Freud has suggested, and everything we do is a sublimation of sex. Release our sexual powers, and we not only will be fulfilled but will be set free for all sorts of artistic and intellectual creativity.

These primitive drives, perhaps overdrawn, nonetheless describe us. One or more of them may become dominant, take control, and run off with us. There is a fourth category, popular a century ago, and more optimistic:

We are *thinking* animals. Unlike other animals, we can reason. And years ago it was popularly thought that if we were educated to know what's right, we would do the right. Only ignorance stands in our way.

The Christian faith does not quarrel with any of these descriptions. They all have something important to say about us. But—and here's where faith takes issue—we are more than animals. *We are children of God.* And at our best, under God, neither food nor power nor sex, nor even our reason alone will be in control.

When God takes control, these drives are not annihilated; they march to a new drum. Instead of being power for aggrandizement, they become instruments for serving others. No longer do they compel us into a jungle anarchy. Harnessed and ordered by the will of God, they become the constructive forces in people's lives and in society.

Of his own will he brought us forth by the word of truth that we should be a kind of first fruits of his creatures (James 1:18).

Love is a widely used word and has many meanings. Understood in the Christian sense, it concerns feeling, but more than feeling; it concerns care of the neighbor, but even more. P. T. Forsyth, a leading British theologian in the first part of this century, writes:

The greatest product of the Church is not brotherly love but divine worship. And we shall never worship right nor serve right till we are more engrossed with our God than even with our worship, with His reality than our piety, with His Cross than our service. It is well to dream and to talk much of brotherly love. But the brethren who love best and the love that loves longest are made by the Gospel. It is this they confess in loving, as they confess it in other ways also. Christian charity is not the sweet reasonableness of culture, nor is it natural kindliness of temper. To the lover of righteousness it does not come easy. It grows only on the stem of Christian faith, which is the tree of the Cross and its righteousness. Never did Paul dream that his song of Christian love (1 Cor. 13) would be turned to belittle or to belabour the Christian faith on which alone it grows. The Church is the greatest product of history, and the greatest product of the Church is a holiness answering the holiness that made it, which is Holy Love. The first commandment of the Cross is "Be ye holy, for I am holy." It calls for the confession, worship, and service of that divine Holiness of love which is the spring of our Redemption. The service of God is the root, the service of man is but the fruit. True, by their fruits shall we *know* them; but not *produce* them. The fruits are the evidence, not the principles. Love does more to show faith than to produce it. Grace produces it. We live by that faith in holy Love whose fruit is to be a love not only kind, but, still more, holy. . . .

A very rich man was asked what was the best time he ever had. His answer was: "When I was in the hospital two months with typhus . . . . I had a nurse, an angel for sweetness and patience . . . in eight weeks I never saw on her face anything but the same shining kindness, never agitated, never morose. It was like heaven."

There is nothing that can continue to make Holy Love, to make love holy, steady, and of everlasting kindness, but the Gospel of our regeneration from human nature in Christ Jesus, and Him crucified.

Make love your aim (1 Cor. 14:1).

When on his return from Oxford, England, in 1960, our son Paul was killed in a street accident ten minutes from home, we found in his billfold these prayers in his handwriting. Not until later did we find them in George Macdonald's *Diary of an Old Soul,* 365 sonnet-prayers, then out of print, but since republished by Augsburg Publishing House:

> Not in my fancy now I search to find thee;
> Not in its loftiest forms would shape or bind thee;
> I cry to one whom I can never know,
> Filling me with an infinite overflow;
> Not to a shape that dwells within my heart,
> Clothed in perfections love and truth assigned thee,
> But to the God thou knowest that thou art.

> Not, Lord, because I have done well or ill;
> Not that my mind looks up to thee clear-eyed;
> Not that it struggles in fast cerements tied;
> Not that I need thee daily sorer still;
> Not that I, wretched, wander from thy will;
> Not now for any cause to thee I cry,
> But this, that thou art thou, and here am I.

> Come to me, Lord: I will not speculate how,
> Nor think at which door I would have thee appear,
> Nor put off calling till my floors be swept,
> But cry, "Come, Lord, come any way, come now."
> Doors, windows, I throw open wide; my head I bow,
> And sit like someone who so long has slept
> That he knows nothing till his life draw near.

Those whom I love, I reprove and chasten; so be zealous and repent. Behold I stand at the door and knock; if any one hears my voice and opens the door, I will come in to him and eat with him, and he with me (Rev. 3:19-20).

You are rich in direct ratio to your sense of wonder. If your affairs get so snarled up that you cannot marvel at the color, texture, lines, and fragrance of a rose, you have lost much in life. If you have become so grown up that you can't stand under the night sky with your little girl, and in real wonder, say with her:

Twinkle, twinkle, little star,
How I wonder what you are,
Up above the world so high
Like a diamond in the sky

Then you have forfeited a vast empire of riches.

One evening the winds unleashed themselves in our city. If in that hour you were so busy with closing the windows or so fretful over falling branches that you missed the sheer exhilaration of nature's little display of power—in that moment of fret and fear you failed to cash in on one of your most precious possessions: the sense of wonder. I hope you have shared William L. Stidger's rainstorm imagery:

I saw God wash the world last night
With His sweet shower on high;
And then when morning came
I saw him hang it out to dry.

He washed each tiny blade of grass,
And every trembling tree;
He flung His showers against the hills
And swept the billowy sea.

There's not a bird, there's not a bee,
That wings along the way,
But is a cleaner bird and bee
Than it was yesterday.

However sensitive you may have become to the wonders of the world about you, there is a whole staggering world of wonder that the eye cannot see and the ear cannot hear. It unfolds only to men and women of daring Christian faith. It centers in one Jesus, and how he washed mankind of all the dust and dirt of sin. The majestic splendor of the mountains, the endless reaches of the sky, the myriad sparkling of the stars cannot open the doors upon the wonder of God's love and grace. But there is a place—if in faith you will see and listen. That place is the cross of Calvary!

O Lord, our Lord, how majestic is thy name in all the earth! (Psalm 8:1).

The lover begs his beloved, "Let me be your slave forever." He does not only volunteer; he pleads for the privilege. He covets the right to serve her.

Christians are caught up in some such madness. We are restored to the family of God. We are joint heirs with Christ to a Kingdom. With all these rights, we yet beg to be slaves. We volunteer; we plead for the honor of becoming servants.

Being children of God is neither more nor less than this: each becomes everyone's servant. Children of God, we are brothers and sisters one of another, and therefore slaves of one another. In Christ we have been set free—free to offer ourselves to the task of bearing one another's burdens.

Humanity has fought a long war against all forms of slavery. In many parts of the world the war still rages. In whatever form, we believe that it is wrong for one person to enslave another. Each person and each nation has the right to freedom. No one should be the chattel or the property of another. No single force on earth has opposed slavery as has the Christian faith.

Yet, within this faith we volunteer to be slaves. But we do this as free people. As servants, we yet are free; as free, we yet are servants. In Christ we are set free from the passions that chain us to ourselves. We are set free to turn to another's need.

The secret of this turnabout is the cross. Here the Lord of heaven and earth, to whom all power is given, lets himself become the servant of all people, dying to give new life to the world. In her *Interior Castle*, St. Teresa of Avila says, "Fix your eyes on the Crucified and nothing else will be of much importance to you. . . . Do you know when people really become spiritual? It is when they become slaves of God and are branded with His sign, which is the sign of the Cross, in token that they have given Him their freedom. Then He can sell them as slaves to the whole world, as He Himself was sold."

There's something repugnant about being "sold" into service for the world, even by God. Most of us have had a taste of what this means, and it's been an exhilarating discovery. To be set free from anxiety about ourselves, to be set free from defending our own rights, and turning to "swing free" in the service of others—these are the truly rich moments of life. We know the joy of a slavery that is freedom!

For he who was called in the Lord as a slave is a freedman of the Lord. Likewise he who was free when called is a slave of Christ (1 Cor. 7:22).

In his widely read book, *The Greatest Story Ever Told,* Fulton Oursler has Annas and Caiaphas, the high priests who plotted Jesus' death, engage in a conversation after the resurrection.

Both had heard the reports of the appearance of Jesus to His disciples by the Sea of Tiberias; and how He had appeared to others on a mountain in Galilee. Now, in the moist warmth of the torrid night, Annas and Caiaphas sat together in the dark, remembering so much of this man whom they had ordered killed, yet who still could plague their peace of mind.

"But has it occurred to you, Caiaphas, that this brave death contradicts all that you had to say earlier this evening? Would any man be willing to die—in a heroic, glorious martyrdom like this—for some conjurer's trick involving the stealing of a corpse in a hoax, a sham?" . . .

"I still don't see."

"Probably you never will. But I shall try to give you a gleam of light. On the night we killed Him, you remember that two of His disciples followed Him into Jerusalem, but one of them denied Him three times and both kept themselves hidden. What happened to the other nine? They went back to Galilee because they were afraid." . . .

"But what makes them brave now?" asked Annas sternly. "Why do they no longer care whether they live or die?"

"Because they have seen their leader rise from the dead; they expect to do the same; to them, now, life and death are mere words for temporary things and do not really matter. Since the resurrection, that is what it means to be a Christian."

"But, Caiaphas, I have a horrible feeling that we have blundered. History may blame us . . . the guilt that belongs so much to you and me and our rich and powerful friends—who are afraid of the truth."

"What is truth," Caiaphas was sarcastic. "Do you know the answer?"

"No, but now I believe it is truth itself that we nailed to the cross and then buried. And truth, as usual, rose again."

Thomas said to him, "Lord, we do not know where you are going; how can we know the way?" Jesus said to him, "I am the way, and the truth, and the life; no one comes to the Father, but by me" (John 14:5).

If someone has wronged you, he ought to ask your forgiveness. How can you forgive him, if he does not come? He ought to take the first step.

For one reason or another, he does not come. He may be too ashamed to come, and his shame weighs upon him and robs him of joy. He may not have the courage to come, willing as he may be. He may fear your rebuff. Or he may be trying to convince himself that he did you no wrong. In any event, a barrier has risen for him, and he doesn't quite know how to get through it. It could be that he wishes the whole matter could be done away with somehow. Something holds him back, and he is miserable.

Someone must take the first step. And Jesus tells us that we, his disciples, must be "big" enough to do it. If someone has defrauded you, lied about you, and even hated you, for whatever reason, you still have the obligation to seek him out for reconciliation.

This is Christ's way. We humans had sinned against him, in far greater measure than any person has ever sinned against other people. But Christ did not sit around in his heaven, waiting for us to come pounding on the door. The first move should have been ours. But God made the first move. He came to win the sinners back to him. And he went to the lengths of a cross to do it.

It's well for us to remember that it is harder for a person to ask for and receive forgiveness than it is to forgive. To forgive is, in George Macdonald's words, "the luxury of the Christian life." To ask forgiveness is to repent, and repentance is always a difficult thing for the ego. It may therefore be easier for the "wronged" one to make the first move than it is for the offender.

We who have been caught in the glorious net of God's forgiveness, we are to move out into this world of our estranged brothers and sisters, to forgive and to be forgiven. We are to shatter the walls that separate us, as God himself has shattered the walls that kept us from him.

It is no easy task. But there is no other way. The ministry of reconciliation is ours. We are the reconcilers of the world.

All this is from God, who through Christ reconciled us to himself and gave us the ministry of reconciliation (2 Cor. 5:18).

God surely wants us to take reasonable precautions for tomorrow, but not at the expense of today's responsibilities and joys. There may be no tomorrow. Jesus had some strong words to say on this point, "Do not be anxious about tomorrow. . . . Let the day's own trouble be sufficient for the day."

Many a person has had his eye so fixed on tomorrow's needs that he has neglected today's duties. Because he is concerned to provide shoes for his children tomorrow, he lets them go barefoot today.

It may seem a bit naive to concentrate on today's needs and tasks, but the fact is that we are put together to find life's fullness by this formula. Let tomorrow's needs and anxieties elbow out today's concerns, and you are in trouble. Your little ship can carry today's cargo; but try loading it with tomorrow's freight too, and it very likely will flounder and sink.

You are on daily rations for God's help. Moment by moment, day by day, he will give you grace or strength as you need it. He deposits enough grace for each day as it comes, and he expects you to draw upon that grace as you need it. But draw more than you need, and the check will bounce. God's great bank does not tolerate an overdraft.

In a strange way, perhaps the greatest affront to God, and maybe the greatest hurt, is to worry. It would hurt a father deeply if his child were no longer to count on him. If she were to ask her father, but live as if her father would not hear or respond, how sad for the father.

Anxiety is natural, perhaps inevitable. Who knows what tomorrow may bring? Resist it as we will, all sorts of possibilities for disaster loom up and rob us of today's joy. Whatever wealth or influence or knowledge we may command, we cannot possibly take all the precautions necessary to put our minds at ease.

But this we know. God will be around tomorrow too. He has more resources than we can know, and he hears us and loves us with an everlasting love. This really should be enough.

Let us deposit our anxieties with him, and fill today full of the duties and joys that await us—today!

But seek first his kingdom and his righteousness, and all these things shall be yours as well (Matt. 6:33).

I was first drawn to Robert G. Ingersoll, much reviled agnostic of the early part of our century, by the beauty of his imagery. I include excerpts from this sermon, given at the grave of his younger brother. I find in its wistfulness a yearning for faith.

The loved and loving brother, husband, father, friend, died where manhood's morning almost touches noon, and while the shadows still were falling toward the west. He had not passed on life's highway the stone that marks the highest point; but being weary for a moment, he lay down by the wayside, and using his burden for a pillow, fell into that dreamless sleep that kisses down his eyelids still. Yet, after all, it may be best, just in the happiest, sunniest hour of all the voyage, while eager winds are kissing every sail, to dash against the unseen rock, and in an instant hear the billows roar above a sunken ship. For whether in midsea or among the breakers of the farther shore, a wreck at last must mark the end of each and all. And every life, no matter if its every hour is rich with love and every moment jeweled with a joy, will, at its close, become a tragedy as sad and deep and dark as can be woven of the warp and woof of mystery and death. Life is but a narrow vale between the cold and barren peaks of two eternities. We strive in vain to look beyond the heights. We cry aloud, and the only answer is the echo of our wailing cry. From the voiceless lips of the unreplying dead there comes no word, but in the night of death hope sees a star and listening love can hear the rustle of a wing.

We can tell all the Ingersolls of the world that we have more than an echo. Across the gulf God has broken his silence and has given us his Word. The writer of Hebrews has these bracing lines: "In many and various ways God spoke of old to our fathers by the prophets, but in these last days he has spoken to us by a Son." We have more than wistful longings and yearnings. Christ is our glorious assurance that we need no longer walk in darkness. The heavens have opened in him and we both see and hear the everlasting love of a heavenly Father.

The Lord is not slow about his promise as some count slowness, but is forbearing toward you, not wishing that any should perish, but that all should reach repentance (2 Peter 3:9).

Our life can be a prison with many cells. We dig ourselves out of one cell only to find that we have burrowed into another. Is there no end? Will we never reach the sunlight—and freedom?

A man begins his life in poverty. With industry and skill, he digs himself out of poverty into plenty. He has money. Now he is free to travel, to buy anything his heart desires. But something is wrong. New places and new things only bore him. Freedom from poverty is really not freedom at all. He is still in the darkness of the prison.

Or, he begins his life unnoticed and unrecognized. He digs himself into power, prestige, and popularity. The world fawns over him. But applause satisfies but for a moment. Darkness settles upon his spirit again. He knows he has not found freedom.

Or, he begins his life in ignorance. With a fine mind and a disciplined will he masters knowledge. He becomes a recognized specialist in his field. The world seeks him out and stands in awe before him. But the dawn does not break. His spirit is not yet free.

Neither wealth nor power nor knowledge is enough for our soaring spirits. We were made to live with God and to work with him in his kingdom's enterprises of justice and mercy. We were made to live and breathe in the world of the Spirit. For this freedom Christ has set us free. Christ ushers us into this world of wonder. Here we find the forgiveness for our sins, release from the unsatisfying chase for wealth, fame, or knowledge alone, and a taste of glory which is God's alone to give.

Nor need we renounce our money or station or knowledge. The Lord has allowed us to achieve these ends. But they no longer control us, nor are they any longer our source of meaning and major satisfactions. They become means toward a higher end. They are ours to use *for others*. That which we have received we are now free to give. We no longer need them. We are grateful to have them as resources the better to be of help to others.

Here, at last, we emerge from all the cells of the prison. The gray walls that held us captive are behind. A whole new world lies before us. With a freedom we never dreamed possible, we stride with courage and gladness into the world that waits for our affection and service.

So if the Son makes you free, you will be free indeed (John 8:36).

You may remember Jesus meeting the woman from Samaria at Jacob's well. Among other things, Jesus said, "Go, call your husband," to which she replied, "I have no husband." And Jesus said, "You are right. You have had five husbands, and he whom you now have is not your husband." Then followed their conversation about God, the Messiah, and eternal life.

Arndt L. Halvorson, professor at Luther Theological Seminary, says that the most important lesson we may learn from this encounter is that she left her water jar and went into the city to tell them about Jesus.

She met Jesus, and forgot her water jar—the symbol of her security, her driver's license, her credit card, her Linus blanket, her peace symbol, her American flag sticker, her long hair, her Ph.D., whatever—even her job. She met Jesus.

Jesus brought down her whole world. Nobody in all Palestine would think of questioning the superiority of the water supply in Jacob's well, but Jesus did. He said that if she knew who he was she would be begging him for water, and his water would not only quench her thirst but make her a thirst-quencher for others. She asked for some of this "water." . . .

Her old world lay at her feet, already a relic of an outworn past. The water well was temporary, the husbands were false, and her god was just a small-time local tin god. But she seemed unaware of losing anything. Rather, she was overwhelmed by the stature of this man, Jesus. She seemed quite unsurprised by his disclosure that he is the Messiah. She ran as fast as possible to her village to tell about him. She left her water jar, the symbol of her old life.

Now she *forgot* it, she did not throw it away! She *forgot* it, she did not renounce it! Gathering food and water was not evil; this world's daily cares are not sin; they simply are not ultimate. . . .

Have you forgotten anything? If we could see into the rooms of your inner self, what would we see? Is everything neatly put in place, packed, tucked away, because, as you say, you never know when you'll need it . . . or is there a kind of divine disorder—a forgotten date, a forgotten spite, a forgotten cause, or even a forgotten life purpose?

So the woman left her water jar, and went away into the city, and said to the people, "Come, see a man who told me all that I ever did. Can this be the Christ?" (John 4:28-29).

The dimension of our sin is in direct ratio to our high station. If we are no more than complex arrangements of protoplasm, we are no sinners at all. If we are only people among other people, engaged in a network of horizontal interpersonal relationships, our offenses are relative and indefinite. But if we are children of God, created to the royalty of God's household, under obligation to live the life of holiness in God's family, then our disobedience becomes of colossal proportions. It was Absalom who rebelled against his father, David the king. Had he been a peasant, it would have been but an incident, but it was a son who rebelled, and this shook the kingdom and broke the king's heart.

We steal our existence from God. This is the supreme theft of all time. We receive our existence from God, and every moment of our lives is dependent on God. We cannot keep our hearts beating a single moment by willing it. Yet, totally dependent as we are, we embezzle our lives from God. If we use one talent as if it were our own to use as we please, if we live one hour as if that hour were ours, if we manage our property or money as if these were ours, then we become frauds, pretenders, thieves.

We affront God in unbelief. Luther's explanation of the First Commandment, "We should fear, love, and trust in God above all things," summarizes our obligation to God. The most elemental of all obligations is trust or belief. To distrust God is the sin that pierces his heart like a sword. As an earthly father I can overlook my child's burst of anger, I can easily forgive a petty theft, but if my child should conclude that I did not love her or that I was really not her father at all, and she should, therefore, no longer come to me for anything or ever count on me for anything—in fact, should ignore me—this would be the greatest hurt of all. This absence of trust and presence of indifference and anxiety is our deepest offense against a God who loves us with an everlasting love, and who went to a cross to recover us and hold us.

It is only in relation to God that we become great sinners. Over against other people we are little more than troublemakers; over against ourselves we are but betrayers of our own humanity or integrity. It is as we stand before God, royal children who have been assigned the management of the earth and the care of our brothers and sisters—it is then that our obedience becomes divine and our infidelity demonic.

Against thee, thee only have I sinned, and done that which is evil in thy sight (Psalm 51:4).

The notable thing about us, even us Christians, is not that we are loving and forgiving. We always fall short in performance. The noteworthy thing is that we are *the loved ones, the forgiven ones*. This is the word of the gospel. God takes the initiative to love us and to forgive us. It is by God's grace alone that we are restored. We are children, by grace through faith, and not because we look like children, talk like children, or perform like children. The only begotten Son has won for us the right to be children of God. Our righteousness is the righteousness of Another. Our favor with God is the favor given us by Jesus Christ, the Son of God and the Son of Man. Nothing in all our imaginations can shake us to our depths as can the staggering news that God receives us through grace, quite apart from any inventory of our own goodness. If this good news cannot reach us and win us, nothing can. God has risked everything on the gospel of forgiveness in Christ. Failing this, we are forever lost, separated from God, from ourselves and from our brothers and sisters.

Luther made forgiveness the center of all God's gifts. He said, "Where there is forgiveness of sins, there is life and salvation." God gives light and victory, but it is forgiveness that plumbs the depth of his love.

Forgiveness also defines our deepest need. We are the blind ones who need light. We are the defeated ones who need victory. We are the bewildered ones who need meaning for our lives. Neither blindness nor defeat nor meaninglessness describes our elemental need. We are the disobedient ones who need forgivness! We need feel no guilt over being blind or bewildered or defeated. We are guilty only if we are disobedient. As the disobedient ones, we separate ourselves from God and face the judgment of God. Now we need redemption, reconciliation, forgiveness.

It is when law and gospel are proclaimed together as *the* Word of God that confession of sin becomes more than a plea in a courtroom. Only against the background of God's immeasurable love in Christ, and the amazing offer of forgiveness—only against this background will we, out of broken hearts, cry for mercy and praise God for mercy. Law without forgiveness breeds defiance; forgiveness without law elicits indifference. Law and gospel, joined in *one Word*, will yield repentance, gratitude, freedom, peace, joy, and glad obedience. These are the fruits of the Spirit in the life of the forgiven one!

Fill me with joy and gladness; let the bones which thou hast broken rejoice. Hide thy face from my sins, and blot out all my iniquities (Psalm 51:8-9).

Americans have traditionally praised self-reliance (do-it-yourself, which translates into economic *capitalism*), and at the same time they have had an aversion to big government (to handouts, which translates into economic *socialism*). In the best traditions of America, its people have wanted to meet their own needs, and the needs of others, voluntarily, with a minimum of reliance upon or control by government. This, obviously, means that they must be willing to give. And this, in turn, implies that they are moved by compassion for the needs of others—which is at the heart of the Christian way of life. C. S. Lewis speaks to all of us:

> In the passage where the New Testament says that everyone must work, it gives as a reason "in order that he may have something to give to those in need." Charity—giving to the poor—is an essential part of Christian morality; in the frightening parable of the sheep and the goats it seems to be the point on which everything turns. Some people nowadays say that charity ought to be unnecessary and that instead of giving to the poor we ought to be producing a society in which there were no poor to give to. They may be quite right in saying we ought to produce that kind of society. But if anyone thinks that, as a consequence, you can stop giving in the meantime, then he has parted company with all Christian morality. I do not believe one can settle how much we ought to give. I am afraid the only safe rule is to give more than we can spare. In other words, if our expenditure on comforts, luxuries, amusements, etc., is up to the standard common among those with the same income as our own, we are probably giving away too little. If our charities do not at all pinch or hamper us, I should say they are too small. There ought to be things we should like to do and cannot do because our charitable expenditure excludes them. I am now speaking of "charities" in the common way. Particular cases of distress among your own relatives, friends, neighbors, or employees, which God, as it were, forces upon your notice, may demand much more; even to the crippling and endangering of your own position. For many of us the great obstacle to charity lies not in our luxurious living or desire for more money, but in our fear—fear of insecurity.

Give, and it will be given to you; good measure, pressed down, shaken together, running over, will be put into your lap. For the measure you give will be the measure you get back (Luke 6:38).

Napoleon once said, "He who would be victor must know his enemy." The enemy may be unchanged, but the terrain on which he does battle has changed radically. The Christian church has identified the enemy as a triple threat: the devil, the world, and our own sinful nature. These urge us to self-centeredness, to pride and envy and lust. From the dawn of history, the enemy has tried to destroy us by distracting us from the will of God and from God's great truths and values. The enemy is at it still.

Today there are new tools for the enemy, especially in the family—mobility, for instance. Fifty years ago in an agrarian society, a family was anchored in one place, surrounded usually by an extended family of uncles, aunts, grandparents, and friends. All of us, so to speak, had bleachers full of these people, who cheered us on when we ran well and who groaned when we ran badly. These support groups are now scattered. In our urban society our neighbors hardly know us, and perhaps could care less what happens to us.

Formerly the roles of father and mother were clearly defined. Father was the breadwinner. Mother had a full-time job at home, caring for the needs of the family. Today many mothers work outside the home. Modern technology has removed much of the drudgery from homemaking, and there is time left over for the mother to find fulfillment in other ways. Her additional income may enable the family to be released from economic anxieties. It is a new day, and new vigilance is required to give the family the cohesion which in an earlier day was virtually automatic.

Another, and more subtle, factor is society's general level of anxiety. The uncertainty of the future threatens everyone. Until a couple decades ago we all assumed that the world had need of us. We're not sure of that anymore. The father fears losing his job at 50, the children wonder if doors will be closed when they finish school. Cynicism and hopelessness are not far away. Some time ago a Nobel Prize winner, now 80, was asked what he would do if he were now 20. He replied, "I'd go to drugs and fornication." Excess in drugs, alcohol, and sex are symptoms of this cynicism that hovers near.

On an airliner I sat next to a businessman from Denver, who told me that whenever he was transferred to another city the first thing he and his family did was to find a church home, where they could be anchored among friends who believed in God and who could support them in this uneasy and mobile age.

They devoted themselves to the apostles' teaching and fellowship, to the breaking of bread and the prayers (Acts 2:42).

In a profound sense we can never be alone, not even with God. When we pray to him and invite him to come to us, we discover that we have no private party with him. He brings with him all who are his. He also brings with him all who are in need and says, "Whatever you have done for the least of these, you have done for me." So, as we go to our private rooms or sit alone with God, we sense the vast company to which we belong in him, and we cannot escape those whom the Lord asks us to help and to love.

Even the Lord often withdrew from the crowds, and even from the disciples, to be alone with his Father. When he foretold that they would all leave him, he added, "Yet I am not alone, for the Father is with me." And while on the cross, abandoned by his own and surrounded by the angry mob, he seemed to withdraw into the presence of his Father, and addressed him in those memorable last words from the cross, "Father, forgive them."

None of us can hope to capture the intimacy that held the Father and his only begotten Son together, but it is the will of our Lord that we try. After all, he won for us the right to be sons and daughters again, and to call God "our Father."

God comes to us in the person of Jesus. We are not left to guess what God is like or to conjure up some image of him out of our fancies. Jesus told us that he and the Father were one. We touch the mystery of the triune God by coming into the presence of Jesus, our brother and Lord.

As we ask him for things, let us not forget that above all else he has given us *himself*. He has given us a universe, a land, air and water, our bodies and our minds. But above all that which he has given, that which cannot be taken from us against our will, is himself. He doesn't come empty-handed. He is ready to give everything our hearts desire, unless what we desire is harmful for us or for others.

It is important, however, not to look just for what he may bring, but to focus simply on him. If someone we love, a son or a daughter, has been far from home and now walks in through the door, it would be childish to ask, "What did you bring?" We are overwhelmed by a presence, and we say simply, "Oh, how good it is to have you here." God has given us the supreme right always to say, "Oh, how good it is to have you here!"

Whither shall I go from thy Spirit? Or whither shall I flee from thy presence? If I ascend to heaven, thou art there (Psalm 139:7).

Dorothy Sayers, best known for her early detective stories, and later for her celebrated life of Jesus, *The Man Born to Be King*, has as the theme of her play, *The Just Vengeance*, the doctrine of the atonement. In these lines God is made to ask after the Fall of Adam and the murder of Cain:

> What did you do? What did you do for Us
> By what you did for yourselves in the moment of choice?
> O Eve, my daughter, and O my dear son Adam,
> Whose flesh was fashioned to be My tabernacle,
> Try to understand that when you chose your will
> Rather than Mine, and when you chose to know evil
> In your way and not in Mine, you chose for Me.
> It is My will you should know Me as I am—
> But how? For you chose to know your good as evil,
> Therefore the face of God is evil to you,
> And you know My love as terror, My mercy as judgment,
> My innocence as a sword; My naked life
> Would slay you, How can you know Me then?
> Yet know you must, since you were made for that;
> Thus either way you perish. Nay, but the hands
> That made you hold you still; and since you would not
> Submit to God, God shall submit to you,
> Not of necessity, but free to choose
> For your love's sake what you refused to Mine.
> God shall be man; that which man chose for man
> God shall endure, and what man chose to know
> God shall know too—the experience of evil
> In the flesh of man: and certainly He shall feel
> Terror and judgment and the point of the sword,
> And God shall see man's face like flint
> Against Him; and man shall see the Image of God
> In the image of man; and man shall show no mercy.
> Truly I will bear your sin and carry your sorrow,
> And, if you will, bring you to the tree of life,
> Where you may eat, and know your evil as good,
> Redeeming that first knowledge. But all this
> Still at your choice, and only as you choose,
> Save as you choose to let Me choose you.

Then the Lord God said to the woman, "What is this that you have done?" (Gen. 3:13).

The psalmist says, "A thousand years in thy sight are but as yesterday" (Psalm 90:4). God is not harried by the clock. He can wait. One would think that a God who designed the universe to function with such precision that we can predict moonflights with computerized accuracy would be completely intolerant with waiting.

But he is a waiting God. He has infinite patience with his children—not with the galaxies, nor with the rising and setting of the sun—only with his children.

To understand this, we must remember that he gave the gift of freedom to his children. We may obey or disobey. He deals with us as sons and daughters, not as pieces of the game, or as cogs in his machine.

When he sees his children turning away from him and going on paths that will lead to pain and ruin, he has no option but to let us go. He does not withdraw the gift of choice from us. He does not, in impatience, change us into puppets or robots. We might wish that he would, when we plunge ourselves into wars and other disasters. But he wants us with him as a family, not as an army camp or a zoo. He grieves, he is indignant, but he does not try to force us to turn about and find his will. He waits.

Helmut Thielicke has a series of sermons on the story of the prodigal son which he calls *The Waiting Father*. No parable of Jesus is so poignant a picture of God as this. When the son asked for the inheritance and went to the far country, the father could have refused, locked him up, and spared him that sorry chapter of his life. But this is not the way of God. Or he could have sent his servants to the far country, kidnapped the son, and brought him safely home. But he didn't.

Yet the father did not forget his son; he yearned for his return. Day after day, he waited. What sorrow there must be for our heavenly Father to have us wander off, squander our lives in selfish pursuits, while he must wait and wait for us to discover that we are lost.

In a profound sense, of course, he does pursue us. He does this through the Word and sacraments, the means of grace through which the Holy Spirit keeps calling us. But in pursuing us, he is not a hunter who forces his prey. God may be at our heels, but he will not trap us, catch us in some net, or bring us down by force. He is nearer than the air we breathe, but he waits.

There is joy before the angels of God over one sinner who repents (Luke 15:10).

HOW SHAMEFUL OF GOD August 1

Friedrich Nietzsche, a German philosopher and the son of a Lutheran pastor, held the Christian faith in derision. He contended that it was impossible to respect, much less worship, a God who shamefully allowed himself to be crucified by hoodlums. He dubbed the way of Christians "the morality of slaves."

It has never been easy for the secular mind (even for Christians) to think of God in terms of suffering. To conceive of him as all-powerful, all-knowing, everywhere-present, holy and just—this makes sense. But to have him victimized by his own mercy to the point of having mortal man put him to death—this is an "offense," "a stumbling block," and "foolishness."

The Israelites, nursing the promise of a Messiah or deliverer all those centuries, had trouble with that great picture in Isaiah 53 of the Savior as the suffering servant. They chose to believe that the one to come would deliver them from their many oppressors and usher in a new era of national glory, as in the days of King David. When Jesus came, he fulfilled the prophesies of the Old Testament in his life, death, and resurrection, but did not reveal his power and overcome the legions of Rome. Most of the people therefore could not accept him as the promised one. Why should God have to suffer?

We, too, may have some trouble keeping a dying Lord in focus as the suffering servant. We may prefer to worship a risen Lord whose church is a billion strong, a Lord who will come in glory to confound all his enemies. On the other hand, it is not likely that a single church would have been built had our Lord not given his life on a cross for us. The cross is the most powerful symbol of the church, more moving than the empty grave. It is in our Lord's sufferings and death that we find the God of infinite love.

His sufferings did not end with the cross. We see him still, 2000 years later, as the man of sorrows, the lamb of God. He is not only high and lifted up, he is in the thick of our sorrows, grieving with us.

What a comforting thing it is to worship a God who not only sits in the bleachers to watch our struggles, but who "weeps with those who weep."

For we have not a high priest who is unable to sympathize with our weaknesses, but one who in every respect has been tempted as we are, yet without sinning (Heb. 4:15).

There's nothing quite like being bitter to make everyone around you miserable. It could well be, too, that bitterness is the seed of mental illness. You may have a right to be bitter. Someone has wronged you. You hurt. Or, growing older, it may seem that life has passed you by. The dreams and aspirations of youth are long gone. Harry Emerson Fosdick, former pastor of New York's Riverside Church, says:

How easy it is to grow bitter about life! And in personal human relationships, as on an autumn day one walks through a rough country field and comes back covered with nettles, how easy it is to walk through life and accumulate stings! One knows well that some people here this morning are sorely tempted to bitterness and therefore to mental ill health.

For as soon as you see the other thing, an unembittered soul, generous, magnanimous, full of radiant and undiscourageable goodwill, you know that *that* is healthy-mindedness.

Consider a homely illustration of this. A century ago a French citizen left to the French Academy a fund which, increased by others, year after year furnishes prizes for conspicuous exhibitions of virtue discovered in the French population. Here is a typical case: Jeanne Chaix, the eldest of six children—mother insane, father chronically ill; she with no more money than the wages she earns in the pasteboard factory where she works, brings up the family, maintains the entire household, which, says the record, "subsists, morally as well as materially, by the sole force of her valiant will."

With these few facts, what do you know about Jeanne Chaix, standing there to receive her prize from the French Academy? You know this: she had not grown bitter; life had done hard things to her but she had not been embittered; she must have been sustained by an undiscourageable goodwill. She was a healthy-minded girl. . . .

Bitterness imprisons life; love releases it. Bitterness paralyzes life; love empowers it. Bitterness sours life; love sweetens it. Bitterness sickens life; love heals it. Bitterness blinds life; love anoints its eyes.

See to it that no one fail to obtain the grace of God; that no "root of bitterness" spring up and cause trouble, and by it the many become defiled (Heb. 12:15).

We have no trouble with the word *saint* when it is given to a Paul or a Peter or a Francis or a Teresa. But we do have trouble with it when it is applied to people of average, or below average, excellence, such as we are. Yet on Sunday morning we confess glibly that we believe in the church, "the communion of saints"—which means us.

Yet, if on the street someone greets us "you old saint, you," we'd probably feel uneasy—perhaps more uneasy than if he had slapped us on the back and said, "You old sinner, you." For most people the word *saint* has gotten an altogether wrong meaning—a person who is gentle, perhaps a bit naive, someone you'd hardly elect president of the local union or bank.

In the rough and tumble world of ruthless competition, one might conclude that even the great saints would hardly qualify. Peter the fisherman, erratic and stubborn. Paul, rather sharp, who went overboard on a vision he had on the Damascus road. John the disciple, a mild dreamer carried away by emotions of love and ending his days writing the rather unintelligible last book of the Bible, Revelation. And Francis who gave away his money and princely station to become a voluntary beggar, writing sweet things about birds and angels. Hardly a crowd to elect to the board of General Motors.

But—why not a saint winning the world's heavyweight title, or being the whip in Congress, or amassing a fortune in wheat, or standing up unflinchingly to death in a concentration camp, or spanning the seven seas for a cause? Why not?

Just what is a saint? Simply stated and most important, he is a person whom Jesus has saved and taken to himself. To be sure, that's not the picture of a hero standing up to God or battling him on even terms in the ring. You are a saint not because you have held your own with God. In repentance and faith you have capitulated to him. But from that point on you do not go on capitulating. You, the saint, are surrendered to God; but you do not go on surrendering to anyone *but* God.

Nor is the word *surrender* the whole story. It is not as if your will is gone in a weary collapse to the will of the Lord. You *embrace* his will. You make it your own—freely—in gratitude for the incredible fact that he loves you, that he gave his life for you, that he honors you with a firm place in his kingdom and its enterprises on earth. You have been enlisted, with all your faculties, as a saint!

Paul, an apostle of Christ Jesus . . . to the saints who are also faithful in Christ Jesus (Eph. 1:1).

FREEDOM AND RIGHTEOUSNESS August 4

God wants to give us both freedom and righteousness, not freedom alone or righteousness alone, but the two together. There are people who think of freedom as that state where they may do willy-nilly as they please, quite outside of any authority or standards. And there are people who conceive of righteousness as a kind of negative obedience to law. Freedom without righteousness becomes personal license; righteousness without freedom becomes personal bondage.

God is free and he is righteous, and he wants his children to share this dual character. To be given this dual gift, we must be brought back—really *reabsorbed*—to God. And it will be a gift. In our blindness, we go about to climb the ladder of discipline and good works, confident that if we succeed in climbing high enough we will at last reach the rung on which God stands awaiting us. If we slip a step or two, we reassure ourselves that if we try, and try again, at long last we most surely will succeed.

There is something gallant, and even something pedagogically necessary, in making the try. Without trying, we will never know personally the blazing truth of grace alone. How can we know if we have not earnestly tried the ladder of discipline and good works?

Luther gave himself a good workout on the ladder. As an Augustinian monk he not only submitted to the rigorous disciplines of his order, but he imposed on himself added self-denials in a fierce attempt to reach the favor of God. It was not until he had climbed and climbed and had succeeded only in plunging to greater and greater despair that he was ready for the glorious alternative.

But many do not climb high enough to make Luther's discovery. Many settle down on the second or third rung and live in the illusion that they have arrived. They become glued to a few trivial rules and settle back into a spiritual smugness, a priggish pride and moral mediocrity. They have a form of godliness but have none of the spirit. They become a caricature of freedom and righteousness.

It was not so with Luther, nor with Brand in Ibsen's play. Brand, the preacher, senses the grim demands of the ladder, all or nothing, and only when in the final scene the avalanche rolls toward him does he hear through the thunder, *Deus caritas*, God is grace.

Indeed I count everything as loss because of the surpassing worth of knowing Christ Jesus my Lord. For his sake I have suffered the loss of all things, and count them as refuse, in order that I may gain Christ and be found in him, not having a righteousness of my own (Phil. 3:8-9).

Most of us are not good listeners. In our eagerness to be heard, we often interrupt someone who is talking. We are at once thoughtless and rude. There is a little verse:

There was an old owl liv'd in an oak,
The more he heard, the less he spoke;
The less he spoke, the more he heard,
O, if men were all like that wise bird!

We may learn much by being silent, even from people who are not especially wise. But this habit becomes crucial when it concerns God. After all, God does speak. "In many and various ways God spoke of old to our fathers by the prophets; but in these last days he has spoken to us by a Son, whom he appointed the heir of all things."

We need not lapse into some kind of spell in order to hear God. It is in and through the 66 books of the Bible that God most clearly addresses us. The Holy Spirit broods and lurks in this book to have us hear God and come to him. If we read the Bible in order to get information about Noah, for instance, we use the Bible for secondary purposes. Or if we become absorbed in verifying the cosmology and history of the Bible, we become sidetracked from its main purpose. Kierkegaard called such people "parentheses hounds" who break into a gallop over side issues. The chief purpose God has with us is to tell of his will and his love, so that we may yield ourselves to him.

The Scriptures are full of the wisdom of God. They make clear the laws that he wants us to live by. They reveal the purposes of God. Most of all, they disclose God's great love for us, and tell of the lengths to which it has gone to save us. It would be tragic if we did not hear him out.

If we hear him clearly in his Word, our ears will be open to hear his voice in many places and circumstances. The cries of the world's needy will be his voice. Nor will this be primarily the corporate cry of suffering mankind; the cry will best be heard in some suffering, lonely, oppressed, hungry and sick *one*, someone perhaps at your very elbow. All nature may begin to speak his voice: the surf of the sea, the roar of thunder, the wind in the trees, the laughter of children at play. The Scriptures will have attuned our ears to hear him everywhere.

He was still speaking, when lo, a bright cloud overshadowed them, and a voice from the cloud said, "This is my beloved Son, with whom I am well pleased; listen to him" (Matt. 17:5).

Most of us can stand some comfort. We are not Sir Galahads, mounted on great prancing steeds, eager to hear the charge, "Forward!" Our spirits are not too high. More than likely, we are rheumatic riders on some spavined nags, with trembling hands and fearful hearts. We have deep wounds of the spirit to be healed, aching and tired muscles of the will to be massaged. Before God can talk the language of hope to us, he must fill our ears with his message of comfort. Before our spirits will be stirred with the challenge, "Be strong . . . acquit yourselves as men," our hearts will have to be comforted by the invitation, "Come unto me, all ye who labor and are heavy laden, and I will give you rest."

Precisely at this point is where the weight of the Scriptures lies. The God of the Bible is not principally a field general pressing you on into the fight; much more often he is a field physician bending over your wounded spirits and your broken dreams. The kingdom of heaven is not pictured as an army regiment, with God the commander; the kingdom is rather a family, with God as father. And do you recall from your own family or home what characterized it more than any other quality? Is it not there, more than in any other place in the world, you have found refuge and security and sympathy and comfort? Of course it was there that you learned the great lessons of right and wrong. There you may have been first inspired to noble living. But above all else, it was there that you could retreat from the indifference of the school, the shop, or the office to find someone who cared and who would give you comfort. Who among us does not feel the nostalgia of these lines:

> Backward, turn backward, O Time, in your flight,
> Make me a child again, just for tonight.
> Mother, come back from the echoless shore,
> Take me again to your heart, as of yore.
> Kiss from my forehead the furrows of care,
> Smooth the few silver threads out of my hair.
> Over my slumbers your loving watch keep.
> Rock me to sleep, Mother, rock me to sleep.

Comfort, comfort my people, says your God. Speak tenderly to Jerusalem, and cry to her that her warfare is ended, that her iniquity is pardoned, that she has received from the Lord's hand double for all her sins (Isa. 40:1-2).

You can have fun as a sinner, and you can have fun as a saint. But in between, as a reluctant, cautious Christian, you will be intolerably bored. And the pity of so much of our discipleship is that we have never gotten to the point where we are having fun being Christian. We are like bathers who have left the ease of lounging on the beach to take to the water, but have been wading only up to our ankles or knees, all the while with chattering teeth, looking longingly back to the beach or occasionally gazing a bit wistfully out to the deep where real swimmers and divers are having a rollicking time.

There are Christians who, having left the tents of wickedness, have failed in courage to stride into the palace and join the company of the King. Of those in the palace, the Bible said, ". . . and they were filled with the Holy Ghost." These were the people who were tasting some new-found joy and peace and power. They had thrown caution to the winds; they were caught up in a quiet ecstasy; they had the glint of excitement and adventure in their eye. They had made a clean break with some things and they were in clean, certain stride toward something.

Why, do you suppose, is it that we run-of-the-mill church people are missing so much of that joy? Someone from the outside will say of us, and quite justly so perhaps, that he has no desire to get involved with us who pretend to be better than the open sinners and yet are critical, harsh, unforgiving, glum, humorless, without imagination and without laughter. And he may go on to point out that for all our talk about a great King and a Kingdom, we are as plebeian a crowd as you can find.

The great message of the gospel is that you need not be a hero to reach the palace, battling your lonely way up some steep and craggy ascent. You reach the palace by being *led*. A divine companion, the Holy Spirit, ushers you upward and into its spacious halls. Here you will find joy, new and terrifying responsibilities, and glory. The native element of the bird is the air; the native element of the fish is the water; the native element for us is the kingdom of God.

Do not get drunk with wine, for that is debauchery; but be filled with the Spirit (Eph. 5:18).

Oscar Wilde once said: "If a friend of mine . . . gave a feast, and did not invite me to it, I should not mind a bit. . . . But if . . . a friend of mine had a sorrow and refused to allow me to share it, I should feel it most bitterly. If he shut the doors of the house of mourning against me, I would move back again and again and beg to be admitted, so that I might share in what I was entitled to share. If he thought me unworthy, unfit to weep with him, I should feel it as the most poignant humiliation, as the most terrible mode which disgrace could be inflicted on me . . . he who can look on the loveliness of the world and share its sorrow, and realize something of the wonder of both, is in immediate contact with divine things, and has got as near to God's secret as anyone can get."

Dear Mr. Wilde, you must realize that it's not easy to let someone, even a dear friend, into my house of mourning. The pain is deep, and I fear that you may treat it lightly, apply some ointment of cliché, when the wound is far down somewhere. If I could be sure that you would settle for silence, a touch, an embrace, I would have courage to open the door.

You'll have to remember that if the hurt is of my own making, my guilt may close the door on you. I've made my bed, and it's mine to sleep in. And should you, even by a lilt in your voice, say, "You know you had it coming," I don't need you. Even if you bring no note of blame or reproach, you have no power to forgive me. Only God, and those I have wronged, can bring healing.

One of my sons once told me he thought my generation kept our hurts, our worries and cares, too much to ourselves. He shook me with his logic. He said, "Doesn't the Bible tell us that we are to bear one another's burdens and to weep with those who weep?" Then he added, "How am I to weep with you, Dad, if you don't let me know that you're weeping?"

Yes, Mr. Wilde, you are right. If I open my house of mourning to you, I am honoring you far more than inviting you to a feast.

So then, as we have opportunity, let us do good to all men, and especially to those who are of the household of faith (Gal. 6:10).

He came meek! Have you ever thought how things might have been if Christ had not come lowly as a babe in Bethlehem's stable, or meek as a commonplace preacher on a donkey, or unresisting as a sacrifice on Calvary's cross? He could have chosen a blazing pathway through the skies, flanked by millions of armored angels. He could have circled the earth with the thunder of a thousand tornadoes and typhoons, and with a fireworks display of bursting galaxies. He could have established his throne on the peaks of the Himalayas or the Swiss Alps, and ever after policed every household with secret cherubim and seraphim. He could have brought to swift and unrelenting justice any budding Nebuchadnezzar or Nero or Stalin. And he could have won the paralyzing obedience of every trembling child of men. Why did he come meek?

It is not for us to make a brief for God. His ways need not pass inspection before our feeble minds. But this much seems certain, that the response he would have elicited from you and me by an explosive display of his power was not the response he wanted.

He could have won our *fear*. But he was playing for bigger stakes. He had set out to win our love, and with love, our freedom. Fear always imprisons, paralyzes, and drives a person into the narrow cell of extreme self-concern. Love, on the other hand, casts out fear, sets a person free, and gives feet and wings to escape the prison walls of self-anxiety, self-defense, and self-pity. God had created us to be sons and daughters in his Kingdom, comrades of God and the angels in this business of managing and enjoying the universe. Could he, the great God, be a bungler, and for the small and immediate prize of enforced obedience, crush our spirits into the cowering slavery of fear? Better to lose us altogether than to win us on any other terms than love and freedom.

Tagore in his little volume, *Fireflies*, says, "The clumsiness of power spoils the key and uses the pickax." Whatever else may be said of God, he is not clumsy. He chose to use the key of infinite love and suffering and not the pickax of power.

It took none less than the great King himself, God the Son, "who for the joy that was set before him endured the cross, despising the shame," to teach us the sublime lesson of love and suffering and freedom.

Rejoice greatly, O daughter of Zion! Shout aloud, O daughter of Jerusalem! Lo, your king comes to you; triumphant and victorious is he; humble and riding on an ass (Zech. 9:9).

Does anyone feel safe, really safe? You have robust health, but you know a heart is one beat from death, and you know that a healthy athlete may be killed by a drunken driver. You have a good job, good salary, a portfolio of good stocks and bonds, but you know that these cannot guarantee that your wife will love you, and you know that an economic crisis could eliminate both your job and your investments. We live in an insecure world.

Knowing this, as we all do, we still try in countless ways, most of them fraudulent, to take all sorts of precautions against misfortune and disaster. Chief among them is accumulating money. Yet no one is agreed on how much is needed. A person with no reserves thinks that $1000 in a savings account would be security. Having $1000, he goes for $5000, then for $10,000, and on and on. If and when he reaches 1 million, he is as uneasy as ever, perhaps more. Now every vibration in the stock market sends his blood pressure up.

The bewildering madness of our day is the spectacle of nations seeking security by an unprecedented amassing of arms. A statistical analysis provided by the Quakers in 1975 disclosed the following:

The nations of the world have spent $4.5 trillion for "military security" since 1946.

This year they will spend upwards of $240 billion for "military security."

The United States accounts for over ⅓ of all military expenditures on the planet.

The nuclear arsenal of the United States now holds the equivalent of 615,000 Hiroshima-sized bombs, enough to annihilate every major Soviet city 36 times. The Soviet Union can level every major American city 11 times.

How much will it take until we feel safe? Neither an individual nor a nation can feel safe no matter what money or power they may command. Safety or security is a gift of the Spirit, and rests in the heart of man.

Unless the Lord watches over the city, the watchman stays awake in vain (Psalm 127:1).

Heaven is greedy. God and the angels yearn to have you and me forever. Christ died on a cross to make it possible. When we accept his grace, heaven tingles with joy.

The incredible message of grace is that you are accepted. Despite anything you are or have done or have failed to do, you are accepted in and through Christ. That which is greater than you enfolds you. Do not try to do anything at the moment; perhaps later you will do much. Simply rest back now in the glorious fact that you are accepted. Let the eternal moment of grace sink in upon your troubled heart. You are loved; you are cradled in the everlasting arms. You are swallowed up, and your life is hid in Christ. That is grace.

Your old capricious and competitive self is in death throes; a new life is born. Nothing in all God's universe is as momentous as this event in you. That which excites God is what happens to you—an eternal soul. He did not die to create new heavens; he died on a cross to capture you.

Only once in my memory has the fate of one person captured the imagination of the world, and for an hour crowded all else. At 24 minutes after 10 on the night of May 21, 1927, over the airport of Paris there slipped out of the darkness a gray-white airplane and lighted on the far side of the field as 100,000 people pressed forward to welcome the first man to fly alone across the Atlantic from New York to Paris. That afternoon the *New York Times* was flooded with 10,000 telephone calls of inquiry. The *Times* for May 22 reports, "New York bubbled all day yesterday with excitment and expectancy, first yearning for word of Captain Lindbergh, then half-doubting, gaining confidence as the afternoon progressed, finally acclaiming victory in the greatest demonstration the Western world had seen for a decade," all because a boyish looking man whose fate was undetermined until his craft came to rest in a firm place.

Your flight has heaven all astir. God and the legions of angels are observing you with bated breath, hoping you will come to rest on the firm rock of your salvation, restless until your life is hid with Christ in God, until you rest back in the wondrous fact of grace. As you do, all heaven bursts forth in paeans of joy and hallelujahs.

I tell you, there will be more joy in heaven over one sinner who repents than over ninety-nine righteous persons who need no repentance (Luke 15:7).

The Bible often uses the word *return*. To return, or go back, is not altogether a popular cry, least of all in this 20th century with its worship of progress. We have learned to exalt that which is new or modern, until we often assume that because a thing is new it therefore must be better than that which is old. A new book, a new fashion, a new friend, a new wife must necessarily be an advance over the former. So we press on in adventure and anticipation for something novel.

There are people who disclaim this god, progress, and just as foolishly extol that which is old. They speak of "the good, old days," as if the old days were all good. They praise the simple life of the pioneers, as if life was so much simpler when drinking water had to be carried in a pail. They see greatness in people who are dead and gone, but regard their neighbors as stupid or immoral.

Then there are people who worship the status quo. The present order is best. They disdain the past, and they fear future change as revolutionary. They want neither the hard road back nor the perilous road forward. They have neither the repentance required for turning around and going back, nor have they the gallantry to press on and go forward. They sit smugly by, protesting any change.

The prophets of the Lord were unanimous in calling on people to return—not to some golden age of the past, however. The call was always to return *to the Lord*. And that's a long cry from a return to some vague, idealized past. It is the journey of the soul back to the Creator who made him and to the Savior who redeemed him.

To return, in that type of journey, is a more rigorous and exacting passage than any other. For it implies that a man has been going in the wrong direction and that he faces squarely the folly and sinfulness of his ways. How much more palatable to our pride if the prophets had called on us to press on to God, you gallant ones. But they cry, return! Take the road of sorrow and penitence, abandon the bravado of self-sufficiency, turn about and find the God who awaits you. This journey, at first so unattractive, has the wonder of ushering the soul into adventures and enterprises that never grow old.

Let the wicked forsake his way, and the unrighteousness man his thoughts; and let him return to the Lord, that he may have mercy on him, and to our God, for he will abundantly pardon (Isa. 55:7).

Obedience is not one of the popular virtues. Few firms, looking for an executive, will ask, "Can he obey orders?" They ask for his qualities of leadership: "Can he give orders?" Few people with their lives snarled up are told by their psychologist, "The trouble with you is that you fail to obey."

With God, obedience is one of the cardinal virtues. In fact, the whole orientation of life centers about obedience. The whole miserable catalog of man's troubles began with disobedience, when Adam and Eve failed to obey the simple command of God.

It is obedience to God that is the key to being rescued from the chaos of our own erratic desires, to finding the meaning of life. Once we have surrendered the sovereignty of our lives to another command, the will of God, we are on the road to finding ourselves, to integrity, to healing, to a fullness of living.

Søren Kierkegaard has a striking analogy:

> Once upon a time there was a rich man; he ordered from abroad at an exorbitant price a pair of faultless and highbred horses which he would use for his own pleasure and for the pleasure of driving them himself. Then something like a year or two passed. Anyone who previously had known these horses would not have been able to recognize them again. Their eyes had become dull and drowsy, their gait lacked style and decision, they couldn't bear anything, they couldn't hold out, they hardly could drive four miles without having to stop on the way, sometimes they came to a standstill while he sat and drove his best; besides that, they had acquired all sorts of vices and bad habits. . . . Then he had the King's coachman called. He drove them for a month—in the whole land there was not a pair of steeds that held their heads so proudly, whose glance was so fiery, whose gait was so handsome. . . . How came this about? It is easy to see—the owner, who without being a coachman gave himself out to be a coachman, drove them according to the horses' understanding of what it is to drive; the royal coachman drove them according to the coachman's understanding of what it is to drive.
>
> So it is with men. Oh, when I think of myself and of the countless men I have known, I have often said sorrowfully to myself: Here are enough talents and powers and capacities—but the coachman is lacking.

They who wait for the Lord shall renew their strength, they shall mount up with wings like eagles, they shall run and not be weary, they shall walk and not faint (Isa. 40:31).

Many a person has lost faith in God because the world seemed topsy-turvy. The innocent suffer, the righteous are persecuted and the wicked prosper. If that's the sort of world God has made and manages, how can a person put any faith in God?

Why can't God at least be fair? This is the cry. Why should a good son suffer because his father is in prison, and a renegade son be excused because his family is wealthy? Why in war should a God-fearing soldier be killed and a drunken nobody be spared? Why in industry should a cunning and ruthless scoundrel become rich and his hard-working, honest employee get cancer and die?

There is no easy way to resolve these questions, but God does speak for himself in our Holy Scriptures. There it is clear that the pain and sorrow and injustice of the world are not God's doing. These are all intruders, thieves who came in through the back door against God's will. When God had completed his work of creation, crowning his work with the creation of man in his own image, the Bible declares that he beheld his work and, lo, it was all very good. Then sin came. God's perfect plan was violently disturbed. A horde of enemies descended: hatred, murder, selfishness, vice, sickness, and death.

It is clear, too, that while life is unfair in many ways, there is a justice that is silently at work. There are compensations, or rewards, for the upright which are not quickly evident. There are punishments for the wicked which no law court need administer: the uneasy conscience, the restless heart, the fear of discovery and reprisal, self-reproach, and the dread of overhanging judgment. "Day and night thy hand was heavy upon me," said David in his hour of wrong.

But faith in a just world is not very comforting, even for the best of people. Who among us would like to stand before God and ask for what we had coming, no more and no less? If God should be fair, and mark every iniquity, who could stand? Our hope is that God will not be fair, that he will be much more than fair. With the publican in the parable, we will all cry, "God be merciful to me, a sinner."

We do not want a fair God, after all, unless he is also a God of mercy. And he is a God of infinite mercy. Meeting him at the foot of the cross of Christ, we know him as a God who has left justice far behind and deals with us in the wonderful world of mercy.

If thou, O Lord, shouldst mark iniquities, Lord, who could stand? But there is forgiveness with thee, that thou mayest be feared (Psalm 130:3-4).

The Christian church really has but one book. Of course thousands of books have been written about the faith, but all draw from one book, the Bible. The Bible is the basis for our faith.

We who are Christians believe that the Bible is different from all other books. It is not an encyclopedia where you can look up information about birds or stars. The whole world of chemistry and biology, for instance, is not in this book. God gives us this kind of knowledge largely through studies in science.

The Bible is God's book, and God reveals himself in it. He does not tell us everything about himself in this book, but he does tell us all that we need to know about him. It is an old book. The last parts were written at least 1800 years ago. If you're studying aeronautics, you certainly will not go to the Bible. But for knowledge about God, an old book may be better than a new one. Plato's dialogues and Shakespeare's plays are old too, but they remain the best of their kind in every university of the land. And the Bible, an old book to be sure, is in a class by itself. It is the Word of God.

The strange thing about the Bible is that God uses it as a door through which he comes to us. It is almost as if he leaps out of the pages to enter our hearts. Or, think of the Bible as a lake. You sit on the bank fishing for knowledge about God. Suddenly God himself—not knowledge about him—takes the hook and pulls you in. God catches *you*.

By far the most important fact about the Bible is that Jesus Christ is in it. Luther said that the Bible is like a cradle holding Jesus. If you are starting from scratch to read the Bible, you should probably first read the four Gospels, the accounts of Jesus' life and sayings. Something remarkable then will happen; you find that Jesus is more than the total of what he said and did. Jesus himself becomes the Word. You not only learn about God through him. You know God and are brought to him through Jesus.

It is when we do more than hurry through a few verses—as we frequently do—and begin living with and loving certain parts of the book, it is then that it becomes alive for us, and we begin to know it as a great treasure.

All scripture is inspired by God and profitable for teaching, for reproof, for correction, and for training in righteousness, that the man of God may be complete, equipped for every good work (2 Tim. 3:16-17).

Much has been made of the difference between the Greek and the Hebrew manner of dealing with and expressing truth. The Hebrews (as in the Old Testament and in the parables of Jesus, for instance) dealt in pictures and concrete events. The Greeks, as in Plato and Aristotle, dealt in abstractions and universals. The Western world has inherited more from the Greeks than from the Hebrews and tend, therefore, to want to extract a philosophy of some kind from the biblical revelation. William F. Lynch, in his book, *Christ and Apollo,* quotes from a French biblical scholar, Claude Tresmontant:

> In the Biblical mode of expression, it is enough to be human to understand that which is proposed. The Biblical parable is as intelligible for the Galilean peasant as for the Corinthian docker in the time of St. Paul, as it is for the worker in the factories of Paris in our time. We must even add, by them above all. Greco-Latin culture is often an impediment to an understanding of these parables, which imply a sense of the real and of work, and such a love of the concrete element as seems a defect to a Platonic mentality; the latter is more or less unconsciously dualist, and too aristocratic to prove the depth and richness of the mystical content of these daily realities of working with the elemental . . . . the particular in the Biblical universe is neither negligible or insignificant. It is a vehicle of sense.

> God has chosen a particular people among the nations to manifest the truth. To do this He called a particular man who is named Abraham, at one particular time and in one limited place. The Incarnation is the choice of the particular, of the real with all its historical and geographic contingencies; a particular woman, a particular epoch. . . . God Himself becomes someone particular for us, concrete, an individual with his name, country, his face, his history. The choice of the particular to manifest universal truth, to teach the truth which by right is universal, is without doubt the most profound intellectual scandal, the scandal par excellence for the Greek mind.

For since, in the wisdom of God, the world did not know God through wisdom, it pleased God through the folly of what we preach to save those who believe . . . . we preach Christ crucified, a stumbling block to Jews and folly to Gentiles (1 Cor. 1:21-23).

The most important family you have is the big family of God—the one, holy, Christian and apostolic church. At baptism you were brought into this family. The family circles the whole world, and it even includes those who have left this world and now live in heaven.

The family next in importance is your own—parents and children, brothers and sisters. God loans us to each other to love one another.

You did not choose your parents, nor your brothers and sister. In a sense, they did not choose you either, even though they wanted you. Before you were born or before you were adopted, they didn't know precisely what sort of person you would be. Now we are thrown together, and we all have the privilege and the task of wanting each other and loving each other.

If you are a son or daughter, remember it might have been easier for your parents if they did not have you—or any children. Without children they would be free to come and go whenever they chose, and they would have more money to spend. They would not have to worry about you when you are sick. But they want you.

If you are a parent, remember that, more than anyone else, you will determine the outcome of your child's life. If making money and having fine things are your important concerns, these are the values your children will have. If you are indifferent about the church, it will be difficult for them to take God and his will seriously. If success (however that's defined) is more important to you than honesty and compassion for others, you'll probably have children who will use people for their own purposes instead of being true friends. By what you say or do, you are your children's prime teachers.

We have much power over each other in the family. Children have frightening power. They more than anyone else can make their parents glad or sad. Parents have awesome power. By their love and wise counsel they can encourage love for God and become God's agents, giving their children a sense of worth and security, compassion, and courage for the future.

But no person, and no family, is sufficient unto itself. If a family is marooned by itself, turning in upon its own needs alone, lavishing things upon themselves, even if they achieve love among their members, the family itself becomes selfish, indulgent, and spiritually impoverished. The family, too, needs to be lost in love of God and the neighbor.

And these words which I command you this day shall be upon your heart; and you shall teach them diligently to your children (Deut. 6:6-7).

One night, while I watched a favorite old movie on television, a repetitious commercial kept dinning in my ears with the obvious truth that I deserved a bargain priced round trip to Hawaii, at least a low priced round trip to Las Vegas. The refrain was, "You need it, you deserve it." The wind chill at the moment, as I remember, was 58 degrees below zero, so perhaps we did need it. Moreover, our neighbors (fine people, but no finer than we!) had just gone to Hawaii; we deserved a trip as much as they, didn't we?

For the advertising industry to stir my desires and make me covet is one thing, but to become moral and have me *deserve* it, is quite another. The subtle thrust of most advertising is the implication that if you desire something, you need it and you deserve it. Other people have it, why not you?

We ought to ask, who deserves what? Something, surely. Even Jesus said that a laborer is worthy of his hire; he deserves his wages. No economic system, whether socialist or capitalist, can ignore that rule. That a great athlete or rock singer deserves fifty times more than a teacher or a field worker is sheer nonsense, of course. And Jesus could hardly have meant that Americans deserve ten times more than an African or Pakistani.

In a very profound sense, we deserve nothing. We own nothing, after all. The heart that beats, the brain with its powers of reason, the air and water that sustains us—everything, including our very lives, is a gift from him who owns it all, and who has entrusted it all for us to manage for him. Even the just wage is ultimately a gift.

Our Father's rule of management is that all his children should share equitably in the resources necessary for life. Those who, because of their skills, hard work, and fortunate opportunities, have more than they need are for that very reason under the more stringent accountability. "To whom much is given, of him shall much be required" is the standard by which God judges our management.

You may or may not need it, but assuredly you do not deserve it!

I do not mean that others should be eased and you burdened, but that as a matter of equality your abundance at the present time should supply their want, so that their abundance may supply your want, that there may be equality (2 Cor. 8:13-14).

WHAT TO REMEMBER ABOUT THE CHURCH
August 19

If you are tempted to be disillusioned with the church, you need to retreat a few steps to take a second, hard look. P. T. Forsyth, eminent churchman of this century in London, invites you to such a look:

When we have written off the Church's mistakes and wickedness, past and present, which we are not likely to forget, let these things also be remembered:

1. Let us remember its historic work after all; in spite of its defalcations its survival today in such power and blessing; the lie given by its immortal remnants in every age to the principle of the big battalions; its minority victory through the ages; its principle of an elect; its consecration for the man's sake of the choice few.

2. Yet is the true Church not in a huge and standing majority among the powers that settle things at last? For before God the Church in heaven and on earth is one. There is not an organic severance. The Church in the Unseen comes in aid. The dead we call the majority; and surely the number of those who now live to God, seen and unseen, exceeds those around us on earth who are God's enemies.

3. But let us also add always to its numbers Christ Himself. If the presence of Napoleon on the field was worth 50,000 men, what is the value to the Church of His presence Who is more than worth the whole human race?

4. Consequently, the Church is the only society on earth whose battle is already won. The Church chiefly exists to certify that that battle was won in what was done by Christ, and that we have but to follow the victory up. Here again we see the radical difference between Church and State. The State only works forward through history to a life and a freedom always *to be* won; the Church works out a freedom already won once for all. The State can do with the legacy of the past what it will; the Church has, in its final Gospel from the past, a trust which it may not tamper with, which fashions and colours all it wills to do.

5. That is to say, the Church is the only society with a fulcrum outside the world; and therefore the only one that can move the world as a whole. Every Church has the whole true Church at the back of it, and the one full salvation.

But you have come to Mt. Zion and to the city of the living God, the heavenly Jerusalem, and to innumerable angels in festal gathering, and to the assembly of the firstborn who are enrolled in heaven, and to a judge who is God of all (Heb. 12:22-23).

Does anyone live without fear of impending disaster? Even a child, separated from his mother in a bus depot, suddenly is overcome by panic. His little world seems to collapse.

We live with an uneasy feeling that catastrophe may be just around the corner. We are human, and as such are dependent and independent beings. We know that we don't have everything under control. In a twinkling of an eye our lives can be changed, or gone. We do our best to build our little forts, but we know they rest on sand.

We've done a lot to keep nature from dealing us unexpected blows. With modern medicine we may never again have a bubonic plague, a Black Death that broke out in Constantinople in 1347 and decimated half of the world's population. Nor need Johnstown, Pennsylvania, destroyed in 1889 by floods, or Galveston, Texas, in 1900 by hurricane seas, fear similar catastrophes.

We humans are not as easily tamed as is nature. We continue in every age to blunder in avarice and hatreds, and to set the stage for gigantic upheavals. After a thousand years Rome fell in 410 when Alaric the Goth put the finishing touches on an empire that had rotted from within. In 1517 Luther's 95 Theses triggered the convulsion of a church grown proud and greedy, and released forces that reshaped the face of Europe and the form of the Christian church itself.

What of the 20th century? Already we have called it The Volcanic Century. We've had two world wars, plus Korea and Vietnam, the Communist upheavals in Russia and China, the genocide in Nazi Germany. This century has dislocated and killed more people than all previous centuries.

Nor has the world settled down. What catastrophes may lie ahead staggers the imagination. For the first time in history, the United States is clearly a military nation. And at long last the world has the capacity for nuclear suicide. It is said that the Trident submarine in our arsenal carries more destructive force than all the military establishments of Great Britain, Italy, Spain, Brazil, Argentina, West Germany, Japan, the Philippines, India and Pakistan put together. The world lives on the brink.

Only our lives in God are sure!

God is our refuge and strength, a very present help in trouble. Therefore we will not fear, though the earth should change (Psalm 46:1-2).

St. Paul said, "Let a man examine himself" and Socrates urged us, "Know thyself." But neither Paul nor Socrates, had they lived now, would have had any truck with the modern fad of psychological self-analysis. Each of these great sages embraced a moral universe. It was against the standard of truth, in all its moral and spiritual reality, that they urged us to examine and know ourselves. Do we measure up? That is the issue.

Simply to explore what you do, and why, with no other purpose than to know, is not only useless but most likely harmful. There is the legend of the centipede who, walking merrily along, was stopped by a friend who asked how it was possible for his numerous legs to function without colliding or becoming entangled. He had never once thought about that. But he began a process of self-examination, watching closely the movement of his legs, only to have them all tangled up and he rolling over into the ditch.

I may sound too skeptical. Most likely a person who sets out to examine his life may be dissatisfied with it and wants it changed. He may not yet have a model or a standard, but he doesn't like what he is and does. This makes him a candidate for the real thing. Paul and Socrates would take him on.

The professional counselor, and the world is full of them now, had better be committed to a standard of truth or morality or religion. Without this commitment, the counselor can be no more than a good photographer, taking psychological pictures of a person, and letting him see the dour result. And it will be dour. Or if the counselor should point beyond the "patient," and blame his troubles on parents that didn't love him, or grandparents with nasty dispositions, the consequence may only be that the patient now adds new hostilities.

To be examined against the law of God, and to discover the depth of one's sin and self-centeredness, may be more dreadful than any other kind of self-analysis. We not only see the abject picture, but are driven to the wall. No one, pastor or other professional, should subject anyone to this searing self-disclosure, unless he or she is ready with a cure.

And there is one: the overarching mercy and forgiveness of God. This wonderful truth is the healer, the power that can put together the broken pieces of a person's life.

He heals the broken hearted and binds up their wounds (Psalm 147:3).

Dag Hammarskjöld was Secretary General of the United Nations until his untimely death in 1961. Not until a collection of his "notes" was published later as *Markings* did the world know him not only as an economist and statesman but as a poet and mystic of profound spiritual insight. This is one of his notes.

He was impossible. It wasn't that he didn't attend to his work: on the contrary, he took endless pains over the tasks he was given. But his manner of behavior brought him into conflict with everybody and, in the end began to have an adverse effect on everything he had to do with.

When the crisis came and the whole truth had to come out, he laid the blame on us: in his conduct there was nothing, absolutely nothing to reproach. His self-esteem was so strongly bound up, apparently, with the idea of his innocence, that one felt a brute as one demonstrated, step by step, the contradictions in his defense and, bit by bit, stripped him naked before his own eyes. But justice to others demanded it.

When the last rag of a lie had been taken from him and we felt there was nothing more to be said, out it came in stifled sobs.

"But why did you never help me, why didn't you tell me what to do? You knew that I always felt you were against us. And fear and insecurity drove me further and further along the course you now condemn me for having taken. It's been so hard—everything. One day, I remember, I was so happy: one of you said that something I had produced was quite good—"

So, in the end, we were, in fact, to blame. We had not voiced our criticism, but we had allowed them to stop us from giving him a single word of acknowledgment, and in this way had barred every road to improvement.

For it is always the stronger who is to blame. We lack life's patience. Instinctively we try to eliminate a person from our sphere of responsibility as soon as the outcome of this particular experiment by Life appears, in our eyes, to be a failure. But Life pursues her experiments far beyond the limitations of our judgment. This is also the reason why, at times, it seems so much more difficult to live than to die.

Brethren, if a man is overtaken in any trespass, you who are spiritual should restore him in a spirit of gentleness. Look to yourself, lest you too be tempted (Gal. 6:1).

After one of my classmates dropped in his tracks from a heart attack at his church in Portland, Oregon, another classmate wrote me of the funeral. He said, "They told me it was a triumphant service, but I only wanted to cry."

In the last decade or two the churches have had a veritable epidemic of "celebrating" every life event with joy and triumph, as if grief does not belong in the repertoire of the Christian. The disposition to emphasize victory may be a subtle compensation for the pessimism that infects our age. But grief, remorse, fear, and even anger are marks of our humanity. To celebrate when we should grieve is a denial of being human. The writer in Ecclesiastes says, "For everything there is a season, and a time for every matter under heaven . . . a time to weep, and a time to laugh; a time to mourn and a time to dance."

Our family learned this lesson following the death of our son, Paul, in 1960. He had been in England for two years as a Rhodes scholar. Upon his return, ten minutes from home, accustomed as he now was to the flow of British traffic, he stepped from the curb into a truck and was instantly killed. Grief had come to our house.

The grief that struck with such wrenching pain, though now diminished in intensity, has remained like a minor chord among the more jubilant majors of our lives. Life lost some of its merriment and mirth, but we now know sorrow as a natural and not an ugly ingredient in life. To love is human and to grieve is human, and they belong together. We do not want to reject either.

The Bible calls death "the last enemy," but it may not be the most cruel. There are wounds of the human spirit more pervasively painful than death. We had not lost love. The love that held our family together suffered no loss with the life of one of us being transferred to a station on the other side of death. We now have Paul in the eternal bleachers (Hebrews 12:1) cheering us on. Once separated from us by an ocean, he now is beyond immediate reach across the silent river. But he is alive again in the consummate part of the Lord's empire. For this we can celebrate, but grief is still our legitimate companion.

Truly I say to you, you will weep and lament . . . you will be sorrowful, but your sorrow will turn into joy (John 16:19-20).

The word "experience" troubles me. I get uneasy when someone says "I had a wonderful worship experience at church this morning." We do not go to church to collect experiences. We go to worship and to praise God. Worship is not designed to create or stimulate a mood or a feeling in the worshiper. If the worshiper, and not the one worshiped, becomes the focus or the center, then everything has gone wrong. God then is the one used, someone employed to serve the worshiper. If God doesn't do it well at one church, then try another. Or, if he doesn't seem to do it in any of the churches, drop the churches and drop God.

The moment we allow this turn-about, where our feelings or moods become the objective, we are on an endless chase. If God is unable to give us a feeling of calm or ecstacy or of pleasure, try drugs or rock music or fornication. The field of exploration is wide open.

Experience-centered religion has this subtle temptation. People, and not God, take the center of the stage. Humans, and not God, become the measure of all things. True religion, of course, produces profound experience, the profoundest of all. But it is never experience-directed. It does not *set out* to produce feelings; it sets out to thank and praise and serve God. It rests not on the quality of the experience, but on the promises or Word of God.

The apostle Paul had a meteoric experience on the road to Damascus. He was not looking for it. Nor did he spend the rest of his life trying to reproduce it. He did not go to Macedonia, for instance, because there he might again have some striking experience. He went because they cried for help.

The Christian life is rich with experience. What is Psalm 23 but a moving confession of the Psalmist's experience with God? Each of us, if we try, can marshal moments when God has seemed very near, or when flashes of insight have seemed very near.

We do not worship God in order to generate peace of mind; we worship him to thank and praise him. We do not undertake a task in order to learn something or to feel something; we do a task to obey and to serve. Experience will come, but we do not make it our goal.

The Lord is my shepherd, I shall not want; he makes me lie down in green pastures. He leads me beside still waters; he restores my soul (Psalm 23:1-3).

In our Christian creeds we confess that we belong to the *one* church, "the one, holy, Christian (or catholic) and apostolic church." How can we speak of *one* church, when we belong to the Lutheran, the Baptist, the Methodist, or Episcopal church? P. T. Forsyth, eminent British theologian, in his book *The Church and the Sacraments* attempts an answer:

I will offer an illustration. When strangers come to Cambridge, and when they have seen the colleges, it would be natural to say, "Now take me to the University." It is a puzzling request. The Senate House—it is not there. The Library—it is not there. The Schools—it is not there either. It has a personality of its own; it is not a mere group, or sum, or amalgam. It has a history, a tradition, a life, a power, a spell, which is not simply the added-up history of the colleges. To the curious stranger you cannot show the University—which yet is Cambridge. Who can deny the University? It is a great reality, a great spiritual reality, in which its colleges inhere. It gives the colleges their true value. It is that which they serve. It is the one spiritual corporation in which the palpable sodalities of the colleges hold together. It dignifies them all. It is the mother of them all from above.

So it is with the true Church. The universal Church is, so to say, the University of the churches. They are all, as it were, collegiate churches in the great Church they express and serve. They are true churches in proportion as they lay hold of this spiritual reality, which is their life. To ask to see the one Church among the churches is like asking to see the University when you have done the colleges. And to refuse to believe in a true Church which is not identical with some visible company is like refusing to believe in the University because it cannot be shown you by your guides. . . . Such is the great Church subsisting in the many churches, which only have their right to be in proportion as they contribute to its fulness. All the churches draw their right from the Church which Christ created in His blood and equipped with His Gospel.

Because there is one bread, we who are many are one body (1 Cor. 10:17).

Tolerance is not the same as indifference. A person may seem to be politically tolerant because he doesn't care whether we have democracy, socialism, capitalism, or totalitarianism. He may appear tolerant because he has no religious convictions. A person should be concerned about truth and values, and feel that he has a right, even a duty, to win others to his convictions.

Indifference, parading as tolerance, is cruel. We may have the mistaken notion that it's enough that a person be sincere, whatever his beliefs. But what he believes determines his life. "As a man thinketh in his heart, so is he." Suppose a friend of mine believes in ghosts. He believes sincerely, even intensely, so much that he dares not walk alone at night, will never enter a darkened house, even in sunshine, lives in dread of the coming night. There'd be no kindness in tolerating his destructive beliefs.

The fact is that if we have any real kindness we must be meddlesome in the matter of ideas and beliefs. Ideas sprout wings and fly off with us. If your neighbor is attacked by a robber you'd go to his defense. If he is stricken with a disease, you'd try to help. Now, if he's captured by false beliefs, is it not your duty to wage battle against what may be more destructive than either thieves or disease? Gangsters can take his property, and bacteria, his health, but the idea can take him—the whole person, body and soul.

The church is vigilant about this matter of ideologies or doctrines. It has pledged itself to seek the truth, and by the truth to make people free. It believes that truth is revealed to us by God in and through the Holy Scriptures, and singularly through Jesus Christ who said, "I am the truth."

Victories of truth are never won with threats or clubs or bombs. You do not convince a person he is wrong by bashing his nose; you only convince him that you have a hard fist. The only legitimate tool for a strong, tolerant person is persuasion, the persuasion of reason and love.

I therefore, a prisoner for the Lord, beg you to lead a life worthy of the calling to which you have been called, with all lowliness and meekness, with patience, forbearing one another in love, eager to maintain the unity of the Spirit in the bond of peace (Eph. 4:1-3).

There is a legend of an Indian chief with three sons, living at the foot of a great mountain range. One day he told his eldest son to strike out alone up the mountainside, and return with some token from the highest point which he had reached. The next day he returned, with some rare blossoms. He had gone to the very end of the timberline. The chief then sent his second son, and he returned with some unknown bit of mineral. He had climbed high, beyond the timberline. The youngest, the bravest, of the sons then set out. Two days later he returned empty-handed, and said, "Father, I have nothing in my hands, but I climbed to the summit, and from where I stood I caught sight of the sea."

Life can be great, not because of what we have of tokens in our hands, but because we have caught a vision, a glimpse of an expanse which is beyond our reach. In our national hymn, "America the Beautiful," we sing of a vision yet unattained,

Thine alabaster cities gleam
Undimmed by human tears.

To give up the vision and cynically to regard dreams and aspirations as futile is to give up on life itself.

Visions are not for contemplation alone. What we see in the distance drives us on. There was a day in the Christian church when people who had caught a vision of God thought it best to retire as hermits to keep the vision from being sullied by the world. This was not the way of Christ, nor of Paul, for instance. Paul told Agrippa, "I was not disobedient to the heavenly vision." Having caught the vision of what Christ and his eternal Kingdom could mean, he embarked on a turbulent, restless course to share this vision with the world. It has been so with every great saint.

Jesus lamented, "They have eyes but don't see; they have ears but don't hear." If we lift our eyes, if we attune our ears, we may catch sight of the turrets of a kingdom and hear its surging symphonies. We were made for that.

And it shall come to pass afterward, that I will pour out my spirit on all flesh; your sons and your daughters shall prophesy, your old men shall dream dreams, and your young men shall see visions (Joel 2:28).

Christianity is a religion for failures, for people who fall short of the mark. Jesus once said, "Only the sick need me, not people who are well." David Swenson, late professor of philosophy at the University of Minnesota, put it this way, "I need a religion for bad men." We may be successful by the standards of the world, but before the high court of God we know we have no case. We need, therefore, more than anything else, a place to leave our failures. William James in his celebrated book, *Varieties of Religious Experience* said that everyone needs "a gospel of relaxation," by which he meant a religion of grace. These are his words:

> To begin with how can things so insecure as successful experiences of this world afford a stable anchorage? A chain is no stronger than its weakest link, and life is after all a chain. In the healthiest and most prosperous existence, how many links of illness, danger and disaster are always interposed? . . . Take the happiest man, the one most envied by the world, and in nine cases out of ten his inmost consciousness is one of failure. Either his ideals in the line of his achievements are pitched far higher than the achievements themselves, or else he has secret ideals of which the world knows nothing, and regard to which he inwardly knows himself to be found wanting.

> What single-minded man was ever on the whole as successful as Luther? Yet when he had grown old, he looked back on his life as if it were an absolute failure. "I am utterly weary of life," he said. "I pray the Lord will come forthwith and carry me hence. Let him come, all above, with his last judgment: I will stretch out my neck, the thunder will burst forth, and I shall be at rest."

> Failure, then, failure! So the world stamps us at every turn. We strew it with our blunders, our misdeeds, our lost opportunities, with all the memorials of our inadequacy to our vocation. And with what damning emphasis does it then blot us out. No easy fine, no mere apology or formal expiation will satisfy the world's demands, but every pound of flesh exacted is soaked with all its blood.

Restore to me the joy of thy salvation, and uphold me with a willing spirit (Psalm 51:12).

If I ask, "What do I have a right to expect from my church?" I have certain obvious claims to make.

I have the right to be given the Word of God and the sacraments. These are the means, the channels, through which God the Holy Spirit conveys knowledge, comfort, and power. God comes to us through these instruments. If on a Sunday morning my pastor has been distracted into discussing some contemporary issue and has overlooked giving me the glad good news that in Christ I have forgiveness of sins and the assurance of a life everlasting, I feel cheated. I need to be exhorted to the good life, but I need to be reminded that I hold my rights to the kingdom of God not through an inventory of my performance, but through the gracious work of God for me.

I have a right to be deeply disturbed. If I am ushered before God, which the church should do for me, I cannot expect to be complacent. The expectations of the kingdom should be so vividly presented that I am left crying, "God be merciful to me, a sinner."

I have a right to be encouraged and prodded. The glorious assurance of forgiveness should be ringing in my ears. The right to begin each day anew, without dragging along the rubbish and debris of the past, should be made clear. The style of life which our Lord gave us while on earth should haunt me and lure me on. I should leave the church with the praises of God echoing in my spirit and with firm resolutions to try harder anchored solidly in my will.

I have a right to be filled with gratitude. Even if my path is littered with pain and sorrows, I should have a continuing and pervasive gratitude—because the love of God has been rhapsodically proclaimed in the cross, the guarantee of the constancy of God's love.

Gratitude to God is the only power comprehensive enough and sustaining enough to enable a person to turn from himself to others. It is the key to the ethical dilemma. For our problem is not primarily to know what is good. Our problem is to find something which will make a person *do* the good. The church, with its gospel, has that power.

For the love of Christ controls us, because we are convinced that one has died for all; therefore all have died. And he died for all, that those who live might live no longer for themselves but for him who for their sake died and was raised (2 Cor. 5:14-15).

God is not an austere judge in the sky who loves to throw the book at all evildoers. He is not a capricious old uncle who loves to be pampered with praise and sacrifice. He is not an exalted landlord who has tenanted his world with crawling and cowering slaves. Nor is he a kindly and venerable grandfather who absentmindedly overlooks the shame and reproach of his children.

God is a hunter who pursues us relentlessly with his justice and his love. He is a lover who woos and courts our favor. He is a rescuer who suffers and dies to save us from our sins. He is a servant who rolls up his sleeves and waits tables at the heavenly banquet for us, his children. There is no other religion in all the world that has had the incredible audacity and boldness to picture God as a seeker, a lover, a savior, a servant.

Our Lord is king of heaven and earth. And what a strange and wondrous king! Can you imagine an earthly king, say Louis XIV of France in his splendor, waiting tables in his castle at Versailles, except in royal jest? Normally the king is the *sought one,* someone people seek out for patronage and favors. He is the *adored one,* someone people praise. He is the *served one,* to whom hundreds and thousands give their service and protection.

The Bible sketches the Great King in a daring reversal of roles. "God so loved the world, that he gave his only begotten son." "He humbled himself and took the form of a servant." "He will make them sit down to meat, and will come and serve them."

But we may not like to be hunted. The prospect of being hunted or sought may be comforting or discomforting, depending on the disposition of our hearts. Until the end, he will keep pursuing us. In his celebrated poem, *The Hound of Heaven,* Francis Thompson describes one hunted of God:

I fled him, down the nights and down the days:
I fled him down the arches of the years, . . .
I hid from him . . . up vistaed hopes I sped . . .
From those strong Feet that followed, followed after . . .
The Voice is round me like a bursting sea . . .
"Lo, all things fly thee, for thou fliest me."

What man of you, having a hundred sheep, if he lost one of them, does not leave the ninety-nine in the wilderness, and go after the one which is lost, until he finds it? (Luke 15:4).

When the Lord said that except as children we cannot enter the kingdom, he most assuredly did not mean that we be as capricious as children, nor as naive, nor with their endless questioning. It is commonly thought that the Lord meant trust—counting on God, come what may. For the believer God is not an academic subject for speculation; God is reality, he is fact. A little boy who, offered $10 if he'd be willing to be lowered down over a cliff on a rope to recover a camera caught in a tree, said he'd be willing only if his father would hold the rope. He had the kind of "blind" trust that God asks of his children. Walter Lippmann, for years a leading American commentator, in his *A Preface to Morals,* makes this observation:

> We should not forget that the religions which have dominated human history have been founded on what the faithful felt were undeniable facts. These facts were mysterious only in the sense that they were uncommon, like an eclipse of the sun, but not in the sense that they were beyond human experience. No doubt there are passages in the Scriptures written by highly cultivated men in which the Divine nature is called mysterious and unknowable. But these passages are not the rock upon which the popular churches are founded. No one, I think, has observed the religious life of simple people without understanding how plain, how literal, how natural they take their supernatural personages to be.
>
> The common man is an unconscious pragmatist: he believes because he is satisfied that his beliefs change the course of events. He would not be inspired to worship a god who merely contemplates the universe, or a god who created it once, and then rested, while its destiny unfolds itself inexorably. To the plain people, religion is not disinterested speculation but a very practical matter. It is concerned with their well-being in this world and in an equally concentrated world hereafter. They have wanted to know the will of God because they had to know if they were to put themselves right with the king of creation.

Satisfy us in the morning with thy steadfast love, that we may rejoice and be glad all our days . . . establish thou the work of our hands upon us (Psalm 90:14, 17).

What really did Adam and Eve lose through disobedience and separation? What precisely is it that we must recover if our tomorrows are to be joined to the glories of the past?

I am intrigued by Genesis 3:7: "And the eyes of them both were opened and they knew that they were naked." Why were they not aware of their nakedness before the fall? A child of one is not aware of nakedness. He will toddle into a crowd stark naked and feel no embarrassment. The mother may, but not the child. Why? He's totally absorbed in the world of people and things around him; he yet has no self-consciousness. Even when he plays with his toes, it is as if his toes belong to another world.

Perhaps this is the key to the bliss of Eden. Adam and Eve were completely lost in the wonder of a world outside themselves. Their lives were caught up in three centers, three foci.

First, God. They were captured by the greatness and goodness of God. They rested back into his care with no trace of distrust. Second, they were fascinated by the beauties of the Garden. Everything was theirs to enjoy. They walked through the Garden as possessors. Third, they were absorbed in each other, Adam in Eve and Eve in Adam. They lived in the innocence of lovers that ask nothing of each other but to give each other gladness.

In one tragic moment they lost all three centers. They hid from God. They were driven out of the Garden to become fugitives in the earth. They turned in upon themselves and lost each other, as evidenced in Cain's cynical retort to God when he had murdered his brother Abel, "Am I my brother's keeper?" God, the Garden, and the brother were all lost. Man turned in upon himself as the one focus, and history is one long story of man's self-concern, self-defense, self-accusation, self-aggrandizement and self-pity. This is his sin, his tragedy, his hell.

The recovery of joy and of meaning for life is the recovery of these three centers, and emancipation from the tyranny of self. To the extent that we can again be lost in wonder and awe over the goodness and greatness of God, to the extent that we can repossess the earth as a Garden to care for and to enjoy, and to the extent that we can turn from ourselves to our brothers and sisters—to this extent will we recover Eden.

The Lord God took the man and put him in the Garden of Eden to till it and keep it (Gen. 2:15).

There is infinite comfort in the assurance that we are the called ones, the elected ones. We are Christ's prisoners, as Paul calls himself, by the wonder of God's own initiating work. The wonder is not that we volunteered; the wonder is that God took us captive. When the Apostle poses the question in his letter to the Romans, "Who shall separate us from the love of Christ?" his own jubilant reply rests upon the glorious fact that we are the chosen ones of God.

On this fallen planet, we are the new Israel, called to suffer and to triumph as God's people. The call is to everyone, the world over. Those who respond are now with vocation to *live* as God's people. Among the qualities required for our calling are those that seem to be passive —lowliness, meekness, longsuffering, forbearing one another in love. These are qualities of endurance rather than conquest.

In the wars of this century, America has been spared the sufferings of much of the world, and the American church has not had to endure persecution and martyrdom. Our mood, therefore, is still activist; we still sing lustily, "Like a mighty army moves the church of God." Our European brothers and sisters know what it is to dig in, to hold fast, to be longsuffering. We think of ourselves as a people to press on; they have to think of themselves as a people primarily to endure.

When the church falls on evil days, as it has often done in its long history, or when in our own lives we fail to win any significant conquests of the Spirit, at such times we could very well give it all up— if we could not be reassured that we belong to God *because he has chosen us,* come what may, and that our real victory is the victory *given* us in Christ Jesus.

As Christians we are to have the mind of our Lord who "endured on the cross." Whether in days of good or ill, our calling is to remain in character, to become what in Christ we are—a people chosen of God.

I know your works, your toil and your patient endurance, and how you cannot bear evil men. . . . I know you are enduring patiently and bearing up for my name's sake, and you have not grown weary (Rev. 2:2-3).

WHAT GOOD IS THE CHURCH?   September 3

One of the most beloved leaders of the Lutheran church in our country during the middle-twentieth century was O. P. Kretzmann, for a generation the president of Valparaiso University in Indiana. *The Crescent* carried his column, "The Pilgrim" for many years, through which he expressed his wisdom in the poetic language which was his hallmark. During the late 1960s, when young people were skeptical about all institutions, including the church, he, in his irenic spirit, reminded his young friends of the essential character of the church:

> I turn my chair to face the window toward the north. . . . At my left is a campus clustered around a towering chapel. . . . The Church built that chapel—a poor woman in Iowa, a business man from Fort Wayne, a struggling preacher in Canada. . . . They, the Church, the people of God—built that chapel as a sign in stone and glass that neither hell nor high water would finally prevail against its message and life. . . .
>
> The solution of the problem of the Church lies not in becoming more *this-worldly* but by the alchemy of heaven in becoming more *other-worldly.* . . . After all, the Church is the organism thrust into time and history paradoxically by the helpless hands of a child and the helpless hands of a crucified criminal. . . . No human laws, no idea of progress, no histories of civilization really and finally apply to the Church. . . . The Church of Christ has no liberty to become the slave even of its own history. History is great, but Christ is greater. . . . He is a present Lord with a present will, and the Church becomes truly contemporary only by doing His will on earth as it is done in heaven. . . .
>
> Will you understand if, for the time being, I quote from the end of Dostoyevsky's "The Grand Inquisitor" in my own conclusion. . . . His Christ figure, who has listened to all the Inquisitor's accusations without saying a word, at the end "suddenly approached the old man in silence and kissed him softly on his bloodless, aged lips." That kiss was the eternal answer to the question, "What is the Church?" It is to follow the Lord in kissing the new bloody but still cold lips of your world—and mine.

These all died in faith, not having received what was promised, but having seen it and greeted it from afar, and having acknowledged that they were strangers and exiles on the earth. . . . Therefore God is not ashamed to be called their God, for he has prepared for them a city (Heb. 11:13-16).

In his novel, *By Love Possessed*, these words of James Cozzens leaped out at me: "Victory is not in reaching certainties or solving mysteries; victory is in making do with uncertainties, and supporting mysteries."

Aside from God, are there any certainties, and is God Himself not the greatest of all mysteries, which we transmute into life's greatest certainty, but only by faith?

As a young father of six children, ages one to thirteen, the question would strike me, usually as I was falling asleep, "What will happen to them if I die?" I began listing the "certainties," and they quickly evaporated into uncertainties. Nora and I had a small savings account, I had modest life insurance. Neither would last long. Our children had nine uncles and one aunt, all younger than I; they could hardly expect to constitute a certainty. Finally I fell asleep on the thought, "God will find a way for them." I rested on the "certainty" of a mysterious being whom I had never seen or touched or heard.

Isn't this what life demands of us, "the assurance of things hoped for and the conviction of things not seen?" To build on that which people normally regard as certainties, solid and undeniable, will leave us little to build with. What we see, said Paul, is transient and passes away; what we don't see lasts forever.

Some people—maybe all of us at some time or another—will feel uneasy about building on "stuff" we can't touch and see. Is this fantasy? Wishful thinking? By the inner transmutation of faith, the miracle of God's spirit, the stuff takes on the shape of blocks more solid than the ground we walk on. God becomes "a mighty fortress," his Word the "firm foundation," his promises "the bread of life."

Driving through the countryside, I am always cheered by church spires that suddenly catch my eye, the brave fingers pointing upward to a God and a kingdom that will outlast my swift years, and even the earth itself. I am conversely depressed at times over the skyline of the city, the massive piles of stone that swallow up the brave spires of churches built in an earlier day, and that tell of the pride of man which now in a twinkling may be destroyed in a moment of nuclear madness.

I am driven to build on something, and Someone, "who was, is, and ever shall be."

Blessed be the Lord God of Israel, from everlasting to everlasting! Amen and Amen (Psalm 41:13).

Is there no end to asking and seeking and knocking? Must there not come a time when we have gotten everything we need, found what we have been looking for, gone through the door, and no longer need to knock?

The world has always felt that the great answers have eluded us. What is the meaning of life? Where did we come from and where do we go? The universe seems silent at the point of our greatest need. It yields its secrets for food and shelter and clothing. But why—why are we here at all?

In Omar Khayyam's *Rubaiyat* the complaint is put in these poignant lines:

There was a Door to which I found no Key;
There was a Veil through which I might not see;
Some little talk awhile of Me and Thee
There was—and then no more of Thee and Me.

Jesus reverses the imagery and says that he stands at the door knocking, and that if we will, he will come in. We believe, therefore, that with and in him we have a necessary clue to the meaning of life. The great answer is ours. By grace through faith we are in his kingdom.

But he still wants us to keep asking and seeking and knocking—in pursuit of the riches of the kingdom that may escape us. He does not want us to sit down and smugly claim that we have arrived. St. Paul said, "Not that I have already obtained this . . . I press on." God is both revealed to us and hidden from us. We *have* the Lord, we have the saving truth, we have his righteousness. But until the end we will constantly be pushing farther and farther toward the center of the kingdom with its untouched and unclaimed riches.

But in the very act of pressing on, we can have the strange peace of knowing that our Lord has caught up with us and holds us fast. His Word gives us this assurance.

We may feel discouraged, wondering whether we are in the kingdom at all because we sense so little of the joy, the love, the patience, and the courage that we ought to feel—if indeed we are in the kingdom.

The Lord does not ask that we have certain feelings. He asks simply that we trust his Word. There we rest, as we still ask and seek and knock.

Ask, and it will be given you; seek, and you will find; knock, and it will be opened to you (Matt. 7:7).

Leo Tolstoy, one of the great novelists of all time, known best for his *Anna Karénina* and *War and Peace,* was born into wealth and station in Russia, and after years of spiritual wanderings, came to a simple faith in Jesus Christ. He speaks of this great discovery:

> I lived in the world for fifty-five years, and after the first fourteen or fifteen of childhood I was for thirty-five years a nihilist . . . in the sense of an absence of any belief.
>
> Five years ago I came to believe in Christ's teaching, and my life suddenly changed; I ceased to desire that I had previously desired, and began to desire what I formerly did not want. It happened to me as it happens to a man who goes out on some business and on the way suddenly decides that the business is unnecessary and returns home. All that was on his right is now on his left, and all that was on his left is now on his right; his former wish to get as far as possible from home has changed into a wish to be as near as possible to it . . . good and evil changed places.
>
> Not all can be initiated into the deepest mysteries of dogmatics, homiletics, patristics, liturgies, hermeneutics, apologetics, etc., but all may and should understand what Christ said to all the millions of simple, unlearned people who have lived and who are living. . . .
>
> This discovery was made by me thus . . . what touched and affected me most of all was Christ's teaching of love, meekness, humility, self-sacrifice and repayment of good for evil. Such always was for me the essence of Christianity—that in it which my heart loved, and for the sake of which, after passing through despair and unbelief, I accepted as true the meaning the labouring Christian fold attributed to life, and submitted myself to the faith professed by them.

. . . as I drew near to Damascus, about noon a great light from heaven shone about me. And I fell to the ground and heard a voice saying to me, "Saul, Saul, why do you persecute me?" And I answered, "Who are you, Lord?" And he said to me, "I am Jesus of Nazareth" (Acts 22:6-8).

Anywhere you turn you run into rules, laws, or commandments. Some of them are made by God, some by people. All of God's rules are good; most rules made by people are good.

Everything that God made in the universe is governed by his rules, which are sometimes called the laws of nature. And all of nature, from galaxies to insects, follow these laws automatically or instinctively. Human beings alone have the freedom to obey or disobey. They alone can rebel.

In the Garden of Eden God gave Adam and Eve a commandment which they disobeyed (Genesis 3:3, 6). This was the beginning of a long history of human disobedience and rebellion.

Much later, God gave the people the Ten Commandments. Moses was leading the people out of their bondage in Egypt. They were stranded in the desert, dissatisfied and rebellious. That is when God took Moses up into the mountain and gave him the Ten Commandments to govern his people. The Commandments contain the basic principles for those who want to know the will of God. In fact, they have become the basis and guide for almost all the rules and laws that people and governments have made.

Most rules or laws are good. Some are not. Human history is one long struggle to get laws that are good and just. We do not always succeed. For many years there were laws that gave white people the right to buy and sell black people. In every country there is the danger of having the rich and powerful make laws unfair to the poor and powerless. Rules and laws made by people often fall short of the justice and mercy of God.

It is different with the Commandments of God. If we obey them, God has a chance to bless or reward us. If we break them, God, like a good Father, has no option but to punish us. He must try to stop us from doing those things which eventually would hurt us and others.

The fact is that none of us can obey the Commandments perfectly, no matter how hard we try. God knows this. He gave us the Commandments to show us our desperate situation. He knows that we shall face his judgment, guilty and condemned. He knows that we will have to cry out for mercy and for forgiveness. And he has made provision for just that need.

Jesus Christ, the Son of God, became man, became our brother, and obeyed the will of God perfectly. He died on a cross for us to give us a right to be God's restored and pardoned children. This is the heart of the Bible's message to us.

I will praise thee with an upright heart, when I learn thy righteous ordinances (Psalm 119:7).

In many ways Dr. Albert Schweitzer is the most celebrated example in our century of a life given to others. Already in his early 30s, he was a distinguished theologian and philosopher and the most acclaimed organist in Europe. Suddenly he puzzled everyone by turning to medicine and going to the interior of Africa to spend his life healing people there.

The term *reverence* for life describes Schweitzer's attitude. He went to such extremes that he would not knowingly kill any living thing, not even the ants that busied themselves on his table.

Reverence for human life is etched deeply in all humanitarian circles, certainly in the Christian faith. We take seriously that God is the giver of all life. We also believe that death is not one of God's gifts, but in biblical language an enemy, "the last enemy" which God has set out to oppose and at last to overcome. If we take seriously God's command, "Thou shalt not kill," we are arrayed with God in opposing anything that destroys human life. And as a consequence of Christ's resurrection from the dead, we are confident that life, not death, will have the last word.

For these reasons questions concerning war, capital punishment, abortion, and euthanasia become perplexing. Do we ever, under any circumstances, have a right to destroy or end life? Must we not do everything we can to preserve life? Are there values even greater than life itself that warrant either destroying it or giving it up?

There is a still deeper level of life to consider for those of us who are Christian. We believe that in addition to physical life there is a life with God, eternal life, the life of the soul, the life that is restored after death so we can live with God forever. Jesus said that if anyone causes another to lose eternal life, it would be better had he never been born.

Reverence for life will be taken seriously only if we believe that people are more than organisms that breathe and think. If we are no more than high-grade mammals, complex animals that write oratorios and invent computers, but animals still, cousins of the rat and the chimpanzee, then we shall tend to treat each other as animals. But we are children of God, our bodies the dwelling places for God himself. Thou shalt not kill sons and daughters of the eternal king!

You shall not kill (Deut. 5:17).

Gerhard E. Frost, professor, preacher, and poet, in his volume, *Bless My Growing*, gives us the following insight:

I won't forget a small child
who wouldn't say "thank you."
It happened in the doctor's office.
Only a routine check,
but this was followed by a shot,
and the little one cried.
Now the tears were dried
and it was time to go.

Without thinking, I said,
"Tell the doctor, 'thank you.' "
Bless her, she wouldn't say it;
and, of course, she was right.
She wouldn't say what she didn't feel;
she wouldn't be false
to please a parent.
Such is the integrity of the child.

I think how we rear our altars
of adult pride,
encouraging hypocrisy and hollow courtesy
by unwise and thoughtless commands.
How we need to subject each request
to the rigid test of a child's integrity,
remembering that a wise man once said:
"Nearly all the truth that is told in this world
is told by children."

At that time the disciples came to Jesus, saying, "Who is the greatest in the kingdom of heaven?" And calling to him a child, he put him in the midst of them, and said, "Truly, I say to you, unless you turn and become like children, you will never enter the kingdom of heaven. Whoever humbles himself like this child, he is the greatest in the kingdom of heaven" (Matt. 18:1).

BUILDERS OR DESTROYERS September 10

As far back as we have historical records, the human race has been both builder and destroyer. It may be difficult to measure how well we have built. The population has expanded many times over. Continents have been explored and developed. One secret after another in nature has been uncovered and put to use. People have not been idle. And now we have begun to explore other worlds.

But every now and then our world has exploded into violence and destruction. The years are littered with wars, those of this century most devastating of all. Nor has the record of our getting along with other members of the family of nations and races been encouraging.

It wouldn't be difficult to conclude that human beings are more destroyers than builders. At times we are like children who laboriously and patiently build castles of blocks, and having looked at them awhile, on a momentary impulse, kick them all over the living room floor.

Despite these destructive spasms, our race has expanded the enterprise so much that demand may now exceed supply. If we are not careful in using what we have, and if God does not unlock new secrets of available resources, there may not be enough food, enough clean air and water, enough energy to support the race. Moreover, with the atom bomb we now can destroy a great city with one blow and end civilization as we have known it.

God took a big risk in making us his children and putting us here as managers of the earth. He took another risk when as God the Son he came personally to become a part of the enterprise and to bail us out of an impossible situation by dying on a cross for us. What a staggering maneuver of love and trust!

If we will but understand God's own stake in us and in the world and comprehend even in part the love he has for us, out of sheer gratitude to him we may yet have the wisdom and the will to care for this earth —his earth—and for one another, so that our grandchildren will possess some of the good life he has planned for his children.

Thou hast given him dominion over the works of thy hands; thou hast put all things under his feet (Psalm 8:6).

WHY PRAY FOR SOMEONE?   September 11

Most of us pray for someone. Why? Do we think we can persuade or wheedle God to do something he otherwise will not do? Won't he heal our loved one unless we remind him? Won't he give wisdom to our leaders to keep the peace unless we prod him? If he is a good God who loves all his children on earth, is he not already doing what he can for them?

These are difficult questions, and, if we dwell on them long enough we conceivably might stop praying for people.

There are those who say that in praying for others, we ourselves become involved in doing what we can for them. That's right, but is that all? Others say that since the Lord wants us to be a family, concerned about one another, intercessory prayer is one way of welding us together as a family. So it is, but is that all? Still others say that to pray for another ennobles the one who prays; it frees him from selfishness. It does, but is that all?

Jesus prayed for others, and told us to do so. He said to Peter, "I have prayed for you that your faith fail not." He interceded for the people, "so that they may believe that thou didst send me." Did he not tell us to pray for those who persecute us, "so that you may be sons of your Father who is in heaven"? Also, he urged us to "pray therefore the Lord of the harvest to send out laborers into his harvest." In his great high-priestly prayer, he prayed for his disciples and "also for those who are to believe in me through their word." Whatever mystery there is in intercessory prayer, if Jesus prayed, certainly we must. Who knows what changes come with praying.

Only God really knows what is good for us and for others. Our judgment dare not be pitted against his. "For my thoughts are not your thoughts, neither are your ways my ways," says the Lord. Nor is it possible in this sinful world, where we ourselves in ignorance and wickedness block him out, for him to have his way with us, however much he would want to.

But with all these limitations, conditions, and mystery, we pray. In so doing we rest back into his good and gracious will for us and for others.

The Lord is a stronghold for the oppressed, a stronghold in times of trouble . . . .he does not forget the cry of the afflicted (Psalm 9:9, 12).

261

In Dostoevski's *Brothers Karamazov*, this moving interlude, "The Grand Inquisitor," tells of Jesus appearing in Seville, Spain, during the Inquisition, when people were executed for heresy. The Inquisitor, a cardinal of 90, orders Jesus thrown into a cell and comes to him at night. He tells him that on the morrow he will die as the worst of the heretics for leaving man with the frightening gift of freedom, instead of heeding the devil's counsel in his temptation in the wilderness.

Judge Thyself, who was right—Thou or he who questioned (tempted) Thee then? Remember the first question: its meaning, in other words, was this: "Thou wouldst go into the world, and going with empty hands, with some promise of freedom which men in their simplicity and their natural unruliness cannot even understand, which they fear and dread—for nothing has ever been more insupportable for a man and a human society than freedom. But seest Thou these stones in this parched and barren wilderness? Turn them into bread, and mankind will run after Thee like a flock of sheep, grateful and obedient, though forever trembling, lest Thou withdraw Thy hand and deny them Thy bread." But Thou wouldst not deprive man of freedom, and didst reject the offer, thinking, what is that freedom worth, if obedience is bought with bread? Thou didst reply that man lives not by bread alone.

Thou didst promise them the bread of Heaven, but, I repeat again, can it compare with earthly bread in the eye of the weak, ever sinful and ignoble race of man? And if for the sake of the bread of Heaven thousands and tens of thousands shall follow Thee, what is to become of the millions and tens of thousands of millions of creatures who will not have the strength to forego the earthly bread for the sake of the heavenly? . . . Instead of taking men's freedom from them, Thou didst make it greater than ever! Didst Thou forget that man prefers peace, and even death, to freedom of choice in the knowledge of good and evil?

Jesus then said to the Jews who had believed in him, "If you continue in my word, you are truly my disciples, and you will know the truth, and the truth will make you free (John 8:31).

It's a bit easier to handle Jesus as a hero than as a Savior. We like him when at 12 he baffles the scholars in Jerusalem; we like him when he outmaneuvers the Pharisees who try to trip him up with tricky questions. We are drawn to him as he feeds the five thousand and heals the sick. We applaud him as he drives the money changers from the temple. There's something splendid about the way he refuses to cower before Pilate. And what of the sheer moral grandeur of his praying God to forgive his enemies as he dies on a cross? What in all history can compare with the resurrection, where "our hero" conquers even death? Nor do we forget his march across the centuries, over borders and oceans, to be emblazoned in the majesty of a thousand cathedrals and in the soaring rhapsodies of a thousand oratorios.

This is our hero. But he doesn't want to be a hero; he came to be a Savior. He came to save us from our sins. We are not an army that needs to be commanded; we are not the lost and scattered ones who need rescue. We are not budding heroes who need a leader; we are sinners who need a redeemer.

It has always been more comfortable for man to deal with a God who triumphs than with a God who suffers. Why should God suffer the "slings and arrows of outrageous fortune," why should God bow to the injustices and cruelties of men, why should we have to die? We tend often to regard this "humiliation" as an interlude, not quite real, a strategy of guile to distract the devil, when all the while Jesus knew that he had the trump card in his hand (the resurrection) which would leave his short term of suffering far behind. When on that Friday he had said, "it is finished," he would throw aside his disguise and march off as the hero we've always wanted him to be.

But he suffers still, and he invites his followers to suffer. This is where the going gets a bit rough for us. We want to sing, "Onward, Christian soldiers," with banners flying and our Lord of Hosts leading the way. But he turns us away from flags and bands to an inner death struggle with our own selfish desires and ways, and then sends us into the byways to find the sick, the poor, the homeless, the lonely, the lost. We had wanted to build soaring temples for him, and he tells us he needs only our hearts to be his temple. We had wanted to crown him with pomp and pageantry, and he chooses to be our companion on the road.

Of course there is triumph, quite hidden until that glorious day when he will finish that which he began at creation and again in redemption.

Are you able to drink the cup that I am to drink? (Matt. 20:22).

Jesus could have said, "I will show you the way, I will point you to the truth, and I will guide you to the good life." But he made the strange and glorious claim, "I am the way, and the truth, and the life."

None other in all history has made such a claim. And hundreds of millions of people throughout the centuries have believed it. They have not thought him demented or a fool or a charlatan for using this language. They have believed him to be God come to earth, and this is the language of God.

We do talk about his way, the way of the cross. The finest minds of the world have wrestled with the question of truth as a value to be pursued. And we do speak of a style of life. But we who are disciples of Christ come back to this quiet claim, "I am the way, the truth, and the life," and stand in wonder and awe before this *person*, Jesus of Nazareth. In the final analysis, it is *he* who holds us, not a way of life or a style of life, or any philosophical or theological system of truth. We are held fast by him, the Lord of our life.

Our son, Paul, while at Oxford was on the crew. He told us that none of the men, including the coxswain, were believers in the traditional sense—seekers, probably, or agnostics. At times, he said, he was hard-pressed to keep his faith. It wasn't the fact that his father was a pastor, nor that he found the teachings of his church clear and always persuasive, nor that to let it go he would be retreating from the faith of his family. Strong as these bonds were, he said, he could have let them go, but he couldn't let Jesus Christ go. He who was the way, the truth, and the life held him.

This may sound like something too vague, too intangible, too mysterious to be real. But doesn't our experience in human love give us the real clue? Life does get wrapped up in a person—a person we love and who loves us. We are held fast by a person, not by a common way of life, nor by a truth that we both accept. And Jesus is supremely that kind of person. He has given us himself, and we give ourselves to him.

He is indeed the Son of God—God of God, Light of Light—and all the truth and beauty and goodness of the universe are brought together in him. The highest goal of life is not to embrace a truth, but to be embraced by him.

He is the image of the invisible God . . . all things were created through him and for him. He is before all things, and in him all things hold together (Col. 1:15-17).

In my 20 years as administrator of a theological seminary, charged by the church to train pastors and, upon their graduation, to certify that they were suited for Christian ministry, I often had the uneasy feeling that we should not rely too much on psychological tests to ascertain qualities that may not yield to measurement at all. Dr. Robert Coles, eminent psychiatrist and author, expresses this same caution:

> Why not make sure that prospective ministers have clean psychological bills of health? Why not, as people like me are all too inclined to put it . . . bring to bear "modern scientific knowledge" upon the "selection process" that the various religions ask of their men and women? Sometimes it does indeed help. But there are many psychiatrists who have no real understanding of what a religious vocation is all about, and some of us are narrow-minded, smug, possessed of our own sectarian, ideological faith—hence the last persons in the world who ought to be writing letters of evaluation to bishops. . . . Psychiatrists, like others, are thoroughly caught up in a given cultural and political order, and so quite inclined to accept as "normal" or "deviant" what various "principalities and powers" want so defined . . . a psychology of "adjustment" and "adaptation" is so often an acquiescence to the most banal and crude, if not blasphemous, in a given society.

> Is it not sometimes an abdication of faith, faith in their own God-given judgment, that prompts some religious authorities to give so much weight to psychiatric opinion? Perhaps the real issue is religious dissatisfaction—expressed in the all too eager embrace of the secular world, two of whose obsessions are psychology and psychiatry. I am appalled at the excessive way some ministers have taken to pastoral counselling, to group therapy, to an endless self-consciousness (in turn demanded of others). . . . Psychological categories are used by so many of us to dismiss, refute or chastise others, or to show how clever *we* are—a contemporary version, alas, of the sin of pride.

Now a bishop [pastor] must be above reproach, the husband of one wife, temperate, sensible, dignified, hospitable, an apt teacher, no drunkard, not violent but gentle, not quarrelsome, and no lover of money (1 Tim. 3:2-3).

Our Lord could well say "If you have me, you have all." For we were made for God, and if we have him, and he has us, everything else is of secondary importance.

God has promised himself to us. That's really the only promise he has made unconditionally, with no strings attached. To be sure, he gives life (but we may die), he give us food (and we may run out), he gives us friends (and they may leave us). In fact, all these good things of life he gives us—or better still, loans to us, we have no sure promise that we will always have them.

A husband might tell his wife, "I have you, and that's enough." She may cook his meals and mother his children. But he did not marry her to get a cook, or even to get children. He married her because he loves *her* and wants *her*. If she should become ill and couldn't cook his meals or bear children, he would certainly not divorce her—if indeed he loves her.

Many of our religious television programs, and sometimes even our churches, tend to offer God as a cure-all. If you accept Christ, your emotional problems will disappear, your marriage will be saved, your energies will be freed from fear so that you'll prosper in your work, your health will improve, and best of all, you'll have heaven when you die. Except for heaven, God has made no such deal with us. We may still have emotional problems; our marriages may be beyond saving; we still may lose our jobs; cancer may still strike; and we may die early. God may want to spare us from these adversities, but we live in a fallen world where tragedy and death often strike with no apparent design.

But we can have him, here and hereafter—if we will. He has gone to long lengths—the length of a cross—to give us himself. And with himself, the forgiveness of sin and the promise of life everlasting.

To be sure, having him can make a profound difference in our lives here. He does have ways of giving us joy, the joy of guilt gone, the joy of hope restored, the joy of knowing that, come what may, he is at hand to strengthen and comfort. But these are the built-in joys in having him. They are not dividends or bonuses that dangle off to the side.

With him, we are given tasks in his kingdom—the care of the earth, the care of one another. This too is a built-in gift, the honor he gives us as sons and daughters.

Happy the people whose God is the Lord (Psalm 144:15).

In the early years of my ministry I visited a girl in her late teens who knew she was dying of a terminal illness. As I was leaving one day she asked if I'd like her to recite a poem. These lines from Kipling's "L'Envoi" I heard first from her lips.

When earth's last picture is painted,
  and the tubes are twisted and dried.
When the oldest colors have faded, and
  the youngest critic has died.
We shall rest, and, faith, we shall need
  it—lie down for an eon or two,
Till the Master of all good workmen
  shall set us to work anew!

And those that were good shall be happy;
  they shall sit in a golden chair;
They shall splash at a ten-league canvas
  with brushes of comet's hair;
They shall have real saints to draw from—
  Magdalene, Peter, and Paul!
They shall work for an age at a sitting
  and never be tired at all!

And only the Master shall praise us, and
  only the Master shall blame;
And no one shall work for money, and
  no one shall work for fame;
But each for the joy of the working, and
  each, in his separate star
Shall draw the Thing as he sees It for
  the God of Things as They are!

So we do not lose heart. Though our outer nature is wasting away, our inner nature is being renewed every day. For this slight momentary affliction is preparing for us an eternal weight of glory beyond all comparison, because we look not to the things that are seen but to the things that are unseen (2 Cor. 4:16-18).

God has set out to attack our sinfulness with three powerful thrusts. First, he annihilates its guilt. Second, he reduces its presence. Third, he removes its ultimate punishment.

Guilt is like the debris of a crumbling building; it keeps piling up, higher and higher. Before there can be any rebuilding, the debris must be cleared away. It is folly for a person to think that he can make a fresh start as long as his life is cluttered up with haunting memories, nagging remorse, festering guilt. These immobilize him for any new effort. In the book of Hebrews, we are told to "lay aside every weight," if we are to run the race. How can we make any great strides if the heavy chains of unresolved guilt weigh us down?

It is not by accident that the supreme gift of the cross is the forgiveness of sin. To have the Lord say that he will not remember our sins, that he has removed them as far as the east is from the west— this sets the stage for healing and rehabilitation.

The guilt of sin is gone, but of course its presence is still with us. There is no instant sanctification. Its power is still abroad, within us and pressing upon us from outside. It cannot crush us nor control us as before, because the power of guilt is gone. We are free to swing against it now, with resources from the outside. We are free to build a new life, because the rubble of past failures has been cleared away. As long as life lasts, sin will continue to harass us, luring us into pride, indifference, envy, lust, and selfishness. But its tyranny is broken.

Sin will continue to exact its punishment, but the greatest punishment of all—separation from God here and hereafter—is gone. There is no condemnation to those who rest in Christ. If the sin of infidelity, for instance, has broken up a family, there is no way to avoid the hurt. If the sin of gluttony and drunkenness has taken its toll in loss of health, forgiveness will not be a ticket to recovery. Wounds may be healed, but the scars will remain. The bird with the broken wing never flies high again. But there is amazing comfort, and therapy for healing, in the love of God that forgives all.

Let us also lay aside every weight, and sin which clings so closely and let us run with perseverance the race that is set before us (Heb. 12:1).

God must despise uniformity. Children may have the same parents, but how different they are. No two leaves on a tree are the same. A billion snowflakes may fall, each with a different design.

A tyrant loves uniformity. For him the ideal is that every man have the same ideas, the same values, and that finally a whole people become one unambiguous mass.

We have some difficulty living with diversity, because diversity implies freedom to be different. And each of us has a bit of the tyrant spirit. We tend to coerce others to our point of view, sometimes by persuasion and sometimes by threat. It is not easy to give others the same freedoms we want for ourselves. If we succeeded in coercing all others to our way, we would have a very drab world on our hands. It would be as if we were to eliminate all color but one, gray for instance. Ask any color-blind person how delightful this would be.

In accepting diversity, many of us make the mistake at times of wishing that we were someone else, or at least like someone else. Why couldn't I have the intelligence, the appearance, the opportunities, the money, or the power, of another? Wishing this is a dead-end street. God has given me a certain set of gifts. They may not be spectacular. That may not rank high in the marketplace of the world. I may even say that I am not as "gifted" as others. Who but God is to measure gifts? Whatever mine are, if I use them to the full, may it not be that God will work as many wonders through me as through another?

The church itself has a hard time with diversity. Most congregations tend to have people of the same economic class, the same race, the same general outlook. To have someone of a different race or radically different political views seek membership may send a tremor through the parish. Also, the church has had difficulty accepting some variety in theology, even though the variety is quite faithful to the central teachings of the Bible. Churches have been known to be so intolerant of differences in theological emphases that they have closed their altars and pulpits and fellowship to those who have had difficulty conforming.

It is well for us to remember that God's nature and God's Son enjoy diversity.

For just as the body is one and has many members . . . so it is with Christ. For by one Spirit we were all baptized into one body—Jews or Greeks, slaves or free—and all were made to drink of one Spirit (1 Cor. 12:12-13).

However slender our hope as we survey the enormous issues that face our world, can we who confess faith in God have any other stance toward our tomorrows than to entertain expectations of a better day? "If God is for us, who is against us?" said Paul, and "he that spared not his own Son, but gave him up for us all, will he not also give us all things with him?"

Our tomorrows simply cannot be a dead-end street. The future is open-ended. We may not subscribe to the poet's exultant lines, "God's in his heaven, all's right with the world," but we can rest in the assurance that "the earth is the Lord's," and go on from there to believe that the Lord will not let his earth go without a struggle. He is on the side of the abundant life for his children, and he has resources far beyond our most extravagant calculations.

His strategy is to focus on the hearts and wills of people. His revolutions always begin with people one by one. He turns us around, from fear to love, from indifference to mercy. He releases us from the prison cell of selfishness to roam in freedom the wide world of the needs of our brothers and sisters. He takes from us the fear of death and empowers us for the enterprises of life—life in justice and compassion for all.

God invades and builds bridgeheads in the hearts of people. If he can have some bridgeheads here and there, whole communities and nations can change. These people become leaven and salt. They are true nonconformists, the quiet revolutionaries that change the world. They are under higher orders. They love, because the love of God has captured them. They do not ask what the world can give them; they ask what they can give the world. Even when rebuffed, even when the odds seem too great for any success, they keep trying.

Every hope that we have is somehow anchored in God. He created us to be his own and to live with him here and hereafter forever. He sent his only Son to redeem the world and to usher in an imperishable kingdom. He who has begun this good work has promised to see it through. Nor, of course, is he limited to the confines of this planet alone. If the planet blows up, and all of us in the twinkling of the eye are vaporized in a holocaust, this is not the end for us or for God. He has other holdings in his empire, and transportation facilities to put us to work again in another and better sector of his estates. We believe in the resurrection of the dead and life in the world to come.

If God is for us, who is against us? (Rom. 8:31).

The great question is not "Is there a God?" The really critical question is, "Does God really care?" If he is but the great architect and engineer who designed, created, and manages the billions of bodies in the universe, but no more, then it really doesn't matter to any of us whether there is a God or not. Vote for him or against him—it is quite unimportant, merely academic. *Does he care?* That's the important question. It is the deep cry of the whole human race.

When Job in his anguish cried, "Oh, that I knew where I might find him, that I might come even to his seat," he was yearning for some assurance that God cared. Few people have known the perplexing sufferings of Job, but every human being has a burning need to know that God cares.

A man tells of walking to church one bright spring morning, the birds singing in the trees, the leaves sparkling in the sunlight, when suddenly across his path darted a mouse with a cat in pursuit. The cat caught it, played with it, tantalized it, tortured it, finally crushed it and devoured it. Seated in the pew, he couldn't erase the spectacle from his mind. Soon there were two mice, then three, then ten, then a hundred, each pursued by a cat, and the cats catching, torturing, crushing, and devouring. He couldn't worship. It seemed to him, at the moment, that this was the microcosm of all life, where the weaker were always overtaken and crushed by the stronger—and where, in that kind of a world was a loving God?

Nature cannot tell us that God cares. Too often the pattern seems tooth and claw. Even the lives of people and nations take on this pattern. Where will we find the clue to a caring God?

Strange as it will always seem, our starting point is back 2000 years to a little knoll outside of the city gates of Jerusalem where a young man from Nazareth writhed to his death on a cross. For the Christian church this is not only the starting point; there we rest our case!

To be sure, we find other clues—but only after we have found the fixed one in the life and death and resurrection of our Lord for us and for the whole world.

When I came to you, brethren, I did not come proclaiming to you the testimony of God in lofty words or wisdom. For I decided to know nothing among you except Jesus Christ and him crucified (1 Cor. 2:1-2).

YOU ARE NOT EXPENDABLE September 22

The world may get along without you, but God can't. He counts you of infinite worth. He created you to be his own, and in Christ he died on a cross to reaffirm your value.

We all have a hard time believing that we are important, really important. The rich man is haunted by the suspicion that it is not he, but his wealth, that is important. The man of power may strut his way, but what would be left if he were stripped of his power? This question troubles him. In and of ourselves, quite apart from our wealth, power, skill, intelligence or appearance—are we of any value? If we are not, then we plunge into a fierce race of accumulating something which will give us significance.

It's often as we grow old that we look back and wonder if our life has added up to anything significant. Is the world any better for our having lived, and couldn't the world have gotten along very well without us? Alfred B. Nobel discovered nitroglycerin a century ago. If today he could assess his amazing discovery, would he be able to balance off the good dynamite has done against the devastation of the hundreds of cities? And what of our atomic scientists—might they not wonder if their discovery could best have been left forever lost? Perhaps most of us can understand the mood of the Preacher in the book of Ecclesiastes:

> So I became great and surpassed all who were before me in Jerusalem; also my wisdom remained with me. And whatever my eyes desired I did not keep from them; I kept my heart from no pleasure, for my heart found pleasure in all my toil, and this was my reward for all my toil. Then I considered all that my hands had done and the toil I had spent in doing it, and behold, all was vanity and a striving after wind, and there was nothing to be gained under the sun (2:9-11).

If our only stage is the swift years between birth and death, and add the grim fact that at death we can take nothing with us—then it would be difficult to conclude that we were needed and not expendable.

It is as we broaden the stage, so that our three score and ten years are but a tiny spot on the vast panorama of God's infinite stage, that we arrive at the blazing awareness that we are important—important to God, and therefore important to ourselves and to one another.

Thy hands have made me and fashioned me (Psalm 119:73).

It is comfortable to hide behind, "I can't help being what I am or doing what I do." This excuse is okay for tigers and pigs, but not for human beings. Yet our age has elevated these weasel-words into a sophisticated description of human beings. Everything we do, however rational it appears, is but the bubble bursting on the surface, forced into action by primitive appetites over which we have no control.

Leslie Paul in his *The Meaning of Human Existence* speaks of the devastating consequences of such a view of humanity:

> Man is gifted with a passion for truth, for devotion, for sacrifice, for moral and ethical decisions, for the risk of his life in order to fulfill certain ends rendered necessary by conscience. If these come out of appetite, are merely hedonism of a disguised order, then it is difficult to regard ethics, values, and intellectual activities as having independent validity. It is doubly difficult, for in the first case Freud traces the permanent form of the mind from events occuring at an age when no independent moral judgment is possible, and secondly, he derives the energy of the mind for the whole of life from the quite primitive sexual libido. The judgments which emanate from powers determined in such a fashion are going to be purely capricious.

> R. G. Collingwood has reminded us that "distinctions like that between truth and error, knowledge and ignorance, science and sophistry, right and wrong, good and bad, expedient and inexpedient . . . form the armature of every science; no one can abolish them and remain a scientist."

> Yet the theories of the many schools of psychology which from the early 19th century assumed that reason and will were only concretions of sense and appetite involve denial of the independence and reality of the intellectual and moral qualities of man. It is for reasons of this kind that Collingwood writes with considerable bitterness that "psychology, therefore, regarded as the science of the mind, is not a science. It is what phrenology was in the early 19th century and astrology and alchemy in the Middle Ages and the 16th century: the fashionable scientific fraud of the age."

Then God said, "Let us make man in our image, after our likeness; and let them have dominion" (Gen. 1:26).

There are many kinds of singing. There is the dirge, the song of death. There is the ballad, the song of the lover. There is the tempo of marching feet, the song of the soldier.

In Christ Jesus, God gave us a new song—the song of salvation. We sing of the goodness of God who delivered us from the bonds of sin and who ushered us into his wondrous home again.

This is the song of all songs. It blends its strident notes with the minor chords of the dirge. It hallows the joyous melodies of the lover. It hovers over the militant marches of the soldier. It weaves its music in and out of all the events of life. From the moment it reached the earth that Bethlehem night in the voice of the angels, the earth has never been the same again.

Nor has the world of music been the same. The new song, finding a home in the creative spirit of a Bach or a Handel, and in hundreds of lesser artists, has given us oratorios, chorales, symphonies, and a hymnody that for sheer musical excellence has no rival in the world of art.

The story of Christ's death for the sins of the world becomes the motif around which all the glorious music of Christendom is built. How can such a story do other than reverberate into every nook and cranny of the universe? It must have been this truth of God's love that set the morning stars to singing and the children of God dancing for joy.

The new song reaches its crescendos with the crucifixion and the resurrection. But it reaches back into the story of creation, when God said, "Let there be light" and when the touch of his hand on clay created his sons and daughters. It soars to rhapsody that night in the fields of the shepherds. Through these long centuries it has been on the lips of old and young, rich and poor, learned and unlearned. It has yet to reach its final fulness—when one day in the presence of the angels and archangels and all the hosts of heaven we join our tiny notes with theirs to praise him forevermore.

After this I heard what seemed to be the mighty voice of a great multitude in heaven, crying, "Hallelujah! Salvation and glory and power belong to our God" (Rev. 19:1).

How often do we say of people, "He was a successful farmer—or business man—or doctor," or, "She was a successful homemaker—or teacher—or nurse." How seldom do we say simply, "He was a successful man," or "She was a successful woman." David F. Swenson, Kierkegaard scholar and professor of philosophy at the University of Minnesota, addressed this question in his *Faith of a Scholar:*

We have too long lost ourselves in anxious considerations of what it may mean to be a shoemaker or a philosopher, a poet or a millionaire; in order to find ourselves, it is needful that we concentrate our energies upon the infinitely significant problem of what it means simply to be a man, without any transiently qualifying adjectives. When Frederick the Great asked his Court preacher if he knew anything about the future life, the preacher answered, "Yes, Your Majesty, it is absolutely certain that in the future life Your Highness will not be king of Prussia." And so it is; we were men before we became whatever of relative value we became in life, and we shall doubtless be human beings long after what we thus became or acquired will have lost its significance for us. On the stage some actors have roles in which they are royal and important personages; others are simple folk, beggars, workingmen, and the like. But when the play is over and the curtain is rolled down, the actors cast aside their disguises, the differences vanish, and all are once more simply actors. So, when the play of life is over, and the curtain is rolled down upon the scene, the differences and relativities which have disguised the men and women who have taken part will vanish, and all will be simply human beings. But there is a difference between the actors of the stage and the actors of life. On the stage it is imperative that the illusion be maintained to the highest degrees possible; an actor who plays the role of a king as if he was an actor, or who too often reminds us that he is assuming a role, is precisely a poor actor. But on the stage of life, the reverse is the case. There it is the task, not to preserve, but to expose, the illusion; to win free from it while still retaining one's disguise. The disguising garment ought to flutter loosely about us, so loosely that the least wind of human feeling that blows may reveal the royal purple of humanity beneath.

Let the lowly brother boast in his exaltation, and the rich in his humiliation, because like the flower of the grass he will pass away (James 1:9-10).

Are we not all like Peter? We are fond of Jesus, as was Peter. We count ourselves his disciples. We would not hurt him. In fact, we work for his cause—in church and in our homes. We give money—too little it is true, but we do give something for his kingdom. But there is a limit, as there was for Peter. We dare not risk all. In some critical issue, we may, like Peter, deny him. We may not say openly, "I never knew him," but by our silence and our shoddy behavior we in fact let him down.

The risks for Peter were high. Warming his hands before the fire that Thursday night, had he admitted to being Jesus' disciple he may very well have been crucified too. Rarely are the risks that great for us, if ever. Our denials therefore are more shameful than his.

Legend tells us that years later Peter was crucified for his faithfulness to Christ, and that he requested his executioners to crucify him with his head down, feeling unworthy of being crucified as his Lord. And that tragic night before Jesus' crucifixion, seeing Jesus and hearing the cock crow three times, Peter did repent. He went out and wept bitterly.

It is at this point where we may part company with Peter. Denying Jesus, as he did, we may nonetheless go our casual way and do nothing about it. We may feel no shame, weep no tears, and go on through life denying him again and again. For Peter, the denial was a revolutionary moment. He was never the same again. He became a leader of Jesus' followers, and died rather than letting him down again.

It was after the resurrection that Jesus asked Peter, "Simon, son of John, do you love me?" Three times he asked it, and three times Peter answered, "Yes, Lord, you know that I love you." Jesus said, "Feed my sheep." He entrusted his kingdom to Peter.

And he entrusts it to us—to us, who like Peter, may fail him. It is Christ's way. He sends no angels to take over if we fail. He forgives, and forgives, and forgives—and keeps on trusting us to carry on. This is the risk he has been willing to take. He counts on you and me with all our weaknesses to carry his mission to all the world.

And the Lord turned and looked at Peter. And Peter remembered the word of the Lord, how he had said to him, "Before the cock crows today, you will deny me three times. And he went out and wept bitterly" (Luke 22:61-62).

WHAT WILL IT BE LIKE FOR THEM?   September 27

I have grandchildren. What will life be like for them in the next 50-70 years? I am frank to say that I swing between hope and fear. I struggle for hope, but fear often holds the stage.

The bomb was a turn in the road for me. Hiroshima and Nagasaki were a watershed. Up to that time I was optimistic; from that moment on I knew that the world could destroy itself. Nor has the madness of the arms race between Russia and America in the years following given me any reassurance; it has only increased my fear. It has puzzled me that even the most ardent patriot could any longer rely on military might to give the world, or any nation, security. Every other issue of our lives, individual or corporate, now fades into insignificance compared with the one towering issue of war. And since nuclear war would be suicide, is there any hope that we may say so openly in the company of the other nations of the world?

Frankly, this is my hope. The longer we live with the spectacle of gigantic powers that can blow up each other's cities in an hour, must not the sheer horror of such a prospect finally become so much a part of our international thinking that the congresses and parliaments and even dictators will take dramatic steps to disarm? I am told that the nations now have enough arms to assign 6000 pounds of dynamite (or its nuclear equivalent) to every man, woman, and child on earth.

I cannot forget the words of Norman Cousins of *Saturday Review:* "Men caught up in games of international realpolitik tend to delude themselves with the thought that 'hard' matters of military policy are the only ones that count. History, however, is littered with the relics of civilizations whose leaders felt uncomfortable or scornful in the presence of moral questions."

There are voices like that of Cousins, yet too few to be sure, but voices that summon us to a new day of international negotiations and mediation as the only escape from world suicide. With the dawning of possible catastrophes for everyone, perhaps we'll take seriously that we are one world and be ready to support our leaders in every attempt at disarmament. Unprecedented as it will be, this, under God, must be our hope.

I will deliver them by the Lord their God; I will not deliver them by bow, nor by sword, nor by war, nor by horses, nor by horsemen (Hosea 1:7).

Jesus tells the parable of the man who in the early morning hired workers for his vineyard and continued, at intervals during the day, to hire others. At the end of the day he paid them all the same wage. The early workers protested, of course. The point of the parable is the *vineyard*, God's kingdom—and the privilege and joy of being there at all. A parallel might be this: should a man who has lived 50 years with a loving wife and served her deserve a greater "reward" than the man whose dear wife died after five years? Helmut Thielicke in his *The Waiting Father*, makes this point:

> The whole parable gains meaning on only one condition. And that is that we let it tell us that this is work which takes place in the *vineyard*, and therefore it should be service for the Lord, and for this very reason cannot be viewed as something earned or merited. On the contrary, it says that this work is itself a gift and carries its reward in itself; for it brings the workers near to their fatherly Lord and his care. We shall understand this parable only if we see that Jesus is here speaking against legalistic religion, against *all* religion of the kind that dwells in our hearts by nature. It is a good thing to realize very clearly how men have toiled, and still toil, in the sphere of religion to earn heaven; they pile high the altars with sacrifices, they tell their beads, they do good works, they even go to such lengths as those strangest of all saints who spent their whole lives sitting on high pillars, enduring the wind and the weather, growing old and gray in the process, solely in order to gain merits for heaven. We must realize once and for all that these people are not doing all this as children who live and move about freely and happily in the Father's house, but that they are doing it as slaves, doing it out of fear, that all this comes not so much from the heart but is for them a means of making themselves worthy of heaven. *If* these people were right, *if* fellowship with Jesus were a business transaction with a definite *quid pro quo*, with accounts of earnings which we could present to God and receipts entitling us to entrance into heaven—then it would in fact be shamefully unjust if the person who entered the Lord's service at the evening of life were to receive the same as did all those who had toiled and sweated and come home at evening with all their bones aching. . . .

> The person who knows that he has been given the grace to love God—for that person this is in itself a joy, an undreamed of fulfillment of life.

Count it all joy . . . when you meet various trials (James 1:2).

TOO MUCH OF THE WORLD September 29

We are in the world, said Jesus, but not *of* the world. We march to a different drummer. We are to manage the world, but not by the standards of the world. We take our orders from Someone other than "the voice of the people." We are pilgrims and aliens, never naturalized in this world.

One of the perils for the Christian and for the church is to be swallowed up in the prevailing culture of their times. Today we need to be alarmed by the extent to which the Christian church has accepted the values of an all-too-permissive society, and have actually domesticated them under the rubric of "situational ethics."

The sexual revolution of our day is perhaps the most pervasive of the new culture. With the advent of contraception and abortion the social inhibitions that once were supportive of a way of life are largely gone. In the wake of the new freedom, men and women live together without marriage, not clandestine, but openly. Homosexuality, spoken about in whispers before, is often advocated as a licit option among Christian life-styles. Divorce is taken for granted, and we now have liturgies for the dissolution of marriage covenants as well as for their making. Woe to the church that is both in the world and of it too!

When Jesus said that the Sabbath was made for man and not man for the Sabbath, he did indeed say that institutions and practices which did not serve the happiness and fulfillment of man did not deserve to be respected or followed. But, not by the wildest stretch of the imagination, can one conclude that had Jesus lived today, he would have been complacent with our turn of events.

The person is the highest value, not the state nor laws. But people are eternal beings. They are not animals, with unerring instincts for their own fulfillment. They will find happiness and joy and satisfaction only as they conform to the standards for which they were created. And they don't create their own standards. These are of God.

Many of the standards by which we now live, and which we, even in the church, tacitly accept, are destructive. They are illusions given us by the devil. To follow them is to end in misery. Far from finding fulfillment, we find meaninglessness, guilt, and loneliness. The ways of the world lead to a desert; the ways of God, to a kingdom.

I do not pray that thou shouldst take them out of the world, but that thou shouldst keep them from the evil one. They are not of the world (John 17:15-16).

Much as we would like to deny it, there is in most of us a little rogue who just loves to hear that someone has gone wrong. Pushing someone far down on the other end of the teeter-totter has the pleasant effect of elevating us on our end. Tidbits of scandal have a better chance in the chain of gossip than some noble deed.

The Bible speaks of us as fallen creatures, and theologians talk about original sin. There is in each of us a perverse twist that makes us use people instead of helping them, that makes us feel sorry for ourselves instead of for others, that makes us envy, instead of enjoy, another's good fortune, that makes us enlarge on someone's faults instead of excusing them.

Occasionally someone asks the question, "Why does the newspaper print bad news instead of good news?" Could it be that it's the bad news that we want, and that sells papers? If the columns of the press were filled with stories of the integrity of politicians, the social consciousness of the industrialists, the commitment of the churches, the valiant efforts of voluntary organizations to rehabilitate people, would we be in a hurry to get the first edition?

It is not that our free press is irresponsible. It is a cornerstone of our democracy, and its function is to monitor our lives, government, industry, and labor. Thomas Jefferson once said that given a choice between government without the free press and free press without government, he would have to choose the latter, yet Jefferson was more vilified by the press than any other president in American history, with the possible exceptions of Abraham Lincoln and Franklin D. Roosevelt. With all its biases and shortcomings, a free press remains a bulwark of democracy.

We return to the twist in our own natures. We do want the spectacular instead of the commonplace; we do find the good more bland than the bad; we do chatter about people's faults more than about their virtues.

There is within us, however, a counterforce, the gospel, which turns us around to weep with those who have fallen into evil ways and to rejoice with those whose lives reflect the honorable and noble.

First take the log out of your own eye, and then you will see clearly to take the speck out of your brother's eye (Matt. 7:5).

HE HELD HER FAST   October 1

The great novels of the world show remarkable insight into human nature and, in many instances, a deep understanding of the Christian faith. Among these is the trilogy *Kristin Lavransdatter*, by Sigrid Undset of Norway, winner of the Nobel Prize for literature in 1928. The following is a scene from the deathbed of Kristin:

Kristin woke up fully again with a start, and fixed her eyes upon her hand. The gold ring was gone, that was sure enough—but there was a white, worn mark where it had been on her middle finger . . . she deemed she could make out two round spots on either side where the rubies had been, and somewhat like a little mark, an *M*, where the middle plate of gold had been pierced with the first letter of Mary Virgin's holy name.

And the last clear thought that formed in her brain was that she should die ere this mark had time to vanish—and she was glad. It seemed to her to be a mystery that she could not fathom, but which she knew most surely nonetheless, that God had held her fast in a covenant made for her without her knowledge by a love poured out upon her richly—and in despite of her self-will, in despite of her heavy, earthbound spirit, somewhat of this love had become *part* of her, had wrought in her like sunlight in the earth, had brought forth increase which not even the hottest flames of fleshly love nor its wildest bursts of wrath could lay waste wholly. A handmaid of God had she been—a wayward, unruly servant, oftenest an eye-servant in her prayers and faithless in her heart, slothful and neglectful, impatient under correction, but little constant in her deeds—yet had he held her fast in his service, and under the glittering golden ring a mark had been set secretly upon her, showing that she was his handmaid, owned by the Lord and King who was now coming, borne by the priest's anointed hands, to give her freedom and salvation.

Every Christian knows that he comes to the Lord not only empty-handed, but with a wretched cargo of wrongs done and good undone. The marvel of grace is that God receives us still.

But we are bound to give thanks to God always for you, brethren beloved by the Lord, because God chose you from the beginning to be saved, through sanctification by the Spirit and belief in the truth (2 Thess. 2:13).

You can't argue with experience. Try it on any level. A man has pain. Someone tells him, "The pain is only in your head." The man replies, "Sorry, my friend, but it's my pain, and it's in my knees." A man sees a strange disc-like craft with twinkling lights hovering over the earth at night. His friends arch their eyebrows, and he says, "But I saw it!" An economist proposes that the more a nation spends the richer it'll be, but the old storekeeper shakes his head and mumbles, "That ain't the way I've learned it." The philosopher constructs a logical brief against the idea of a personal God, and the silver-haired grandmother lays her knitting aside, "But, my good man, I know him; I rest myself each day into his everlasting arms." You can't gainsay that sort of experience.

Most of us are a bit skeptical about relying on experience alone for our Christian faith. The cults are filled with people who have had "experiences," many bizarre and destructive. We fall back on something more constant—sound reason, conscience, and above all, the Word of God, the promise that we have in the Scriptures.

On the other hand, more than we perhaps know, we find assurance in the experiences we have had, or in the experiences of other believers, or in the aggregate experience of the Christian church. My mother was a person of deep faith. How much my experience in faith is a reflection of hers or a flow from hers, I will never know. In any event, I have longings which point to something greater than the longings themselves. I have an inner joy or peace that points beyond to the Giver of joy and peace. I see and know there is a sun; I hear and know that there is music; I feel and know the touch of a beloved; I believe and know that there is a God.

From the time we were little children most of us have had experiences that have come from God or point to him. Rarely have they burst upon us with a searing certainty. But they have become a sort of reservoir to reinforce what we call faith—a profound intuition that God is at hand to judge, to guide, to comfort, and to hold us in all the days of our lives. The world may regard it as fantasy. No matter. We know him, because we have experienced him.

But I am not ashamed, for I know whom I have believed, and I am sure that he is able to guard until that Day what has been entrusted to me (2 Tim. 1:12).

Whether it's my age, now over threescore and ten, or whether the world is really "going to pot," I don't know. I only know that I have a struggle looking into the future with hope. Luther had his struggle too, as the following "table talk" reveals:

> When God wills to punish a people or a kingdom, he takes away from it the good and godly teachers and preachers, and bereaves it of wise, godly, and honest rulers and counselors, and of brave, upright and experienced soldiers, and of other good men. Then are the common people secure and merry; they go on in all wilfulness, they care no longer for the truth and for the divine doctrine; nay, they despise it, and fall into blindness; they have no fear or honesty; they give way to all manner of shameful sins, whence arises a wild, dissolute, and devilish kind of living, as that we now, alas, see and are too well cognizant of, and which cannot long endure. I fear the axe is laid to the root of the tree, soon to cut it down. God of his infinite mercy take us graciously away, that we may not be present at such calamities.

This was Luther's world over 400 years ago, and the world has survived. To be sure, our ills are more complex today, but perhaps qualitatively no different. People are people, and calamities have always followed in the wake of man's sinfulness. We have no right to take comfort from the fact that in every age there have been cries of doom. The old woman of 90 used poor logic when she said that she was glad that it was the month of May again and, asked why, said that she had lived 90 months of May and had never died in the month of May.

But there is comfort. God is around; he loved this world so much that he gave his only Son to die for it; and he can use us as salt to keep the whole from decay and death. It is not the best of all possible worlds, but it is his world. It is a part of his vast kingdom, and we are his children—his family. What we sow, we shall reap: this is the law of his universe. But with our Lord is mercy—and with mercy, hope.

First of all, then, I urge that supplications, prayers, intercessions, and thanksgiving be made for all men, for kings and all who are in high positions, that we may lead a quiet and peaceable life, godly and respectful in every way (1 Tim. 2:2).

METEORS OR NO METEORS October 4

Suddenly for one swift moment a meteor streaks across the night sky—for only a moment, then we're back with the twinkling stars.

Christian life is like that. At some unsuspecting moment, God may seem very near. Your girl is desperately sick. You pray and pray. The doctor comes, examines her, and tells you, "She's out of danger." Your heart overflows with joy, and you feel God very near. You'll never forget that soaring moment. Or, maybe Sunday after Sunday at church you are edified, but one Sunday, either through the sermon or a hymn, you sense a surge; your heart overflows with praise and thanksgiving. It must have been such a moment for John Wesley at fifteen minutes before nine on an evening at Aldersgate. Suddenly his heart was "strangely warmed," and life was never the same for him again. A meteor had streaked across his spirit-sky.

Few of us will have an Aldersgate, nor Isaiah's vision the year King Uzziah died, nor, like Jeremiah, have the Lord touch our mouths, nor, like Paul, be striken blind on a Damascus road. But there will be moments when the Lord seems to break through in ways that are not the run-of-the-mill, day-by-day experiences.

We have no right to demand that the Lord give us meteors. He has given us the eyes of faith to see his hand in the commonplaces of life. When the rich man pleaded with the Lord to have someone return from the dead to arrest the attention of his brothers so that they might believe, the Lord said, "They have Moses and the prophets." They have God's Word. Like them, we have the Scriptures. We cling to them, meteors or no meteors.

If we have never had moments when God seemed very near, when our souls welled forth in thanks and fresh commitment to him, it just could be that we are not keeping our eyes focused right. If we're always looking for earthworms, we're likely to miss the meteors. If we are so preoccupied with making money, keeping our health, and pleasing other people, why should we expect any burst of insight from the world of the spirit?

We walk through the darkness of this world, not with a cavalcade of meteors, but with the light from the faithful flickering stars. If you do have shining moments, thank God for them, tuck them away among your memories, but don't demand encores from God.

Arise, shine; for your light has come, and the glory of the Lord has risen upon you. For behold, darkness shall cover the earth . . . but the Lord will arise upon you (Isa. 60:1-2).

To believe that Jesus Christ is the light of the world gives me no trouble. But when he tells me that I, too, am to be the light of the world, I become uneasy. After all, do I want to be that bold or presumptuous? Do we dare to parade ourselves as being so good that Christ can point to us as examples, as light? Should we not, as *humble* followers, disclaim that honor?

Like it or not, when we travel abroad, for instance, we represent our country. The book *The Ugly American* stated the bald truth that no American traveling abroad could escape being a credit or discredit to his country. We would not nullify our individual citizenships for a month and become international neutrals. We cannot enjoy the privileges of citizenship and be spared its responsibility.

Citizenship in the kingdom of God implies the same troublesome truth. There are no neutrals, no hidden followers, no secret citizens. Either we will let the light of Christ shine through what we are, what we say, and what we do—or we will, by our defections, block out the light.

We would be most comfortable if God were to give us two choices. First, that we receive his love, the forgiveness of our sins, and only rest back in the assurance of everlasting life to come. The second, that we enlist actively in his enterprises of love and righteousness on the earth, that we undertake to be his light in the world. The second option gives us pause.

But these two options are rolled into one. We are accepted into his kingdom freely—no entrance fee, no qualifying tests. We are in because someone has died for us and has given us the right to citizenship. We dare not hide the fact that we are of his kingdom. We may, if we choose, reject it altogether, in indifference and unbelief. But if we elect to receive his gift of salvation and become citizens, we become involved in the style of life of the kingdom. We are the reflected light of the great Light, which is Christ. Frightening as the logic may be, the world will know him because it knows us.

We may not shine brightly, and sometimes our lives are only a glimmer of what they ought to be. But even so, they are of the light and not of the darkness.

You are the light of the world. A city set on a hill cannot be hid. Nor do men light a lamp and put it under a bushel, but on a stand, and it gives light to all in the house (Matt. 5:14-15).

As far as the New Testament records go, only one thing did the disciples explicitly ask Jesus to teach them—how to pray. They were praying men already, of course, but in watching Jesus withdraw to pray to his Father, they sensed that he was in touch with a radiance and a power which had escaped them. So Jesus taught them the prayer, "Our Father," which most of us have prayed, thoughtfully or thoughtlessly, a hundred times over. Speaking of this incident, Harry Emerson Fosdick, a leading American preacher in the first half of our century, says:

> The more they lived with him the more they saw that they never could explain him unless they understood his praying. . . . It is an impressive experience to face a personality whom we cannot explain until we understand his prayer. A superficial brook can be explained without going far, but the River Nile is inexplicable until one knows the high mountains in the center of the continent and the rains that fall there. Personalities like that we do discover, not simply among great figures in history, but in homely places. Here, for example, was a woman who, comparatively young, was left a widow with five children and who resolutely shouldered the practical and spiritual responsibilities which that entailed. By careful management she saw the children through college. On the day of her burial, in her ninety-sixth year, one of the children said they had never seen her impatient or distraught to the point of giving up, even in the most troubled times. One son became president of a great railway system; another became president of a state university; another became a leading pioneer in his department of medical research. That kind of consequence in a family is no accident. That mother was an extraordinary personality. It was the university president who said to me that no one could understand her who did not understand her prayer. It was a force, he said; it released radiance and power.

In a very profound sense, prayer is resting back in God, relaxing in the everlasting arms. But these arms go places. Jesus did. And resting back in them, we go with their power, not simply with our own. This is one of the secrets of prayer.

Truly, truly, I say to you, if you ask anything of the Father, he will give it to you in my name (John 16:23).

To be meek, in Christ's terms, is not to be pushed around. It is rather a sort of endurance in the face of all adversity and opposition, a refusal to fight the battles of life on the world's terms, giving up everything, if necessary, except one thing—the integrity of a person's life in Christ. There is no strength to compare with this. Little wonder that Jesus pointed out these people as those who would last. The earth belongs to them. They are the baffling, terrible meek.

What can the world do with a Polycarp, Bishop of Smyrna in the second century, who when told that his life would be spared if he would deny his Lord, said, "Eighty-six years have I served him, and he has never done me wrong. How can I deny my King and my Savior?" What power does a totalitarian government have over a Hanns Lilje in the Nazi prison, threatened with death, who replied, "I don't need to live"? Or what can the world do with a Luther, who for the sake of conscience, faced the combined powers of the church and the empire at Worms and quietly told them he could not recant? What can you do with a person who can't be bribed or threatened, who refuses to be lured by the prospect of money or power or rank—but stands his ground, come what may, simply because he is loyal to truth and justice? All the world can do is to kill him. He is one of the terrible meek!

Jesus himself is the prime exhibit. If he had been willing to bend, just a little, Pontius Pilate could have saved him. If he had been willing to be just a little less meek, just a little more willing to fight on the world's terms, he need not have died.

The Bible speaks of dying with Christ and living with Christ. Paul said, "It is no longer I who live, but Christ who lives in me." And at one point he writes to his friends, "I am going to Jerusalem. Imprisonment and afflictions await me. But I do not account my life of any value nor as precious to myself, if only I may accomplish my course and the ministry which I received from the Lord Jesus, to testify to the gospel of the grace of God." Obviously Paul had desires and needs. He was human, after all. And he took some normal precautions for his safety, as we do. But safety was not the top priority for him. He would give up safety, even life itself, rather than betray his Lord.

People like these are the salt of the earth. They keep the whole of life from rotting. They are the cement that holds the structure from crumbling. Put to the test, even you may give up life itself rather than betray your Lord.

Blessed are the meek, for they shall inherit the earth (Matt. 5:5).

Throughout the history of the church, the question of the arts, in color, form, and music, has been an issue of controversy. Do they assist a person in reaching God, or do they deflect him from God?

The use of statues and pictures became a burning issue, and had not a little to do with the separation of the church in the East (the Orthodox) from the church in the West (the Roman Catholic). In much of early Protestantism, there was a strong bias against the use of art. Symbolism was reduced to a minimum. A Presbyterian friend of mine told me that in his early ministry he would have been forced to resign had he introduced a cross into the church. No doubt the fear lurked that a person would stop with the symbol and not go on to God himself. A statue or a picture would become an idol.

Music, too, was suspect. There have been churches which allowed no instrument, organ or piano. Only the human voice was acceptable to God.

The issue probably was one of esthetics over against the ethical. A person may be absorbed in beauty, but have his character unchanged. And if beauty in the church, whether in pictures, statuary or music, should distract the worshiper from the hard, sturdy virtues of doing God's will, then out with beauty.

Unlike many of the other reformers, Luther found beauty a support for Christian living. He retained much of the symbolism in the church and was especially fond of music. In fact, he composed hymns, including the celebrated "A mighty fortress is our God."

In one of his table talks he exalts the role of music. He says, "Besides theology, music is the only art capable of affording peace and joy in the heart like that induced by the study of the science of divinity. The proof of this is that the devil, the originator of sorrowful anxieties and restless troubles, flees before the sound of music almost as much as he does before the Word of God. This is why the prophets preferred music before all other arts, proclaiming the Word in psalms and hymns. My heart, which is full to overflowing, has often been solaced and refreshed by music when sick and weary."

Praise him with trumpet sound; praise him with lute and harp! Praise him with timbrel and dance; praise him with strings and pipe! Let everything that breathes praise the Lord! (Psalm 150:3-6).

EQUALLY GUILTY? October 9

Reinhold Niebuhr is an eminent American theologian of the 20th century, especially as theology relates to our common life. Two of his early books, *Leaves from the Notebook of a Tamed Cynic* and *Moral Man and Immoral Society*, were helpful to me in my early ministry. He, better than most theologians, probed the deep sinfulness of the human being and of society. I quote from his major work, *The Nature and Destiny of Man:*

Obviously men who are equally sinful in the sight of God may also be equally guilty in a specific situation. The equality of their sin must, in fact, lead to the general assumption that their guilt is more equal than it will seem to be upon cursory analysis. Two nations involved in perennial war may thus be equally guilty, even though only one was responsible for the latest act of provocation. A ruthless father may be more equally guilty of the waywardness of his son than a superficial analysis would reveal. An abandoned wife may share equal guilt with her faithless husband though the overt act of desertion was his alone. The Christian doctrine of the sinfulness of all men is thus a constant challenge to re-examine superficial moral judgments, particularly those which self-righteously give the moral advantage to the one who makes the judgment. There is no moral situation in which the Pauline word does not apply: "Therefore thou art inexcusable, O man, whosoever thou art that judgest: for wherein thou judgest another, thou condemnest thyself; for thou that judgest doest the same things" (Romans 2:1).

Yet men who are equally sinners in the sight of God need not be equally guilty of a specific act of wrongdoing in which they are involved. It is important to recognize that biblical religion has emphasized this inequality of guilt just as much as the equality of sin. . . . Specially severe judgments fall upon the rich and the powerful, the mighty and the noble, the wise and the righteous (that is, those who are tempted to spiritual pride by their attainment of some relative, socially approved standard of righteousness, the Pharisees). . . . Prophetic judgment is leveled at those "which oppress the poor, which crush the needy" (Amos 4:1), those who "lie upon beds of ivory, and stretch themselves upon their couches" (Amos 6:4).

The Lord watches over the sojourners, he upholds the widow and the fatherless; but the way of the wicked he brings to ruin (Psalm 146:9).

It wasn't that he was a pastor for 21 years, or his becoming a bishop and the president of two colleges, or that he had been a star pitcher in college baseball, or that he sang the bass solos in Handel's *Messiah* and ballads to my children, or that he remained the tender lover of the mother of his six children for their 45 years together. All this would not be enough to set him apart for greatness.

He loved people. He never used them or manipulated them. He grasped the calloused hand of a farmer and the manicured hand of a senator with the same respect and warmth. He knew the value of money, but sought it only to distribute it. When I had a call to a congregation at a substantial increase in salary, I asked him if he wanted me to make sure that his grandchildren had shoes. He asked, "Do they have shoes now, and are they paid for?" When I said yes, he said, "Well then, why do you ask?" He belonged to a whole generation of church leaders who managed the affairs of its institutions with financial adroitness but with almost prodigal disregard for their own personal gain.

In conversation, whether theological or practical, we thought him exasperatingly deliberate, only to discover that in his wisdom he was surveying a far larger terrain of facts than others with more ready conclusions. I always thought he would have been a superb jurist. (Not until years later did the family learn that he had earned a Doctor of Jurisprudence degree.) He was sagacious, just, firm, kind, and disquietingly intelligent.

His years as a parish pastor were his happiest. He could not hide this fact from me as I prepared in 1934 to take his daughter with me to my first parish. With a twinkle in his eye he gave me a bit of counsel. "They are eager to love you. Remember, however, that they have gotten along without you and your ideas for 45 years, so you can afford to ride along with their ways for a year before you start changing things." Only from a sense of duty had he turned from the parish to posts of leadership in the church. When he was 68, a heart attack led him to leave administration, and he had the joy in his two remaining years of again serving as pastor of a small parish—he preaching and his wife playing the organ, as they had in their early years.

Do your best to present yourself to God as one approved, a workman who has no need to be ashamed, rightly handling the word of truth (2 Tim. 2:15).

Moses is the symbol of God's law; Jesus Christ is the symbol of God's grace. Both are of God. Each has its proper place in the life of the Christian. One cannot stop with Moses, nor can one reach Christ by bypassing Moses. To stop with Moses is to have a Christian life of rules and regulations alone. To bypass Moses and go directly to Christ is to have a life where redemption, forgiveness of sin, is not the center, and where Christ is a pleasant friend instead of a Savior. Unless a person has faced the law of God and his demand for holiness and righteousness, and has discovered his abject failure to meet God's demands, he cannot be aware of the great gift of mercy and pardon in Christ Jesus.

Writing in his *Commentary on Galatians,* Martin Luther says:

"God is the God of the humble, the miserable, the oppressed and the desperate, and of those that are brought to nothing; and his nature is to give sight to the blind, to comfort the brokenhearted, to justify sinners, to save the very desperate and damned. Now that pernicious and pestilent opinion of man's own righteousness, which will not be a sinner, unclean, miserable and damnable, but righteous and holy, does not let God come with his own natural and proper work. Therefore God must take this maul in hand [the law] to beat in pieces and bring to nothing this beast with her vain confidence, that she may so learn at length by her own misery that she is utterly forlorn and damned. But here lieth the difficulty, that when a man is terrified and cast down, he is so little able to raise himself up again and say, 'Now I am bruised and afflicted enough; now is the time of grace; now is the time to hear Christ.' The foolishness of man is too great that then he rather seeketh to himself more laws to satisfy his conscience. 'If I live,' saith he, 'I will amend my life: I will do this, I will do that.' But here, except thou do the quite contrary, except thou send Moses away with his law, and in these terrors and this anguish lay hold upon Christ who died for thy sins, look for no salvation."

Law and gospel, works and grace—these are the recurring motifs in the Christian life. To arrive at the wonder of *grace alone* is its goal.

But God, who is rich in mercy, out of the great love with which he loved us, even when we were dead through our trespasses, made us alive together with Christ (by grace you have been saved), and raised us up with him, and made us sit with him in the heavenly places in Christ Jesus (Eph. 2:4-6).

In his essay, "God's Lonely Man," Thomas Wolfe expresses both the poignancy of loneliness and Christ's assault on it:

The most tragic, sublime, and beautiful expression of human loneliness which I have ever read is the Book of Job; the grandest and most philosophical, Ecclesiastes. . . . The lonely man, who is also the tragic man, is invariably the man who loves life dearly—which is to say, the joyful man. The one condition implies the other. . . . For the tragic writer knows that joy is rooted at the heart of sorrow, that ecstasy is shot through with the sudden crimson thread of pain, that the knife-thrust of intolerable desire and the wild, brief glory of possession are pierced most bitterly, at the very instant of man's greatest victory, by the premonitory sense of loss and death. . . .

What Christ is saying always, what he never swerves from saying, what he says a thousand times and in a thousand different ways, but always with a central unity of belief, is this: "I am my Father's son, and you are my brothers." And the unity that binds us all together, that makes this earth a family, and all men brothers and the sons of God, is love.

The central purpose of Christ's life, therefore, is to destroy the life of loneliness and to establish here on earth the life of love. The evidence to support this is clear and overwhelming. It should be obvious to everyone that when Christ says: "Blessed are the poor in spirit: for theirs is the kingdom of heaven," "Blessed are they that mourn: for they shall be comforted," "Blessed are the meek: for they shall inherit the earth," "Blessed are they which do hunger and thirst after righteousness: for they shall be filled," "Blessed are the pure in heart: for they shall see God,"—Christ is not here extolling the qualities of humility, sorrow, meekness, righteousness, mercy, and purity as virtues sufficient in themselves, but he promises to men who have these virtues the richest reward that men were ever offered.

And what is that reward? It is a reward that promises not only the inheritance of the earth, but the kingdom of heaven as well. It tells men that they shall not live and die in loneliness . . . but that, through love, they shall destroy the walls of loneliness forever.

No man has ever seen God; if we love one another, God abides in us and his love is perfected in us (1 John 4:12).

It cannot be denied that in our day God has drifted off to the edges of daily life and perhaps for many has disappeared altogether. An emptiness and loneliness have overtaken modern man. A vacuum yawns before him. He has longings and yearnings for something—he knows not what—something that will give meaning and completeness to life. This something is God. Left alone, we yield to panic or paralysis, or both. We can stand to be the co-pilot, but we cannot stand to be the pilot; we can stand to be children of God, but we cannot stand to sit on the throne.

With God gone, the category of authority disappears. We no longer say, "We must obey God rather than man." We are at sea; we find no certain focus for authority. We are left alone without a sovereign and without law. Made for obedience, we find no one to obey. We are left to create moral order in a universe that has no transcendent basis for order. We cry for a judge, but the bench is empty.

Finally, hope is gone. Spectacular as our achievements are in the field of technology, our triumphs give us no hope. We see looming up before us the angry clouds of the hurricane, the mammoth problems of our time. And behind the clouds there is no one to lean on, no everlasting arms in which to rest, no power greater than our own to come to the rescue. Lonely people go their lonely way to a vast and lonely grave.

This is modern humanity—without God!

But God is still here. He has not abdicated. His judgment hangs heavy over a people who go their heedless way. But his love hovers even more surely over these, his children, who are groping their way. He weeps for them as they find no overarching meaning for their lives. He suffers with them as they stumble and fall into ways that yield only hurt and misery. He yearns for them.

After all, he has prepared a place for them from the foundation of the world. In Christ Jesus he has a kingdom planted firmly in their midst. The cross of Christ is eloquent guarantee that he loves with an everlasting love.

Perhaps the emptiness, the longings, the hurts and anxieties of our day are but the prelude to a better day, when his children, hearing the wonderful gospel, will be captured again by hope and joy and love.

Therefore, lift your drooping hands and strengthen your weak knees, and make straight paths for your feet, so that what is lame may not be put out of joint but rather be healed (Heb. 12:12-13).

JANE COULD NOT LET HIM GO October 14

Jane had tried to let Jesus go. She had ignored him, pushed him aside, tried to forget him. Many times she had wanted to let him go.

He was not like a policeman who would not leave his beat. He was not even like a lover, who, when rebuffed, kept pushing his attentions on her. He was more like a haunting, tender memory. But he was more than a memory. He was never really gone. His presence seemed to swallow her up. She could never quite let Jesus Christ go.

For months on end she had been able to let the church go. She had been fed up with sermons that seemed dull, hymns that she did not know too well, the youth meetings that seemed pointless. Even the people were too conventional, too smug, outwardly too decent. Finally she had dropped out of this colorless routine. Even so, at the most unsuspecting moments, Jesus Christ would cross her mind. And at night, before falling asleep, either from long habit or from some inner compulsion, she would pray to him.

She knew the church had often failed. It had failed to fight the evils of the day as it ought. It had failed to champion the cause of the under-privileged as it ought. It had seemed content to turn in upon itself, whipping up larger memberships and more impressive budgets, but insensitive to some great, magnificent mission. Jane knew enough about the early church, from the book of Acts, to know how restless it had once been to follow its Master, Jesus Christ.

In the fall a new girl had enrolled in her college class, an American Indian. At first she was a curiosity. Not too attractive in her rather ill-fitting dresses, she went about her studies scarcely daring to smile. She grew more withdrawn as the weeks went on. Jane's sorority had three vacancies to fill, and Jane nominated this new girl. A mild storm of protest arose. But Jane was firm, and after much persuasion the other girls reluctantly consented. The Indian girl was in, and the year blossomed into warm friendships for her.

Jane asked herself why; why had she gone to bat for this stranger? She was not especially drawn to her, any more than were the other girls. Then she realized that Jesus had gotten involved. This is what he would have wanted her to do ". . . to the least of these my brethren . . . I was a stranger and you welcomed me."

Let brotherly love continue. Do not nelect to show hospitality to strangers, for thereby some have entertained angels unawares (**Heb.** 13:1-2).

The age of the Enlightenment, with its optimistic appraisal of man, had brushed aside the whole cargo of evil—the Fall and original sin, the devil and demons—and had been lured by the evolutionary hope that man and civilization were becoming better, day by day, century by century, millennium by millennium. Our volcanic twentieth century has given us a fresh look at the brutality of man—Buchenwald, Dachau, the wars. We are more ready to take seriously the profound dimensions of evil, both in man and his culture, and to at least entertain the scriptural warnings of celestial beings of evil lurking "to devour us."

Mark Twain obviously doesn't sound like a preacher, but in his own inimitable way he pays tribute to this evil power:

I have no special regard for Satan, but I can at least claim that I have no prejudice against him. It may even be that I have been a little in his favor, on account of his not having a fair show. All religions issue Bibles against him, but we never hear his side. We have none but the evidence for the prosecution, and yet we have rendered the verdict. To my mind this is irregular. It is un-English, it is un-American. Of course, Satan has some kind of case, it goes without saying. It may be a poor one, but that is nothing; that can be said about any of us. As soon as I can get at the facts I will undertake his rehabilitation myself, if I can find an impolite publisher. It is a thing which we ought to do for anyone who is under a cloud.

We may not pay him reverence, for that would be indiscreet, but we can at least respect his talents. A person who has for untold centuries maintained the imposing position of spiritual head of four-fifths of the human race, and political head of the whole of it, must be granted the possession of executive abilities of the loftiest order. In his large presence the other popes and politicians shrink to midgets for the microscope. I would like to see him. I would rather see him and shake him by the tail than any other member of the European Concert.

Finally, be strong in the Lord and in the strength of his might. Put on the whole armor of God, that you may be able to stand against the wiles of the devil (Eph. 6:10-11).

FOLLOWERS FIRST

In our day it isn't very popular to be called a follower. Corporations look for leadership qualities, young people aspire to be leaders, and obituaries usually call attention to the leadership a person has provided in his lifetime.

Did Jesus ever call for leaders? I look in vain through the Gospels to find him asking for anyone but followers.

There's a delightful story about a young man applying for admission to a men's college which admitted only 250 freshmen each year. The boy's father got a questionnaire to fill out, in which, among other questions, was this one, "Is your son a leader or is he a follower?" The father pondered the question, and concluded that while his son was a very able boy, he probably was more a follower than a leader, and this is what he indicated. In due time he received a letter from the college's admissions office stating that his son was admitted, with the notation added, "We are pleased that in a class of 249 leaders we will have one follower."

What was it about Luther that made him, a peasant monk, stand at bay the combined power and pomp of the church and the empire, and say, "I can do no other"? Was it the mantle of leadership that he felt? He was a *follower* of Jesus Christ, and his conscience, and that gave him the strength to obey.

It is questionable if anyone has a right to leadership who is not first a follower. If he is not committed to some high principles—to follow them, come what may—is he leadership stuff?

It is doubtful if any of the early disciples felt the weight of leadership. They were followers; they were sent, and they obeyed! That Paul became the leader of the church's outreach into the Gentile world, and that Peter became the leader of the early flock—these were the accidents of their lives. Their mandate was to follow, not to lead.

We who confess Christ are followers. If, by chance, or by the turn of events, we are thrust into places of leadership, and if we do well, the greatest tribute will still be that we excelled in following.

Then Jesus told his disciples, "If any man would come after me, let him deny himself and take up his cross and follow me" (Matt. 16:24).

It hardly seems fair. Why should God expect us to be perfect when he knows well how far short we will fall? Couldn't he tailor his demands to match our best performance? After all, none of us can be perfect.

If a family has expectations of its members, like honesty and integrity and industry, would you think it right for a father to reduce those standards for a son who was inclined to cheat and lie and waste his time? You'd say, no! You would say that the son should face squarely the expectations, try his best to shape up, and not bring shame on the family standards. To abandon the standards to fit the boy would be to scuttle the quality of the family itself.

God's family is one of holiness, of righteousness, of justice. Nor is there any halfway point in holiness and righteousness. God will not settle for a person to be half righteous and half unrighteous. And you wouldn't want him to.

To try earnestly to meet the standards, and to fail, is not a betrayal. To abandon the standards is the betrayal. Jesus, whose whole life was one of compassion for the people who failed, reminded his people that "till heaven and earth pass away, not an iota, not a dot, will pass from the law until all is accomplished." Holiness will be demanded, even though no one attains holiness. The standards will stay.

God has a marvelous way of dealing with us who try but fail. Only we have to try. We have no option but to give our best to fulfilling the law. And we need to know sorrow and repentance for failing.

But God does not let us lie in the rubble of our failures. He puts us on our feet, again and again. This he does through the amazing turnabout of having his only Son, Jesus Christ, fulfill the law for us. He became one of us; he was tempted in every way as we are, yet without failing; he, in some strange way, accredits us by faith, with his holiness. The standards of God's family, which are holiness, are not reduced to match our performance, but are fulfilled in Jesus Christ, our brother.

There will come a day when we, too, will have no trace of sin, unrighteousness, or unholiness. He plans to make perfect that which he has begun. It will take him beyond the borders of death, into eternal life, to finish it. But he will!

You, therefore, must be perfect, as your heavenly Father is perfect (Matt. 5:48).

To accept injustice and cruelty without fighting back is not one of our American virtues. Many of us, however, may have had to endure adversity, with no hope of change. *Bontshe the Silent* by Isaac Peretz, Yiddish writer in Poland, is a touching account of someone who learned to endure without bitterness.

Here, in this world below, the death of Bontshe produced no impression whatever. . . . Like a shadow he passed over the face of the earth. . . . He lived, a grain of sand on the seashore, among the millions of its kind. And when the wind at last carried him off to the other side, no one noticed it. Born quietly, he lived in silence, died in silence, and was buried in a silence even greater.

But it was not thus that things happened in the *other* world. There, the death of Bontshe produced a deep impression. . . . The bugle-call of the Messiah, the sound of the Ram's horn, was heard throughout the seven heavens. "Bontshe the Silent has died." . . . Very young angels, with eyes of diamond, gold-threaded wings, wearing silver slippers, were rushing out, full of joy, to meet Bontshe.

The Patriarch Abraham stationed himself at the gate of heaven, stretching out his right hand to Bontshe in cordial welcome: "Peace be with you," a sweet smile illuminating his delighted old countenance.

"But the Supreme Court has not yet pronounced judgment?" ask the astonished saints, not without a tinge of jealousy. "Bah!" reply the angels, "That will only be a formality . . . the case will not last five minutes."

Terror-stricken, Bontshe did not even hear the President of the Court call out in a loud voice: "The case of Bontshe the Silent!"

The voice of the angelic advocate reached his ears . . . "Never," said the advocate, "never has he uttered a complaint against God or men. Never has a spark of hatred flamed up in his eyes, never has he lifted his eyes with pretensions to heaven."

"My child," said the President, "the Supreme Tribunal will never pass sentence against you . . . Everything here belongs to you; take whatever your heart desires."

"Really?" Bontshe asks. . . . "Then, if such is the case, I should like to have every morning a hot roll with fresh butter."

Do all things without grumbling or questioning, that you may be blameless and innocent, children of God without blemish" (Phil. 2:14).

It would not be hard for a leper, suddenly cleansed, to praise him. Or for someone recovering from cancer. Or when a fine promotion comes along. Even then we may forget to thank or praise him, and simply enjoy our good fortune. We may be absorbed in the gift and forget the giver.

But can we praise him when we don't recover and when no promotion is there? Is there something so constant, so unchanging, and so overwhelming in value that in both "good and evil days" we keep praising him, whatever happens?

If our lives are not to be one long series of ups and downs, one day full of joy and praise and another day heavy with pain and bitterness, if we are to be protected from the ebb and flow, we must find something for which we can always be thankful. It will need to be something that soars above the flux of time, something beyond the caprice of fortune or luck, something that nothing can change or take away from us.

For us who are Christians, we focus on a cross outside of the city gates of Jerusalem 2000 years ago. It is a strange place to find the fixed, the unchanging, the eternal, and that which nothing can take from us. This is where we discover that God loves us with an everlasting love.

The lover gives his beloved the gift of his heart. In addition he gives her a lovely bracelet. It would be a tragedy if she treasured the jewelry more than his love.

Most of us find ourselves doing just that. We may be overwhelmed by the gifts. If things go well, and we have the blessings of family, of friends, of health, of security, we may be so enrapt by these that we overlook the greater gift hovering behind all others—the gift of himself and his love. It may just be that when the secondary gifts are gone, when health goes, when loved ones die and leave us lonely, when adversity strikes and security is gone—it may be then that we become aware that we still have the dearest gift.

Thanksgiving and praise belong in all ups and downs. Some day, when death draws near and we see all else slipping away, we will know in all its wonder the gift of life with our Lord, which not even death can take from us.

For I am sure that neither death, nor life, nor angels, nor principalities, nor things present, nor things to come, nor powers, nor height, nor depth, nor anything else in all creation, will be able to separate us from the love of God in Christ Jesus our Lord (Rom. 8:38).

Once through the great main door of the castle, we find all sorts of doors inviting us to enter.

The main door of God's castle is repentance and faith. We face his judgment, and are stripped of all pretense. Here, where all hearts are open, there is no point trying to present a good front. There's something purging about finally coming clean, hiding nothing, even if it means that we are bankrupt. "If thou, O Lord, shouldst mark iniquities, Lord, who could stand?" asked the psalmist. We are judged and found wanting. But that's not the end. The judge sentences. And then, wonder of wonders, he steps down from the bench to take our sentence upon himself, and we are free! We are free to go through all the doors of his wondrous castle.

The door of praise and adoration beckons us. Our hearts fill with gratitude, and we lift our spirits into the sheer joy of thanking him.

The door of merriment swings open. Released from the melancholy burden of sin and guilt, we discover all life gives gaiety and mirth. We are restored to God, and we are heirs to his whole universe. We revel in friends and family, we bask in the sunshine, we throb with the pulsating life of nature about us, we tingle at the winds that blow. Everything has a touch of rhapsody—the song of birds, the laughter of children—everything.

The door of glad service to those in need is there to enter, with its profound satisfaction. It is within this castle that the sublime secrets of the kingdom yield themselves. We learn that it is more blessed to give than to receive. To be a servant, we discover, is far more gratifying than to be served. Outside of the castle we may have wandered furtively, trying to find the meaning of life. Now we find it. Dag Hammarskjold speaks of entering the door, "and from that hour I was certain that existence is meaningful and that, therefore, my life, in self-surrender had a goal."

And, of course, there is a final door, when within the castle we leave death behind and enter the glories that have been prepared for us from the foundation of the world.

Not to us, O Lord, not to us, but to thy name give glory, for the sake of thy steadfast love and thy faithfulness (Psalm 115:1).

HOW CERTAIN CAN WE BE?

Many Christians are troubled by questions such as: "How can I be sure that I have faith?" "What must I do to be sure that I am saved?" "I have doubts; does that mean that I have slipped away from the Lord?"

Paul Tillich, exiled from Nazi Germany, became in America one of the leading religious voices of our century. Speaking of certainty, he says,

> But let us look more exactly at the nature of that certainty which Paul and Luther defend. The words of Paul clearly show that it is not *self*-certainty: ". . . Even if *we* . . . should preach to you a gospel contrary to that which we preached to you. . . ." The truth of the gospel Paul has preached is not dependent on Paul. The certainty he has is not dependent on the changes in his personal experience. He can imagine that some day he might preach a distorted gospel; he can even imagine that an angel from heaven might bring another message than that which the Church has already received. He is not sure of himself and he is not even sure of angelic visions.
>
> The gospel . . . *is* our certainty, but it is lost the moment we begin to regard it as our certainty. We are certain only as long as we look at the content of our certainty and not at the rational or irrational experiences in which we have received it. Looking at ourselves and our certainty as *ours*, we discover its weakness, its vulnerability to every critical thought; we discover the small amount of probability which our reasoning can give to the idea of God and to the reality of Christ. We discover the contradictions in the emotional side of our religious life, its oscillation between ecstatic confidence and despairing doubt. But looking at God, we realize that all the shortcomings of our experience are of no importance. Looking at God, we see that we do not have Him . . . but that He has us. . . . Looking at God we feel that we cannot escape Him even by making Him an object of sceptical arguments or irresistible emotions. . . . *We* may not comprehend, but we *are* comprehended. We may not grasp anything in the depth of our uncertainty, but that we are grasped by something ultimate, which keeps us in its grasp and from which we may strive in vain to escape, remains absolutely certain.

I have looked upon thee in the sanctuary, beholding thy power and glory. Because thy steadfast love is better than life, my lips will praise thee (Psalm 63:2-3).

If we are at all earnest about having the Lord Jesus Christ dwell in our hearts and direct our lives, there are some simple disciplines to observe.

First, we go to church. This may sound too institutional, but it is no accident that the church as an establishment has survived throughout the long centuries. Here, gathered with others who are seeking the Lord and who are gathered to worship him, we are exposed to the stirrings of the Holy Spirit. In Word and sacrament the Spirit broods over us. As we pray and as we sing, and as we hear his Word proclaimed and feast at his table, we open our hearts to our Lord in ways that are not as likely if we remain alone.

Second, we assign some moments of solitude to him. Most of us are not attuned to meditation. We will need helps. Scripture is full of helps. There are books on prayer and devotion. We may need these as catalysts to usher us into God's presence.

Third, if possible we arrange a time when as a family we worship together in our home. This is not without its difficulties, since so many families are on broken schedules. Prayers at mealtime, and even a familiar hymn or two will be a touch of heaven.

Fourth, a rather fixed schedule for reading the Bible. You may follow the readings which the church has recommended, found, for example, in a hymnal. You may want to go beyond snatches, and read a whole book at a time, one of the gospels, for instance. This is the book of all books for us as Christians, and we ought to let it speak to us.

Fifth, we strive for a calculated and deliberate concern for people. After all, we are Christ's agents on earth. His love reaches people through other people. Busy as we all are, if we will have our radar out for people who are lonely and in need (nor are they far away), we will find ourselves companioned by him who loves us all.

These disciplines are not for the purpose of enticing or luring the Lord into our hearts. He needs no manipulating to come. He said, "Behold, I stand at the door and knock." These are but little helps to make sure that we open the door.

Let us hold fast the confession of our hope without wavering, for he who promised is faithful; and let us consider how to stir up one another to love and good works, not neglecting to meet together, as is the habit of some, but encouraging one another, and all the more as you see the Day drawing near (Heb. 10:23-25).

If God is perfect, does he suffer? If he is all-powerful, all-knowing, everywhere-present, holy and eternal, can we possibly cause him to suffer? Would it not be beneath his dignity to let small people like us cause him pain?

If, in addition to all these other sovereign qualities, he should be a God of love, then how can he escape suffering? If we love someone, we give that person the power to hurt us. We place a whip in his hands. To the degree that we love, to that degree we may have to suffer. A loving wife who is betrayed by a faithless husband knows what suffering love is like. A father and mother who lose a child know. The only certain way to be spared suffering is never to love at all—never to give to another the whip that can hurt.

God opened himself up for suffering when he created us to be his sons and daughters. Had he made us like all other creatures, beasts and birds and fish, he could have escaped the risk. In the very first book of the Bible, we see him broken-hearted over the betrayal. Adam and Eve chose the enemy of God instead of God. And throughout the long chapters of the Old Testament, as he lavishes his love upon Israel, only to have them turn to other gods again and again, we watch him suffer.

One would think his patience would run out. It would have, had his love run out. But he loves with an everlasting love. Once committed to his children, he could not abandon them, though they grieved him a thousand times. His anger would flare, but it was anger out of a broken heart. Not only was it anger at his children, but more often high indignation over the evil that caused suffering for his children. He wept for them and with them.

Anyone who has lost a dear one in death, anyone who has watched a dear one in agony, anyone who has had his dreams shattered, anyone who has writhed in pain has known what great comfort there is in having a God who, in love, suffers with us. If, when our son was killed, I would have had to think of God sitting detached as a spectator, I could not have prayed to him. It is good to remember I had a Lord who wept at the grave of his friend Lazarus. It is of great comfort to have a God who loves and suffers.

Let us then with confidence draw near to the throne of grace, that we may receive mercy and find grace to help in time of need (Heb. 4:16).

When, as Christians, we believe that Christ lives in us, and we in him, we are speaking of more than memories and affection. We believe that he is a strange and palpable presence within us. We become one with him.

It is difficult to find parallels for this truth. No two people are ever fused or merged into one. Even the most loving husband and wife who have become "one flesh" are yet like two pebbles rubbing against one another in the ebb and flow of life. They remain two. Weeping together at the death of their child, they are yet two people, joined in grief, but two still. Only *in Christ* do we become one.

It is as if Christ takes up residency within us. He doesn't stand on the outside, giving encouragement and instructions. He comes in, to dwell. George Macdonald, in his *Diary of an Old Soul*, says,

> The house is not for me—it is for him.
> His royal thoughts require many a stair,
> Many a tower, many an outlook fair. . . .
> Thou being in me, in my deepest me,
> Though all the time I do not think of thee,
> Shall I not grow at last so true within
> As to forget thee and yet never sin . . .
> Not conscious think of thee, yet never from thee stray?

There's something in the experience of every Christian that understands the words of Macdonald. Goodness, or doing the Lord's will, can become an instinctive and even effortless way of life. By nature we are deeply egocentric, on guard for our own interests. With Christ dwelling within us, there is a strange turnabout. Now, to be concerned with others, to love and to forgive, becomes a new dynamic. Something —someone—within us makes it easier to do the right thing than the wrong. To do the wrong sets up barriers of shame and remorse; in doing the right we are caught up and carried along in a flow of joy and power. We need no longer suffer the anguish of decision at each turn. We do good because it is the nature of the Christ in us to do good. Goodness becomes fun!

. . . that they may all be one; even as thou, Father, art in me, and I in thee, that they also may be in us, . . . I in them and thou in me, that they may become perfectly one (John 17:21-23).

Most of us have grown up in what we may call normal Christendom, in the traditional churches, and we may be less than tolerant of that part of the Lord's family that goes to "excesses" of one kind or another. We must remember that the Lord has a big family. Some worship him in stately reserve, some with unrestrained enthusiasm, some in quiet meditation. Nor are the needs of people the same at all times. In a penetrating story of his family, *Brother to a Dragonfly*, Will D. Campbell tells of his brother Paul, whose wife abandoned their two daughters and their affluent home after 20 years of marriage, and left him crushed. Mr. Campbell says,

> He did not then turn to drugs or booze but joined the Church of God, actually joined what we as children had called the "holy rollers" and considered children of the devil. But the split-level Baptists, now grown rich, could offer him nothing but a weekly appointment on the counselor's couch with a young Th.D. probing his psyche. The "holy rollers" could, and did, offer him a place where he could cry out loud to an empathizing audience who would cry with him because they loved him, a place where he could laugh out loud and shout God's goodness out loud and roll on the floor and scream in either agony or joy when he felt like it. And the "holy rollers" could, and did, offer him ex-prisoners to take home and care for, and homeless boys to whom he could, and would, give his land and houses to be their own ranch and home, bringing life and laughter to the barns and meadows neither the barns and meadows, their giver, nor the homeless boys had ever known before.

Most of us recognize that our churches sometimes become so staid, so orderly, and so cautious that warmth and enthusiasm are hard to come by. On the other hand, it would be nonsense to abandon our long traditions in the naive hope that the Holy Spirit can do his work only by radical change in forms. It is equally important not to look down our noses at churches and groups that respond to their Lord in more uninhibited ways than we. The Holy Spirit blows where he wills. He has more than one way to meet our needs.

Now there are varieties of gifts, but the same Spirit; and there are varieties of service, but the same Lord; and there are varieties of working, but it is the same God who inspires them all in every one (1 Cor. 12:4-6).

Greatness is found in the most unsuspecting places. Invariably people who meet the test point beyond themselves. Intuitively we know that they are committed to something or someone greater than they.

They were poor, abjectly poor, and their years were running out. When I first met them they were living in quarters hardly more than a corner of the warehouse where he was working as the night janitor. They had no car, but on a Sunday morning, arm in arm, they trudged their way to church.

The first time I visited them, a lonely tin can on a shelf in the corner arrested my attention. The shelf was obviously a place set apart, like one reserved for a family picture or the image of a saint, and here was a can, perhaps a pork and bean can stripped of its label. The wife caught me looking at it, and with a smile she told me that that's where their weekly offering to the Lord was kept. Later I learned that the husband earned $19 a week, and that the first thing he did upon being paid was to put $1.90 in the tin can. Never in all these years have I been able to forget the feeling of wonder, admiration and pity—and shame for myself—that overwhelmed me that day.

I learned to love them dearly. Later, scratching together their meager savings, they were able with the help of some carpenters in our church to enclose a small 3-room home on the outskirts of town. They were overjoyed with their little nest.

They had no children, and now in their sixties, they could easily have given way to gloom. I kept asking myself, what power is theirs to make two people pray, "Give us this day our daily bread," and to believe that God did answer. What inner springs are there to bring gratitude and patience and kindness into lives that could with good reason collapse into bitterness, emptiness, and even despair?

Once I thought to tell them that the church certainly could get along without their $1.90. I never did. They had learned the Lord's lesson, so hard for us to learn, that it is more blessed to give than to receive. I'm sure that the $1.90 they emptied from their can each week gave them more joy than the $17.10 they had left.

There is great gain in godliness with contentment; for we brought nothing into the world, and we cannot take anything out of the world; but if we have food and clothing, with these we shall be content (1 Tim. 6:6-8).

Unless checked and transformed by a deep commitment to Christ and his ways, the sin of greed and pride will control any person, rich or poor. It is a perennial delusion that if the "have-nots" can unseat the "haves," conditions will be much improved. On a grand scale this has been tried in the Russian revolution, designed to give equality to all. It is reported that the present Soviet President owns a Rolls Royce, a Cadillac limousine, a Mercedes Benz sports coupe, a Citroen-Maserati, a Lincoln Continental, a Matro Rancho cross-country car, and most recently a $50,000 Aston Martin V8 Vantage. Reinhold Niebuhr in his *The Nature and Destiny of Man* addresses this all too-human quality:

The Biblical analysis agrees with the known facts of history. Capitalists are not greater sinners than poor laborers by any natural depravity. But it is a fact that those who hold great economic and political power are more guilty of pride against God and of injustice against the weak than those who lack power and prestige. Gentiles are not naturally more sinful than Jews. But Gentiles, holding the dominant power in their several nations, sin against Semitic minority groups more than the latter sin against them. White men sin against Negroes in Africa and America more than Negroes sin against white men. Wherever the fortunes of nature, the accidents of history or even the virtues of the possessors of power, endow an individual or a group with power, social prestige, intellectual eminence or moral approval above their fellows, there an ego is allowed to expand. It expands both vertically and horizontally. Its vertical expansion, its pride, involves it in sin against God. Its horizontal expansion involves it in an unjust effort to gain security and prestige at the expense of its fellows. The two forms of expansion cannot be sharply distinguished because, as previously noted, spiritual pretension can be made an instrument of power in social conflict, and dominant power, measured socially inevitably seeks to complete its structure by spiritual pretensions.

A too simple social radicalism does not recognize how quickly the poor, the weak, the despised of yesterday, may, on gaining a social victory over their detractors, exhibit the same arrogance and the same will-to-power which they abhorred in their opponents and which they were inclined to regard as a congenital sin of their enemies.

If we say we have no sin, we deceive ourselves, and the truth is not in us (1 John 1:8).

We are almost afraid to think of what God may want to give us. Perhaps it's much more than we want.

What does God really mean when he wants to give us salvation, or the kingdom, or life abundant? If salvation, what are we saved from and what are we saved for? If the kingdom, what is the style of life of that kingdom? If the abundant life, just how does God define that kind of life? It may be that we are reluctant to have any of it—salvation or the kingdom or the abundant life.

He sets out to save us from our sins, their guilt, and their power. That may not be what we want. We know it's wrong to hold a grudge, but we secretly enjoy it. We know it's wrong to ignore the needs of our neighbors, but we hate to get involved. We know it's wrong to pile up wealth when others are in need, but it's fun to see the pile grow.

And if he gives us a kingdom—which he has promised as a gift through Christ—what changes may we have to make in our manner of life? We are not sure that we mean it when we pray, "Thy kingdom come." And what does he mean by the abundant life? Perhaps it does not include expensive recreation or even many things we've counted as necessities.

An army recruiting officer, for instance, may point out all the benefits of enlistment. There is a reasonably good salary, much better than years ago. In addition, there is free medical and dental care. Clothing is provided. Free education in various kinds of technology is there. Moreover, if one remains in the service, there are promotions and upon retirement a good pension. At that moment the prospective enlistee may ask, "But what is asked of me?" The officer says, "You will have to obey orders, go where your country needs you, and, if there's a war, be ready to give your life."

We are given the gift of salvation, the kingdom, the abundant life. This will mean that we lose the comfort of being average and unimportant. It means that we lose the pleasures we find in self-indulgence, in self-pity, in defending our rights. It means that we are enlisted in a kingdom, to take orders from our king, and find life by losing it.

Little wonder that we may pause. Is this really what we want? Deep down, we know it is, cost what it will. There is no other option if we want fulness of life!

I came that they may have life, and have it abundantly (John 10:10).

When in Psalm 23 I get to the lines, "Thou preparest a table before me in the presence of my enemies," I pause. Can it be true that in this world of danger God keeps throwing a party for me? For me to close my eyes to the grim issues that face the world and forget the war that rages and celebrate in my little corner—that I can understand. But that God would do it for me is another matter.

Often I wonder, have I a right to joy, when there is so much misery and unhappiness in the world? Have I a right to relish a good meal, when half of the world is underfed? As I read a good book, must my pleasure not be dampened by knowing that my friend down the block can't see to read anymore? And as I take a brisk walk, must I not be haunted by my former student who last week had both his legs amputated?

Yet, if I understand the psalmist, he is saying that in the midst of all this, God spreads a feast before me and tells me to have joy. It's almost as if he insists that I *claim* joy, no matter what the world is like.

Nor do I think he means that my joy should come primarily from comparing myself to the less fortunate and say, "God, I thank thee that I am not as other men." It's inevitable, of course, that I should be grateful for eyes when I've been with someone blind.

But there is a deeper joy that pervades life at this banquet. It's a joy that my blind neighbor still has, and that my student, who expects to ski again, still has. It's the joy of knowing that, come what may, they are held fast in the loving care of their heavenly Father. I become aware that they are there at the feast with me and that their joy doesn't seem lessened by their losses.

If Psalm 23 was written by King David, his life certainly wasn't one of untroubled ease and safety. From the time he faced Goliath, he was in the thick of intrigue, violence and war. Nor was his private life without its shame. In the forgiving mercy of God he must have found a refuge, a table spread with joy.

It isn't as if the Christian forgets the world of pain and evil. No force to counter the hurts of the world has been released to rival the love and concern which the followers of the Lord have had these many centuries. They leave the feast to find their suffering brothers and sisters the world over.

Thou preparest a table before me in the presence of my enemies; thou anointest my head with oil, my cup overflows. Surely goodness and mercy shall follow me all the days of my life, and I shall dwell in the house of the Lord for ever (Psalm 23:5-6).

We take a hundred freedoms for granted. Entering church on a Sunday morning, or giving gifts to support our colleges and seminaries, or reading Christian literature, who pauses to thank God for this high privilege. In our land we are free to worship God according to our own conscience. Our government not only gives us this freedom, but in many ways gives encouragement to the churches.

I read a letter by the celebrated Russian exile, A. Solzhenitsyn, addressed to the Soviet leaders of his country, pleading, among other things, for the freedom of religion in his land:

> So that the country and people do not suffocate, and so that they all have the chance to develop and enrich us with ideas, allow competition on an equal and honorable basis—not for power, but for truth—between all ideological and moral currents, in particular between *all religions:* there will be nobody to persecute them if their tormentor, Marxism, is deprived of its state privileges. But allow competition honestly, not the way you do now, not by gagging people; allow it to religious youth organizations (which are totally nonpolitical; let the Komsomol be the only political one), grant them the right to instruct and educate children, and the right to free parish activity. (I myself see Christianity today as the only living spiritual force capable of undertaking the spiritual healing of Russia. But I request and propose no special privileges for it, simply that it should be treated fairly and not suppressed.) Allow us a free art and literature, the free publication not just of political books—God preserve us!—and exhortations and election leaflets; allow us philosophical, ethical, economic and social studies, and you will see what a rich harvest it brings and how it bears fruit—for the good of Russia. Such an abundant and free flowering of inspiration will rapidly absolve us of the need to keep on belatedly translating new ideas from Western languages, as has been the case for the whole of the last fifty years—as you know. Our country is not without its grave faults, to be sure, but should we not each morning raise our hearts and voices to God in thanksgiving for the rights and freedom we undeservedly enjoy in this good land?

Praise the Lord. Blessed is the man who fears the Lord, who greatly delights in his commandments! (Psalm 112:1).

WHAT OF THE SOUL?

I like the word *soul*. Some friends of mine resist dividing up a person into body, soul, spirit, even heart and mind. Didn't God create the whole person, they ask, and didn't he redeem the whole person, and doesn't he plan to have the whole person with him in paradise? I must agree with them, but I still like the word *soul*. I don't know how I'd get along without it.

If someone says, "I haven't taken time for my soul," I know what he means. "I haven't taken time for my whole person" would hardly convey the same meaning.

The reluctance to use the word *soul* has a valid basis. In non-Christian cultures, the Greek for instance, it was sometimes thought that God created the soul, and the devil the body. The soul was good, the body bad. That way of salvation was to deny the claims of the body, to suppress all desire, and to retreat from the "bad" world. This, of course, is not the Christian faith at all. We believe that God created a good world and gave people good bodies. The appetites of the body, food and sex, are good appetites, and salvation doesn't mean to kill them but to have them under the control of God's laws:

Also, by separating the soul from the body, heaven threatens to become an unreal, even ghoulish, place, with souls, like wisps of vapor, floating around. This clearly is not Christian. We confess, "I believe in the resurrection of the body." Heaven is full of bodies, glorified bodies, far more real than earthly bodies, so real that pain and death can no longer touch them. The imagery in C. S. Lewis's *The Great Divorce* does a great service in making heaven a real, even substantial place.

We will still keep the word *soul*. Our language has no substitute. Our liturgies and hymns use it, and certainly the Scriptures. Without chopping up a person into parts, we will speak of the soul, the heart, the spirit. These words will remind us that we are eternal beings, that the world we see and touch and measure is not the whole of life. When the Lord says, "My son, give me your heart," we'll understand, and when the psalmist prays, "Gladden the soul of thy servant," we'll join him.

You shall love the Lord your God with all your heart, and with all your soul, and with all your mind, and with all your strength (Mark 12:30).

When someone greets me with "What's new?" I have an uneasy feeling. Must there always be something new to make life worth living? Isn't an old book as good as a new book, perhaps better? What of the old songs? Old friends?

On the other hand, must we not hope for something better? And may this not mean something new? Perhaps there is a new day dawning—when wars will be no more, nor hunger, nor racial hatreds. We have no option but to hope and to work for a new day. To give up on our longings for the better day is to settle for the melancholy cynicism of the writer of Ecclesiastes, "There's nothing new under the sun," or the sad commentary of Shakespeare's Macbeth, "Tomorrow and tomorrow and tomorrow creeps in this petty pace from day to day . . . and all our yesterdays have lighted fools the way to dusty death."

But there is something new under the sun, and life has a more noble end than death. God, the Ancient of Days, is new with his mercies each morning. He is the one new and radical factor in the world's cycles of seasons and civilizations. He can alter the shapes of empires and the hearts of men, but only he. Left to ourselves, there is nothing more new than struggle and death.

He has invaded this planet in his Son, Jesus Christ. He invades it still, in every heart that will give him room. And when he invades, he makes all things new. He erases our sins, he lifts our fears, he releases our wills. This he does through the power of his Word, the preaching of his gospel and the administration of his sacraments.

Most of us who count ourselves God-fearing will probably be hardpressed to identify what is new about us. There's too much of the old still cluttering up our lives—old grudges, old anxieties, old envies, old regrets, old vanities. The Bible tells us that these (sometimes called the old man over against the new) will harass us until we die. But there is a new power at work within us. Sometimes we feel it, sometimes not. Most often it works quietly, like a yeast in our souls. Some crisis comes along, and suddenly we know that it's there, like a hidden or forgotten reservoir with life-giving waters of healing. Something new has been at work in us all along. Almost to our surprise we find springs of hope and love and patience and courage to carry us through.

And he who sat upon the throne said, "Behold, I make all things new" (Rev. 21:5).

"The universe is safe for souls," said Evelyn Underhill, one of the leading Christian voices of the first part of our century. Born into a barrister's family in England in 1875, by 1911 she had published her first great book, *Mysticism,* and later what probably is her finest book, *The School of Charity.* Bernhard Christensen in his *The Inward Pilgrimage* says of her, "Evelyn Underhill was a scholar and a thinker of the highest order. Her books deal profoundly with the whole field of Christian spirituality—its intellectual basis, its liturgical expression, its history in the lives of the saints, its daily application in present experience." While pursuing a brilliant educational career at King's College, London, she spent two afternoons a week among the poor in the slums and near-slums of the city. She speaks of Christ as Rescuer:

It was like this when He went up to the disciples in the ship, "and the wind ceased and there was a calm." Then the situation was transformed by his presence. . . .

Sometimes it is on our soul that He lays His tranquilizing touch and stills the storm; sometimes on the hurly-burly of our emotional life, sometimes on events that we think must destroy us or the people and causes we love. . . . We do feel sometimes as if we are left to ourselves to struggle with it all. He is away praying on the mountain, or He is asleep in the boat; the waves seem to be getting decidedly higher, the night is very dark . . . we begin to lose our nerve for life and no one seems to mind. Certainly life is not made soft for Christians; but it *is,* in the last resort, safe. The universe is safe for souls. The disciples were frightened, exhausted, soaked to the skin, but *not* destroyed. At the critical moment He went up into the ship and restored safety, sanity, peace. . . .

So Christ stands over against history and in its darkest and most dangerous moments we receive a new revelation of His power.

And a great storm of wind arose, and the waves beat into the boat, so that the boat was already filling. But he was in the stern, asleep on the cushion; and they woke him and said to him, "Teacher, do you not care if we perish?" And he awoke and rebuked the wind, and said to the sea, "Peace! Be still!" And the wind ceased, and there was a great calm. He said to them, "Why are you afraid? Have you no faith?" (Mark 4:37-40).

Three conditions make any task pleasant. First, if we like the work; second, if we do it well; and third, if people approve and praise us for it. None of these conditions, nor all three together, will guarantee that the enterprise ought to be done. For instance, if we like to gamble, if we do it well, and if we win the reluctant praise of others for our performance—this does not justify our gambling.

God promises that if we undertake any worthwhile work, any noble cause, however difficult, he will fulfill these three conditions.

Initially we may not like the work. In fact, we may never quite enjoy it. But if it is a good work, God will give us satisfactions which draw us to the task in a strange kind of pleasure. He will work in and through our blundering efforts to provide a singular kind of skill. And, if we fail to gain the plaudits of men, we can be assured of the approval of God.

It is in the context of this help and approval of God that we can actually enjoy the hardships that the task may involve.

In Hebrews 12, the writer tells us to "run the race," undertake the hard tasks of the kingdom, "looking to Jesus . . . who for the joy that was set before him endured the cross." There is a sustaining, pervasive satisfaction in doing what we ought to do, even when every instinct of safety and self-interest cries out against even trying.

In this day of psychological testing it is quite common to arrive at a vocational choice by the two initial conditions. First, what are your aptitudes; is mathematics easy for you? Second, do you like mathematics? If you can say yes to these two criteria, perhaps you should be a banker or an engineer, both honorable occupations that likely will give you honor in society. But this may not be enough. Perhaps you should go into politics, unpleasant as this may be, and fight for laws that create justice in society. Perhaps you should be a preacher and enlist people for God.

It is easy to cop out. We can say, "I don't like it. I'm no good at it, my friends are against it." But if it's something we know God wants done, God himself can and will fill in the gaps. He will help us to will and to do that which pleases him, and he will give us strange pleasure in doing it.

For it is better to suffer for doing right, if that should be God's will, than for doing wrong (1 Peter 3:17).

All of us are given to moods. They come and go. If God is left out of our reckoning, all our moods will tend to demobilize us for any courage, even for any effort in the struggle.

I describe these various moods as pessimism, skepticism, indifference, optimism, and despair.

In my moments of pessimism, I tend to see only the dark side. I recognize that man may choose, but dominated by self-interest, his choices always tend away from the good. Or I may conclude that he is no more than "a helpless piece of the game," which blind fate keeps tossing about with no pattern or design. I see nothing but disaster for him in his future.

On a slightly brighter side, I may only be skeptical. I have grave doubts. I see man as capable of both good and evil, but I have my grave misgivings about the good ever holding the field. My doubts get in the way of any concerted effort for betterment. I simply cannot muster any gallantry, any boldness, any hope.

Indifference is a mood more common, and ultimately more damaging, than any other. This presupposes that nothing matters. The universe itself is indifferent. We are but accidents of biology that "strut and fret our hour upon the stage." Why bother with anything, except perhaps to avoid pain, and pillage a bit of pleasure these few swift years?

We applaud optimism as a good mood, but it has its dangers for the struggle. If our optimism is based on the belief that we are good, that our failures are only a bit of mischief, that everything will turn out well "in the wash," then this rosy-hued outlook may be as treacherous as pessimism. Why bother to fight if the battle is not a serious one, and if the future will largely take care of itself and rather automatically usher us into a better day? Optimism, as commonly understood, is not the same as Christian hope.

Cynicism is skepticism gone sour. Only a century ago the intelligentsia of our western civilization wrote extensively of a new day dawning in the world's history, because man is now governed by reason. That day is gone. We are now tempted to believe that reason is but a thin veneer that camouflages the irrational, passionate, and primitive drives of man, and that the future is plunging on to catastrophe.

In the face of these moods we are reminded that we are the children of God who has redeemed us and empowers us to care for the earth and for each other in the swift years given to us.

Thou hast given him dominion over the works of thy hands; thou hast put all things under his feet (Psalm 8:8).

When our son was killed enroute home from two years of study abroad, questions surfaced for me, questions that had been quite academic until then. Would he now continue to pray for us, as I was sure he had? Would I ask him to do so? Was he now so far separated from us that our welfare was of no concern to him? I had long believed that the saints below and the saints beyond, the church militant and the church triumphant, did have some mystical communion. So, would I, in my prayers, ask him to pray for me? I haven't. I give you the words of C. S. Lewis on the subject:

> There is clearly a theological defense for it; if you can ask for the prayers of the living, why should you not ask for the prayers of the dead? There is clearly also a great danger. In some popular practice we see it leading off into an infinitely silly picture of Heaven as an earthly court where applicants will be wise to pull the right wires, discover the best "channels," and attach themselves to the most influential pressure groups. But I have nothing to do with all this. I am not thinking of adopting the practice myself; and who am I to judge the practice of others? . . .
>
> The consoling thing is that while Christendom is divided about the rationality, and even the lawfulness, of praying to the saints, we are all agreed about praying *with* them. "With angels and archangels and all the company of heaven." . . . One always accepted this *with* theoretically. But it is quite different when one brings it into consciousness at an appropriate moment and wills the association of one's little twitter with the voices of the great saints and (we hope) of our own dear dead. They may drown some of its uglier qualities and set off any tiny value it has.

Even though I have not asked Paul to pray for me, I hope that all those dear ones who have gone on before me are still somehow supportive of my life on this side.

Therefore, since we are surrounded by so great a cloud of witnesses, let us also lay aside every weight, and sin which clings so closely, and let us run with perseverance the race that is set before us (Heb. 12:1).

We don't like to get letters that are unsigned. Usually they are bitter or complaining, and that's not pleasant. Even if they are letters of appreciation or praise, they fall a bit flat when the writer remains unknown.

God has not left himself without signature. Even the heavens declare the glory of God, says the psalmist. If we have the eyes of faith to look for the signature, every good and perfect gift comes from God. We know that it did not pop out from nowhere.

Our trouble lies in the fact that we overlook the signature. We accept the message. We eat our food, we see the color of the sunset, we feel the wind and the rain, we revel in our health. All these are gifts, or letters, from a great and good someone—God.

Life is immeasurably richer if we see God behind all these blessings —and thank him. To receive them day after day and year after year without bothering to think of who might have sent them robs us of a dimension of life which enriches and ennobles.

Who is it that inspires us to love and to hope? Who has given us the capacity for wisdom and knowledge? Who endows us with the capacity to exult in that which is beautiful? Who has put us together in such a way that we probe this vast universe for its treasures? To overlook these questions and to have no answer is to have an absentmindedness which cheats us of our essential humanity.

In some of these letters God's signature may be a bit blurred, and people may be excused for not seeing clearly. But in one letter, the most superb of all, the signature is bold and clear. He has not left us in doubt about the cross, and what he gives us there. All other gifts, the gift of life itself, pale before this one. Here he gives us himself. And with himself, he gives us the forgiveness of our sins, victory over the evil one, and the assurance of a life everlasting with him. Here he assures us that he loves us with a boundless love.

Seeing his signature there, we are ready to see it in a thousand different places and circumstances.

Where were you when I laid the foundation of the earth? Tell me, if you have understanding. Who determined its measurements—surely you know! . . . when the morning stars sang together, and all the sons of God shouted for joy (Job 38:4-5, 7).

THE THIRST FOR VIOLENCE November 7

A well-traveled friend of mine said, "You can walk the streets of Calcutta at night without fear, but not the streets of Detroit or New York or Chicago." It is a disturbing fact that the past quarter of a century has vastly increased the phenomenon of violence in our country.

And what is even more alarming is the observations of publishers that if a book of fiction is to sell well in America it must deal with thugs, abnormal sex, and murder. Not that thugs read books, but we who are not sex perverts want more exciting reading than Charles Dickens or Thornton Wilder.

Reasons given for the growth of violence are varied. World War II and Vietnam, for instance, taught millions the science of the ruthless. Television and the advertising industry create hunger for things, and people will steal and kill to get them. The threat of nuclear war hangs heavy, so that giving up any hope for an ordered future, people plunge into a frenzied chase after today's pleasures. There may be no tomorrow. A half a century ago, Pitirim Sorokin, the Russian-born Harvard sociologist, warned that our sensate society would catapult into a period of violence before the pendulum would swing back to the life of the spirit.

Pendulums have swung before. The Old Testament has episodes of sheer brutality; then there's the bloody entertainment of the Roman amphitheater, the age of the Vikings, the savagery of America's winning of the West. Nestled in our well-manicured suburban estates, we can hardly imagine that there once were people and epochs of this kind.

In every age of violence there have been followers of Christ who resisted the tide. Some of them were swept away, but others survived in the midst of chaos to keep alive and nourish the fruits of the Spirit—love, tenderness, kindness, hope, self-control. The wheels of God grind slowly, but throughout the centuries his mercy and courage has again and again eroded the power of hatred, greed, and lust. However feeble at the moment are the signs that recovery is under way, we must cling to hope, and in our own families, schools, and communities we must be vigilant to exalt the way of Christ as the only way that can bring joy and meaning into this harried world.

Blessed is the man who walks not in the counsel of the wicked. . . . He is like a tree planted by streams of water. . . . The wicked are not so, but are like the chaff which the wind drives away (Psalm 1:1, 3-4).

The church is a worshiping community. It approaches God in many forms, but always with adoration and praise, in thanksgiving and prayer. It comes to receive from God the gifts of love, forgiveness, wisdom, and hope. Most people find it more edifying to worship in forms familiar from childhood. Few people vote for novelty and change. On the other hand, people of the 20th century have needs different from people of the first or 16th centuries, and the church cannot but be sensitive to how God can best meet his people, and they meet him, in every age.

Michael Rogness, in *The Church Nobody Knows*, addresses this issue:

> The church stands in the middle of the clash between ancient liturgical traditions and new ideas. It must take the 20th century into its liturgical life, just as every age has left its imprint on the development of the liturgy. Consider how many songs Luther literally pulled in off the street to make hymns. Some of the liturgical footprints of our century will survive, and many more will expire with the passing of time. But the church can never ignore the present age in its worship.

> Yet on the other side, those ways of worship which have served for centuries can hardly be discarded lightly. There is a magnificent continuity in Christian worship, a richness in knowing that I am praying the very prayers uttered by Augustine, Francis of Assisi, Thomas Aquinas, Luther, and others. When we sing the threefold kyrie, or the sanctus of the Eucharist, our voices blend with the echoes of voices throughout the ages. The Lord's Prayer unites in spirit with the disciples on that day when our Lord taught it to them, and through Aaron's benediction ("The Lord bless you and keep you . . .") we stand with those receiving God's blessing in the wilderness after the Exodus. Treasures like these are ageless. Their language and musical forms might change, but they continue with the universal church.

It is good to give thanks to the Lord, to sing praises to thy name, O Most High; to declare thy steadfast love in the morning, and thy faithfulness by night, to the music of the lute and the harp, to the melody of the lyre (Psalm 92:1-3).

We Christians cannot escape; we must be evangelists. Whatever we do and whoever we are, we have no other option but to become ambassadors of the Good News. It was this Good News that changed our lives.

The Good News is not a complicated story, but it is a sweeping one. It begins with God creating the heavens and the earth and creating human beings to be his children. To these children he gave the radical gift of choice and commissioned them to care for the earth and for their brothers and sisters.

We are on earth for a brief assignment before we are ushered into the eternal kingdom to live with God and the hosts of heaven forever. But the assignment has its perils. The earth may trap us. In fact, we are born into the trap of sin and death. Instead of leaving us there, God sent his only Son, Jesus Christ, to free us. This is the heart of the Good News. If we want this freedom, God, the Holy Spirit, will release us into a full and abundant life, even here on earth.

The Good News has its own built-in power. We, the ambassadors or the witnesses, are to tell the story. We may do a blundering job of it. We may be afraid to try. But we are under orders; we have no choice. And, more than we know, we carry a portfolio of enormous authority. We represent the Lord of the universe. The world may renounce the story with disdain, even try to destroy it. But the world is no match for its owner. For 2000 years God has used this gospel to change civilizations and to free hundreds of millions of people.

Nor are we alone in the telling. The Holy Spirit is there at our side. It is as if we are the salesmen, charged with making as good a presentation as we can, but at the moment when the sale is to be finished off, the Spirit steps in to "sign him up." It is not by our skills or eloquence or cleverness that people are won for the Lord. It is the work of the Good News itself, empowered by the Spirit.

The evangelist has two tools: words and life. By what we say and by what we do we present the Lord to the world. It is when the word of the gospel is reinforced by a life of love that the world begins to understand.

Go into all the world and preach the gospel to the whole creation (Mark 16:15).

The earth is the Lord's, and we have no right to let anyone else have it. Its governments, its industries, its schools, its homes—everything should be held and managed for him who owns all.

Ownership belongs to God; management has been given to us. Neither animals nor angels are given stewardship of the planet. We, created in God's image, are assigned the awesome task of subduing and governing the earth.

But man has a bad record of embezzlement, fraud, and rebellion. With devices of deeds and titles he creates the illusion that everything belongs to him. He thinks the money in his bank account is his. He thinks that because stocks and bonds bear his name that they belong to him. He boasts skills and lands, as if he himself manufactured his brain and hands and formed the land. He struts his way in the eternal courts a most comic and tragic figure. For everything is God's!

Man is not only a comic figure, he is a destructive one. In his competition and rivalry for wealth and power, he unlooses centrifugal forces that put constant strain on the structures of life. It simply is not true, as some economists and political scientists have contended, that unchecked competition creates a balance of forces that give order and stability to the world. When people and nations turn in on themselves to guard their own interests alone, they become poor managers of God's earth. We are one human family on one shrunken planet with one Lord. The welfare of one must also be the welfare of all.

No one can be certified as a manager in good standing unless he first is a *servant* of all. This is the clear policy of the owner. And whenever that policy is followed, centripetal forces are released to counter the erosions of ruthless self-concern, and to give the world some hope, even hope for survival.

In our day it is quite common to believe that the destructive forces have taken over, and that there is no hope. But in every family, community, and nation there are people who have been captured by the Lord's policies of management and who have become a quiet, sometimes unnoticed, leaven for keeping life from falling apart.

The earth is the Lord's and the fulness thereof, the world and those who dwell therein; for he has founded it upon the seas, and established it upon the rivers (Psalm 24:1-2).

Jonah the prophet was sent by God to pronounce judgment on the wicked city of Nineveh. In his book, *The Message of Jonah,* Terence E. Fretheim suggests that Jonah initially refused to go because he feared that God might "go soft" and in mercy let Nineveh off. When he finally did go, and when God did show mercy to Nineveh, Jonah was bitter and crestfallen. Fretheim draws from the story this lesson:

> The conclusion seems inescapable. God is far too indulgent a father. When it comes to turning on the mercy, he doesn't seem to be able to help himself. . . .
>
> We never seem to learn. The kingdom of God cannot be compared with IBM and its labor relations board or to a democratic republic with its judicial system. In their own spheres such orders have their proper place. In letting the punishment fit the crime, the community and its judges are necessary guardians of moral responsibility. They witness to a moral order that must command deep respect. But, even if they carefully take into account the differences among persons in their application of justice, they only begin to approximate what is involved in the mercy of God.
>
> The good news of God's mercy goes beyond justice. Here careful calculations of the relationship between what has been done and what is deserved as a consequence are blatantly put aside. The rules associated with individual responsibility and one's proper dues are broken. God creatively and miraculously intervenes into the system of retributive justice and breaks it wide open. He is gracious toward those who deserve nothing but punishment. He bestows favors quite disproportionate to just deserts. He welcomes the prodigal home without exacting a penalty. He extends salvation on the wicked city (which repents!) in the same way as he has on Jonah, on those who have "borne the burden of the day and the scorching heat" (Matt. 20:12). God looks beyond the sinful actions to the persons, to the masses (4:11), those created in his image, and has mercy. Such love is costly, however, for God takes the burden of guilt on himself.

Seek the Lord while he may be found, call upon him while he is near (Isa. 55:6).

We have many needs. We need to eat, to be clothed and sheltered, to love and to be loved. But we have one towering need. We need God. If every other need should be met, but without God, we would remain deeply lonely, empty and forlorn.

Every gift which the church has to offer is but a means toward one great end: that we might have God again. We receive the forgiveness of sins in order that we might be eligible to live with God. We receive peace in order that we be fit to live with the Prince of Peace. Holiness is credited to us by faith in Christ in order that we might not be out of place as we walk with God.

Our minds play tricks on us, and we put the cart before the horse. We who are tormented by guilt are beguiled into thinking that we need Christ in order to be rid of our guilt. We who fret over our fears get the notion that we need Christ in order that we might gain peace of mind. Christ becomes a kind of medicine which we take to achieve health. And having achieved health, we need the medicine no longer. Having had our sins forgiven and being restored to peace, we then need Christ no longer. Like a rich uncle who comes to bail us out of our debts, he has done his work for us, and we're glad not to have him on our hands.

Let us suppose that a husband has been estranged from his wife. In the months apart from her he discovers how much he loves her and needs her. He returns with the simple plea, "I need you." Then let us suppose that she replies, "You think you need me, but all you really want is someone to make your meals, share your bed, give you children, and nurse you when you're sick." But he says, "It's you I need. I can get someone to do all these things for me if I want to. I don't need things. I need *you!*"

Quite apart from what may happen when we have God, or what we may get from him, or how we might change—it is God himself we need. We need him, whether we get dividends or not. He is all in all for us. If the world drops away and there is nothing left to us except the Lord, and him alone, we yet have all.

I stretch out my hands to thee; my soul thirsts for thee like a parched land (Psalm 143:6).

Whoever heard of the gospel called scandalous? Precisely this is what the New Testament calls it, the Greek *skandalon,* which means stumbling block or snare. Men were outraged in hearing it, and they put to death those who proclaimed it.

The gospel is the message that God loves men. Certainly there is nothing offensive about that, is there? A nice God who does nice things to nice people dressed in nice clothes sitting quietly in a nice church on a nice Sunday morning? What could be nicer?

Unfortunately, that is not the gospel. A gory death on a cross, a carpenter who told the nice people that thieves had a better chance at the Kingdom than they, a message that implies that everything, absolutely everything, we have is not ours, and that there is no chance except we repent our sinful ways. All this is the gospel.

To see the gospel in this light is deeply disturbing. This Jesus, who suffered rejection, endured universal scorn, and at last died his lonely death on a despised cross, is not our idea of a hero. None of us wants our children to follow him and lose everything but some sort of invisible Kingdom. Moreover, it angers us to think that it was necessary to pay such a price for the kind of sins we have—minor sins, like cursing a little, cheating a little, and fretting our lives away trying to look respectable and have a little money in the bank.

There is a more profound dimension to the scandal. It is that an innocent one should suffer for the guilty. This is neither decent nor fair. It violates every good rule of order. If our courts should administer justice in this shabby way we would end in chaos. Albert Camus said that the injustices we see rampant in the world are only compounded by having God himself suffer injustice. It could be that the deepest reason the world has rejected Christ is that he let the high court become a cross, and that he asks us to join him, not in judging the world but in carrying a cross.

We plot to take the scandal out of the cross. We play with it in the architecture of our churches, giving it sleek symmetry. We sentimentalize over some trivial loss and say, "we all have our little crosses." We polish our sacramental cups and make soothing music with our organs. And Jesus, writhing and twisting on the cross for our sins, cries, "Father, forgive them, for they know not what they do."

He who does not take his cross and follow me is not worthy of me. He who finds his life will lose it, and he who loses his life for my sake will find it (Matt. 10:38-39).

From his years as a British reporter in U.S.S.R. in the early 1930s, Malcolm Muggeridge speaks of two episodes which provide by contrast insights into the tragic life of the Revolution:

I tried to describe it all—the abandoned villages, the absence of livestock, neglected fields; everywhere famished, frightened people and intimations of coercion, soldiers about the place, and hard-faced men in long overcoats. One particularly remarkable scene I stumbled on by chance at a railway station in the gray early morning; peasants with their hands tied behind them being loaded into cattle trucks at gunpoint; . . . all so silent and mysterious and horrible in the half light, like some macabre ballet. . . .

In Kiev, where I found myself on a Sunday morning, on an impulse I turned into a church where a service was in progress. It was packed tight, but I managed to squeeze myself against a pillar whence I could survey the congregation and look up at the altar. Young and old, peasants and townsmen, parents and children, even a few in uniform—it was a variegated assembly. The bearded priests, swinging their incense, intoning their prayers, seemed very remote and far away. Never before or since have I participated in such a worship; the sense conveyed of turning to God in great affliction was overpowering. Though I could not, of course, follow the service, I knew from Klavdia Lvovna little bits of it; for instance, where the congregation says there is no help for them save from God. What intense feeling they put into these words! In their minds, I knew, as in mine, was a picture of those desolate abandoned villages, of the hunger and the hopelessness, of cattle trucks being loaded with humans in the dawn light. Where were they to turn to for help? Not to the Kremlin, and the Dictatorship of the Proletariat, certainly; nor to the forces of progress and democracy and enlightenment in the West. Honourable and Right Honourable Members had nothing to offer; *Gauche Radicale* unforthcoming, free press, Duranty's pulpit. Every possible human agency found wanting. So, only God remained, and to God they turned with a passion, a dedication, a humility, impossible to convey. They took me with them; I felt closer to God then than I ever had before, or am likely to again.

O Lord, thou God of vengeance, thou God of vengeance, shine forth! Rise up, O judge of the earth; render to the proud their deserts! O Lord, how long shall the wicked, how long shall the wicked exult? (Psalm 94:1-3).

All our sorrows flow, like a river, into the heart of God. This is the mystery of the cross. If there were no God and if there were no cross, where could our suffering go—your suffering and mine?

You are tormented by fears. You are overcome by suspicion. You are crippled by grief. Where can your fear, your suspicion and your grief go—if not to God? Is there any other to take them?

"He has borne our griefs and carried our sorrows. . . . He was wounded for our transgressions, he was bruised for our iniquities." This is how the Bible describes this God of the cross.

The Cross of Calvary is the great harbor of all man's sorrows. There the suffering Savior, at once God and man, died for us. Before he died, he had gathered into his bosom all the sorrows of the world. Our sin and shame and fear were all in him that day.

The human tragedy is that we try to find some other place to deposit his sorrow and pain. Grief overcomes us when a dear one has died, friends try to reach in to carry our grief for us, but they can only touch the surface. A marriage is in trouble, and there is pain; a well-meaning counselor tries to ally the pain, but without God there's really no place for the pain to go. A person has wronged a friend, and the friend forgives, but it's not enough. The hurt is deeper. With David who cried, "Against thee, thee only, have I sinned," we need to rest our hurt in the overarching forgiveness of God.

Then there are the continuing fears of the morrows. They hover over us like a cloud, blotting out the sun. Who can take these from us? Neither wealth nor power, nor parliaments nor kings, have the power to lift them. The unpredictable tomorrows are in God's hands. Until the fears are deposited there, they keep weighing us down.

God keeps his great heart open. Today, as on that Friday long ago, all our sorrows and pain and fear can flow to him. He makes your sin his sin, and he has it be crucified once and for all. Its guilt and power are destroyed. You are free.

All that is ignoble and unworthy, all regrets and terrors, are gathered in the cross. All the righteousness and mercy and power of God are also in that cross. Beneath that cross we find the glory that is his and that can be ours.

And the ransomed of the Lord shall return, and come to Zion with singing; everlasting joy shall be upon their heads; they shall obtain joy and gladness, and sorrow and sighing shall flee away (Isa. 51:11).

God holds us responsible. He gave us the gift of freedom, the right to choose, the faculty of independence. He charged us with the management of the planet for him. He commands us to care for one another.

He does not leave us unattended, on our own. He stays around.

He stays around to check on our performance. When we abdicate, he meddles with his judgment and punishment. He is on hand to give us help when we turn to him. He has gone to the lengths of a cross to assure us that he wants us in his kingdom, whatever our failures or betrayals.

But, in a profound sense, he puts us on our own. We cannot retreat from the responsibilities he has given us and turn it all over to him. We cannot rest passively, pray to him, and simply wait for him to perform some miracle. He expects us to take charge. He holds us responsible for the outcome of history.

It is as if he is the pilot of the airplane and we are the copilot. He turns the craft over to us. We have him at our side, to be sure, and this is the kind of assurance we need. But the controls are given to us. We have to make the decisions, make the moves, and manage the flight the best we can. And, taking the assignment seriously, we will do pretty well, knowing all the while that he is at our elbow to help whenever the course becomes turbulent. We are glad that he is there. It would be frightening to be completely on our own. We could very well freeze up in fear or panic.

We have great issues to face in the management of this earth. Even in our own private lives, the problems get out of hand at times. We need him. We have no right to expect that he will release us from doing the best we can. But he has given us the right to expect that when the tasks simply get to be too much for us, he steps in. In strange and unknown ways, he can make even our failures yield dividends for good.

Archibald MacLeish once said, "Now we are the gods," by which he meant that having given up belief in ghosts and spirits, and finally in God, we are left alone and unattended to manage life. And he added, "This is too much for us." We need God at our side, but he has entrusted us with the high honor of management.

The Lord takes pleasure in those who fear him, in those who hope in his steadfast love (Psalm 147:11).

Of all Jesus' parables of the Kingdom, the one about the wheat and the tares is the most puzzling. Weeds had been sown by an enemy at night. Servants asked if they should clear out the weeds; the owner said to wait until the harvest when the wheat would be gathered into barns and the weeds burned. What does the parable mean?

It has been suggested that it is a philosophy of history. Until the coming of the Lord in glory, good and evil will live side by side. Try as we will, we'll never create utopia—a Kingdom of God on earth where good emerges triumphant and evil is totally destroyed. Or, does it mean that there are good people and bad people, and that in a final judgment the good will be rewarded and the bad will be destroyed? Or, is there good and bad in each of us. Martin Bell in his charming book, *The Way of the Wolf,* comments:

> The kingdom of God, Lord, is like so many things. Yet like nothing at all that I have ever known. Perhaps my poor head will never even grasp a single strand from your complex multiplicity of images. But the story about the wheat and the tares will always be hardest of all for me to understand. Because, in the end, the man burns the tares. And if tares represent people, Lord, I'll never understand that. Never.
>
> Did you mean for the wheat to represent good people, Lord? And are the tares then desperate and evil men whose willful sins are so bound to them that there is no release—only the fire? . . . Is this what the story means, Lord? That God created good men? And that somehow a stranger brought into being a number of bad men? And that the good men and the bad men must continute to live together side by side until the day of judgment when they will be either rewarded or punished. God, I hope that's not what the story means. Partly because I am an evil and desperate man. . . . Dare I hope that the tares do not represent people, but rather alienation and despair, the universal condition of existing men? . . . I pray, Lord, that in the end it will be this alienation that is destroyed and the whole of mankind that is gathered into the Kingdom. If so, then there is no longer any mystery as to the identity of the stranger who sowed the seed. He is none other than myself. We have each of us sown tares, and we are all of us virtually strangled by them.

The kingdom of heaven may be compared to a man who sowed good seed in his field; but while men were sleeping, his enemy came and sowed weeds among the wheat, and went away (Matt. 13:24-25).

We would be less than honest if we were not to acknowledge that we are profoundly self-centered. We are given to self-concern, to self-indulgence, to self-defense, to self-pity. Our own aches and pains concern us more than those of our neighbors.

Jesus is practical. He wants us to be concerned about other people. This is the key to his kingdom. So, he starts with our self-concern. He does not tell us first to get rid of self. He says, "Do for others what you want them to do for you." You want security for yourself; see that your neighbor has security too. You want justice for yourself; there's nothing wrong with that, but make sure your neighbor gets justice too.

One might have thought Jesus would start with himself. He thought nothing of security for himself. He never defended himself against injustice, even in that flagrant miscarriage of justice before Pilate. Why didn't he say, "I never bothered to protect myself, why should you?"

He did, in fact. He said, "Love one another, as I have loved you," and in obeying that command, we would be shorn of our self-concerns altogether.

To do for others as we want them to do for us is a halfway point. It can be the beginning of the real thing. This is probably what Jesus intended his counsel to be. If he could get us turning toward the rights and needs of others, yet being concerned about our own, he would put us on the path that would usher us into his kingdom, where thoughts of self would eventually be swallowed up in the will of God and the needs of our neighbors. Certainly he never meant us to stop at some calculating point where we would serve others *if* they would serve us.

There's something absurd about the kingdom. Caution is thrown to the winds. If a person lose his life, Jesus said, only then will he find it. Within the center of the kingdom, thoughts of self-defense, self-pity, or self-protection are gone. A person's life is swallowed up in the purposes of God.

He who loves his life loses it, and he who hates his life in this world will keep it for eternal life (John 12:25).

Time is a stage. Across its span of minutes and millennia God and Satan, angels and demons, men and women enact the drama of existence. The stage does not determine the plot nor the passion of the actors. The stage is coldly indifferent. It lends itself to murder and to love with heedless impartiality.

It is sheer folly to say that time will heal. Within time wounds may heal or they may fester. Time may see things grow better or worse, and whichever direction they take, time itself cannot and will not do anything about it. Scientists have conjectured that life on earth has evolved from simple forms to complex, and we have naively concluded that man himself has been growing better and better through the centuries, and that the only medicine he needs is time.

On the stage of time great achievements have been made. We have cures for many of the old killers—pneumonia, smallpox, peritonitis, diphtheria. But time did not provide them. Nor will time cure cancer or old age. And it is sheer nonsense to think of time as the therapist who will rid us of hatred and greed and lust, the deep-rooted cause of most of our ills.

An unseen Physician does move across the stage. With him there is healing for most of the wounds of earth, a radical healing for our elemental illness, sin and guilt.

Already he has put to rout the ancient tormentor, Satan. This he did on a cross outside the city gates of Jerusalem. No longer do we need to be in the enemy's concentration camp, brainwashed to love darkness rather than light. We are free to seek the Physician and be healed.

But the Physician will not force his cure. He refuses to manipulate us into unsuspecting healing. Gently, through the prodding of his Word, he helps us realize the root of our misery. He leads us through the corridor of repentance into the place of healing, where grace with its forgiveness surges through us with newness of life.

This is the drama which God waits to enact on the stage of time. By all odds, it is the most decisive of the plots. The rise and fall of civilizations are trivial compared with this. Someone has said, "I invite you to a one-to-one revolution, the only kind of revolution that's coming." When God meets us, and turns us around, there is healing and hope and joy.

The Lord has done great things for us; we are glad (Psalm 121:3).

In his Lenten book, *Pathways of the Passion,* Per Lonning, a pastor and professor in Norway, once Bishop and member of Parliament, reviews the trial and sentencing of Jesus, and says:

The sentence is pronounced. The court decrees that he deserves to die because he has declared himself to be the Messiah, the Savior-King whom the Jewish people had awaited according to God's promise.

Why do his enemies react so violently to these words, shouting, "Blasphemy!" and tearing their garments? Is it not that a miserable, helpless person, one who has been utterly unsuccessful, a loser whose wretched game is up at last—that *he* claims to be God's Messiah?

Had he come to them as a victorious general, had he come to them in power and wealth at the head of his twelve legions of angels, the situation would have been different. Such an appearance would have been becoming to the Messiah. But to link the holy name to a defeated and lonely figure was to insult it. Honor and power are becoming to the Messiah. To attach his name to a wretched, suffering man is to divest this name of the honor which it deserves.

The hatred which sweeps in upon him like a flood, however, stems from a deeper source. When I am in the presence of an unusually intelligent, wealthy, and successful man, it is not difficult for me to bow to him. For I realize at once that this man, with his prestige and his dignity, may become a useful friend, yes, even a valuable aid, one who with his resources may be able to rescue me from failure and misfortune—a powerful political Messiah I can hail as Savior without its detracting in the least from my honorable position, yes, even if I were high priest in Zion. . . .

What advantage does he have over me? . . . What kind of salvation is it he insists that I need, which he—and he alone—can provide? . . . Perhaps the terrifying fact is beginning to dawn on me: This man is in dead earnest in his insistence that what I need is deliverance from myself, from the life I have wasted, and from the judgment of God which hovers over me. In *him* are truth and light and life; in me are only deceit and darkness and death. . . . Either I sentence him to death, or he sentences me—to life.

And the soldiers plaited a crown of thorns, and put it on his head, and arrayed him in a purple robe; they came up to him, saying, "Hail, King of the Jews!" (John 19:2).

His life had not been altogether untroubled. But he had overcome the obstacles. He finished the university with honors. He married a lovely girl. He gained the confidence of his company and went from one promotion to another. Life was full. At 52 he was "on top of the world." Then his doctor told him he had but six months to live.

He had been given many hard assignments in his work. Now he faced the most difficult assignment. How would he meet illness, pain, and death? Would life remain full to the end?

He could collapse into self-pity. He could seethe in anger. He could let pain make him irritable and bitter. He could make life miserable for his family, his friends, and for the people who were assigned to care for him. Or, given inner resources, he could make the last months more full and memorable than any other.

E. Stanley Jones, the eminent missionary to India, describes an eagle caught in a sudden mountain storm. The fury of the winds threatens to dash the bird against the crags. The bird wheels into the storm, tilts its wings at a given angle, and seems to be poised, unmoving in the winds. Gradually the gale lifts it up and up until at last it rises above the storm and the crags. The power that might have destroyed it brings it to calm.

This kind of "fulness" is available because God is at hand. He does not promise to eliminate pain or fear. In the midst of anxiety and distress, he releases a power which enriches the spirit of man with patience and love and hope. He points man beyond the hours of pain, beyond the moment of death, to an everlasting life of peace and glory. In faith, a person takes hold of this coming splendor, and it casts its radiance back into the hours of loneliness and pain and death.

Even so, there are no heroes in hospital beds. Pain and death levels us all. If you have strength for that stretch of the road, it will be a given strength. God turns you around from bitterness to gratitude. If you are able to exercise patience, love, cheerfulness, a sense of humor, and hope in such an hour, you may be giving your family and friends the most treasured memories they'll ever have of you.

For you shall go out in joy, and be led forth in peace; the mountains and the hills before you shall break forth into singing, and all the trees of the field shall clap their hands. Instead of the thorn shall come up the cypress; instead of the brier shall come up the myrtle; and it shall be to the Lord for a memorial, for an everlasting sign which shall not be cut off (Isa. 55:12-13).

In the year A.D. 410, Alaric the Goth thundered down from the North to conquer Rome. For almost 1000 years Rome had withstood every attack. For centuries it had stood as a symbol of that which did not change, until it had become known as "the eternal city." Sixteen years after its fall, Augustine of Alexandria published his book entitled, *The City of God.* This work was a great scholar's attempt to face a world which now had nothing firm or fixed anymore, and to rediscover for it something which still "towered o'er the wrecks of time."

We, in the middle 20th century, have had the comfortable props of recent centuries knocked out from under us. The cultural values which we had assumed were rather firm and fixed after centuries of painful struggle—values such as life, liberty, and the pursuit of happiness—have now disappeared at an alarming rate in our Western world. Our highly touted scientific age threatens to betray us to chaos and destruction.

The sober diagnosticians are not hopeful. Even before 1939 titles such as Spengler's *Decline of the West,* Berdyaev's *The End of Our Time,* and Albert Schweitzer's *The Decay and Restoration of Civilization* told the story of our plight. Schweitzer said in 1923, "It is clear now to everyone that the suicide of civilization is in progress. What yet remains of it is no longer safe. It is still standing, indeed, because it was not exposed to the destructive pressures which overwhelmed the rest, but, like the rest, it is built upon rubble, and the next landslide will very likely carry it away!"

Long years ago Isaiah stood watching the last landslide sweep into bondage and oblivion the remnants of the once proud nation of Israel. It was indeed a dark hour, for Israel was more than a nation; it was the cradle of a magnificent religious culture. But God had plans for Israel. The mighty conquerors of Israel—Babylon, Assyria, Persia—are now quite swallowed up in their moldering dust, but Israel, with its one God of law and mercy, has pervaded almost every phase of this civilized world. Flowering into the Christian church, it has overturned empires and survived every crumbling age, to reappear in new triumphs in the next.

There may never be another England; France, the flower of Western culture, may be in its last hour; the doctrine of "white supremacy" may become a fable. But somewhere, on the changed landscape of time, the gospel of Christ will push up its new shoots and make another garden.

The tempest shall scatter them. And you shall rejoice in the Lord (Isa. 41:16).

WHEN I AM STRONG

Life is more than a race you run in competition with other people. There are other competitors—cancer, war, swift death. How do you outdistance them and win against them?

People become rivals of one another in winning more customers, more clients, more patients, more promotions, more this and that. But people are pitted also against fear, anxiety, depression, loneliness. I may be strong enough to outrun my brother, but be roundly beaten by these "unseen" rivals.

For the whole of life's race, I need God. Only as I rest back in him do I win. He takes over. He carries me. To swim across the Atlantic—to attempt it—might be a sign of courage and heroism, but it would in fact be sheer lunacy and foolhardiness. It could end only in disaster. To surrender—and take passage on an ocean liner—would, on the other hand, be both necessary and wise.

The Christian life is not only to "do justice, and to love kindness, and to walk humbly with your God," as Micah counsels. It is that, but first it is to rest back in God. We start by doing nothing. We let ourselves be overwhelmed by what God has done and is doing for us. It is folly to start running the race until we have been entered. It is futile to start fighting until we've been enlisted in the army. We "surrender" to God before we win. Nor is this a weary collapse. It is rather to be caught up in a will and a strength not our own. Do you remember the lines of George Matheson's hymn?

Make me a captive, Lord, And then I shall be free;
Force me to render up my sword, And I shall conqueror be.
I sink in life's alarm When by myself I stand;
Imprison me within thine arms, And strong shall be my hand.

To rest ourselves in God is not as uneventful as it first may seem, however. The fact is that if we are captive to him we go where he goes. And God plunges full into the hurts and travail of all men. He pits himself against all injustice, and so do we. He enters into the sorrows of all, and so do we. He is about the business of reconciling people to him and to one another, and so are we. He heads into the storms of life, and so do we. We are not immobile cargo which he carries around. When we rest back into him, he empowers us to become his partners in all his enterprises on earth. It is terrifying business. But it is the only way for glory and for ultimate victory for us all.

I will all the more gladly boast of my weaknesses, that the power of Christ may rest upon me. For the sake of Christ, then, I am content with weakness, insults, hardships, persecutions, and calamities; for when I am weak, then I am strong (2 Cor. 12:9-10).

God did not count on either beauty or power to move us. Jesus displayed neither. His entrance in a Bethlehem stable was not of beauty, nor his writhing to his death on a cross. Neither a stable nor a cross is likely to send us into ecstasy.

Let us start with the cross and stay there. With whatever imagination faith will give you, declare to yourself that he who died there was God. Then the cross cannot possibly be an accident, a simple incident of miscarried justice. The cross must then be a part of a plan and pattern willed by God himself. Go on from there, if you will, to the belief held by the writers of the Scriptures. They believed that God willed the cross and Christ's death as an atonement, a payment, for the sins of the world. Christ was doing more than demonstrating loyalty to truth and steadfastness of purpose by dying. Thousands had done that before, and thousands have done that since. There was no need for God to come to earth merely for such a display. The early Christians would never have become a new and unique fellowship of faith if that were all. They believe, as has the church ever since, that Christ's death on the cross was an event that shook heaven and earth and changed the relationship of God to men. Through it the sacrifice for sin was once and for all time made, Satan was conquered and his power eclipsed, and God and man were reconciled to each other. Actually, what has been claimed for the cross is greater far than what has been achieved by all the power and rank and beauty the earth has ever known.

Before you leave the cross, let the full impact of human sinfulness reach you. What demonic quality was there in those people of Jerusalem that they allowed the Holy One to be crucified? But you won't feel too indignant, because, with a little more imagination, you find yourself there. Indifference, selfishness, fear, disregard for another's pain—these qualities, yours and mine—were there to plan and to allow the tragic crime.

While the cross forces us to a sense of utter unworthiness, it has the strange power to lift us to a station of unparalleled worth. If God had willed the cross so that we might be forgiven and restored to fellowship with him, then we cannot escape the conclusion that we must be of infinite worth. Our shame is so great because our worth is so great.

For he grew up before him like a young plant, and like a root out of dry ground; he had no form or comeliness that we should look at him, and no beauty that we should desire him (Isa. 53:2).

In the book, *His Only Son Our Lord,* Kent S. Knutson speaks of the mystery of time:

> Imagine that you are on a New York subway. For some of you (who do it every day) that may not be an altogether pleasant idea, but come along, it is useful for our illustrative purposes.
>
> If you stand at the back of the train while it is hurtling through the dark tunnel, you will see only the shadows swallowing up the track you have just passed. In the front of the train you may see a green or red light glowing in the distance, but again everything else is hid from you. You move constantly—the past recedes into oblivion and the future has not yet arrived. In a certain sense, it is only the present which is real. It is only the lighted subway car in which you are that is your existence. Augustine, in one of his more psychological moments, said that the past was really only memory and the future only hope. . . . You cannot reach out and touch the past—it is always retreating. You must wait for the future to arrive. Only an occasional warning or bit of hope lights it up for you. . . .
>
> Suddenly you come to a station. The train stops for a moment. The station is all lighted up. It extends for some distance forward and some distance behind—if you are in the center car. It is as though the whole world, and it *is* the world of the subway car, were suddenly expanded. The future and the past become more real. . . . This is somewhat the meaning of time which the New Testament calls *kairos.* There is a kind of time which assumes special significance and has content and meaning which is not encompassed in the simple passing from the past into the future. This is a "full" or "ripe" time.
>
> When Jesus came to Galilee, preaching and opening his public ministry, he said, "The time is fulfilled, and the kingdom of God is at hand" (Mark 1:15). . . . The time of Jesus was so significant that it engulfs all of history. . . . He is the beginning and the end, the terminus, the goal of all times.

And he said to me, "It is done! I am the Alpha and the Omega, the beginning and the end" (Rev. 21:6).

A few years ago even *Time* magazine carried a story on the "God is Dead" philosophy. It was probably ludicrous for a major publication to bother with such a story at all. After all, there was nothing newsworthy about it. Long years ago, Friedrich Nietzsche had announced to the world that he had a new gospel: God is dead. He cynically declared that even Christians lived as if he were dead, and that moreover if there were no God mankind would be rid of its most crippling fear, the fear of God.

If God were dead, or if there were no God at all, what difference would it make? To most of us it would make a vast difference.

If God were dead, would the universe itself have any meaning? Self-contained, as a huge machine, whirling inexorably, could it have any purpose, other than having it finally run down and stop, or explode, or erode into nothing? And we with it!

If God were dead, would there be any basis for law—a moral law or a universal law of equity and justice? And if no basis, why should nations enact constitutions? Why should mothers and fathers talk about fairness, about right and wrong? What nonsense to be concerned about mercy and compassion.

Most important of all, if God were dead, where would we deposit our sins and guilts, our fears and anxieties?

The incomparable message of the Bible is that God is very much alive, not only to manage this vast universe which he has created, but far more important, alive in the lives of the people whom he created to be his sons and daughters. The supreme guarantee of his life among us is Jesus Christ, God the Son come to earth to become one of us and to save us by his death and resurrection. He is the revelation of God, God as an almighty and loving Father.

There will be other pundits who will seek to startle us with the death of God. They may have a short day, but the great human family will brush them aside and go on to believe that behind it all, above it all, and even within it all, there is Someone who is in charge. And the Christian family will know him as both judge and Savior, as creator and sustainer—as the great and good friend who companions us all the way, through the portals of death into an everlasting life with him.

The fool says in his heart, "There is no God." They are corrupt, they do abominable deeds, there is none that does good (Psalm 14:1).

If Jesus were to give us a test, he might ask three questions:

1. Do you *believe,* or confess, the right things about God?
2. Do you *feel* joy and hope and love in your heart?
3. Do you *do* the will of my Father?

To believe the right things about God is important. The church has always been vigilant about doctrines. That Jesus Christ is the only Savior from sin and guilt—this is a doctrine so important that the apostle Paul declared that if anyone, even an angel, should preach any other doctrine, he should be condemned. As a man believes in his heart, said the Lord, so is he. What a person believes finally determines what he does; beliefs sprout wings and carry us off.

What we feel, too, is important. Feelings are quite often the fuel that give us noble purposes and speed us on to generous deeds. Someone has said that no great cause has gone forward except on the wings of song. The surge of emotion is an elemental need for the human being.

The success of the test will probably rest with question number 3: Do you *do* the will of my Father? Even correct doctrine, knowing and believing the right things about God, comes from *doing.* Jesus said, "If any man's will is to do his will, he shall know whether the teaching is from God or whether I am speaking on my own authority" (John 7:17). All the speculative theology of the world will veer off into some dead-end street, unless the theologian is a follower of his Lord. And think of how many of us have learned the reality of loving someone by first going to help him, even when we didn't initially like him at all? We have learned to feel love, by first doing love.

It isn't as if God, seated high on his throne of judgment, will face us with an audit of what we have done or not done. We know better than that. We know that we are accepted by him through relying on his mercy in Christ Jesus. We are received by grace through faith. But the rich gifts of joy and hope, the strange knowledge of truth about God, that which we believe and confess about him, all this comes with our experimenting with doing his good and gracious will.

Not every one who says to me, "Lord, Lord," shall enter the kingdom of heaven, but he who does the will of my Father who is in heaven (Matt. 7:21).

Faith is never the result of proofs. It does not rest on proofs, nor does it grow strong because of proofs, whatever the nature of the proofs. To say that you believe in God because the universe must have a creator (as a watch must have a watchmaker), or because God answers your prayers, or because belief in God creates a feeling of calm or a flow of courage, or because most everybody believes in some sort of God—these "supports" for faith are ultimately false. Faith is trust—trust in God—in a Being you've never seen or touched or heard. As a Christian your faith is even more astonishing—you entrust yourself to a Jewish carpenter who was crucified at 33 and believe that in his life, death and resurrection he forgives your sins and flings wide the door of the Father's house for you. Of faith Luther says, "I believe that I cannot by my own reason or strength believe in Jesus Christ my Lord, or come to him; but the Holy Ghost has called me by the gospel."

Søren Kierkegaard has a beautiful picture of the believer as a swimmer:

> If one were to say that to swim is to lie upon dry land and squirm, every one would regard him as mad. But to believe is exactly like swimming, and instead of helping a man to get his feet on land, the preacher should help him to get out into the deep. So if one were to say that to believe is to lie upon dry land and go through the motions, all the time sure of the result, he is really saying the same thing as the above, only people perhaps do not notice it. . . . For a finite being—and surely that is what man is so long as he lives in the temporal sphere—the negative infinity is the highest attainable, and the positive is very questionable reassurance. Spiritual existence, and the religious existence in particular, is by no means easy; the believer lies constantly out upon the deep, with 70,000 fathoms of water under him. Long as he may lie there, he gets no comfort from the expectation that little by little (because of accumulated proofs) he will find himself on land, stretched out at his ease. He may, indeed, become calmer, more accustomed, find a sense of security which enables him to take pleasure in fun and light-hearted merriment—but until the last instant he lies above a depth of 70,000 fathoms.

By faith Abraham obeyed when he was called to go out to a place which he was to receive as an inheritance, and he went out, not knowing where he was to go (Heb. 11:8).

If it had been up to you, would you have chosen to be born at all? There may have been moments in your life, like that of the preacher in Ecclesiastes, when you wish you had never been: "I have seen everything that is done under the sun; and behold, all is vanity and a striving after wind."

Would you have chosen your parents, your country, your century? These are meaningless questions, of course, because you had no choice.

Most of us may wish we were more gifted, richer, more handsome—but it is not likely that we would be willing to lose everything we have and are in order to be someone else in some other part of the world or time.

It is for us to believe that God put us together as we are, placed us in this family, in this country, and in this moment of history—and that he had a reason for doing so. You may seem to be a biological accident, but remember that there is no other person quite like you in all the world—there never has been, and there never will be. This sobering thought ought to open your mind to the possibility, and probability, that God does have a unique spot for you in all existence.

It is a staggering thought. In a family of 12 children, for instance, some may resemble others, but they are all different. In the billions of people in God's family, you included, there are no two people alike. And if a father and mother can love each of their 12 children, different as they are, our heavenly Father, with infinite powers and love, can love each of us.

Let us not feel trapped. We didn't choose to be born, nor did we elect this family and this country. But God did, for us. Had it been up to us, would we have done as well? Must we not believe that in his infinite plan, accidents of birth as we seem to be, he has a specific purpose in having us be alive? To believe other than that is to give up on ourselves and ultimately on God.

We do have a choice. We can believe that we are caught in a web of birth and death that has no meaning, or we can believe that we are children of our heavenly Father, with a destiny on earth of great meaning, and a destiny that defies death and puts us in his hands forever.

See what love the Father has given us that we should be called children of God (1 John 3:1).

No one, even in his most discouraging moments, would like to think that there's nothing more to come. You might fear what is to come, but you would not like to turn the switch and say, "That's the end." Or, maybe you would.

In Shakespeare's play, Hamlet is overwhelmed with tragedy and contemplates suicide. "To be, or not to be: that is the question: . . . To die, to sleep: No more; and by a sleep to say we end the heartache and the thousand natural shocks that flesh is heir to, 'tis a consummation devoutly to be wish'd. . . . But that the dread of something after death, the undiscovered country from whose bourn no traveller returns, puzzles the will and makes us rather bear those ills we have than fly to others that we know not of."

For many people the future looms before them with faint hope and much fear. Our Christian faith is a corrective for both. It inspires hope, it diminishes fear.

No matter how many adversities come, and there may be many, we believe that our days are in God's hands. He will not allow more hardships than he provides strength to bear them. We may face tomorrow with the hope that tomorrow will be better. If not better, tomorrow will bring new strength from the Lord to endure. When we say, "There's yet more to come," we think not only of the ills of life, but of its blessings.

When death is at the door, we do not look through the veil into emptiness. There is a glorious fulfillment beyond the door, a city not made with hands, a new Jerusalem, where tears are no more, nor pain, and where all the yearnings and longings of the heart are stilled, and where the rhapsody of song bursts forth.

That grim Friday the followers of Jesus saw their dreams ended. Their hopes with Christ and for him were over. Yet, there was more! There was a resurrection, and with his resurrection something utterly new broke into the world. Not even death would now be the end. There would always be yet more.

It was this discovery that sped his followers into the world with the glorious good news that ever since has captured hundreds of millions. It has captured you and me.

Therefore do not be anxious about tomorrow, for tomorrow will be anxious for itself. Let the day's own trouble be sufficient for the day (Matt. 6:34).

STILL A MYSTERY December 1

In his *Letters to Malcolm* C. S. Lewis speaks of the mystery of Holy Communion:

Some people seem to discuss different theories of this act as if they understood them all and needed only evidence as to which was best. This light has been withheld from me. I do not know and can't imagine what the disciples understood Our Lord to mean when, His body still unbroken and His blood unshed, He handed them the bread and wine, saying *they* were His body and blood. I can find within the forms of my human understanding no connection between eating a man—and it is as Man that the Lord has flesh —and entering into any spiritual oneness or community or *koinonia* with Him. And I find "substance" (in Aristotle's sense), when stripped of its own accidents and endowed with the accidents of some other substance, an object I cannot think. My effort to do so produces mere nursery-thinking—a picture of something like rarified plasticine. On the other hand, I get on no better with those who tell me that the elements are mere bread and mere wine, used symbolically to remind me of the death of Christ. They are, on the natural level, such a very odd symbol of that. But it would be profane to suppose that they are as arbitrary as they seem to me. I well believe there is in reality an appropriateness, even a necessity, in their selection. But it remains for me, hidden. Again if they are, if the whole act is simply memorial, it would seem to follow that its value must be purely psychological, and dependent on the recipient's sensibility at the moment of reception. And I cannot see why *this* particular reminder—a hundred other things may, psychologically, remind me of Christ's death, equally, or perhaps more—should be so uniquely important as all Christendom (and my own heart) unhesitatingly declare. . . .

I am not saying to anyone in the world, "Your explanation is wrong." I am saying, "Your explanation leaves the mystery for me still a mystery. Yet I find no difficulty in believing that the veil between the worlds, nowhere else (for me) so opaque to the intellect, is nowhere else so thin and permeable to divine operation. Here a hand from the hidden country touches not only my soul but my body. Here the prig, the don, the modern in me have no privilege over the savage or the child. Here is big medicine and strong magic.

The cup of blessing which we bless, is it not a participation in the blood of Christ? The bread which we break, is it not a participation in the body of Christ? (1 Cor. 10:16).

We belong first to the "animal" family. We have much in common with rats and monkeys. In laboratories scientists experiment on these "lower cousins" of ours to discover many valuable, even lifesaving truths about us.

Then we belong to the human family, that special group of mammals known as men and women. There are perhaps around four billion of us on this spaceship called earth.

We who have been captured by faith in Jesus Christ belong to a third family, the holy Christian church. We have no choice but to belong to the first two. We may, if we choose, reject the third.

Be grateful that we belong with the rats. Countless of these relatives have died as martyrs for us in medical research. There are cynics who conclude that we are no more than "high grade" animals who write symphonies and invent computers, but animals still, with no more freedom and self-determination than the rest of the family. They believe that we can't help doing what we do any more than the rat can decide for himself what to do. If that be true, then we are no more than one vast veterinary society.

There's more to being human. We dream, we reason, we remember, we choose, we regret, we hope—in ways that are alien to our cousins in the animal kingdom. We have more in common than to eat and find shelter. Our tears and our joys have the same roots. Neither creeds nor color nor culture can erase the fact that we are one human family. We may rear barriers to separate ourselves from our brothers and sisters, but we are one. Living as we do now on this shrunken planet, it is of utmost importance that we understand our one family tree.

It is the Lord's hope that all may be gathered around him into one eternal family. This is the calling of his church. The whole human race has been redeemed by his death and resurrection. He claims them all.

For you did not receive the spirit of slavery to fall back into fear, but you have received the spirit of sonship. When we cry, "Abba, Father!" it is the Spirit himself bearing witness with our spirit that we are children of God, and if children, then heirs, heirs of God and fellow heirs with Christ, provided we suffer with him in order that we may also be glorified with him (Rom. 8:15-17).

If we wait until we have our own tangled up lives unraveled and healed before we turn to help others, we'll never start. It may very well be that our own fears and lusts may retreat the moment we begin to be concerned about other people. In any event, Jesus made it quite clear that if we are to be the people he wants us to be, the direction of our lives will be outward, toward others. To turn in on ourselves is to be mired in an endless morass.

Before we can generate any zest for serving others, we must have a rendezvous with God himself. We journey upward to him before we journey outward to our neighbor. Our interest in our neighbor is a consequence of our interest in God. We face God and discover that he accepts us, loves us, and even enjoys us just as we are. He lets us come to him, tangled up as we are. This he does because Christ intercedes for us. He died on a cross to give us the right to come to God—as we are! We need not wait to be healed before we come. We come, and then he begins the healing.

Of course, it's not always that step two follows step one. They may be going on simultaneously. For, in helping others, we draw into God's very presence. That's his business too—helping others. God lurks wherever there's a helping hand.

When in that great judgment scene in Matthew 25 the Lord says, "I was hungry, and you gave me food," the people respond in surprise, "When did we see thee hungry and feed thee?" And Jesus tells them that when they fed the hungry it was as if they were feeling him. He was there.

It is well to remember, too, that the Lord was not on some high throne of power when he was here helping people. He had taken our weaknesses upon him. He was one of us.

Nor need we be strong, healthy, emotionally well-balanced, all our problems well under control. Sometimes we minister best out of our weaknesses instead of our strengths. Two mothers, each having lost sons, may be of greater comfort and healing for one another than if one had no grief to share. Each, entering into the grief of the other, may have her grief lifted.

If you pour yourself out for the hungry and satisfy the desire of the afflicted, then shall your light rise in the darkness and your gloom be as the noonday (Isa. 58:10).

WHEN GRACE GOES SOUR

In one of his parables Jesus tells of two men who come to the temple for prayer. Both thank God; the Pharisee explicitly, the Publican implicitly. Both count on God's grace; the Pharisee for grace already given to improve his life, the Publican for grace he expects. Unfortunately, the Pharisee's recital of what God has done for him turns out to be a parading of his virtues. This, says Helmut Thielicke in *The Waiting Father*, is grace gone sour.

I cannot help thinking of many of the stories of conversions which pious people and also many moral movements love to tell in these days. First they paint a picture of what they were before in the blackest possible colors. They work themselves up to an almost masochistic pitch of self-accusation. Then they tell how they came into contact with the Spirit of God when they met up with a particular group or sect, and now their eyes are enlightened, now they can rejoice all the day, they are liberated children of God.

The fact is that this does not actually happen; one *can* have this experience with God. And anybody who has had it will always be grateful to God for it. But the more one talks about it, the more one trumpets abroad these stories of one's experience with God, the more one's attention becomes focused upon oneself, and suddenly the devil has turned the whole thing into a pious and vain autobiography. After all, I must have been pretty good raw material for him to have picked me out the way he did. God must have found something rather special in me; otherwise he wouldn't have entered into my life and given me this privilege above so many others. . . . The grace of God actually can be corrupted by spiritual vanity. And the so-called non-Christian is quick to note this and is repelled by it. . . .

In the figure of the Pharisee we are confronted with a shocking exposure of the sin of Christianity, your sin and mine, the sin of us who have subtly made of our Christianity a sign of virtue and given it the unpleasant smack of privilege. Pharisaic pride is one of the most dreadful and also one of the most infectious diseases of Christianity.

The Pharisee stood and prayed thus with himself, "God I thank thee that I am not like other men, extortioners, unjust, adulterers, or even like this tax collector. I fast twice a week, I give tithes of all that I get" (Luke 18:11-12).

In the language of our creeds, Jesus is Son of God and Son of Man, the second person of the Holy Trinity, God of God, Light of Light.

He is *Savior*. By his life, death, and resurrection, he became the atonement for our sins and for the sins of the whole world. John the Baptist, pointing people toward him, said, "Behold, the Lamb of God, who takes away the sin of the world!"

He is *Lord*. All power in heaven and on earth is his. His kingdom is eternal. It is here in our midst, and he presides over it. We hail him as Lord of lords, King of kings.

He is *Friend*. We sing, "What a friend we have in Jesus." He said, "Greater love has no man than this, that a man lay down his life for his friends. You are my friends."

He is *Teacher*. Through sublime parables and exalted ethical insights, he teaches us the meaning of life. He teaches with an authority unlike all others.

He is *Shepherd*. He guides, he comforts, he protects, he gathers us into a flock, his church.

He is *Example*. In him we see what it means to be human. Compassion for the poor and suffering, indignation against evil and oppression, mercy for the erring, patience under trial—these are the qualities that give nobility to humanity.

No person in all history has tantalized, comforted, disturbed, and enthralled the world as this carpenter from Nazareth. He stands quite alone, like a mountain peak rising abruptly from the plains.

Before a Nero or a Hitler, we would stand in fear; before a Beethoven or a Shakespeare, in admiration; before an Einstein, in awe; before a Lincoln, in respect. If Jesus were to walk into the room, we would fall on our knees.

Most of the world's great are tucked away in encyclopedias, or in mouldering volumes of *Who's Who*. Jesus walks the paths of the world still, no longer among the hills of Judea alone, but on the highways and byways of every continent, and into the hearts of people of all races and nationalities. He is Savior and Lord!

Grace be with all who love our Lord Jesus Christ with love undying (Eph. 6:24).

THE WONDER AND THE TREACHERY OF FEELINGS
December 6

Thank God that he has given us the capacity to feel deeply. But don't trust your feelings. If we feel that our sins are forgiven, that's fine. If we don't, we turn to the promises of God. He tells us that if we confess that we are sinful and trust his forgiveness no matter how we feel, we are forgiven. We have his Word for that. What more do we want?

If we feel like forgiving someone who has wronged us, that's excellent. If we don't, we have the Lord's command to keep on forgiving anyway, seventy times seven. If we are inspired by a church service and leave deeply moved, thank God. If we don't, remember that we came to church not primarily to get something, like excitement and rhapsody. We came to thank God for his great goodness, no matter how we feel either before or after.

If you have had some high moments of ecstasy, as in a conversion or hour of assurance, be grateful. Tuck these moments into your memory. Don't demand that God give you encores. What right do we have to dictate to God what kind of feelings he should give? He has given us his Word, and through the Word a faith—a faith that may or may not be buttressed by high feeling.

Some people are caught up in a tragic chase after one inspiration or another. If they don't find it in their own church, they tramp around to others. They have made an idolatry of feelings, and God himself becomes less important than their feelings of God.

One of the disturbing and sad phenomena of our day, it seems to me, is the multiplying of cults, most of them promising spiritual food for the impoverished and bewildered people of our time. Some groups are "foster children" of our established churches, some are under earnest if misguided leadership, but many are fraudulent exploiters of human emotion. The bizarre character of many frightens us. Feelings that should be inspired by truth, should lead to lives of love and service, and should inspire hope and patience, become fuel for suicidal violence.

Even in traditional churches, some leaders have deflected their people from the glorious message of grace in Christ, away from the sober tasks of caring for the planet and meeting the needs of people to an introspective search for feelings.

God gives us deep feelings, but they steal upon us as we walk the path of love and gratitude in obedience to his command to follow him.

If any one serves me, he must follow me; and where I am, there shall my servant be also; if any one serves me, the Father will honor him (John 12:26).

Simone Weil was a special kind of "saint," called forth from today's maelstrom of industrialism, revolution, and war. She died in 1943 at the age of 34. Born in Paris of Jewish parents, precocious and with no contact with a worshiping community, Christian or Jewish, until a few years before her death when she became a friend of a Dominican priest, she had abandoned the academic world to become one with workers and revolutionaries. It was when praying the Lord's Prayer that, in her words, Christ himself "descended and took her." She steadfastly refused formal Baptism, feeling that this would separate her from the other children whom God loves. Here are some of her thoughts:

Since the commandment "Thou shalt love the Lord thy God" is laid upon us so imperatively, it is to be inferred that the love in question is not only the love a soul can give or refuse when God comes in person to take the hand of his future bride but also a love preceding this visit, for a permanent obligation is implied.

This previous love cannot have God for its object, since God is not present to the soul and has never yet been so. It must then have another object. Yet it is destined to become the love of God. We can call it the indirect or implicit love of God. . . .

The implicit love of God can have only three immediate objects, the only three things here below in which God is really though secretly present. These are religious ceremonies, the beauty of the world, and our neighbor. Accordingly there are three loves.

The combination of these loves constitutes the love of God in the form best suited to the preparatory period, that is to say a veiled form. They do not disappear when the love of God in the full sense of the word wells up in the soul; they become infinitely stronger and all loves taken together make only a single love.

The veiled form of love necessarily comes first however and often reigns alone in the soul for a very long time. Perhaps, with a great many people, it may continue to do so till death. Veiled love can reach a very high degree of purity and power. At the moment when it touches the soul, each of the forms that such love may take has the virtue of a sacrament.

As a hart longs for flowing streams, so longs my soul for thee, O God. My soul thirsts for God, for the living God. When shall I come and behold the face of God? (Psalm 43:1-2).

We speak of a series of great events in the past as God's guarantee of his love for us. He delivered his people from Egyptian bondage, he brought back a remnant to Jerusalem from one exile after another. He kept his promises. Then came Bethlehem, Calvary, and the empty tomb. The logic is clear: if God had such steadfast love, and if he finally sent his only Son to die for us, can there be any question of his presence among us right now, to bless us in countless, unknown ways? These are his pledges from the past.

He holds before us a glorious future as another guarantee. He will come in glory to end this sorry state where tragedy and sin and pain and death can destroy our fondest hopes. If things go wrong for us and for the world now, are we not sustained by what has been and what yet shall be?

Of course, this is a matter of faith. Without faith, we would look upon Jesus as a misguided peasant who in his idealism failed to consider the harsh facts of life and got himself snuffed out one Friday. And we would attach no meaning to his vision of a great day when suffering and death would be totally overcome. But we are people of faith.

In this faith we believe that God's love reaches us now, in the present, in ways we cannot easily see. We believe that, despite the threat of cataclysm, we, and history itself, are on a pilgrimage toward some wonderful consummation. To believe this is not easy. Doubts will arise. Conditions throughout the world today seem no better than in the days of Rome. There is violence and crime. And human beings in general seem woefully indifferent to the cries of their neighbor, whether in the same block or across the oceans.

But, as believers, we have a past with God, and we have a future with God. Therefore we plunge into the teeming tasks of the present with some courage. We may not change the world, but the world cannot claim or overcome us. We have his guarantee from the past and from the future that he is with us all the way.

For whatever is born of God overcomes the world; and this is the victory that overcomes the world, our faith. Who is it that overcomes the world but he who believes that Jesus is the Son of God? (1 John 5:4-5).

We tend to be a bit uneasy about people who say they know for sure that God wants them to do this or that. I once picked up a hitchhiker who was on his way from Kansas City to Laporte, Minn. Upon hearing that Laporte was my destination, he said, "I knew it! God be praised!" Upon leaving Kansas City he had told God that if a ride did not come along within a mile, he would know that God did not want him to go to Laporte. Just before he had walked a mile, a car picked him up. I found myself mildly envious of his easy way of finding God's will.

God does reveal his will. We can hear his voice. His command to love, to have patience, to hold on to hope, to help our brothers and sisters—these commands are quite clear, and when we obey, we can be reasonably sure that we are doing his will.

We cannot tolerate someone who says he had some inner communication from the Holy Spirit to leave his wife and children to run off with someone else's wife. I knew a young man like that. Two sets of children were abandoned, but even later he wrote me from prison, still persuaded that God had told him to destroy two homes. Not often, but sometimes, people piously justify their most flagrant wrongs by claiming to have a directive from God.

It is more difficult in the hundred-and-one situations where a decision for right or wrong has to be made. Try as we will to use the best of our reflective powers and weigh the pros and cons, we still wonder which is the better course. We get no cablegram from heaven, but a decision must be made. And most of us make it with a prayer that this may be pleasing to God, and that if not, in some way he will forgive and do the best he can with us.

God has not left us adrift. He does guide us. He has given us his Word, the Holy Scriptures. He surrounds us with earnest friends. He works within us, through conscience, to give us wisdom, a kind of heavenly intuition. And through prayer we open channels of communication for him to reach us.

Of one thing we can be sure. He loves us. This he has revealed supremely through the cross of Christ. It is his unqualified will to save us for himself and for his kingdom. He will forgive our errors and blunders, patch things up for us as best he can, strengthen us for every good work attempted, and when life is done, take us home to be with him. This we know to be his will!

If any of you lacks wisdom, he should pray to God, who will give it to him (James 1:5).

PACKAGING YOUR BURDENS December 10

It was in 1954 that my attention was first drawn to Charles Williams and his strange Christian novels, fantasy and reality intertwined to express some of the great truths of our faith. I went to the city library in Sioux Falls to ask for his books and discovered that the librarian, who loved the books, was almost ecstatic to have someone else learn to know him. Since then, I've read most of the strange titles, *War in Heaven, All Hallows Eve, The Greater Trumps*. In *Descent into Hell* he tells of a woman who for years has been tormented by a totally irrational fear of meeting her alter-self coming toward her on the streets. She has told no one, until one day she confides to a friend, Peter Stanhope:

> "You have friends; haven't you asked one of them to carry your fear?"
>
> "Carry my fear!" she said, sitting rigid in her chair. . . . "How can anyone else carry my fear? Can anyone else see it and have to meet it?" . . .
>
> "Come . . . when you go from here, when you're alone, when you think you'll be afraid, let me put myself in your place, and be afraid instead of you. . . . It's so easy, easy for both of us. . . . Haven't you heard it said that we ought to bear one another's burdens?"
>
> "But that means—" she began, and stopped.
>
> "I know," Stanhope said. "It means listening sympathetically, and thinking unselfishly, and being anxious about, and so on. Well, I don't say a word against that; no doubt it helps. But I think when Christ, or St. Paul, or whoever said *bear*, he meant something much more like carrying a parcel instead of someone else. To bear a burden is precisely to carry it instead of. If you're still carrying yours, I'm not carrying it for you—however sympathetic I may be. . . . If you give a weight to me, you can't be carrying it yourself; all I'm asking you to do is to notice that blazing truth. It doesn't sound very difficult."
>
> "And if I could," she said, "If I could do—whatever it is you mean, would I? Would I push my burden on to anybody else?" . . .
>
> "If you will be a part of the best of us, and live and laugh and be ashamed with us, then you must be content to be helped. You must give your burden up to someone else, and you must carry someone else's burden. . . . Not to give up your parcel is as much to rebel as not to carry another's."

Bear one another's burdens, and so fulfil the law of Christ (Gal. 6:2).

Do you want the boy to become a criminal or a customer? This was the question asked of a community to support a halfway house for juvenile offenders. The logic was clear: as a criminal he would cost the community thousands of dollars; as a customer he would sustain the community's economy. From a purely selfish point of view, a citizen should support the project.

Enlightened self-interest is a wise and prudent motive, but basically a selfish one. If it pays to give, give. The gift is a long-range investment—for you.

One should not deprecate this kind of giving. In fact, our whole system of voluntary support for Boy Scouts and Girl Scouts, the YMCA and the YWCA, the Red Cross, even the churches, is our way of saying that we want to do freely some honorable and necessary things for the community's well-being, without turning it over to the government for support and control.

But there is clearly another kind of giving. Our Lord, invited to a dinner for important people, suggested to the host that he might want sometime to have a dinner for the poor, the maimed, the blind—for people who couldn't possibly return the favor. It is when giving is uncalculating, spontaneous, cheerful—with no thought for return of any kind—that it most approximates the giving of God.

Kierkegaard once said that giving should be done with two invisible hands. First, the hand of God, which obviously is invisible. "Every good and perfect gift is from above," said James. Everything we have is a gift from him, given silently by God without any boasting on his part, nor with any demand for amortization. When we, in turn, become givers, remembering that what we give is something we have been given, we, like God, should give quietly, with "an invisible hand," expecting neither some favor in return, nor even the gratitude or embarrassment of those to whom we give.

We love, because he first loved us. We forgive, because he first forgave us. We give, because he has first given us. It is then that giving can become pure joy.

Thus, when you give alms, sound no trumpet before you, as the hypocrites do in the synagogue and in the streets, that they may be praised of men. Truly, I say to you, they have their reward. But when you give alms, do not let your left hand know what your right hand is doing, so that your alms may be in secret; and your Father who sees in secret will reward you (Matt. 6:2-4).

In all the history of the world no person has so baffled and inspired mankind as Jesus. Who was he? Who is he? What is there about him that sets people afire for him, not for a day, but for nearly 2000 years?

He commanded no armies. He wrote no books. He amassed no wealth. He had no wife or children. His immediate friends were few. When at 33 on a Friday he was executed on a trumped-up charge of disturbing the peace, his brief story should have ended. His friends thought it was over. In a generation all memory of him should have been gone.

But he rose from the dead the third day!

He had told his friends he would, but they had not taken his words seriously. Suddenly they were electrified. He appeared to them, spoke to them, ate with them. Before leaving them he told them to lay claim to the whole world for him. They set about doing just that.

What has happened since has perplexed the historians the world over. To be sure, nations rise to power from small beginnings, but they die. Civilizations come and go. But this is different. Whoever heard of a person who refuses to be forgotten, who is more *alive* today than ever before, and who, age after age, wins the allegiance of more people than all the kings and philosophers put together?

Can there be any other explanation than that he is God who walks the earth, and who steals into the hearts and minds of men and women? If it is fantasy, it is the greatest hoax ever to infect the earth.

Whatever else is said of the Christian church, it has but one Lord, this Jesus of Nazareth, God the Son and the Son of man. Its theology, its art, its ethics, its culture, and its life are like rays radiating from him who is the Light of Light. And we know that whatever else about Christendom has meaning for us, it is Jesus who holds us fast. Far more than we can ever explain, we know that Jesus is indeed the truth and the way and the life. We may be perplexed about the church's doctrine and be discouraged by its history, but we can't let Jesus go. He has captured us, and he holds us!

In the beginning was the Word, and the Word was with God, and the Word was God. He was in the beginning with God; all things were made through him. . . . And the Word became flesh and dwelt among us, full of grace and truth; we have beheld his glory, glory as of the only Son from the Father (John 1:1-3, 14).

I am now over 70. Sometimes the question haunts me, am I more Christ-like now than I was at 12? Have I, continuously since my baptism, been renewed in the image of God? I dare not say yes, certainly on my own, and I don't know anyone—except God—who knows me well enough across the years to give a verdict. Fortunately, I have been taught the Scriptures well enough to know that my rating with God does not depend on the progress I've made. I am adopted as his child by the grace given me in Christ. On the other hand, I know that it has been the Spirit's full intention to reshape me toward the perfection of a child of God. C. S. Lewis puts it this way:

> When I was a child I often had a toothache, and I knew that if I went to my mother she would give me something which would deaden the pain for the night and let me get to sleep. But I did not go to my mother—at least, not till the pain became very bad. And the reason I did not go was this. I did not doubt she would give me the aspirin; but I knew she would also do something else. I knew she would take me to the dentist next morning. I could not get what I wanted out of her without getting something more, which I did not want. I wanted immediate relief from pain: but I could not get it without having my teeth set permanently right. And I knew those dentists; I knew they started fiddling about with all sorts of other teeth which had not yet begun to ache. They would not sleeping dogs lie; if you gave them an inch, they took an ell.

> Now, if I may put it that way, Our Lord is like the dentists. If you give Him an inch, He will take an ell. Dozens of people go to Him to be cured of some one particular sin which they are ashamed of (like masturbation or physical cowardice) or which is obviously spoiling daily life (like bad temper or drunkenness). Well, He will cure it all right; but He will not stop there. That may be all you asked; but if you once call Him in, He will give you the full treatment.

> That is why He warned people to "count the cost" before becoming Christians. "Make no mistake," He says, "if you let Me, I will make you perfect. The moment you put yourself in My hands, that is what you are in for. Nothing less, or other, than that."

For me, and for you, he will have to finish the work on the other side of death, but then, for sure, he will! We shall be like him!

Beloved, we are God's children now; it does not yet appear what we shall be, but we know that when he appears, we shall be like him, for we shall see him as he is (1 John 3:2).

LIKE IT OR NOT, WE ARE ONE December 14

Sometimes we Christians forget that we belong to a larger group than the Christian church. We are *human beings* before we are white, black, yellow, brown, or red, before we are from West or East, before we are Christian, Buddhist, or Moslem. In a profound sense we are one because we have one Creator, one Father, and we Christians believe that, whether recognized as such or not, there is but one Redeemer.

We are one great human family. We may concentrate on our differences, but that which we have in common really swallows up all differences. The deepest sorrows and the greatest joys are the same for a mother in Beirut as for a mother in Boston, for a father in Moscow as for a father in Minneapolis.

Those of us who have allowed Christ to capture us are in a special group, within the larger family, the body of Christ on earth, the church. We are one with all humanity; we are one with all Christ's followers.

We often deny both of these unities. We divide into nations, races, creeds, cultures—and look across these fragile and illusory borders as if we are strangers and enemies. Even with each nation, there are walls between rich and poor, the trained and untrained, old and young. Perhaps the greatest scandal is among the followers of Christ themselves, who form denominations that look with suspicion at each other and become rivals of one another. The prayer of Jesus becomes muffled, "I do not pray for these only, but also for those who are to believe in me through their word, that they may all be one; even as thou, Father, art in me, and I in thee, that they also may be in us" (John 17:20-21).

A crisis does tend to make us forget our differences. A tornado, a typhoon, a flood suddenly bring all into a fellowship of danger and suffering. In disaster a rich man's son and a poor man's son, a white and a black, coping side by side, become friends, their differences forgotten.

God must love diversity. We know he loves unity. He wants us all, with none of our differences basically changed. And he wants us all to be together as his one family, concerned for one another, serving one another, and growing to love one another.

So God created man in his own image, in the image of God he created him; male and female he created them. And God blessed them (Gen. 1:27).

We are different from our animal cousins, the wolf and the ant. They do not write oratorios nor discover electronics. Neither do they bomb cities nor build concentration camps. People are different. They are human.

What it means to be human may be described in many ways. One clue is to say that to be human means the ability to enter upon something new. The wolf remains the same, century after century, as does the ant. Only people have the capacity and the privilege and the duty to make things—and themselves—new. They are not imprisoned into their own past nor the world's past.

In the last two centuries we have demonstrated in staggering dimensions that we can produce something new. The scientific, technological, and industrial revolutions of these swift years are eloquent evidence that we need not be mired in our past. We can enter that which is new.

Once having turned from these materialistic evidences, however, we may be harder pressed to find proofs that humanity has entered upon a new chapter of inner moral and spiritual life. Are we not on an old treadmill of selfishness, indifference, violence, and crime? And sometimes it seems that the pace has become faster and that the children are plunging faster than their grandparents into ways of destruction.

God's chief concern has always been a newness for each person. The hard rigid stuff that is inside of us may be far less pliable than our universe. In the last analysis it may be of little importance that we travel in a jet plane instead of on the back of a donkey—if we ourselves are not made new.

In an algebraic equation, the sum or the outcome remains unchanged unless and until a digit is changed from minus to plus. Add -3 plus -1 plus -2, and the result is -6. Juggle the digits as you will, -1 plus -3 plus -2, the result is the same, -6. But change the -1 to a plus 1, and the outcome becomes different, -4.

In our society or world, things will remain the same until someone moves from dishonesty to honesty, from selfishness to unselfishness. Without this newness in the individual, social engineering will be nothing but a futile juggling act.

The power to change us comes from the outside, from the intervention and invasion of God himself. The newness he brings is a miracle to dwarf all the wonders of the space age.

Therefore, if any one is in Christ, he is a new creation (2 Cor. 5:17).

Chronicles of Wasted Time is the title Malcolm Muggeridge uses for his autobiography. Like C. S. Lewis, he became a Christian later in life. He writes in his autobiography:

> In other words, the Christian proposition that he that loves his life in this world shall lose it, and he that hates his life in this world shall see it projected and glorified into eternity, is for living, not for dying. After all, it was St. Francis who truly loved the world he so gaily abjured, as his enchanting prayers and canticles convey. . . . All I can claim to have learned from the years I have spent in this world is that the only happiness is love, which is attained by giving, not receiving; and that the world itself only becomes the dear and habitable dwelling place it is when we who inhabit it know we are migrants, due when the time comes to fly away to other more commodious skies.
>
> I have never, I should add, learned anything from any exhortation or homily; any political, ethical, theological or philosophical exposition; any presentation in any form of plans, programmes or blueprints for happy living. Nor from any supernatural visitation or sudden Damascus Road prostration. Only from the experience of living itself, or—what is the same thing—the distillation of that experience in the visions of mystics and the productions of great writers and artists. Learning from experience means, in practice, learning from suffering; the only schoolmaster. Everyone knows that this is so, even though they try to persuade themselves and their fellows otherwise. Only so is it possible to understand how it came about that, through all the Christian centuries, people have been prepared to accept the Cross, ostensibly a symbol of suffering, as the true image and guarantee of their creator's love and concern for them. To climb the highest, stoniest mountain to set it on its peak; to carry it to the remotest, darkest, most forbidding corners of the earth; to build great cathedrals to glorify it; to find in it the inspiration for the most sublime achievements and noblest lives over the last two thousand years.

For in him all the fulness of God was pleased to dwell, and through him to reconcile to himself all things, whether on earth or in heaven, making peace by the blood of his cross (Col. 1:19-20).

Fairy tales are not for children alone. It may just be that adults are in the greater need of flights of fantasy. Myths and legends point beyond the laboratory and the computer to a whole world of truth and meaning and glory that will elude the mightiest telescope.

The great truths of the Christian faith come very near to fantasy: to believe that we are created in the image of God and that to save us from sin, death, and the power of the devil, God would come down from heaven, become one of us, and go to his death on a cross. It is not strange that people may regard the biblical story as wishful thinking.

Contrary to the lines of that delightful song, we are not "climbing Jacob's ladder" to heaven. God and heaven have come down. This is the glorious story of the gospel. If we are left to struggle "higher and higher," we would be in despair. We slip too many rungs. Man's noblest efforts will not reach heaven. Inspired by the Spirit of God, our climbing will be evidence that we want God and heaven. But the wonderful truth is that God has more than met us halfway. He has come all the way down to us.

In coming to earth to die and be raised again for us, Jesus brought the kingdom of God within reach. We need not wait for death to release us for citizenship in this kingdom. Through Holy Baptism we enter here and now. Through the gracious work of the Holy Spirit in us, we have a foretaste of the fullness of heaven.

Think what this means for us! Earth itself is aglow. Our days are not a weary march toward death. Already we live in a kingdom that has no end. We have inherited its riches—the forgiveness of sins, the righteousness of Christ, and life with God. We can come to him in prayer, as children come to their loving father. We can rest back into his everlasting arms with all our burdens and cares. We can count on him to guide us, step by step.

And we have the assurance that there will be a triumphant end to this world of sin and tragedy and pain and death. Christ will come again in glory to claim all that is his. If all this is a dream, don't awaken us!

It is no dream, no fairy tale. Hundreds of millions have staked their lives on the truth of Jesus as Lord and Savior, and have found courage, comfort, nobility, glory.

For God sent the Son into the world, not to condemn the world, but that the world might be saved through him (John 3:17).

No Christmas seems complete for me without hearing again the great message of the Lord's redemption in Handel's *Messiah* and in reading the story of a man's transformation in Dickens' character, Scrooge.

For over 200 years since its premier in Dublin, the *Messiah* has inspired audiences the world over. Opening with the tenor recitative from Isaiah, "Comfort ye, comfort ye, My people, saith your God," and rising to the heights in the "Hallelujah Chorus," and closing with the thrilling lines, "Worthy is the Lamb that was slain," it joins the remarkable selection of Scripture with the inspired musical score to usher the listener, or worshiper, into the vestibule of heaven.

From Ireland it moved to England where in 1759, April 9, at Covent Garden, Handel, then nearly blind, made his last public appearance, dying eight days later on the eve of Easter Sunday. From England it went to Germany, where at one performance there were a thousand singers and instrumentalists. Parts of the oratorio were first sung in the United States in a New York tavern in 1770.

In Dickens' *Christmas Carol* the night visitor, Marley's ghost, warns his partner, Scrooge, that a grim fate like his awaits him if he does not mend his ways. Scrooge says, "But you were always a good man of business, Jacob." Marley replies, "Business . . . Mankind was my business. The common welfare was my business: charity, mercy, forbearance, and benevolence, were all my business. The dealings of my trade were but a drop of water in the comprehensive ocean of my business." And, after the "miracle" of Scrooge's transformation, I like the words that summarize the change, "Scrooge was better than his word. He did it all, and infinitely more; and to Tiny Tim, who did not die, he was a second father. He became as good a friend, as good a master, and as good a man, as the good old city knew . . . and it was said of him, that he knew how to keep Christmas well, if any man alive possessed the knowledge."

Next to the incomparable story in Luke 2, these two pieces, the *Messiah* and *The Christmas Carol*, set the tone for my Christmas. They can for yours, too.

In those days a decree went out from Caesar Augustus that all the world should be enrolled. And Joseph also went up from Galilee . . . to the city of David, which is called Bethlehem (Luke 2:1-4).

Stephen Neill, bishop of the Church of England, spent a lifetime in missionary work, principally in India, and is known the world around as a teacher, pastor, author, and churchman. The following paragraphs are from one of his many books, *The Unfinished Task.*

In the chapel of my old home in India there hangs a reproduction, left by my predecessor, of Piero della Francesca's famous fresco of the Resurrection. With his incomparable genius for giving eternity to a moment, the artist has fixed forever the profound sleep of the guards and the tranquil solemnity of the Risen Christ. On the left of the picture all is winter; in the right the trees are already bursting into leaf. Because Christ is risen, we are between those two worlds. We look out on the dark billows of our world in tempest, on its desperate disappointments, its anxious calculations, its delusive hopes. We are already partakers of the new calm world of reconciliation and achievement. The Gospel we bring to the world is the Gospel of hope because it is the Gospel of the Resurrection. But that Gospel has power only because the Resurrection is the Resurrection of the Crucified.

It is as the Crucified that Jesus draws the hearts of men to Himself. The rendering of Psalm 96:10 given in some manuscripts of the Septuagint is not original, but it is true: "Tell it out among the heathen that the Lord hath reigned from the tree." This is the strangest of all transformations. God has taken that place of horror and disaster and made it the place of peace. In our darkest hours of despair, it is to the Cross that we turn to find consolation. When we are tempted to doubt everything, it is the Cross that tells us plainly that God is love. Bowed down by the sense of failure, we turn to the Cross and receive the grace of forgiveness. When the way is not clear before us, and we hesitate about the vocation of a lifetime, it is the Crucified who says to us, "Follow me."

Have this mind among yourselves, which you have in Christ Jesus, who, though he was in the form of God, did not count equality with God a thing to be grasped, but emptied himself, taking the form of a servant, being born in the likeness of men. And being found in human form he humbled himself and became obedient unto death, even death on a cross. Therefore God has highly exalted him and bestowed on him the name which is above every name (Phil. 2:5-9).

Our daughter, Martha, a few weeks after their twins were born, wrote about the event:

Wayne baptized our twin sons, David and Jonathan, the night they were born. We didn't know if they would live and we wanted God's hand upon them. We didn't necessarily think that this was a ticket to salvation, but we knew that God works in mysterious ways, through water and the Word, and so in faith, Wayne touched our boys' heads with water. They were very tiny, just 2 pounds, 2 ounces, and 3 pounds, 11 ounces.

The next 48 hours were tumultuous. We were both praying. For me it was an emotion-packed time as every postdelivery is. I didn't know what to pray. My concept of "God's will" is perhaps different from others. I could not believe that God would will these babies to die. And, if they did die, I didn't want to be praying madly for life and wonder why they died. . . . And if they lived, I really didn't know if I could, in the same turn, believe that God had somehow granted life to our boys while another 2-pound baby born to a couple with no children might not live. So, I prayed almost like those who would touch the hem of Jesus' robe, not knowing exactly what to expect, yet having faith to reach out.

Now they live and are a part of our lives. They are a miracle of God as all living babies are. We have a lot to be thankful for. However, the simple fact that they are living is compounded in a number of miraculous things. If they had not come seven weeks early, David might have died of starvation, having only two vessels in his umbilical cord rather than three. I think this is a miracle. The wonders of medicine that could nestle these tiny babies in isolettes allowing them to grow is a miracle. I would look at the loving nurses who would gently push a tube down to their stomachs and give them a thimble full of milk every two hours, burping them carefully with one finger. I think this is a miracle.

Now we want sort of officially to welcome them into the community of saints. Patti and Andrew, the babies' aunt and uncle, are to be David Wayne's godparents; and Marci, a second mother to all our children, is to be Jonathan Paul's godmother. This makes us joyful because our boys are ushered into life surrounded by believers, and we know that through this they can grow and be nurtured in Jesus.

Let the children come to me, do not hinder them; for to such belongs the kingdom of God (Mark 10:14).

The family of God is of enormous variety. The experience of one Christian with his Lord is probably never precisely duplicated in any other. The gifts of the Holy Spirit to the church are of intriguing variety. The differences are what gives riches to the whole. If it were not so, the family would be dull, a stodgy uniformity.

Occasionally there will emerge in the church a member who, as ardent and loving as others, yet has a penchant for criticism, someone who has a quarrel with the church he loves. He may see more clearly than others his own shortcomings and the shortcomings of the church. Søren Kierkegaard in mid-19th century Denmark was such a person, who in his sometimes cruelly sharp criticism was misunderstood and suffered rejection by many of his peers. He understood his role, and accepted it. He writes of himself:

> As a skillful cook says with regard to a dish in which already a great many ingredients are mingled: "It needs still just a little pinch of cinnamon"; . . . as an artist says with a view to the color effect of a whole painting which is composed of many, many colors: "There and there, at that little point, there must be applied a little touch of red." . . .
>
> So it is with Governance. Oh, the Governance of the world is an immense housekeeping and a grandiose painting. Yet He, the Master, God in heaven, behaves like the cook and the artist. He says: Now there must be introduced a little pinch of spice, a little touch of red. We do not comprehend why, we are hardly aware of it, since that little bit is so thoroughly absorbed in the whole. But God knows why.
>
> A little pinch of spice! That is to say: Here a man must be sacrificed, he is needed to impart a particular taste to the rest.
>
> These are the correctives. It is a woeful error if he who is used for applying the corrective becomes impatient, and would make the corrective normative for others. That is the temptation to bring everything to confusion. . . .
>
> God knows well him whom He elects to use in this way, and then He knows also how, in the inward understanding of it, to make it so blessed a thing for him to be sacrificed, that among the thousands of divers voices which express, each in its own way, the same thing, his also will be heard, and perhaps especially his which is truly *de profundis*, proclaiming: God is love.

Paul, a servant of Jesus Christ, called to be an apostle, set apart for the gospel of God which he promised beforehand through his prophets (Rom. 1:1).

How much faith must a person have to be accepted by God? P. T. Forsyth, in his book, *The Church and the Sacraments,* points out that this is the wrong question to ask:

> Fix your minds on the fundamental relation between grace and faith which the Sacraments express. They are not there chiefly to testify anything so subjective as individual religion. Their standing witness is the priority of grace, the free, nutritive, creative nature of God's grace, and the most worshipful wonder of it. They do not testify the priority of faith, as if it were a meritorious and qualifying work of ours that determines a Christian Sacrament, and makes the matter worth dividing upon. When we were without strength, Christ died for the ungodly. First grace, then faith. Grace is the cause, faith the effect. The grace is there for us and acting on us long before we believe it; it lies about us in our infancy, when as yet we have no faith. It is only grace that can create the power, and faith itself is the gift of God's grace. Nothing can create the response of faith but grace. . . . If we wait for personal faith and confession, we must keep asking when there is enough faith of the right kind to justify Baptism, and who is to decide. It is an unanswerable question. We are to be much more sure of God's grace in our faith than of our faith in God's grace. Faith is not getting up a certain degree of receptivity and so inviting, facilitating, or even deserving God's grace. It is answering grace's prevenience. And there is no statutory interval between the grace and the faith, between the gift and the response. It may be twenty, thirty, sixty years. Infant Baptism is a means of exhibiting to the whole Church and world this right relation of grace and faith, that grace precedes and is the condition of faith, that it is not its reward, and that the element of time between grace and faith does not change the grace and its power.

It is not fatal to infant Baptism to say that individual faith was absent in Baptism; but it would be if we said that individual grace was absent—that Christ did not expressly in His Church's act claim and commit the child. In the Gospel every child belongs to Christ, and the Church claims every child in the name of Him who reconciled the whole world. So the children are baptized not really to place them in God's grace, but because by Christ's work they are meant to be there.

If, because of one man's trespass, death reigned through that one man, much more will those who receive the abundance of grace and the free gift of righteousness reign in life through the one man Jesus Christ (Rom. 5:17).

ON BEING NEEDED

Everyone needs to be needed. For each of us, this may be the greatest need of all. I think God meant it to be that.

For someone to be unemployed may not be an economic disaster. Unemployment compensation may keep one from begging on the streets. But to lose one's job, or not to find one, may be the world's way of saying that it has no need of you. This is to threaten your very reason for living.

Upon retirement, many a man has floundered. He may have looked forward to the day when he would no longer need to go to the office or the shop or the schoolroom. When the day comes, he faces the stark fact that the office or shop no longer needs him. Who does need him now? His family is grown. He may conclude that should he die, his wife would not collapse. Some well-meaning program of activity may invite him to learn some crafts, play golf, travel, or whatever—all a sort of distraction to help him forget the gnawing suspicion that the world has no further use for him. A tortured loneliness sets in because the elemental requirement of life is gone—he is not needed!

William E. Hulme speaks of this situation in his *Creative Loneliness:* "In stressing the importance of service and action groups I might be giving the impression that the answer to loneliness is in keeping busy. Unfortunately, keeping busy is a way many people in our culture try to cope with their problems, including the problem of loneliness. They pour their energies into their many activities at the expense of their relationships to themselves, to nature, to God, and even to others. Although their activities involve them with others, their task-oriented approach protects them from the hazards of intimacy. Keeping busy is a form of escapism. On the other hand, involvement in activities directed at meeting the needs of others fulfills our own needs."

Whether officially retired, or formally unemployed, every person is needed. The needs of others become the doorway through which we discover that we are needed. We may have to look for the doors, but the moment we open them there will be silent hands reaching out to us and for us—almost as if they had been waiting precisely for us.

"Which of these three, do you think, proved neighbor to the man who fell among the robbers?" He said, "The one who showed mercy on him." And Jesus said to him, "Go and do likewise" (Luke 10:36).

WHERE IS BETHLEHEM? December 24

Bethlehem can be in our hearts. Jesus came to this little village. He can come to us too.

His coming to the earth centuries ago was a part of God's gigantic maneuver to get into our hearts. In fact, if people are not captured for him, there is a sense in which Bethlehem and Calvary will have failed. God's objective is not the conquest of nations, but of people, you and me, one by one. It stretches the imaginations to their limits to believe that God would bother with this tiny planet, and with us who despoil it and who too often ignore him and one another.

He did not come because great hosts of people awaited him. On that first Christmas night only a few scattered shepherds took note. The rest of the world, and even the little village itself, carried on as if nothing eventful had occurred. Even during Jesus' 33 years on earth, there was no surge of interest and loyalty. At Calvary virtually everyone had deserted him.

Only in the wake of the Easter resurrection did things happen, and even then rather quietly. Not until three centuries later did he find a place in the courts of the empire. But since that time the name of Jesus has become the most honored name in the world. Hundreds of millions have acclaimed him King and Lord and Savior.

God's objective remains the same as that Bethlehem night. Not nations, not civilizations, not cultures, not the planet itself (all these are passing away), but people, one by one, are in his eye. And he wants to take up residence within us, to hold and keep us now and forever. We are his Bethlehem, as Phillips Brooks says in his beloved hymn:

How silently, how silently
The wondrous gift is giv'n!
So God imparts to human hearts
The blessings of his heaven.
No ear may hear his coming;
But, in this world of sin,
Where meek souls will receive him, still
The dear Christ enters in.

The shepherds said one to another, "Let us go over to Bethlehem and see this thing that has happened, which the Lord has made known to us" (Luke 2:15).

The legends of most ancient people tell of gods and goddesses visiting the earth. They come and go capriciously, sometimes showing favor, sometimes visiting disaster. They were of little comfort. More often than not their appearances were feared. It may not be unfair to say that people worshiped them, sacrificed to them, largely to keep them at bay. A god was much like a nasty landlord who, if you didn't pay your rent on time, would show up to give trouble. So you paid your rent. Your worshiped, not because you hoped the gods would appear, but for fear that they might. To be unnoticed by the gods was a profound relief. Gods and goddesses never became a part of the sufferings of men; they hovered off at the side.

How different the God of the Bible. He came to us, and comes to us, in Jesus Christ. He became one of us, and remains one of us. Nor did he come simply to find out how we lived. His was more than a visit. He came to suffer and to die for the sins of the world. He came to bring the blessings of heaven to earth. He came to reclaim us for the Father's kingdom.

This is quite different from a Zeus or an Apollo or an Odin. These are characters from myths and legends. Jesus is the Word made flesh, come to live among us. He is God of God, Light of Light—who became man. He is as much man as Peter and John, as Socrates, as Luther, and as any one of us. He belongs to heaven and he belongs to earth. He is more than legend; he is history.

Because he suffered and died as a human being, he could be the "second Adam," the Adam who recovered all the first Adam had lost. Because he was raised from the dead, as God he could raise up that which is human to be fully human again, as God intended us to be from the beginning.

The pivotal event in the history of the world is this visit! It is not the rise and fall of a civilization, the discovery of the wheel, or the breakthrough into space travel. It is infinitely more. We are born, we live, we die. This is true of people and of nations. This melancholy sequence is broken by the visit of Jesus. Death is not the end for us. Forgiven and restored, we shall live with him forever.

But when the time had fully come, God sent forth his Son, born of woman, born under the law, to redeem those who were under the law, so that we might receive adoption as sons (Gal. 4:4-5).

The feverish preparations are over. Cards have been sent and gifts have been exchanged. The guests have arrived, and perhaps have even gone again. Families bask in the delight of one another.

In this hour we can center our minds on the glorious event centuries ago which has inspired this annual burst of warmth and affection. We can turn to the gift of gifts, Jesus, our Lord and Savior.

Not that we need this extravaganza of preparation as a prelude. All the year through we have this Jesus at our side. In dark moments we fly to him for comfort. In good days we approach him in thanksgiving. At all times we have him as the key to life's meaning. He is our Savior from sin and death.

We who are his followers embrace him as the center of all things. We believe that neither the microscope nor the telescope can unlock the mystery of life. We believe that at the very heart of this vast universe is a Person—this Jesus who let the world see him first in Bethlehem's manger. Were the whole visible universe to disappear, he would still be there—to hold us and to keep us forever. This is the audacious dimension of our faith in him.

It would be tragic if we should be so lost in the little side shows of our own making that we would fail to enter the "big tent." The sideshows are delightful—the parties, family reunions and holiday mirth—but the staggering event is the coming of Jesus.

Nor are the side shows wrong or unimportant. They are the joys that filter through from the Great Joy, as the sun's rays playing through the trees are the gift of the great sun in the sky. We may get lost in the woods and see but broken fragments of the sun, but the sun is still there lavishing its light on the world. Were it to set, we would be in darkness. Jesus is the Light of the world. It is his coming that creates all the joys of Christmas and the joys that spread throughout the year.

In Kipling's words, "The tumult and the shouting dies." The bustle is ended. Now is the time to lift our eyes and our hearts to contemplate the wonder of God's limitless love for us in giving us the gift of a Savior. In this gift all other gifts inhere. It is in and through him that we have an endless life with God.

Be not afraid; for behold, I bring you good news of a great joy which will come to all the people (Luke 2:10).

The following delightful Christmas poems are from the pen of Melva Rorem in her book, *I Sing of Mary's Child:*

Oh, I would sing of Mary's Child
Cradled upon the hay,
And of the little birds that sang
For him on Christmas day.
Oh, I would sing of Mary's Child
Who all God's children reconciled.

And I would sing a melody
That echoes through the land,
About the little ones who came
To touch his tiny hand.
Oh, I would sing a melody
Before this Child on bended knee.

Oh, I would sing of Jesus' birth
On that dear silent night,
And of the little stars that shone
On him with heavenly light.
Oh, I would sing of Jesus' birth
That brought great joy to all the earth.

She held him up against the sky,
She heard his infant, new-born cry,
And melody became a part
Of Christmas joy in Mary's heart
Throughout the years her gentle song
Has echoed, swelled, and lingered long
While thousand alleluias ring
In the great crescendos to the King.
With joy she heard his new-born cry,
She held him up against the sky.

But Mary kept all these things, pondering them in her heart (Luke 2:19).

Everything that goes into a good story is found in the Christmas story. A young woman was soon to have a baby. Suddenly an order came from the emperor that all people in the empire must register in their ancestral city. This sent the young wife and her husband on a hazardous journey. The town was crowded; they found room only in a stable, where her baby was born, attended by her husband, and maybe some lambs, cows, and doves perched sleepily in the rafters. If there were no other elements in the story but these, it still would be a moving and tender story. But there is more: shepherds, angels, Wise Men from the East, a villainous king, escape to Egypt.

And still more. Because Bethlehem was but the beginning. There was a Calvary and an empty tomb and an ascension and the promise of return in glory. The conclusion of the story is yet to be written for us: "what no eye has seen, nor ear heard, nor the heart of man conceived, what God has prepared for those who love him."

It is sad, but it is true, that even we, who hail Jesus as Lord and Savior, are caught up with the peripheral things of Christmas. "Did you send a card to the Olsons?" "Have you made the plane reservations yet?"

But let us not become altogether cynical. Granted, the money spent for trips, gifts, and cards could have been given to the poor and hungry. But there is a bright side. All sorts of people, many lonely souls, are cheered by the word they get from friends this one time of the year. While in our affluent society it may be difficult to find a gift that meets a critical need, most gifts are useful, or if not useful, a cherished token of affection. And most trips bring scattered families together. Surely, at no other time of the year is there such a general aura of good will. Perhaps these are, in some strange way, the dividends that flow from the Christmas story into the lives of people.

The anxieties of the long year are minimized, and we remember people who mean something to us. When in a burst of love a woman poured an alabaster jar of very expensive ointment on Jesus' head, the disciples complained that the ointment might have been sold for a large sum and given to the poor. Jesus gave them a mild rebuke, "She has done a beautiful thing to me." There are times when a generous and even lavish act toward someone, though not practical, is the right thing. This may be true for Christmas.

To you is born this day in the city of David a Savior, which is Christ the Lord (Luke 2:11).

There was no laboratory explanation for water becoming wine, nor for five thousand people being fed with a few loaves of bread and a few fish, nor for a leper being healed instantly by the touch of Jesus' hand. In those days they did not have laboratories.

Today, because we have laboratories, we want an orderly explanation for everything that happens. And if something happens that we cannot easily explain, we tend to regard it as phony.

None of us wants to go back to the prelaboratory days. Every advance in medicine, or in any other area of science for that matter, has come about because we count on events following certain "laws." And through science we have uncovered more amazing and startling things than all the magicians ever did in all the centuries. We have learned to live in a world of miracles. We ought to live in daily awe and wonder.

But things become commonplace all too soon. For the Wright brothers the flying machine was something utterly new and wonderful. Today we don't even bother to look into the sky as a jet roars its way overhead. And, most of the time, when I board one, I take my seat and quickly fall asleep. Only a few years ago, radio was a miracle; today our children grow up on television.

This is God's world, and it's full of wonders. You are one of them. You have a heart that pumps away seventy-two or more times a minute for seventy years or more. You have a brain that hatches ideas. The ideas flow into your tongue and lips and you speak. Sound waves are produced, they strike the ear of your friend, are transmitted into your friend's brain, and he gets your ideas. The most amazing automation that man has contrived cannot match this commonplace miracle of communication. Because everyone chatters away, we're likely to forget the wonder of human speech.

Someone gets cancer. Either by surgery or by radiation, the tumor is destroyed. She is well again. But, really, the health she now has recovered *after* cancer is no more wonderful than the health she had *before* cancer. Health itself is the miracle.

There is the miracle of the ordinary, and sometimes the extraordinary. Certainly it should be possible for God to act, without upsetting the orderly universe which he has given us, whenever he wants to, since he is God and is in direct command. We dare not limit God.

And Jesus in pity touched their eyes, and immediately they received their sight and followed him (Matt. 20:34).

THE STORY WITH NO END December 30

I remember from my high-school English class that a good story would have five parts: introduction, rising action, climax, declining action, and conclusion.

The epic we have in the Bible has only three parts. There is an introduction: God made the universe, and he made me in his image to live with him forever. There is rising action: the enemy lured man away from God, and God put in motion a plan for his recovery, a plan he kept alive as a promise through the prophets. There is a climax: in the fulness of time God invaded the earth in Jesus Christ, his Son and now my brother, who died on a cross and rose again to become my Savior, and who established on earth a kingdom for me and for all who believe in him.

Now, at this point, the declining action ought to begin, and inch toward some conclusion. But the sweep of the story keeps going up and up. I am caught up in the life of the kingdom. I am involved in the reconciling work of God on this earth. Every person becomes my brother or sister. Management of the planet is restored to me. Every phase of life, every institution, every relationship will come under the pervasive policies of God's kingdom.

There simply are not hours enough and years enough. Life is full. Even its sorrows, pains, and failures are swallowed up in the story that now has become an integral part of the story of my own life—and of yours.

We don't know how many years may be given us. We may not have even one more day. But until the end we have a significant job to do. Whether we are formally employed or unemployed matters little. The big job, the overarching commission, is still ours. We are sons and daughters of God—to do his will in every concrete situation that meets us. Even on beds of pain, with terminal illness facing us, we have the high privilege of meeting pain and suffering as children of God, spreading what cheer we can in the swift days left to us.

The planet itself is on impermanent tenure. I know he will come again one day—in glory—to usher in the fullness of his kingdom. Death has lost its sting. It now is but a punctuation mark, a comma, in the breathless story that has no ending.

Then I saw a new heaven and a new earth; for the first heaven and the first earth had passed away, and the sea was no more. And I saw the holy city, new Jerusalem, coming down out of heaven from God, prepared as a bride adorned for her husband (Rev. 21:1-2).

Another year of the world's history is gone; another year of your history and mine has slipped into the past. The world is a year older, and we are 365 days nearer heaven.

What do we do with a year that is gone? Its blessings are another cargo of grace for which we thank God. Its sins and failures are a burden that we place in the Lord's hands for forgiveness. Its sorrows are given to him for continued healing. Its unrealized hopes are there to be renewed for another year.

It is we who block time into segments, hours, days, years. Time is rather like a flowing stream. The past, the present, and the future are one. Each of us is a mixture of yesterday's regrets and achievements, today's anxieties and tasks, and tomorrow's hopes. A daughter, for instance, is at once today's student with her books, yesterday's girl with her dolls, and tomorrow's mother with her babies. In the heart of her father and mother she is all three.

Our God is the same yesterday, today, and forever. And he is in the thick of history, your history and the history of the world. He is in the flow of time, not soaring above it. He entered at the time of creation, he walked with his chosen Israel, and in the fulness of time he came in the person of his only Son, our Lord. Until the end of the world he has promised never to leave or forsake us. By his Spirit he calls us into his eternal kingdom which already now is in the midst of everything we do. When death is done with us we shall inherit the kingdom in all its fullness.

For us who are children of God and children of the Bible, God is not a vague spirit that hovers like a bird over existence. He is Jesus Christ, born of Mary, who grew up in Nazareth, who preached and healed and was crucified, and who rose from the dead to be our Savior and Lord. The Word became flesh and dwelt among us. It is he who has redeemed us and restored us to the Father's home. At this very moment by grace through faith we live in that home.

The stream of time flows in ever changing channels. Sometimes there is calm, then the churning rapids, even plunging cataracts. Who knows what is around the next bend? The last years of the 20th century are full of fear for us who sail our frail crafts. But whatever lies ahead, we are in our Father's strong and tender hands, and we hear his word, "Fear not."

All flesh is grass . . . the grass withers, the flower fades; but the word of our God will stand forever (Isa. 40:8).

THE PERILS OF ENTHUSIASM — Palm Sunday

In a great burst of enthusiasm they crowned Jesus King that first Palm Sunday. But enthusiasm was not enough to carry them through. By Friday they were dispirited, and they let the mob harangue him to his death.

High feeling is good. It is wonderful to be carried along on the wings of song, to feel exaltation. But life will not always be braced by noble emotion. There will be days of heavy clouds, and heavy hearts. Everything will look dark and hopeless. These are the days that test the mettle of people, and of our faith.

The Lord has never promised to give us moods of continuous joy. He has promised that, come what may, he will never leave us nor forsake us. Through the valley of the shadow of death, he will be with us.

We will all be tempted to conclude that if God does not deliver us from the dark moods, he obviously is not around. We may go from one church to another, experiment with one religion or another, in a furtive chase after moods. This really is an effrontery to God. What right have we to dictate to him what feelings he ought to give us? He has promised to give us himself, regardless of what enthusiasm or lack of enthusiasm we may have. This should be enough.

Every Christian life has its high moments. They come, said Jesus, unplanned and unexpected. Like the wind that blows, he told Nicodemus, you will not know where it comes from nor where it will lead you. It was so for Paul on the Damascus road that midday, and for John Wesley at nine o'clock one evening at Aldersgate, and for Kagawa in Kobe when the face of the beggar seemed to change to the face of Jesus. The glowing memory of those moments doubtless carried them through many dark and troublesome hours, but they did not insist that God had to reproduce these moments every day. For them, as for us, there was a more constant reassurance of God's presence.

The great guarantee that God is around is the cross. Jesus Christ, God the Son, came to this earth to give his life for us. Believing this and clinging to it, we can walk in peace and in triumph even in those moments when cheer and mirth seem utterly gone. Our sins are forgiven—whether we feel like it or not; a victory has been won for us—even when we feel no song of triumph; the heavens are open to us—even when darkness seems all about us.

And the crowds that went before him and that followed him shouted, "Hosanna to the Son of David! Blessed is he who comes in the name of the Lord!" (Matt. 21:9).

373

One of the saddest spectacles in the life of Christendom is that the Lord's Supper, which certainly our Lord meant to be a meal for his whole family around his table, has become the most striking symbol of our separation. Attempts to explain what the meal actually is have reared walls. C. S. Lewis speaks of this sad offense:

It is almost impossible to state the negative effect which certain doctrines have on me—my failure to be nourished by them—without seeming to mount an attack against them. But the very last thing I want to do is to unsettle in the mind of any Christian, whatever his denomination, the concepts—for him traditional—by which he finds it profitable to represent to himself what is happening when he receives the bread and wine. I could wish that no definitions had ever been felt to be necessary; and, still more, that none had been allowed to make divisions between churches.

Some people seem able to discuss different theories of this act as if they understood them all and needed only evidence as to which was best. This light has been withheld from me. I do not know and can't imagine what the disciples understood Our Lord to mean when, His body still unbroken and His blood unshed, He handed them the bread and wine, saying *they* were His body and blood.

I hope I do not offend God by making my Communions in the frame of mind I have been describing. The command, after all, was Take, eat; not Take, understand. Particularly, I hope I need not be tormented by the question, "What is this?"—this wafer, this sip of wine? That has a dreadful effect on me. It invites me to take "this" out of its holy context and regard it as an object among objects, indeed as part of nature. It is like taking a red coal out of the fire to examine it: it becomes a dead coal. To me, I mean. All this is autobiography, not theology.

I wonder if all of us Christians, even theologians trained in definitions, do not receive the bread and wine like children who, with better imaginations than we and more trust, accept the words of our Lord as given.

And he took bread, and when he had given thanks he broke it and gave it to them, saying, "This is my body" (Luke 22:19-20).

TWO ROADS MEET Good Friday

Two thousand years ago two long roads converged and intersected. One was our sinfulness, the other God's mercy. They met at the cross. The Bible tells the story of Adam and Eve turning from God to follow their own selfish path. Almost simultaneously the Bible tells of God's pursuit in love. He did not want to give up on his children.

Jesus Christ, whom we confess to be both God and man, brought the two long roads into one. He took our sinfulness to himself, and he represented in himself the mercy of God. We humans, with our sins —and God with his mercy—came together in Jesus. We stand in awe of this mystery of the incarnation.

The fears, the intrigue, the indifference, and the cruelty of people are mirrored in the execution of this thoroughly good man. The love of God, who went to his death to win the world back to him, is supremely revealed in the cross.

Nor is this only an event of 2000 years ago. It is a recurring event in our lives. Our record of sin and failure is met head-on by God's record of everlasting mercy at the cross. We stand with the crucifiers and the indifferent crowd. God looks down on us from his cross, and cries, "Father, forgive them, for they know not what they do." Standing there, first with the momentary enthusiasts of Palm Sunday, and then with the silent and indifferent onlookers on Friday, we know that we, too, need the mercy and forgiveness of God. We instinctively echo the phrase, "It was for me he died upon the tree." We bow in repentance, and we feel the surging refrains of praise and thanksgiving forming within our souls:

> Upon that cross of Jesus
> Mine eyes at times can see
> The very dying form of one
> Who suffered there for me;
> And from my smitten heart, with tears,
> Two wonders I confess,
> The wonder of his glorious love,
> And my unworthiness.

But you denied the Holy and Righteous One, and asked for a murderer to be granted to you, and you killed the Author of life, whom God raised from the dead (Acts 3:14-15).

THE BLOW THAT DESTROYED DEATH   Easter

They put him in a cave on Friday afternoon after he had died. They rolled a huge stone against the entrance. Now he was dead. Let no one disturb his body. They even stationed guards at the grave to make sure that no one would smuggle the body away.

They had not counted on God. God had sent him on a mission which included death, but death was not the end of the errand. God raised him from the dead, burst open the grave, and sent him out to invade and capture the hearts of people down the centuries.

The Easter resurrection is as cataclysmic an event today as it was then. Death is destroyed! It does not have the last word. In the wake of Christ's resurrection, a new life is in store for everyone who asks it. Because Christ lives, we too can live—in a kingdom and among riches that are as glorious as they are endless.

We need not wait until death has done its worst before we taste this new life. The kingdom or the resurrection is among us. Just as it marks the end of death, it marks the death of evil and unworthy forces that threaten to kill what could be noble in our lives. Hatred loses its hold, greed begins to retreat, old grudges melt away, fear loses its terror. We sense that something is dying, and something new is rising. Hope and love and joy and courage, long thought to be but ideals and dreams, are taking the field. The Lord of hosts is with us! He who rose, and ascended, and is at the right hand of the Father in power—he is with us.

Without Easter the world would spin on its melancholy axis with no great morn dawning, doomed to keep people in bondage to their anxieties and cupidities in aimless repetition until death overtakes them. The best they could hope for would be simply to endure. Why long for something better? Why aspire to something new?

Nothing in all the world has so enchanted and haunted men down through the centuries as has the event of Easter. Whole civilizations have been changed because men have believed that death does not have the last word. They have clung to the Risen Christ, and he has clung to them, and together they have reshaped the hopes of the world. There is forgiveness, there is victory, there is love and courage and an everlasting future. This is Easter!

If for this life only we who have hoped in Christ, we are of all men most to be pitied. But in fact Christ has been raised from the dead, the first fruits of those who have fallen asleep (1 Cor. 15:19-20).